No Slam Dunk

CRITICAL ISSUES IN SPORT AND SOCIETY

Michael Messner and Douglas Hartmann, Series Editors

Critical Issues in Sport and Society features scholarly books that help expand our understanding of the new and myriad ways in which sport is intertwined with social life in the contemporary world. Using the tools of various scholarly disciplines, including sociology, anthropology, history, media studies, and others, books in this series investigate the growing impact of sports and sports-related activities on various aspects of social life as well as key developments and changes in the sporting world and emerging sporting practices. Series authors produce groundbreaking research that brings empirical and applied work together with cultural critique and historical perspectives written in an engaging, accessible format.

No Slam Dunk

· ·

Gender, Sport, and the
Unevenness of Social Change

CHERYL COOKY AND MICHAEL A. MESSNER

R
Rutgers University Press

New Brunswick, Camden, and Newark, New Jersey, and London

Library of Congress Cataloging-in-Publication Data

Names: Cooky, Cheryl, author. | Messner, Michael A., author.
Title: No slam dunk : gender, sport and the unevenness of social change / Cheryl Cooky and
Michael A. Messner.
Description: New Brunswick, New Jersey : Rutgers University Press, 2018. | Series: Critical
issues in sport and society | Includes bibliographical references.
Identifiers: LCCN 2017033655| ISBN 9780813592053 (hardback) | ISBN 9780813592046
(paperback)
Subjects: LCSH: Sex discrimination in sports. | Sports for women—Social aspects. |
Sports—Sex differences. | Mass media and sports—Social aspects. | BISAC: SPORTS &
RECREATION / Sociology of Sports. | SOCIAL SCIENCE / Women's Studies. | SOCIAL
SCIENCE / Gender Studies.
Classification: LCC GV706.32 .C665 2018 | DDC 306.483—dc23
LC record available at https://lccn.loc.gov/2017033655

A British Cataloging-in-Publication record for this book is available from the British Library.

www.rutgersuniversitypress.org

Manufactured in the United States of America.

No Slam Dunk *is gratefully dedicated to the memory of D. Stanley Eitzen—sport sociology pioneer, prolific author, inspiring mentor, and friend.*

Contents

Part III The Gender of Sports Media

No Slam Dunk

Introduction

• •

CHERYL COOKY AND
MICHAEL A. MESSNER

In recent decades, we have witnessed a dramatic gender transformation in sports, perhaps most evident in youth sports. Buttressed by the enthusiastic support of their parents, peers, and communities, millions of girls have flooded into soccer, basketball, and other sports in recent years (Sabo & Veliz, 2016). Partly as a result of this dramatic increase in participation, there has been a dramatic shift in the cultural expectations for and acceptance of girls' athleticism. No longer do we assume that boys will be on the field and girls will be cheering on the sidelines. Moreover, girls' participation is supported and even celebrated in popular culture, no longer marginalized or stigmatized as it had been just a few decades earlier (Cooky, 2010).

But just below the surface of this dramatic sea change, we can observe currents that run counter to the achievement of gender equality. Girls and boys are still routinely sex-segregated into separate sports leagues. And sometimes, they play different sports entirely: Boys play baseball, while most girls are channeled into softball; boys play football, while very few girls do, and mostly as the lone girl on the boys' team; and transgender and gender nonconforming kids find it hard to figure out where and how to fit in at all (Cooky & McDonald, 2005; Grasmuck, 2005; Ring, 2009; Travers, 2016). Girls of color, immigrant girls, disabled girls, and girls from urban communities have been left behind in the gender transformation of youth sports and frequently confront significant barriers to sports opportunities (Cooky, 2009; Sabo & Veliz, 2008). Girls also quit playing sports at much higher rates during adolescence than boys do. And even though most of today's mothers are young enough to have been part of the 1970s and 1980s sports boom, girls and boys who play youth sports today are far more likely to be coached by men, while most of the women who want to help out are relegated to supplying snacks as "team moms" (Messner, 2009).

Recent years have also in many ways been banner years for high school and college women athletes. Fueled both by surging enthusiasm for women's sports and ignited in the United States by Title IX—a legal statute through which girls and women can claim equal opportunities in school and university sports—girls' participation in high school sports has risen annually for years, as have the number of college and university women's sports teams and athletic scholarships. However, still too frequently, high school girls and college women—often with support of organizations like the National Women's Law Center or the National Organization for Women—have had to press their schools to comply with the letter of the law. Moreover, there is a disproportionate distribution of opportunities at the high school and collegiate level where, outside the sports of basketball and track and field, girls and women and women of color are underrepresented. And what are we to make of the fact that as money has poured into college women's sports in recent decades, the proportion of teams headed by women coaches has dropped, whereas men coaches have poured into the occupation (Acosta & Carpenter, 2014)?

Not long ago, it seemed that a glass ceiling constrained most women athletes to amateur status, with the exception of a few professional golfers and tennis players. Today, the most accomplished women athletes are enjoying an expanding field of opportunities to play professional sports, including boxing, ultimate fighting, auto racing, and team sports like basketball, soccer, and football. However, the pay for these athletes pales in comparison to that garnered by men. A recent public push for better pay for Women's National Basketball Association (WNBA) athletes illuminated a startling contrast: Professional women basketball players in 2016 earned on average of $75,000 a year (with a ceiling of $107,500), compared with the average male NBA player's earnings of nearly $6,000,000. Of course, some might argue that a pay differential is justified, as an NBA season is much longer than a WNBA season and the men's league generates far more revenue than the women's counterpart.[1] Such is not true of professional soccer; several elite women soccer players are household names, and the U.S. women's national team draws huge crowds and television audiences, often exceeding that of the U.S. men's national team. Nevertheless, a 2016 wage discrimination suit filed with the Equal Employment Opportunity Commission (EEOC) against the U.S. Soccer Federation by five members of the champion U.S. women's soccer team revealed that even these highly successful women athletes are paid far less than their male counterparts, who were often less successful on the field. As we write this in 2017, the U.S. women's team has enjoyed a record eight consecutive appearances in the World Cup, including three World Cup wins and four Olympic championships, compared to the men's national team's quarterfinal appearance in the 2002 Olympics. Despite this disparate success rate, at the time of the wage discrimination suit, the men were receiving World Cup bonuses of more than $52,000 for winning third place, $260,000 for second place, and $390,000 for first place, compared with $20,000, $32,000, and $75,000 respectively for the women. The men even received $12.50 more per diem for domestic matches than the women athletes received.

In an even starker contrast, while the National Football League (NFL) thrives, fledgling women's professional football leagues are so far under the public radar that many people are still unaware that women's professional football leagues exist, and the athletes compete almost for free. The fact that participants in the televised pseudosport of "lingerie football" actually earn higher pay than the women who play in women's conventional football leagues speaks volumes about the continuing tendency to value women more as sexual objects than as muscular and powerful athletic subjects (Dworkin, 2001). Meanwhile, the tepid institutional response to the growing mountain of evidence about the long-term impact of head injuries in football speaks to the continuing tendency to think of men—especially men of color—as disposable, even if sometimes highly remunerated, bodies (Anderson & Kian, 2012).

Fans of the 2016 Olympic Games were flooded with triumphant images and commentary that celebrated the domination of U.S. women gymnasts, basketball players, swimmers, and runners. But media coverage of women's sports is still plagued by some of the same issues we've seen over the past several decades. For example, U.S. swimmer Katie Ledecky shocked the world with her breakout performances, including becoming the first swimmer since 1968 to win gold medals in the 200 m, 400 m, and 800 m individual freestyle events. She also broke two world records at the Rio Olympics. Some commentators embraced Ledecky as *the* "World's Best Athlete" ("US swimmer Katie Ledecky," 2016; Loria, 2016). Other media outlets, however, were unsure of what to make of her and seemed unable to describe her athletic prowess outside the context of male performance. She was, according to many media accounts, "the next Michael Phelps" (Warshaw, 2016). Moreover, the media coverage of women of color continues to be plagued by overt and covert racism (Cooky & Rauscher, 2016). Two-time Olympics gold medalist Gabby Douglas was criticized in 2012 for her supposedly too nappy hair, and then in 2016 she drew disdain for her apparent lack of patriotic enthusiasm during the playing of the National Anthem. And whether positive or negative, the bursts of media enthusiasm for women athletes during the Olympic Games tend to be short-lived. If you get your sports information from major news media, then it still might be easy to conclude that only men play sports—or at least that only what male athletes do is newsworthy: ESPN's *SportsCenter*, nightly network news, and the major metropolitan daily newspapers still mostly ignore women's sports (see chapter 10). Perhaps the dearth of coverage of women's sports is related to the fact that sports reporting remains largely a male occupational realm, in which women reporters and commentators are less than welcome (Hardin & Shain, 2005; LaVoi et al., 2007). This is especially true for women who write for online sports media outlets; here, trolling and harassment of women writers have become all too common (Marcur, 2016).

Dramatic but Uneven Change

From youth sports to elite sports, it may seem that today is the best of times for girls and women. In many ways, that is true—but only when we contrast

women's impressive progress with the near-absence of opportunity to participate in sports a few decades ago. Judged against a standard of equality, fairness,
and justice, however, it is clear that the field of organized sports—whether we
focus on participation rates, funding and pay equity, or media coverage—has
undergone a still far from complete revolution. This is especially true when we
avert our gaze from economically privileged communities, focusing on the still
less than equitable sporting landscape in poor communities, among immigrant
populations, and more generally in many of the poor nations of the Global
South (Hargreaves, 2000; Hartmann & Manning, 2016; Jamieson, 1995; Miller
et al., 2005; Thul et al., 2016). To employ a sports metaphor, it is not yet time for
a feminist victory lap.

The title of our book, *No Slam Dunk*, mixes in yet another sports metaphor.
In the worlds of politics, business, or academia, to label something a "slam dunk"
implies full confidence that the chance of success is even better than a "high percentage shot"—more like a done deal, akin to the ball flushing through the net
after a high-flying athlete has jammed it through the hoop. In current narratives
about gender and sport, the slam dunk in the game of basketball has for many
become the potent symbol that differentiates the men's game from the wom-
en's game: Men, so the story goes, play the game "above the rim," acrobatically
soaring and dunking; women play the game with their feet "stuck to the floor,"
relying on the less exciting strategies of passing, screening, and shooting. This
difference, in some people's view, is not only what elevates men's basketball over
women's; it also explains lower fan interest in the women's game, and by extension, justifies less media attention and lower pay for women players. In fact, a
few women basketball players—most notably Lisa Leslie, Candace Parker, and
Brittney Griner—have dunked the ball in college and professional games. But
most top women basketball players have not dunked during a game. By contrast,
most elite men basketball players today can dunk the ball. However, most men
in the population who play high school, recreational, and pickup basketball
can't come close to dunking. This illustrates what Mary Jo Kane (1995) called
"a continuum of difference" that sport reveals among women and men. Though
popular narratives tend to view gender differences categorically (men can dunk;
women can't), sport reveals tremendous overlap between men's and women's
physical abilities: Some top female basketball players can dunk, but most women
can't; many top male basketball players can dunk, but most men can't.

Sport has long played an important ideological role in gender relations, symbolically converting what are actually *average* bodily differences (such as men on
average being about five inches taller than women) to beliefs in *categorical* differences (i.e., men as a group are taller than women as a group; Messner, 1988). In
recent decades, the public celebration of male basketball players' proclivity for
dunking has become increasingly important in constructing a gender boundary
that in many peoples' eyes makes the men's game naturally more exciting and
just plain better than the women's game. We wonder: Is it a coincidence that the
drama of the slam dunk became the litmus test for exciting basketball during the
1980s right as women's ascent in sport was accelerating? A glance back at men's
elite basketball of the 1960s and early 1970s is instructive. Back then, there was

some dunking, but it was neither emphasized nor celebrated in near the same way as it is today. It is conceivable that many NBA stars of that era—Oscar Robertson, Walt Frazier, Pete Maravich, George Gervin, or Rick Barry (yes, even Rick the Stick could pogo before his knees went out)—would be competitive in today's dunkathons if equipped with the proper modern high-tech shoes and given the time to practice. But back then, other skills mattered more. To some basketball fans, the contemporary emphasis on the slam dunk has diminished the men's game. Nevertheless, the dunk today serves as a powerful ideological boundary that is used to disparage the women's game as less exciting.

This book's title, *No Slam Dunk*, is meant to invoke this very real shifting of the ground in what constitutes well-played and exciting basketball, while also suggesting metaphorical meanings that apply more broadly to sports in general: Girls' and women's sports have come a long way in the past three or four decades, but the achievement of equity and fairness is not a done deal. The continuing barriers to full and equal participation for young people, the far lower pay for most elite-level women athletes, and the continuing dearth of fair and equal media coverage all underline how much still has yet to change before we see gender equality in sports.

Our recent research on gender and sport collected in *No Slam Dunk* shows that is this not simply a story of an "unfinished revolution": It is simplistic and rosy optimism to assume that we are currently living a story of linear progress that will end with a certain future of equality and justice. At the same time, it would also be wrongly pessimistic to think that the growth and development of girls' and women's sports has been stopped in its tracks or for some reason "stalled." Instead, as the book's subtitle implies, the gender changes in organized sports reveal what we call "the unevenness of social change." Both changes *and* continuities in gender in/equality are happening simultaneously.

There are four overarching ways that we analyze the unevenness of social change in gender and sport in *No Slam Dunk*. First, we deploy different levels of analysis. At the structural level, we illuminate sport organizations' shifting gender divisions of labor and power (Connell, 1987), for instance, examining the impact of shifts in resources over the past 30 years for girls' community and school-based sports or the continued male dominant gender division of labor in major sports media. At the personal and interpersonal level, we examine the everyday "doing" or "undoing" of gender (Deutsch, 2007; West & Zimmerman, 1987), for instance, the ways that groups of boys and girls interact at a community soccer event or the ways that parents interact and talk about girls and boys in youth sports leagues. And at the level of cultural analysis, we analyze the importance of shared gender beliefs, ideologies, and mediated symbols, for instance, looking at how sports reporters gush about men's sports while mostly ignoring women's or how transgender or gender nonconforming athletes challenge taken-for-granted beliefs in a natural male-female gender binary. As several of the chapters in this book show, it is important to analyze social structure, everyday interactions, and cultural symbols and beliefs as always intertwined aspects of the social construction of gender.

Second, several of the chapters in *No Slam Dunk* consider the importance of social contexts in understanding the unevenness of social change in gender and sport. Forces for change and continuity are at play simultaneously within and between different social contexts. Families, schools, peer groups, sports organizations, and newspaper and television newsrooms tend to differ in their levels of gender equality and inequality (Connell, 1987; Messner, 2002). Daily, individuals move within and across two, three, or more institutional contexts that vary—sometimes dramatically—in their levels of gender equality or inequality and in the sorts of gender beliefs and interactions that are routinely performed, accepted, or challenged in those contexts. Even within one social context, gender relations can shift in salience, meaning, and levels of equality or inequality. For example, Michela Musto's (2014) study of a coed youth swim team shows that during structured practice activities in the pool, the kids are "athletes"; while in the pool, gender boundaries and hierarchy are less salient. By contrast, during less structured time on the deck, the kids tend to divide into two groups—boys and girls—and gender becomes a highly salient organizing principle. Yet Musto (2014) concludes that perhaps the kids' experiences of more egalitarian gender relations in the pool might "spill over" outside the pool, creating the possibility for less gender hierarchy, even as the kids separate in conventional binary ways (p. 361). The social relations of gender, in other words, are complex, multifaceted, and contradictory across, between, and even within social contexts.

The third way we analyze the unevenness of social change in gender and sport is through a critical analysis of boys' and men's relationships to sport. The terms "gender and sport" commonly invoke questions about girls and women. This makes good sense, at least initially, as it was women who made gender visible as an organizing principle in sport and more generally in society (Birrell, 1984; Griffin, 1998; Hall, 1984; Hargreaves, 1983; Lenskyj, 1986; Theberge, 1987). By the late 1980s and 1990s, the emergence of feminist analysis of women's experience with sport had sparked the beginnings of a critical analysis of boys, men, masculinities, and sport (Burstyn, 1999; Crosset et al., 1996; Curry, 1991; Dunning, 1986; Klein, 1993; Messner & Sabo, 1990; McKay, 1997; Pronger, 1990; Sabo, 1985). Rather than accepting men's relationship to sport as a given or, worse, as some social expression of men's biological nature, the growing body of critical feminist research on boys and men illuminated sport's social role in the formation of boys' and men's identities, bodies, relations with men and with women, and ideologies of nation (Messner, 1992; Montez de Oca, 2013). In *No Slam Dunk*, we attend to this focus on boys and men, critically probing both the problems (including injury, violence, and male domination) and the possibilities (including health promotion and learning egalitarian values) of engagement with sport (Drummond, 2016).

A fourth way that we analyze the unevenness of social change in gender and sport in this book is through centering an *intersectional* analysis. Feminist scholars of the 1970s and 1980s argued that ignoring race and class inequalities tended to falsely universalize the experiences of White middle-class women (Baca Zinn, Weber, Higginbotham, & Thornton, 1986; Collins, 1986; Eisenstein, 1979). They demonstrated that it was important for scholars to grapple with the simultaneous and mutually constituting "intersections" of gender, race/ethnicity, social class, sexuality, and nation. By the 1980s and 1990s, it was becoming clear that sport was a laboratory for building an intersectional understanding of how gender relations intersect with race, social class, and sexual orientation and how these intersections play out in differently in sports media, across different institutional contexts, and across national and international regions (Birrell, 1989; Carrington, 1998; Douglas, 2005; Jamieson, 1995, 1998; McDonald & Birrell, 1999; Montez de Oca, 2013; Montez de Oca et al., 2016; Smith, 1992).

Organization of the Book

Taken together, the chapters in *No Slam Dunk* explore and illuminate the complexities and unevenness of social change in gender and sport by deploying a multilevel analysis (structure, interaction, cultural beliefs and symbols), by attending to varying levels of salience and inequalities within and between different social contexts, by examining the experiences of boys and men (and increasingly, transgender and gender nonconforming people) in addition to girls and women, and by centering an intersectional analysis that attends to the simultaneous construction of gender, social class, race/ethnicity, and nation.

We divide *No Slam Dunk* into three sections. The chapters in part I take a bird's eye view of the big questions about gender, sport, and social change. By probing tensions in contemporary youth sports, national debates about gender equity, and emergent transnational disputes about elite transgender athletes, we shed light on the ways in which gender, racial, and sexual relations have changed—or not—in recent years in sport. Part II of the book includes chapters that illuminate the experiences of sports participants—from girls and boys playing youth sports and men and women coaches in youth sports to a transnational nongovernmental organization's (NGO) program intended to build girls' and women's sports participation in a small postsocialist transitioning nation. Part III of *No Slam Dunk* zeroes in on our ongoing research on media coverage of sports. This section includes a report on our most recent update of a 25-year study of televised news and highlights shows, a critical essay on media coverage of men's sports, and two pieces that analyze media coverage of scandals and controversies about race, sex, and gender in sports.

We hope that *No Slam Dunk* will contribute to critically important conversations about gender and sports among athletes, parents, and coaches; in schools and communities; and within the sports media (both traditional "mainstream media" and emerging "new media"). We have also shaped *No Slam Dunk* as a classroom-friendly book by writing a short introduction for each chapter, which provides some background about the text—why or under what conditions we wrote it, what contribution it makes—and by ending with a question or two that instructors and students can use for discussion or further application of the ideas in the piece. We hope instructors, students, and the general reader will find this to be an engaging text, one that provides important theoretical and empirical insights into the contemporary world of sports to help explain the unevenness of social change and how, despite significant progress, gender equality in sports has been "no slam dunk."

Note

1   We would also argue that comparing the NBA and the WNBA is akin to comparing apples and oranges. The fact that the NBA has a much longer season during prime-time viewing months facilitates their already large market share. The 2- to 3-month-long WNBA season is scheduled during the summer when fewer people are inside watching TV and when most sports fans are conditioned to think it is baseball season transitioning into football season.

References

Acosta, R. V., & Carpenter, J. (2014). Women in intercollegiate sport: A longitudinal, national study, thirty-seven year update. http://www.acostacarpenter.org

Anderson, E., & Kian, E. M. (2012). Examining media contestation of masculinity and head trauma in the National Football League. *Men and Masculinities, 15*, 152–173.

Birrell, S. (1984). Studying gender and sport: A feminist perspective. In N. Theberge & P. Donnelly (Eds.), *Sport and the sociological imagination* (pp. 125–135). Fort Worth, TX: Texas Christian University Press.

Baca Zinn, M., Weber Cannon, L., Higginbotham, E., Thornton Dill, B. (1986). The costs of exclusionary practices in women's studies. *Signs: Journal of Women in Culture and Society, 11*, 290–303.

Birrell, S. (1989). Racial relations theories and sport: Suggestions for a more critical analysis. *Sociology of Sport journal, 6*: 212–227.

Burstyn, V. (1999). *The rites of men: Manhood, politics and the culture of sport*. Toronto, Canada: University of Toronto Press.

Carrington, B. (1998). Sport, masculinity, and black cultural resistance. *Journal of Sport and Social Issues, 22*, 275–298.

Collins, P. H. (1986). Learning from the outsider within: The sociological significance of black feminist thought. *Social Problems, 33*, 14–32.

Connell, R. (1987). *Gender & power*. Stanford, CA: Stanford University Press.

Cooky, C. (2009). "Girls just aren't interested": The social construction of interest in girls' sport. *Sociological Perspectives, 52*, 259–284.

Cooky, C. (2010). Do girls rule?: Understanding popular culture images of "Girl Power!" and sport. In S. Spickard Prettyman & B. Lampman (Eds.), *Learning culture through sports: Perspectives on society and organized sports* (pp. 210–226). Lanham, MD: Rowman & Littlefield.

Cooky, C., & McDonald, M. G. (2005). "If you let me play": Young girls' insider-other narratives of sport. *Sociology of Sport Journal, 22*, 158–177.

Cooky, C., & Rauscher, L. (2016). Girls and the racialization of female bodies in sports contexts. In M. A. Messner & M. Musto (Eds.), *Child's play: Sport in kids' worlds* (pp. 61–81). New Brunswick, NJ: Rutgers University Press.

Crosset, T., Ptacek, J., MacDonald, M., & Benedict, J. (1996). Male student athletes and violence against women: A survey of campus judicial affairs offices. *Violence against women, 2*, 163–179.

Curry, T. (1991). Fraternal bonding in the locker room: Pro-feminist analysis of talk about competition and women. *Sociology of Sport journal, 8*, 119–135.

Deutsch, F. M. (2007). Undoing gender. *Gender & Society, 21*, 106–127.

Douglas, D. D. (2005). Venus, Serena and the Women's Tennis Association: When and where race enters. *Sociology of Sport Journal, 22*, 256–282.

Drummond, M. (2016). The voices of boys on sport, health and physical activity: The beginning of life through a gendered lens. In M. A. Messner & M. Musto (Eds.), *Child's play: Sport in kids' worlds* (pp. 144–164). New Brunswick, NJ: Rutgers University Press.

Dunning, E. (1986). Sport as a male preserve: Notes on the social sources of masculine identity and its transformation. *Theory, Culture & Society, 3*, 79–90.

Dworkin, S. L. (2001). Holding back: Negotiating a glass ceiling on women's muscular strength. *Sociological Perspectives, 44*(3), 333–350.

Eisenstein, Z. R. (Ed.). (1979). *Capitalist patriarchy and the case for socialist feminism.* New York, NY: Monthly Review Press.

Grasmuck, S. (2005). *Protecting home: Class, race, and masculinity in boys' baseball.* New Brunswick, NJ: Rutgers University Press.

Griffin, P. (1998). *Strong women, deep closets: Lesbians and homophobia in women's sport.* Champaign, IL: Human Kinetics.

Hall, M. A. (1984). Toward a feminist analysis of gender inequality in sport. In N. Theberge & P. Donnelly (Eds.), *Sport and the Sociological Imagination.* Fort Worth, TX: Texas University.

Hardin, M., & Shain, S. (2005). Female journalists, are we there yet? 'No.' *Newspaper research journal, 26*, 22–35.

Hargreaves, J. (Ed.). (1983). *Sport, culture and ideology.* London, England: Routledge & Kegan Paul.

Hargreaves, J. (2000). *Heroines of sport: The politics of difference and identity.* London, England: Routledge.

Hartmann, D., & Manning, A. (2016). Kids of color in the American sporting landscape: Limited, concentrated, and controlled. In M. A. Messner & M. Musto (Eds.), *Child's play: Sport in kids' worlds* (pp. 43–60). New Brunswick, NJ: Rutgers University Press.

Jamieson, K. M. (1995). Latinas in sport and physical activity. *Journal of Physical Education, Recreation and Dance, 66*, 42–47.

Jamieson, K. M. (1998). Reading Nancy Lopez: Decoding representations of race, class, sexuality and gender. *Sociology of Sport Journal, 15*(4), 343–358.

Kane, M. J. (1995). Resistance/transformation of the oppositional binary: Exposing sport as a continuum. *Journal of Sport and Social Issues, 19*, 191–218.

Kane, M. J., & Disch, L. J. (1993). Sexual violence and the reproduction of male power in the locker room: The 'Lisa Olsen incident.' *Sociology of Sport Journal, 10*, 331–352.

Klein, A. (1993). *Little big men: Bodybuilding subculture and gender construction.* Albany, NY: State University of New York Press.

LaVoi, N. M., Buysse, J., Maxwell, H. D., & Kane, M. J. (2007). The influence of occupational status and sex of decision maker on media representations in intercollegiate athletics. *Women in Sport & Physical Activity Journal, 15*, 32–43.

Lenskyj, H. (1986). *Out of bounds: Women, sport and sexuality.* Toronto, Canada: The Women's Press.

Loria, Kevin. (2016, August 12). Katie Ledecky is redefining the limits of athletic performance. *Business Insider.* Retrieved from http://www.businessinsider.com/katie-ledecky-olympics-swimming-swimmer-2016-8

Marcur, J. (2016, April 28). Social media, where sports fans congregate, and misogyny runs amok. *The New York Times*. Retrieved from http://www.nytimes.com/2016/04/29/sports/more-than-mean-women-journalists-julie-dicaro-sarah-spain.html

McDonald, M. G., & Birrell, S. (1999). Reading sport critically: A methodology for interrogating power. *Sociology of Sport Journal, 16*, 283–300.

McKay, J. (1997). *Managing gender: Affirmative action and organizational power in Australian, Canadian, and New Zealand sport*. Albany, NY: State University of New York Press.

Messner, M. A. (1988). Sports and male domination: The female athlete as contested ideological terrain. *Sociology of Sport Journal, 5*,197–211.

Messner, M. A. (1992). *Power at play: Sports and the problem of masculinity*. Boston, MA: Beacon Press.

Messner, M. A. (2002). *Taking the field: Women, men, and sports*. Minneapolis, MN: University of Minnesota Press.

Messner, M. A. (2009). *It's all for the kids: Gender, families and youth sports*. Berkeley, CA: University of California Press.

Messner M. A., & Sabo, D. F. (Eds.). (1990). *Sport, men and the gender order: Critical feminist perspectives*. Champaign, IL: Human Kinetics.

Miller, K., Melnick, M., Barnes, G., Farrell, M., & Sabo, D. (2005). Untangling the links among athletic involvement, gender, race, and adolescent academic outcomes. *Sociology of Sport Journal, 22*, 178–193.

Montez de Oca, J. (2013). *Discipline and indulgence: College football, media, and the American way of life during the Cold War*. New Brunswick, NJ: Rutgers University Press.

Montez de Oca, J., Meyer, B., & Scholes, J. (2016). The children are our future: The NFL, corporate social responsibility, and the production of "avid fans." In M. A. Messner & M. Musto (Eds.), *Child's play: Sport in kids' worlds* (pp. 102–124). New Brunswick, NJ: Rutgers University Press.

Musto, M. (2014). Athletes in the pool, girls and boys on the deck: The contextual construction of gender in coed youth swimming. *Gender & Society, 28*, 359–380.

Pronger, B. (1990). *The arena of masculinity: Sports, homosexuality, and the meaning of sex*. New York, NY: St. Martin's Press.

Ring, J. (2009). *Stolen bases: Why American girls don't play baseball*. Champaign, IL: University of Illinois Press.

Sabo, D. (1985). Sport, patriarchy, and male identity: New questions about men and sport. *Arena Review, 9*, 1–30.

Sabo, D., & Veliz, P. (2008). *Go out and play: Youth sports in America*. East Meadow, NY: Women's Sports Foundation.

Sabo, D., & Veliz, P. (2016). Surveying youth sports in America: What we know and what it means for public policy. In M. A. Messner & M. Musto (Eds.), *Child's play: Sport in kids' worlds* (pp. 23–42). New Brunswick, NJ: Rutgers University Press.

Smith, Y. (1992). Women of color in society and sport. *Quest, 44*, 228–250.

Theberge, N. (1987). Sport and women's empowerment. *Women's Studies International Forum, 10*, 387–393.

Thul, C., LaVoi, N. M., & Hazelwood, T. (2016). Physical activity experiences of East African Immigrant girls. In M. A. Messner & M. Musto (Eds.), *Child's play: Sport in kids' worlds* (pp. 165–178). New Brunswick, NJ: Rutgers University Press.

Travers, A. (2016). Transgender and gender nonconforming kids and the binary obstacles of sport participation in North America. In M. A. Messner & M. Musto (Eds.), *Child's play: Sport in kids' worlds* (pp 179–201). New Brunswick, NJ: Rutgers University Press.

US swimmer Katie Ledecky called "world's best athlete." (2016, August 10). *ABC News*. Retrieved from http://abcnews.go.com/GMA/video/us-swimmer-katie-ledecky-called-worlds-best-athlete-41262517

Warshaw, Amelia. (2016, August 6). Who is swimmer Katie Ledecky? Meet the next Michael Phelps at the 2016 Rio Olympics. *The Daily Beast*. Retrieved from http://www .thedailybeast.com/who-is-swimmer-katie-ledecky-meet-the-next-michael-phelps-at-the -2016-rio-olympics

West, C., & Zimmerman, D. H. (1987). Doing gender. *Gender & Society, 1,* 125–151.

Part I
Sport, Gender, and Sexuality

● ●

1

Gender Ideologies, Youth Sports, and the Production of Soft Essentialism

● ●

MICHAEL A. MESSNER

When my two sons, Miles and Sasha, started playing youth sports—mostly Little League Baseball (LLB) and American Youth Soccer Organization (AYSO) soccer—I could not help but notice the contrasts with when I played Little League in the late 1950s and early 1960s. Just like back then, parents today still come out in droves to cheer on their kids. Kids continue today to flock to youth sports by the millions to play on neatly tended green fields. But there is one huge difference. In my youth, "kids" in sports meant almost entirely boys. There were virtually no opportunities for girls to play organized team sports back then. By the time my kids were playing in the 1990s and early 2000s, "kids" most assuredly meant both boys and girls. This massive transformation in youth sports participation, however, did not neatly translate into who was coaching the kids. In my youth, it was 100% dads who stood on the sidelines coaching youth sports. Nearly a half century later, my sons were still seeing almost entirely men coaches, though I noticed a sparse sprinkling of women

Source: "Gender ideologies, youth sports, and the production of soft essentialism," by M. A. Messner, 2011, *Sociology of Sport Journal, 28*(2), pp. 151–170, http://dx.doi.org/10.1123/ssj.28.2 .151. Copyright by Human Kinetics, Inc. Reprinted with permission.

assistant and head coaches. This uneven social change tweaked my sociological imagination: On the one hand, 20 or 30 years after the passage of Title IX in the United States, girls were swarming into youth sports, bolstered by the enthusiastic support of their parents; on the other hand, there seemed to be some invisible barrier holding women out of coaching. After several years of participant observation in LLB/S and AYSO and many interviews with youth sports coaches, I wrote a book, It's All for the Kids, *in which I argued that women's relative absence in youth sports coaching was not due so much to overt discrimination as it was due to daily gendered interactions and deeply ingrained beliefs that seemed to override people's growing ideals of gender equality for their kids. I called this currently shared belief system "soft essentialism," counterpoising it to the rigid "hard essentialism" that justified the "naturalness" of a rigid divide between girls and boys during my youth. Soft essentialism, as the following article elaborates, is a shared belief system about gender that expresses the unevenness of social change in sports. Kids today grow up in a world substantially changed—but not entirely transformed—by feminism. I argue, perhaps surprisingly, that if we want to fully realize the feminist ideal of equality for all, we must substantially rethink the ways in which we raise our boys.*

—Michael A. Messner

I begin with a 21st-century feminist fable:

Once upon a time, girls were believed to be naturally unsuited for sports and were not allowed to participate. Sports were set up exclusively by and for boys and men. But in the early 1970s, Billie Jean King beat Bobby Riggs in the Battle of the Sexes; girls sued Little League for the right to play baseball; and Title IX was passed, a national law that gave girls the legal right to equity in school sports. This opened the floodgates to girls' athletic participation. In the subsequent decades, tens of millions of U.S. girls and women have played community-based youth sports, school sports, and college sports. Today, though equity is not yet achieved, sport is no longer just for boys and men. Thanks to feminism and to Title IX, girls are free to choose to play sports, thus gaining access to the social and health benefits of athletic participation.

Most everybody knows this triumphant feminist tale. Like any story that has legs, this one is based on some core truths. There is no doubt that girls' sport participation has skyrocketed in recent decades, and there is ample research to document the claim that girls who play sports gain access to social and health benefits (Miller, Melnick, Barnes, Farrell, & Sabo, 1999, 2005; Sabo & Veliz, 2008). My concern here is with how shifting gender relations in sport articulate with the larger gender order, and in particular, how the commonsense stories we tell ourselves about girls and sport give us a window not into some final triumph of feminism, but rather into a contemporary reorganization of gender relations and a concomitant emergence of a newly hegemonic professional-class-based gender ideology. Rather than reflecting some straightforward view of "reality," the conventional story of girls' athletic progress outlined above distorts reality in three ways. First, it is a simplistic rendering of history, premised on a linear before-and-after view of progress. Second, the story narrates an undifferentiated view of "girls and women," failing especially to account for the ways that class and race have differently constrained and enabled girls' and women's sports participation in the past and in the present. And third, while positioning girls as postfeminist choosers, the story passively endorses an almost entirely unreconstructed naturalistic view of boys' relationship to sport. In focusing on these points, I hope to illuminate sport's contemporary role in a shifting terrain of gender relations.

More than two decades ago in an article published in the *SSJ* (Messner, 1988), I argued that the exploding athletic participation rates of girls and women highlighted sport as a terrain of contradictory and contested gender meanings and relations. This article follows logically from questions raised by that earlier work, analyzing the recent history of U.S. sport and gender relations. At the conceptual heart of this article, I sketch a four-part periodization of hegemonic and counter-hegemonic gender ideologies in sport (summarized in Figure 1.1) that shows the utility of differentiating two concepts that scholars too often conflate: essentialism and categoricalism. I will offer a brief empirical example from my research on contemporary youth sports—with a focus on professional-class volunteer coaches' views of children and gender—to illustrate an ascendant gender ideology I call "soft essentialism," a belief system that arises out of current tensions between liberal feminist ideals of equal opportunity and stubbornly persistent commitments to the idea of natural sex difference. Rather than being a locus of gender revolution, I will conclude, youth sports has become an ideal site for the construction of adult narratives that appropriate the liberal feminist language of "choice" for girls, but not for boys, in ways that help to recreate and naturalize the continuing gender inequalities in professional-class work and family life.

Gender Ideologies and Historical Gender Formation

It has become common academic practice to dismiss ideas or theorists by labeling them "essentialist." Used as a verb, the accusation that one is "essentializing" a group of people has become a shorthand (and often ill-informed) means of dismissing an idea or even an entire line of thought. I suggest that it will contribute to more precise thinking if we differentiate between two commonly conflated concepts: *essentialism* and *categoricalism*. Essentialism, as I use it, is a viewpoint that assumes natural (usually biological) differences between groups of people (e.g., the assumption that genes, hormones, or brain structure make women more emotional and men more rational). Categoricalism is a belief that all members of a group are one way, while all members of another group are the opposite (e.g., all men are aggressive, while all women are maternal).

Essentialism and categoricalism often go hand in hand. But sometimes they exist separately. It is possible to hold an essentialist but noncategorical belief: Women naturally tend to be shorter than men, though we can see that some men are shorter than some women, revealing a "continuum of difference" (Kane, 1995). It is also

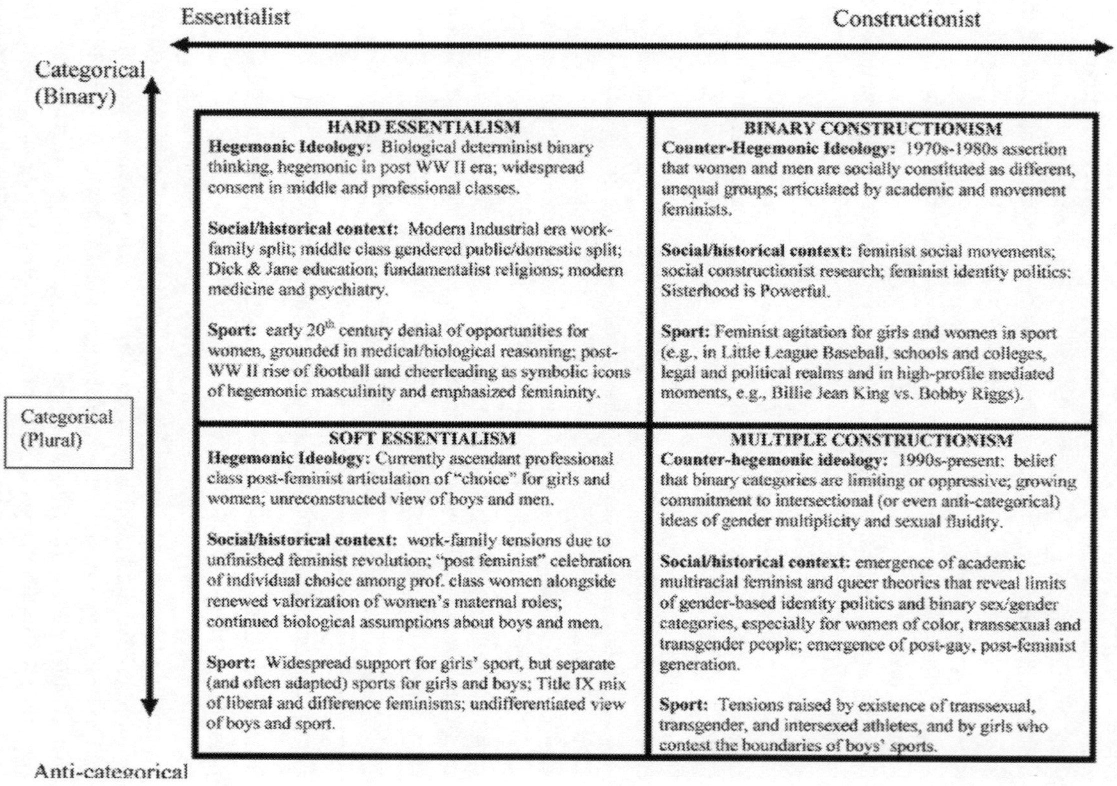

Constructionist

Essentialist

Categorical (Binary)

Anti-categorical

Categorical (Plural)

BINARY CONSTRUCTIONISM

Counter-Hegemonic Ideology: 1970s-1980s assertion that women and men are socially constituted as different, unequal groups; articulated by academic and movement feminists.

Social/historical context: feminist social movements; social constructionist research; feminist identity politics: Sisterhood is Powerful.

Sport: Feminist agitation for girls and women in sport (e.g., in Little League Baseball, schools and colleges, legal and political realms and in high-profile mediated moments, e.g., Billie Jean King vs. Bobby Riggs).

MULTIPLE CONSTRUCTIONISM

Counter-hegemonic ideology: 1990s-present: belief that binary categories are limiting or oppressive; growing commitment to intersectional (or even anti-categorical) ideas of gender multiplicity and sexual fluidity.

Social/historical context: emergence of academic multiracial feminist and queer theories that reveal limits of gender-based identity politics and binary sex/gender categories, especially for women of color, transsexual and transgender people; emergence of post-gay, post-feminist generation.

Sport: Tensions raised by existence of transsexual, transgender, and intersexed athletes, and by girls who contest the boundaries of boys' sports.

HARD ESSENTIALISM

Hegemonic Ideology: Biological determinist binary thinking, hegemonic in post WW II era; widespread consent in middle and professional classes.

Social/historical context: Modern Industrial era work-family split; middle class gendered public/domestic split; Dick & Jane education; fundamentalist religions; modern medicine and psychiatry.

Sport: early 20th century denial of opportunities for women, grounded in medical/biological reasoning; post-WW II rise of football and cheerleading as symbolic icons of hegemonic masculinity and emphasized femininity.

SOFT ESSENTIALISM

Hegemonic Ideology: Currently ascendant professional class post-feminist articulation of "choice" for girls and women; unreconstructed view of boys and men.

Social/historical context: work-family tensions due to unfinished feminist revolution; "post feminist" celebration of individual choice among prof. class women alongside renewed valorization of women's maternal roles; continued biological assumptions about boys and men.

Sport: Widespread support for girls' sport, but separate (and often adapted) sports for girls and boys; Title IX mix of liberal and difference feminisms; undifferentiated view of boys and sport.

FIGURE 1.1. Terrain of Gender Ideologies

possible to hold categorical but not essentialist views: Feminist psychoanalytic theorists have argued that women and men developed categorically different orientations to intimacy and morality, differences grounded not in biology but in the social organization of mothering (Chodorow, 1978; Gilligan, 1982).

In Figure 1.1, I locate beliefs in essentialism at one end of a horizontal continuum, countered on the other pole by beliefs in social constructionism. On a vertical continuum, I locate categorical beliefs at the top, counterposed to anticategorical views of gender plurality and fluidity at the bottom. In what follows, using the two-by-two table created by these two continua, and influenced by Connell's (2002) periodization of gender thought, I will sketch out a schema of hegemonic and counterhegemonic gender ideologies in U.S. society and in sport. Starting with the upper-left cell, I will move clockwise to discuss, in turn:

1. **Hard essentialism:** a categorical and essentialist view of women and men that was the foundation of the hegemonic gender ideology of the post–World War II era White, middle-class, heterosexual family, constructed and naturalized in part within sport.
2. **Binary Constructionism:** emerging in the 1970s out of feminism, a view that challenged naturalized beliefs of gender difference and hierarchy, and mobilized counterhegemonic discourse and actions by strategically organizing around the category *women*.
3. **Multiple Constructionism:** with its roots in late 1970s socialist feminism and 1980s feminist women of color's critique of the White, middle-class basis of feminist binary constructionism, this view developed in the 1990s to the present as a radical anticategorical, antiessentialist impulse in queer and transgender action, and academic de-gendering theory.
4. **Soft Essentialism:** as a currently ascendant hegemonic ideology of the professional class, this view valorizes the liberal feminist ideal of individual choice for girls and women while retaining a largely naturalized view of boys and men—a view that is especially evident, I will argue, in youth sports.

I will outline the first three of these gender ideologies briefly with very broad brushstrokes, spending more space in articulating the dynamics of soft essentialism. Overall, my aim is to illustrate the shifting hegemony of historical gender formation in the United States over the past half century. Hegemony, as it is widely understood, is a consolidation of power based in part on force but most effectively on the development of widespread consent (Hargreaves, 1983; Willis, 1983). Any hegemonic moment of gender formation also creates tensions and contradictions. While consent based on shared ideology helps to contain or manage these contradictions, fissures necessarily occur, often (but not always) resulting in organized opposition, reform, or occasional radical ruptures. Thus in the model presented below, I will attempt to illustrate both the sources of consent and continuity while showing how tensions and contradictions give rise to counterhegemonic ideas and actions. Soft essentialism, I will argue, is a largely conservative, class-based reorganization of gender that resolves some of the contradictions of professional-class work and family life in this historical moment, while giving rise to new and different tensions.

Hard Essentialism

The post–World War II era in the United States ushered in a harsh imposition of strict gender divisions of labor in work and family life. The 1950s is still viewed nostalgically by many as the golden era of "the American family," but scholars have shown that the near hysteria (stretching across popular culture, psychiatry, medicine, politics, education, industrial unions, and sport) that pushed millions of women out of public life and into the home in the postwar years was actually a historical aberration, rather than a manifestation of some long-standing "traditional family" (Coontz, 2000). In the postwar era, hegemonic ideals of motherhood for women and breadwinning for men were grounded in both essentialist and categorical beliefs about women and men.

The consent that consolidated around postwar hard essentialism was never absolute. It was middle- and professional-class women and men who most closely conformed to this hegemonic ideal. Millions of poor and working-class women (disproportionately women of color) remained in the labor force, often out of necessity. Squeezed between the middle-class hegemonic ideal of the housewife/mother and the postwar expansion of women's low-paid industrial and service-sector jobs, these women were judged as deviant, perhaps not fully "women."

A look at post–World War II sport—perhaps the apogee of sex segregation in U.S. sport—illuminates this moment of class-based gender formation. By the mid-20th century, a dramatic burst of women's early century athleticism had been largely suppressed or contained into nearly invisible social spaces (Twin, 1989; Cahn, 1994). By the postwar years, youth sports programs (as well as school and university sports programs) had become almost entirely the province of boys, and though it survived for a few years after the war, women's professional baseball was soon extinguished (Ring, 2009). The ascendance of football, a game that valorizes violent collisions of armored male bodies and heroic metaphors of war and conquest—symbolically linked with the emergence of the cheerleader as symbolic icon of American White femininity—became sport's most celebrated display of hard essentialism (Adams & Bettis, 2003; Messner, 1988; Montez de Oca, 2005).

Just as the gendered public–domestic split in postwar society was structurally manifested more in middle-class (and disproportionately White) families, the flushing out of girls and women from midcentury sport was also closer to absolute among class- and race-privileged girls and women. Cahn (1994) observes, for instance, that African American women's participation in industrial basketball leagues and national amateur track and field competition continued unabated through the middle decades of the 20th century. My own analysis of 100 years of a California high school's annual yearbooks suggests similar patterns, with girls' interscholastic sports disappearing after the 1920s and midcentury participation in the (mostly intramural) sports ghetto of the Girls' Athletic Association (GAA) disproportionately made up of Japanese-American, Filipina, and Latina girls. White middle-class girls achieved social status not as athletes but as cheerleaders. As public exemplars of what Connell (1987) calls "emphasized femininity," cheerleaders helped to construct male football players as midcentury exemplars of hegemonic masculinity.

However, even within the professional class, consent with the postwar hierarchical gendered public–domestic split was not absolute. The restrictions on educated women's lives were reflected in widespread individual discontent—partly contained by a barrage of psychiatric and other medical "expertise" on the natural virtues of the wife/mother role, dispersed through an expanding popular culture. Betty Friedan's (1963) *The Feminine Mystique* was grounded in the experiences of college-educated, professional-class women who had been largely barred from participation in public life. Given the critiques that emerged in subsequent decades of Friedan's conservatism with respect to sexual orientation, class, and race, it is too easy to forget the sharpness of Friedan's critique of how hegemonic postwar gender ideology supported an institutional scaffolding (included in which were the sturdy girders of Parsonian sociology and Freudian psychology) within which women were confined to maternal domesticity. Friedan provided a first voice in what would blossom a decade later into a full chorus of opposition, consolidating by the early 1970s into a powerful counterhegemonic ideology.

Binary Constructionism

The title of the most widely circulated feminist collection of the 1970s, *Sisterhood Is Powerful* (Morgan, 1970), captures the crux of binary constructionism. As feminist movements exploded in the 1970s, women increasingly found collective empowerment in discovering shared experiences of oppression and articulating shared strategies to change society. It is beyond the focus of this article to reiterate the debates and differences among different strains of 1970s feminisms. Here, I simply want to note that the two most public forms of U.S. feminism at that time shared a similar commitment to antiessentialism while asserting a binary, categorical view of women and men. Whether in its more radical articulations of women as a historically oppressed sex class or in liberal feminists' language of sex roles as socially scripted and learned behaviors, the heart of these 1970s feminisms was the idea that women's subordination was a manifestation not of nature, but rather of social forces (Firestone, 1971). By extension, it was believed that when women organized around their shared identity and interests—whether through radical revolution or liberal reform—a state of equality between women and men could be achieved.

By the late 1970s, radical feminism had been marginalized by a cultural and political backlash and also by the increasing social acceptance of liberal feminist organizations like the National Organization for Women and leaders like Friedan and Gloria Steinem. Though they continued to be influenced by radical and socialist impulses in the larger feminist movement, liberal feminists pushed a narrowed agenda of equal rights for individual women in education, politics, workplaces, and other male-dominated public institutions. Equality increasingly came to be defined not in terms of collective efforts to radically transform institutions but as attempts to open existing institutions to individuals from the disenfranchised category: women.

This liberal feminist activism was reflected in U.S. sports. On numerous fronts—from high schools and colleges to Billie Jean King's push for equal pay for women on the pro tennis tour—women struggled to pry open the institution of sport, a stubborn bastion of men's privilege. This effort was dramatic in youth sports. Little League Baseball was started in 1938 and spread rapidly in the postwar years as the flagship youth sports organization for U.S. boys. In the early 1970s, girls successfully sued for the right to play Little League and were subsequently in the 1980s included in the burgeoning youth soccer movement and an expanding field of national youth sports organizations. Today, millions of girls play youth sports, a testament to the successes of feminist organizing from the 1970s to the present and to the widespread social absorption of the liberal feminist ideal of equal opportunity for girls.

Girls' and women's experiences in U.S. sport illuminate the limits of binary constructionism as a counterhegemonic feminist strategy. I point briefly to two points of tension in this expanding field of play for girls. First, reflecting the widely documented White middle-class basis of liberal feminism, the expansion of youth and school-based sports disproportionately benefited White, suburban, professional-class girls (Baca Zinn et al., 1986; Coakley, 2006; Sabo & Veliz, 2008; Stevenson, 2007). Second, the centrality of the body in organized sports exposed the ideological limits of binary constructionism and the feminist strategy of individual equal opportunity. In sport, the presumption of bodily difference between boys and girls—in effect, a creeping back in of essentialist beliefs—precluded a strategy of desegregation of youth sport, serving instead as a foundation for the creation of a kind of "separate-but-equal" ideal of sport for males and females.

The contradictions inherent in a strategy that pushes for both individual equal opportunity and categorical separation of the sexes in sport can be seen at the national level. Title IX reflects a strategic joining of liberal feminist strategies of equal opportunity along with a sort of throwback to what in the 19th century was called "social feminism," a valorization of presumed natural differences between the sexes (Brake, 2010). The Women's Sports Foundation—the largest and most important advocacy organization for girls and women in U.S. sports—has taken this same tack, using an equity-with-difference strategy, advocating for girls' and women's sport organizations that mirror but do not seek to integrate with boys' and men's sports (Messner, 2002). In youth sports, this joining of different feminist traditions can be seen in the shifting gender regime of Little League Baseball. In 1974, a National Organization for Women–sponsored civil rights claim was decided by the New Jersey Superior Court, which ordered LLB to allow 8–12 year old girls to play baseball. Once forced by law to incorporate girls, LLB responded rapidly to create separate gendered tracks: baseball for boys, softball for girls (Ring, 2009). The organization is now called "LLB/S" and the "slash" in this moniker is a visible indicator of the current state of play of the organization's gender regime (Messner, 2009). Essentially LLB/S accommodated girls not by integrating baseball, but by channeling girls into a separate and different sport, thus maintaining baseball as the province of boys and men.

The feminist counterhegemonic articulation of binary constructionism in sport resolved one of the central contradictions of hard essentialism: the blatantly unfair exclusion of girls and women in a society that values individual equal opportunities. However, as a strategy within sport, binary constructionism privileged the interests of middle- and upper-class White girls (Cooky, 2009). Moreover, organizational responses to binary constructionism ushered into youth sports and into national law a revived strand of essentialism. The resultant institutionalized sex segregation created new contradictions, strains, and tensions in gender relations. As we will see, the mainstream response to the limits of binary constructionism, especially among professional-class people, is the emergence of an ascendant hegemonic ideology of soft essentialism. Before I discuss that, however, I will outline the emergence of a radically resistant discourse of multiple constructionism.

Multiple Constructionism

The power of categorical identity politics lies in its simplicity, its ability to provide a discourse of shared experience and interests around which people can rally for change. But that very simplicity tends also to exclude and to wash out differences and inequalities of race/ethnicity, social class, and sexualities that exist within a category like "women." In the latter half of the 1970s, socialist-feminists developed a sophisticated theory and political practice that sought to grapple with the intersection of social class and gender inequalities. To be sure, socialist feminism was still very much a categorical theory, but it was a first attempt to move beyond an oversimplified *binary* view of gender. Instead of dealing with two undifferentiated categories—women and men—socialist feminists now grappled with differences and contradictions between working-class and professional-class women, working-class and professional-class men (Eisenstein, 1979; Tolson, 1977).

Socialist feminism was a precursor to multiracial feminism, a perspective that blossomed in the 1980s and 1990s as an attempt to theorize multiple categories (most often race, class, and gender), utilizing metaphors of "intersectionality," and "matrixes of domination," that emphasize crosscutting systems of inequality and plural identity categories (Baca Zinn & Dill, 1996; Collins, 1990; hooks, 1984). Like socialist feminists, multiracial feminists retained a commitment to categorical thinking, due in part to their concern with the strategic usefulness of categories in pressing politically for distributive justice (Grillo, 1995). In Figure 1.1, I locate plural categoricalism at the midpoint of the vertical continuum between binary categoricalism and anticategoricalism. Advocates of multiracial feminism like Baca Zinn and Dill (1996) and of "multiple masculinities and femininities" like Connell (1987) reject the class and race bias and distortions built into feminist binary constructionism. But they do not embrace a radical anticategorical de-gendering viewpoint. Instead, they are committed to an intersectional structural analysis that highlights how groups (categories) are shaped and constrained by social and historical dynamics. Social justice, to these scholars, is possible not through eliminating categories such as gender and race, but by building coalitions that strategically assert group-based interests. Adapting Spivak's (1995) often-noted concept of "strategic essentialism," I suggest that multiracial feminists oppose biological essentialism, while simultaneously asserting the utility of what is better termed "strategic categoricalism." Strategic categoricalism (by subordinated racial/ethnic groups, sexual minorities, or women) resists, takes up, and recasts categories that have been imposed upon them by superordinate groups with the goal of contesting the privilege of superordinates.

Though they would not necessarily see themselves as such, multiracial feminists are often viewed as transitional precursors to relativized views of gender fluidity and multiplicity that emerged in the 1990s and 2000s, most radically in the anticategorical works of "post-gay" sexual minorities (Sedgwick, 1990). The growing visibility of intersexed children, transsexual and transgender people, and masculine women illuminate the shortcomings of the tidy binaries of 1970s feminism while also illustrating the limits of a radical strategy of anticategorical degendering (Bornstein, 1993; Fausto-Sterling, 2000; Halberstam, 1998). These visible sexual and gendered "others," joined with a growing generational antipathy to categorical identity politics has fueled debates (mostly within academia) about a "de-gendering" strategy of social change that seeks to do away with sex and gender categories (Deutsch, 2007).

Anticategorical degendering strategies have had little influence within sport, an institution defined by rigid categorical boundaries. However, fluid and multiple ways of thinking about gender raise disruptive questions about sex segregation in sport. Despite the cultural work done by mass media and many promoters of women's sports to contain the public image of the female athlete as feminine and heterosexual, the existence of powerful, aggressive, masculine and/or lesbian women athletes has troubled simple categorical assumptions about women (Dworkin & Wachs, 2009; Kane, 1995; Messner, 1988). In addition, others who do not fit within binary sex/gender categories have increasingly placed strains on the conventional gender regime of organized sport. The recent controversy surrounding South African athlete Caster Semenya's inclusion in women's track is a potent example. As Dworkin and her colleagues (under submission) argue, the fact that Semenya—apparently an intersexed person—was forced to undergo "gender verification" tests reveals the oppressive (and in this case, White colonial) imposition of binary sex categorization in sport. It also reveals the asymmetries in cultural assumptions underlying the gender-divided social organization of sport: that "gender verification" tests are required of intersexed, transgender, or transsexual individuals *in women's sports but not in men's* lays bare assumptions about the natural superiority of men's bodies.

An early transsexual challenge in sport was the celebrated and controversial case of professional tennis player Renee Richards, who transitioned from male to female in 1976 and then sought to play on the women's pro circuit (Birrell & Cole, 1994). The International Olympic Committee in 2003 attempted to resolve the question of where transsexuals "fit" by allowing transsexual athletes to compete within their postoperative sex category. But does this resolution really address fully the issues raised by the existence of people who do not "fit" the binary sex categories around which sport is ordered? Feminist biologist Ann Fausto-Sterling (2000) argues that intersexed, transgender, and transsexual people exist not on some continuum "between male and female," but instead reveal "sex and gender as a multi-dimensional space" (p. 19). Radical critics of the IOC's inclusion of intersexed or transsexual people in women's or in men's sports argue that this policy erases this empirical reality of gender as a multidimensional space, instead absorbing and neutralizing trans or intersexed peoples' otherwise radical challenge to assumptions of fixed binary sex categories. The legal inclusion of, say, a female transsexual in a women's sport serves to reinscribe the ideology of categorical sex difference that in turn legitimizes social inequality (Sykes, 2006; Travers, 2008).

Contrarily, Namaste (2000) warns that rather than leading to greater justice and freedom, a de-gendering strategy that seeks to dismantle binary gender categories can result instead in "queer theory's erasure of transgender subjectivity" (p. 9). Similarly, Connell (2010, forthcoming) argues that many 1970s feminists vilified transsexual women because they did not "fit" in the counterhegemonic binary constructionist narrative, while more recently multiconstructionists have deployed transsexuals as heroic exemplars who prove the fluidity and malleability of sex and gender. Connell (forthcoming) concludes that a forced inclusion of transsexual women within the "agglutinative" LGBTI umbrella is wrongheaded: "Far from being fluid, transsexual women's lives are a striking proof of the *intransigence* of gender," an intransigence most notable in the fact that most transsexual women do not want to be included in a de-gendered LGBTI umbrella group of sexual others. Instead, they seek social recognition *as women*.

Connell (forthcoming) argues that "a powerful political agenda need not have the goal of abolishing gender." For transsexual women, the more relevant goal is creating a *just* gender order that moves beyond individual rights to include guarantees of safety from physical violence; material access to education, jobs, and medical care; and respectful social recognition. In concluding that "The best guarantee of justice for transsexual women is a gender-equal society," Connell illuminates the limits of a political strategy of de-gendering. As a discursive "troubling" of gender categories in sport and elsewhere, anticategoricalism is potent. As a way to force broad social changes especially in the realm of distributive justice, anticategoricalism is limited. Much of the social world—including sport—is organized under the categorical assumption that there are women and there are men. Fighting for distributive justice usually involves not abandoning, but rather strategically deploying these social categories. From this point of view, sisterhood—albeit a more radically inclusive and multiple conception of "sisterhood" than that deployed in 1970s feminism—may still be a powerful transformative force for social justice. On the other hand, it is also the case that successfully pressing for gender justice for "women"—especially if this category is firmly delineated through biological essentialist assumptions—will not necessarily lead to greater inclusion of transgender, transsexual, or intersexed people. All categorical projects—even those premised on progressive strategic categoricalism—create boundaries that exclude "others" who do not fit within the categorical definition.

Soft Essentialism

As we have seen, liberal feminism leveraged institutions toward equal opportunities for individual women with a strategic use of the category *women*. However, in sport, whether through development of adapted sports for girls, like Little League Softball, or through legal statutes like Title IX, a strain of essentialism akin to 19th-century social feminism crept back into the strategy, thus complicating what is meant by "equality." Can separate really ever be equal? Codified and endorsed, the separation of boys and girls in sport fed in to the development of an ascendant gender ideology: Soft essentialism is a belief system that assumes natural differences between boys and girls. But in recognizing girls' and women's right to choose participation in public life, soft essentialism does not endorse categorical social containment of women in domestic life. Meanwhile, boys and men are a largely unmarked (and implicitly undifferentiated) category in the discourse of soft essentialism.

I will next illustrate some of the key dynamics of soft essentialism by drawing from my recent study of gender relations among adult volunteers in one community's youth sports programs.[1] I draw from this research to offer illustrative examples of soft essentialist discourse. Youth sport is an ideal site for seeing the workings of soft essentialism. As an institution that makes visible people's bodily abilities and limitations, sport has historically created and conveyed cultural assumptions and values about essential differences between women and men, more so than most other institutions (the military is perhaps equivalent). Though clearly contested by girls' and women's movement into sport, this is still a place where essentialism is constructed through sex-segregated bodily practices. As I will show, many adults are not only "comfortable" with thinking of boys and girls as naturally different—they in fact revel in the pleasure of shared talk about the ways that girls and boys differ (Messner, 2000).

Adults' Narratives about Boys and Girls in Youth Sports

In my interviews, I asked youth soccer, baseball, and softball coaches to talk about boys, girls, and gender. All of the coaches embraced a narrative of equal opportunity for boys and girls to play sports. However, most struggled with how to square this belief in equality with the continued sex segregation in sports and with the fact that the vast majority of coaches are men, while most women volunteers take on the helping roles of "team moms."

Adults I interviewed were very articulate and confident in drawing from well-known cultural narratives about sport as a site of health enhancement and empowerment for girls. By contrast, they fumbled and struggled to find a coherent thread with which to weave a narrative about boys, often falling back on trite clichés about boys being "hyper-active" and "rowdy" with "high energy" and driven by "all that testosterone." Girls are narrated by adults as flexible choosers in the world and boys as narrow, linear, and predestined for public lives in sport and careers.

I was struck by the clear and confident ways in which today's adults talk about girls' lives as a *socially contextualized field of choices*. This way of talking about girls is, without a doubt, one of the major accomplishments of liberal feminism over the past 40 years. By contrast, adults still don't have very sophisticated ways of thinking about boys beyond assuming that everything they do is driven by "testosterone" and by their natural predispositions to be active, aggressive, and competitive. Many of the parents I interviewed saw sports participation as a way for girls to learn more conventionally masculine traits that would benefit them in public life. These same adults seemed to see boys' aggressive and competitive traits as simple expressions of nature, played out within (but not constructed by) sports, while girls were viewed as malleable, their softer natures reformable through sports participation. For example, Gilbert Morales, who has coached both girls and boys at various age-levels, suggested that sports participation creates aggressive traits in girls that make them more like boys:

> They're very, very different in style . . . The girls tend to form a team much easier than boys. Boys seem to have a much more competitive streak in them and a much more aggressive streak in them than the girls do—sometimes to the detriment of the team. They are individuals playing together, not a team working together. I think that changes a little bit as the girls get older and become more trained or conditioned into behaving in a more aggressive manner—over time, girls who would have been aggressive, to some extent, and competitive, to some extent, I think learn to be more so. And I think what happens is as they grow older, those who are willing to be like that—be more similar to boys, I think—stay in the sport. And I think that's where the similarities—they become more similar. So, I think as that happens, as they get older, I think the differences tend to get a little bit more blurred.

Morales, like many coaches I interviewed, assumed that girls are naturally cooperative and group-oriented but concludes that with athletic experiences, they can become aggressively competitive individuals, "more similar to the boys." While girls are viewed as flexible, boys are viewed categorically as aggressive individualists whose essential nature is played out in sports. Boys and girls become more similar—"the differences . . . a little bit more blurred"—when girls play sports and become more like boys. Coaches' narratives rarely recognize any kind of range among boys, tending instead to assume that all boys have a natural affinity with sports. This assumption—especially when compared with the common view of girls as flexible, complex, and fluid—speaks volumes about adults' one-dimensional and still largely unreconstructed views of boys.

Adults who had coached both boys and girls said that they treated them differently because they saw girls as more sensitive and emotionally vulnerable and boys as insensitive and less vulnerable. Mark Daly, who has coached both girls' and boys' soccer, said that boys respond well when he yells at them:

> We had practice last night, and you know I found myself yelling at a couple of them. Whereas when I coached the high school girls I never, I won't say never but almost never scream at them. I find that they kind of go into themselves and its kind of uh, it doesn't work out. Whereas the guys you can yell at him, tell him

that he's going to do fifty laps and, and they don't hate you. There's no problem, do you know what I mean?

Similarly, soccer coach Alan Lindgren said that "girls are a lot more complex [while] the boys tend to be . . . there's just not much going on . . . with the boys it's—it's *subtler*—they don't really push back very much, they just kinda' do it. They keep their thoughts more to themselves I think." Little League coach Ted Miller said that he has read articles on coaching that say that when coaching boys, "male coaches can, you know, come up and grab the face mask and shake 'em and yell at 'em, *'rah-rah!'*" But Miller has learned from these articles that girls "don't seem to respond to that very well, the yelling and screaming." Mitch Flores has coached both girls' softball and boys' baseball, and he took a "very different approach" to coaching them:

> When I coached boys' baseball it was a total different style. The boys are a little more rough around the edges and you can talk to them a certain way and they take it and it just rolls right off 'em, but the girls, no way. I'm boisterous, I have a deep big voice, I can yell at a kid across [the field]. I had some nine year olds on the team and I did "*Come on*" you know, and you see the little girls' faces and you're thinking, I hurt this little girl's feelings, I'm sorry you know, "Are you all right?" And they're standing there and they're quivering and you're going "Oh my gosh" and it, but it's a different, it's a different style.

As these coaches' statements show and as I observed in my years of field research, coaches tend to treat boys and girls differently. To the extent that they are conscious of this different treatment, they believe it to be a reasoned response to the different natures of boys and girls. Coaches' rarely seem to consider how their behaviors might in fact *construct* these differences. Mark Daly's and Mitch Flores's belief that when a coach yells at boys "there's no problem," that "it just rolls right off 'em," is based on an assumption that boys are emotionally invulnerable compared to the emotional vulnerability that seems so visible in girls. What they do not recognize, perhaps, is the many years of gender socialization that nine-year old boys have already endured—from families, peers, popular culture, and sport—that has taught them to hide or repress their emotional and physical pain and not to show their vulnerabilities. Rather than simply responding to some natural ability that boys have to "take it," coaches who yell at boys are simply adding another layer to what psychologist William Pollack (1999) calls "the hardening of boys." Adults—more often men, but sometimes women as well—too often use emotional separation, shame, and fear to toughen boys in ways that prepare them for the cutthroat competition of public life but simultaneously stunt their ability to engage in the kinds of mutual intimacy that are the foundation of close relationships and happy family lives.

In my years of observing boys playing baseball, I've noticed that in the younger age groups, when a boy gets slightly injured, strikes out, or gets yelled at by a coach for a bad play, he will get visibly upset. Some of these younger boys cry—often privately, pulling their caps over their faces in the dugout—and the other boys and coaches usually don't look at or speak to them, respectfully giving the boys private space to express feelings that are not considered fully appropriate. With the older boys—especially by age 11 or 12—these tears and displays of vulnerability are few and far between. Instead, boys' most common response to injuries, making a bad play, or getting criticized by the coach is a short burst of anger—like a thrown helmet after a strikeout—followed by a posture of sullen, determined silence in the dugout. The hardening of boys teaches them to transform any feelings of hurt, pain, or sorrow into the more "appropriately masculine" expressions of contained anger or stoic silence.

Adults tolerate—even celebrate—the toughening of their sons because they assume it to be consistent both with boys' essential natures and with their destinies to compete in future public lives with jobs and careers. It seems that adults assume that boys' primarily adult responsibility will be as family breadwinners, just like most of their fathers. I argue that coaches' different treatment of boys and girls serves as an add-on to differences that have been socially constructed through a myriad of gendering processes that shape boys and girls at deeply emotional levels. In turn, the coaches' actions and discourse about kids serves to *naturalize* these differences, thus helping to reestablish an ideology of gender essentialism.

This idea that boys are defined by their nature, while girls are complex and malleable within shifting social contexts seems an interesting inversion of long-standing tendencies to define women as close to nature and men as aligned with culture. In an influential 1974 article entitled "Is Female to Male as Nature is to Culture?" anthropologist Sherry Ortner wrote that

> woman's body seems to doom her to mere reproduction of life; the male, in con-
> trast, lacking natural creative functions, must (or has the opportunity to) assert
> his creativity externally, 'artificially,' through the medium of technology and
> symbols. In so doing, he creates relatively lasting, eternal, transcendental objects,
> while the woman creates only perishables—human beings. (p. 75)

Through much of the 19th and 20th centuries, this association of women with "nature," and men with "culture" justified a gender dichotomized world that contained women in the domestic, private sphere of supportive and procreative activities while viewing the public world as men's dominion. This belief was foundational to the postwar ascendance of the ideology of hard essentialism.

It is perhaps the hallmark of the contemporary emergence of soft essentialism that boys and men are now seen to be defined by their biology (McCaughey, 2008), while meanwhile girls and women, when given a range of opportunities, are seen to be capable of exercising choice. This view of girls—a result simultaneously of the triumph of liberal feminist discourse and the incomplete feminist transformations of social institutions—allows adults to imagine girls as adult women straddling two contexts—the world of family, home, and hearth, where their true nature presumably draws them, and the public world of education, sports, and work, which they will have a right to choose to participate in or to opt out of. By contrast, this view of boys continues to see the competitive public world of sports, work, and careers as their natural destiny. Since their inflexible biology presumably predisposes boys and men to the public world, they are not viewed as able to "choose" alternative (especially stigmatized feminine) paths. Ironically, fears that their sons may fail to develop properly lead many adults to engage in (or at least tolerate) a hardening and toughening of boys that makes it difficult for boys to develop their full emotional potential (e.g., empathy, care-taking skills) that they need to become healthy adults, good partners, and effective parents. Unchallenged, this socially constructed emotional deficit in boys will leave the responsibility on women's shoulders to, through their "choices," straddle both worlds of public and domestic labor. Clearly, essentialism is alive and well in the ways that adults think about children. But this is not our grandparents' essentialism. It is an emergent "soft" essentialism that accommodates the reality of girls' and women's presence in sports and in public life more generally.

Soft essentialist ideology about children in youth sports meshes neatly with the strains and tensions in work and family life among professional-class adults. If and when they become mothers, highly educated women on professional career tracks face inflexible workplaces and a second shift at home due to husbands who rarely share equally with childcare or housework (Gerson, 2010, Hochschild, 1989, Stone, 2007). When their kids reach school age, they face an accelerating "third shift" of volunteer activities in their children's schools and communities (Messner, 2009). In this context, some class-privileged women choose to opt out of their careers or to scale back to part-time jobs. Those mothers who choose to (or must) stay in their jobs face major juggling of work, family, and volunteer work that often leaves them feeling less than adequate in all three realms. Significantly, the women in my study narrate their decisions related to work and family in the language of "choice," not constraint. Moreover, they describe their husbands as "supportive" of their decisions. Indeed, the men I interviewed uniformly say that they support whatever decisions their wives make about these matters. It is a foundational and usually unspoken assumption of the women's and the men's discourse that men do not face any such choice between work and family life, reflecting what Blair-Loy (2003) calls asymmetrical "cultural devotion schemas" that assume the primacy of men's careers over women's careers.

New mothers also confront what Hays (1996) calls "intensive mothering on behalf of the sacred child," a ramping up of the cultural expectations of mothering (p. 97). Employed mothers must navigate the contradictions between images of warm and nurturing mothers in the home and images of competition and self-interest in the market. "Choice" becomes a mode through which mothers navigate this tension, but not all mothers have the material resources of high-earning families. The idea that women can "choose" to opt in and out of careers is a *class-based work-family formation*: Women who are best able (and constrained into) making the choice to leave (or lessen their participation in) the labor force are women who are married to high-earning men. These professional-class women then feed their considerable talents into what Annette Lareau (2003) calls the "concerted cultivation" of their own kids and into a range of volunteer activities with kids in the community (p. 2).

In short, both professional-class women and men deploy a soft essentialist narrative in which feminism is defined in individualist terms, giving women the choice to stay in their careers while implicitly assuming that men need make no such choices. Soft essentialism's embracing of women's right to choose veils the still unequal social constraints faced by mothers in the contexts of professional-class work and family life. The power of essentialism lies primarily in the widely held assumptions about the tugs and pulls of mothers' supposed maternal natures, symmetrically counterposed to men's supposed natural draw to public life. Parents' discourse projects on to their children the same soft essentialist assumptions about daughters as future choosers and sons as destined for career paths. Put simply, the ideology of soft essentialism views girls as "prechoice" while positioning boys as "precareer."

Conclusion

I began this article with a feminist fable of triumph for girls and women in sport, a story around which a tremendous amount of social consent has congealed in recent years. I argue in this article that this consent signals a new moment of historical gender formation buttressed by a hegemonic gender ideology, soft essentialism. This newly hegemonic ideology emerges as common sense in a moment character- ized by continued gender asymmetries and inequalities in professional-class adults' work and family lives. Youth sports has become a key site for the construction and naturalization of soft essentialism, a shared belief in natural differences between girls and boys that exists alongside more relativized and noncategorical views of girls and women as flexible choosers in social life and still largely categorical views of boys and men. To put it another way, contemporary essentialism is softer when applied to girls and harder when applied to boys.[2]

Hegemonic consent emerges around soft essentialism within the professional class because as a belief system it veils the sources and explains away the conse- quences of continued work-family tensions and gender inequalities in the lives of professionals. Perhaps too, soft essentialism appeals to many highly educated professional-class women because it allows them to rationalize a kind of trade- off: Acceptance of continued gender inequality within their own family appears to support future upward class mobility for their kids. But as with all hegemonic ideologies, soft essentialism has its own contradictions that serve as potential sites of counterhegemonic thought and action. I will conclude by outlining three potential sources of strain, and I will suggest some counterhegemonic strategies that these strains imply.

First, working-class mothers (or middle-class women who are single or do not have high-earning husbands) face different sorts of work-family constraints and are unlikely to have a realistic option to opt out of the workforce. However, many of them are living in communities (such as the one that I studied) domi- nated by the ideological hegemony of professional-class soft essentialism. Just as working-class women and women of color in the 1980s challenged the White middle-class basis of feminist binary constructionism, so too might they object today to the hegemony of soft essentialism. How do women who lack class privilege negotiate this field? What sorts of oppositional networks and discourses might they create? I found, for instance, that many of the most assertive and powerful women coaches in the community I studied were Latina and Asian American mothers working in full-time jobs.

Second, today's largely unreconstructed essentialist and categorical view of boys and men can't help but run up against the reality of the expanding definitions of masculinity that many boys receive in schools, families, and popular culture. Many boys are being exposed to an expanding emotional and sexual repertoire and are also being taught to view girls and women as equals. As some boys internalize these broadened gender and sexual repertoires, they may come to experience youth sports—still largely a homosocial realm run by men—in contradictory ways. However, since youth sports do not simply reflect but also help to construct soft essentialism, we cannot expect change simply to emerge from outside sport. As long as boys and men remain an unmarked category—as long as they are assumed to be driven uniformly by a simple linear nature and are cordoned off from girls and women in homosocial public realms like youth sports—then girls and women will have less hope of overcoming the constraints imposed on them in this historical moment. Surely, any progressive resistance to soft essentialism must include a strategy of broadening boys' emotional repertoires and desegregating adult leadership in sports. In this sense, *a strategic de-gendering strategy* in boys' sports—especially affirmative efforts to break down the sex segregation of boys' sports and men's occupational niches like youth sports coaching—can be a key element of resistance to the oppressive limits of soft essentialism.

Third, the soft essentialist celebration of equal opportunity and free choice for girls can't help but run up against the continued existence of social barriers to equal choice for girls (e.g., girls being routed out of baseball toward softball) and also for their mothers (who continue to face the burdens of making the tough choices between career and family or who bump up against informal barriers to their serving as head coaches in youth sports). Some of the women coaches I interviewed in fact struggled to make sense of the continued sex segregation in youth sports. Most coaches, however, believe it's best for girls and boys to have separate leagues, fearing that putting the kids together might disadvantage the girls, perhaps driving them away from playing sports.

The question of what's best for kids—sex-segregated or integrated teams—is a complicated point of tension, even from a feminist perspective. If one is interested in giving boys experiences that will counter the kinds of sexist attitudes and assumptions that they commonly develop in male-only sports, then one would likely favor coed sports. The more boys can learn early on to fully respect girls and women's full range of abilities, the better off they will be in their future relationships with women as classmates, coworkers, bosses, and family members—and the more they might be nudged in the direction of thinking of men too as having to make choices to navigate between work and family life. However, if one is thinking of girls' interests, this seems a more complicated question. It was decided more than a half century ago in the United States that in race relations, separate is inherently unequal. Some scholars have argued on a similar basis for sex desegregation in sport (McDonagh & Peppano, 2008). Sport scholar Ann Travers takes a nuanced view, arguing that sex segregation in sport "plays an important role in normalizing and legitimizing the ideology of the two sex system" (Travers, 2008, p. 80). In Travers's view, the cordoning off of girls and women contains the ways in which strong and powerful women athletes might otherwise "trouble" stubbornly essentialist views of girls and women as physically inferior. Travers argues for a simultaneous desegregation of boys' and men's sports while retaining for the moment separate leagues for girls and women.

Travers's both/and approach, I believe, intuits perfectly the most promising strategy for pushing the limits of soft essentialism. As I argued above, degendering strategies in girls' and women's sports might today be counterproductive in pushing for distributive justice; after all, girls' and women's sports are still widely underappreciated, underfunded, and undercovered in the media. A program of strategic categoricalism in girls' sports, in this context, still seems necessary in fighting for seemingly mundane things, like access to good playing fields. However, it makes sense to couple this strategic categoricalism of girls' sports with strategic degendering of boys' sports[3] that goes beyond the now-common incorporation of the occasional star girl player (who too often gets defined as a token or fictive boy), instead integrating many girls and opening space for transgender people, thus puncturing the categorical essentialism that still encapsulates boys and men.

This dual strategy—strategic categoricalism in girls' sports coupled with a degendering of boys' sports—presses against the emergent contradictions and fissures within the logic of soft essentialism. Like any strategy in a complex field of power, this one too has its limits and introduces new points of tension and contest. But its future success can be assessed by the extent to which it contests the oppressive social relations of gender, race, class, and sexuality that are reflected in the hegemonic stories we tell ourselves about the place of sport in social life.

Questions for Reflection and Discussion

How do "common sense" stories of the recent past, like the one that introduces this article, affect our understanding of the present? Do you still see evidence of beliefs in "hard essentialism" today? Do "soft essentialist" beliefs exist in fields besides youth sports? In what ways does it limit people when we make categorical statements about boys and girls, women and men?

Acknowledgments

Author's note: many thanks to Raewyn Connell, Cheryl Cooky, Shari Dworkin, Max Greenberg, and Jeff Montez de Oca, who generously read and commented on earlier versions of this paper. Thanks also to Pirkko Markula, Richard Pringle, and the anonymous reviewers of the *SSJ*. Their thoughtful suggestions resulted in revisions that truly improved this article.

Notes

1   The empirical research in this section of the article is drawn from my study of how gender is constructed in a single community's youth soccer and baseball/softball leagues. A several-year participant-observation study, supplemented with 50 in-depth interviews with adult volunteer coaches, this research explored the ways that adult divisions of labor are created in youth sports and how these gender divisions of labor are connected to families, workplaces, and communities. The quotes presented here are used as illustrations of the emergent ideology of soft essentialism, but the broader ramifications of this research are elaborated in my book (Messner, 2009). All names of interviewees are pseudonyms.

2   Here is a point at which the 2 × 2 table in Figure 1.1 reveals its limitations. If we were to properly map the location of the currently hegemonic professional-class view of girls and women, it would be firmly within the lower-left "soft essentialism" quadrant. However, as hegemonic views of boys and men are still largely categorical and grounded in biological essentialism, these views would be located closer to the upper-left "hard essentialism" quadrant.

3   This strategy holds an obvious danger. If the most skilled and competitive girls athletes are siphoned off to play with the boys, then girls' teams and leagues will be face a dilution of talent and probably of parental and community commitment as well. This in turn could spell doom for categorically-organized girls' sports. At least in the short run, this could result in far fewer opportunities for girls to play sports. A historical analogy—not perfectly applicable, but suggestive of these dangers—is the rapid decline and eventual death of the professional baseball Negro Leagues in the mid-20th-century years following the desegregation of Major League Baseball.

References

Adams, N. G., & Bettis, P. J. (2003). *Cheerleader!: An American icon*. Basingstoke, England: Palgrave MacMillan.

Baca Zinn, M., Weber, L., Higginbotham, E., & Thornton Dill, B. (1986). The cost of exclusionary practices in women's studies. *Signs: Journal of women in culture and society, 11*, 290–303.

Baca Zinn, M., & Thornton Dill, B. (1996). Theorizing difference from multiracial feminism. *Feminist Studies, 22*, 321–331.

Birrell, S., & Cole, C. L. (1994). Double fault: Renee Richards and the construction and naturalization of difference. In S. Birrell & C. L. Cole (Eds.), *Women, sports and culture* (pp. 373–397). Champaign, IL: Human Kinetics.

Blair-Loy, M. (2003). *Competing devotions: Career and family among women executives*. Cambridge, MA: Harvard University Press.

Bornstein, K. (1993). *Gender outlaw: Men, women and the rest of us*. New York: Routledge.

Brake, D. L. (2010). *Getting in the game: Title IX and the women's sports revolution*. New York, NY: New York University Press.

Cahn, S. (1994). *Coming on strong: Gender and sexuality in twentieth-century women's sport*. New York, NY: The Free Press.

Chodorow, N. J. (1978). *The reproduction of mothering*. Berkeley, CA: University of California Press.

Coakley, J. (2006). The good father: Parental expectations in youth sports. *Leisure Studies, 25*, 153–163.

Collins, H. P. (1990). *Black feminist thought: Knowledge, consciousness, and the Politics of empowerment*. Boston, MA: Unwin Hyman.

Connell, R. (1987). *Gender & power*. Stanford, CA: Stanford University Press.

Connell, R. (2002). *Gender*. Cambridge, England: Polity.

Connell, R. (2010). Two cans of paint: A transsexual life story, with reflections on gender change and history. *Sexualities, 13*, 3–18.

Connell, R. (forthcoming). Transsexual women and feminist thought: Towards a new understanding and new politics. *Signs: Journal of women in culture and society*.

Cooky, C. (2009). "Girls just aren't interested": The social construction of interest in girls' sport. *Sociological Perspectives, 52*, 259–283.

Coontz, S. (2000). *The way we never were: American families and the nostalgia trap*. New York, NY: Basic Books.

Deutsch, F. M. (2007). Undoing gender. *Gender & Society, 21*, 106–127.

Dworkin, S. L., Swarr Lock, A., & Cooky, C. (under submission). Sport and sex and gender (in)justice: The case of South African track star Caster Semenya.

Dworkin, S. L., & Wachs, F. L. (2009). *Body panic: Gender, health, and the selling of fitness*. New York, NY: New York University Press.

Eisenstein, Z. R. (1979). *Capitalist patriarchy and the case for socialist feminism*. New York, NY: Monthly Review Press.

Fausto-Sterling, A. (2000). The five sexes revisited. *The Sciences, 40*, 18–24.

Firestone, S. (1971). *The dialectic of sex: The case for feminist revolution*. New York, NY: Bantam Books.

Friedan, B. (1963). *The feminine mystique*. New York, NY: Dell.

Gerson, K. (2010). *The unfinished revolution: How a new generation is reshaping family, work, and gender in America*. New York, NY: Oxford University Press.

Gilligan, C. (1982). *In a different voice: Psychological theory and women's development*. Cambridge, MA: Harvard University Press.

Grillo, T. (1995). Anti-essentialism and intersectionality: Tools to dismantle the master's house. *Berkeley Women's Law Journal, 16*, 16–30.

Halberstam, J. (1998). *Female masculinity*. Durham, NC: Duke University Press.

Hargreaves, J. (1983). *Sport, culture and ideology*. London, England: Routledge & Kegan Paul.

Hays, S. (1996). *The cultural contradictions of motherhood*. New Haven, CT: Yale University Press.

Hochschild, A. (1989). *The second shift*. New York, NY: Viking.

hooks, b. (1984). *Feminist theory: From margin to center*. Boston, MA: South End Press.

Kane, M. J. (1995). Resistance/transformation of the oppositional binary: Exposing sport as a continuum. *Journal of Sport and Social Issues, 19*, 191–218.

Lareau, A. (2003). *Unequal childhoods: Class, race, and family life*. Berkeley, CA: University of California Press.

McCaughey, M. (2008). *The caveman mystique: Pop-Darwinism and debates over sex, violence and science*. New York, NY: Routledge.

McDonagh, E., & Pappano, L. (2008). *Playing with the boys: Why separate is not equal in sports*. New York, NY: Oxford University Press.

Messner, M. A. (1988). Sports and male domination: The female athlete as contested ideological terrain. *Sociology of Sport Journal, 5*, 197–211.

Messner, M. A. (2000). Barbie girls vs. sea monsters: Children constructing gender. *Gender & Society, 14*, 765–784.

Messner, M. A. (2002). *Taking the field: Women, men, and sports*. Minneapolis, MN: University of Minnesota Press.

Messner, M. A. (2009). *It's all for the kids: Gender, families and youth sports*. Berkeley, CA: University of California Press.

Miller, K., Sabo, D., Farrell, M., Barnes, G., & Melnick, M. (1999). Sports, sexual activity, contraceptive use, and pregnancy among female and male high school students: Testing cultural resource theory. *Sociology of Sport Journal, 16*, 366–387.

Miller, K., Melnick, M., Barnes, G., Farrell, M., & Sabo, D. (2005). Untangling the links among athletic involvement, gender, race, and adolescent academic outcomes. *Sociology of Sport Journal, 22*, 178–193.

Montez de Oca, J. (2005). As our muscles get softer, our missile race becomes harder: Cultural citizenship and the "muscle gap." *Journal of Historical Sociology, 18*, 145–171.

Morgan, R. (1970). *Sisterhood is powerful*. New York, NY: Vintage.

Namaste, V. K. (2000). *Invisible lives: The erasure of transsexual and transgendered people.* Chicago, IL: University of Chicago Press.

Ortner, S. (1974). *Is female to male as nature is to culture?* In M. Z. Rosaldo & L. Lamphere (Eds.), *Woman, culture and society* (pp. 67–87). Stanford, CA: Stanford University Press.

Pollack, W. (1999). *Real boys: Rescuing our sons from the myths of boyhood.* New York, NY: Henry Holt.

Ring, J. (2009). *Stolen bases: Why American girls don't play baseball.* Champaign, IL: University of Illinois Press.

Sabo, D. F., & Veliz, P. (2008). *Youth sport in America.* East Meadow, NY: Women's Sports Foundation.

Sedgwick Kosofsky, E. (1990). *Epistemology of the closet.* Berkeley, CA: University of California Press.

Spivak, G. (1995). Subaltern studies: Deconstructing historiography. In D. Landry & G. MacLean (Eds.), *The Spivak reader: Selected works of Gayatri Spivak* (pp. 203–236). New York, NY: Routledge.

Stevenson, B. (2007). Title IX and the evolution of high school sports. *Contemporary Economic Policy, 25*, 486–505.

Stone, P. (2007). *Opting out: Why women really quit careers and head home.* Berkeley, CA: University of California Press.

Sykes, H. (2006). Transsexual and transgender politics in sport. *Women in Sport and Physical Activity Journal, 15*, 3–13.

Tolson, A. (1977). *The limits of masculinity: Male identity and women's liberation.* New York, NY: Harper & Row.

Travers, A. (2008). The sport nexus and gender injustice. *Studies in Social Justice, 2*, 79–101.

Twin, S. L. (1979). *Out of the bleachers: Writings on women and sport.* Old Westbury, NY: The Feminist Press.

Willis, P. (1983). Women in sport in ideology. In J. Hargreaves (Ed.), *Sport, culture and ideology* (pp. 117–135). London, England: Routledge & Kegan Paul.

2

Policing the Boundaries of Sex

•••••••••••••••••••••

A Critical Examination of
Gender Verification and the
Caster Semenya Controversy

CHERYL COOKY AND

SHARI L. DWORKIN

In August 2009, 18-year-old South African track and field athlete Caster Semenya won the 800 m event at the World Championships in Berlin, Germany. In that moment, Semenya went from relative obscurity to the subject of international news media debate and scrutiny. Given her "deep voice," "fast improvement in times," and "muscular frame," some of Semenya's competitors suggested she was not a "real woman" and questioned whether she was eligible for competition in women's events. Subject to the International Association of Athletics Federations (IAAF) gender verification policy, Semenya underwent sex testing to determine her eligibility, a process that lasted more than a year and resulted not only in a determination in

Source: "Policing the boundaries of sex: A critical examination of gender verification and the Caster Semenya controversy," by Cheryl Cooky and Shari L. Dworkin, 2013, *The Journal of Sex Research, 50*(2), p. 103–111. Copyright by The Society for the Scientific Study of Sexuality. Reprinted with permission of Taylor & Francis.

which Semenya was deemed eligible for competition in women's events but also in a controversy that spurred the establishment of working groups within the IAAF and International Olympic Committee (IOC) tasked to reassess these policies. This chapter, which is part of a larger project wherein we examined the media framings in the United States and South African mainstream news media outlets (see chapter 12), was written during this period with the goal of serving as public advocacy social science research. As feminist scholars committed to examining and advocating for social justice issues in sports, we are enraged by the media conversations regarding sex and gender, particularly the assumptions that female athletes are "mannish" or "not real" women unless they conform to Westernized standards of femininity and beauty, as well as by the discriminatory treatment of Semenya in much of the international media. There were media accounts of the "leaked" test results, which ostensibly demonstrated Semenya was a "hermaphrodite" (a term considered offensive by many, especially for those in intersex communities), and even worse, news articles, blogs, and comment sections accused Semenya of being a man masquerading as a woman. This chapter deconstructs and challenges the many claims and assumptions by which the logics of sex testing / gender verification are upheld. We advocate for the end of sex testing / gender verification policies and argue that change is necessary not only to protect the rights of female athletes who may be intersex but also to ensure the rights of all female athletes to participate in sport that is free from discrimination. As I write this author note in the lead-up to the 2016 Summer Olympic Games, the IOC has changed its policies, yet it continues to police the boundaries of sex. Moreover, Semenya continues to remain a controversial figure, despite being determined by the IAAF and IOC to be eligible for competition in women's events.

—Cheryl Cooky

Caster Semenya, an 18-year-old track star from rural Limpopo, South Africa, won the gold medal in the women's 800 m at the World Championships in Athletics in Berlin on August 19, 2009. Semenya won the event in 1 min 55 s 45 ms, 2 s slower than the world record, yet 7.5 s faster than her previous times in this event. Media accounts noted that the silver medalist, Kenyan Janeth Jepkosgei, finished a full 2.45 s behind her. On the same day that Semenya won gold, gender-verification tests were requested by the International Association of Athletics Federations (IAAF) to determine whether she was "eligible" to compete in women's sport. Media reports stated that the IAAF requested the tests because of Semenya's "deep voice, muscular build and rapid improvement in times" ("IAAF: Semenya decision in November," 2009). The general secretary of the IAAF stated that Semenya underwent gender-verification testing because of "ambiguity" regarding her sex.

On July 6, 2010, the IAAF "accepted the conclusion of a panel of medical experts that Semenya can compete with immediate effect" ("Athlete Caster Semenya free to compete," 2010). She returned to competition at a low-profile track and field event in Finland on July 15, 2010. Semenya competed in the 800 m event at the 2012 Olympic Games in London, winning the silver medal. The results of her 2009 gender-verification test were not released to the public, and the IAAF stated that Semenya's medical test results would remain confidential.

Semenya identifies as a woman. Family members, friends, South African stakeholders, and leaders in both sport and government have insisted that Semenya is indeed a woman, regardless of what scientific testing may determine (for a discussion, see Cooky, Dycus, & Dworkin, 2012; Dworkin, Swarr, & Cooky, in press). Despite Semenya's performance at the 2009 World Championships, the subsequent controversy regarding her "gender verification" raised issues regarding the eligibility of nonnormatively sexed/gendered bodies to participate in international sporting competition.

It is difficult to ascertain the prevalence of intersexed individuals given a lack of consensus among biomedical scientists regarding what conditions constitute intersexuality (Karkazis, 2008). Some individuals may be born with ambiguous genitalia; in other cases, individuals are born with "normative" genitalia. Moreover, although the incidence of various conditions will vary, estimates are often reported in aggregate. Given a lack of consensus regarding which conditions constitute intersexuality, estimates range based on which conditions are included or excluded from the estimate (Karkazis, 2008).

Adding further complexity to the task of quantifying such conditions is the fact that these often exist on a continuum. For example, the incidence of classical congenital adrenal hyperplasia (CAH), where individuals have variable degrees of genital ambiguity and the most common intersex diagnosis, is estimated at 1 in 15,000 births. For nonclassical CAH, estimates vary between 1 in 100 to 1 in 1,000 births (Karkazis, 2008). Yet there are also a multitude of "disorders" that scientists include under the umbrella term *disorders of sex development* (DSDs), including androgen insensitivity syndrome, Klinefelter syndrome, and Turner syndrome. Despite the lack of consensus on how intersexuality is defined and whether certain DSDs are included under the broader term (see Dreger, 1998; Fausto-Sterling, 2000), within the popular literature and much of the academic literature, the estimate of approximately 1.7% (individuals who can be classified as intersex) is frequently reported (Blackless et al., 2000; Dreger, 1998; Fausto-Sterling, 2000).

Regardless of the challenges of assessing incidence, it is not surprising that a certain number of individuals with DSDs, or intersex athletes, compete in sport. However, the institution of sport is formally organized around the notion that there are only two sexes—male and female—and sport is largely segregated by binary sex categories. Therefore, historically, there has been no formal place within the institution of competitive organized sport for athletes who exist outside of the dichotomous categories of male and female and who subsequently "fail" sex testing.

Female athletes who test positive for DSDs are deemed to have an unfair advantage in sport compared to female individuals without DSDs (those classified by sport organizations as "normal" females). As such, sport organizations attempt to police the boundaries of sex, stating that they do so to maintain a level playing field for "normal" female athletes. Until recently, most individuals diagnosed (or identified through sex testing) with a DSD were barred from sport competition altogether or were asked to quietly fake an injury and retreat from competition

(Cole, 2000; Cooky, Dycus, & Dworkin, 2012). In the aftermath of the Semenya controversy, the International Olympic Committee (IOC) convened a task force to review its policies on gender-verification testing. The IAAF also revised its policies in May 2011, which continue to require female athletes to submit to a medical evaluation should "suspicions" of their sex arise or should an athlete have a known DSD. We review these policies in the sections that follow.

To assess sporting organizations' policies that determine whether intersex athletes are eligible to compete, we first provide a brief history of gender-verification testing in sport. Next, we critically assess the main concepts and claims that undergird gender verification/sex testing in sport, including that (a) sex exists as a binary; (b) sport is a level playing field for competitors; and (c) intersex athletes have an unfair advantage compared to female athletes, and they should be banned from competition to ensure that sport is a level playing field. To conclude, we make three recommendations that are consistent with the attainment of sex and gender justice in sport, which include acknowledging that myriad physical advantages are accepted in sport, recognizing that sport as a level playing field is a myth, and eliminating sex testing in sport.

History of Sex Testing / Gender Verification in Sport

Women began participating in Olympic competitions in 1900. Given that the institution of sport is largely sex segregated, and given emerging fears that some athletes in women's competitions were too "masculine" to be female, international sports governing bodies such as the IOC implemented procedures to ensure that all participants were indeed female. Female athletes were first subjected to a nude parade in front of a panel of doctors whose job it was to verify the sex of the competitors (Cahn, 1994; Cole, 2000; Ljungqvist et al., 2006; Puffer, 2002). This was said to be highly invasive, embarrassing, and humiliating to athletes. The IOC instituted mandatory sex testing in women's sport in 1968 and ended the mandatory aspect of the policy in 1998 (Elias et al., 2000; Ljungqvist et al., 2006). The IOC and other international sports bodies, such as the International Amateur Athletic Federation, implemented various versions of "gender verification" policies or monitoring policies regarding eligibility in female athletic competitions.

At the beginning stages of the implementation of the mandatory policy, the IOC took advantage of advances in technology, specifically the Barr body chromosomal test. This eliminated the need to rely solely on the visual test to verify sex and was thought to be less invasive for the athlete. The Barr body chromosomal test, which was used until 1992, could determine only the chromosomal makeup of an individual, not anatomical or psychosocial status (Simpson et al., 1993). Thus the tests assessed only one component of an athlete's sex/gender and as a result were of limited use.

Numerous limitations existed and continue to exist in the use of scientific technology to determine sex. For example, the Barr body test would categorize individuals with XXY genotypes as women and allow those individuals to compete in women's competitions even though XXY individuals have "male" physical characteristics (Buzuvis, 2010). At the same time, athletes who were anatomically female but had genetic disorders such as 46,XY complete gonadal dysgenesis and 46,XY complete androgen insensitivity would be detected as male under the buccal smear, despite the fact that these individuals would be classified as female based on the appearance of their external genitalia (Genel & Ljungqvist, 2005). Recognizing the limitations of the Barr body test and buccal smear, experts convened at the request of the IAAF in late 1990. What became evident was that the way in which sport organizations measured or ascertained the sex of female athletes often failed to account for (or was unable to account for) the complexity in various chromosomal and genetic variations that exist. However, rather than eliminating sex testing as a means to determine eligibility in women's events, experts determined that laboratory-based sex testing should be replaced with a comprehensive medical assessment of all female athletes to determine their sex. This suggestion was later deemed unnecessary, as it was clearly impractical to implement from a cost perspective.

After 1992, the Barr body test was replaced by the polymerase chain reaction (PCR) test of the SRY gene, a DNA-based form of testing. PCR testing for the SRY gene is a sophisticated test, given that the SRY gene signals the developmental pathway for males and has been found to be 99% accurate (Puffer, 2002). However, as with the Barr body test, this test is not without its limitations. Some argued that the DNA sequences used to prime the PCR were in fact not specific to males. This contributed to a number of false-positive test results in women's events (Buzuvis, 2010; Puffer, 2002; Reeser, 2005). For example, in the 1996 Summer Olympics in Atlanta, eight of more than 3,000 female athletes tested positive using the PCR test, but all eight athletes were allowed to compete, as further medical testing determined that the athletes did not have an "unfair advantage" (Buzuvis, 2010; Zaccone, 2010).

As a result of several high-profile cases involving female athletes who "failed" sex tests and the scientific criticisms of the veracity of the tests in the late 1980s and early 1990s, members of the international medical community argued against the IOC and other international sport federations' use of chromosomal or genetic screening of female athletes to determine eligibility for participation in international sport competitions (see de la Chapelle, 1986; Ljungqvist et al., 2006; Ljungqvist & Simpson, 1992). Scholars—biomedical scientists and social scientists alike—argued that "using a range of sex-tests including the visual test, the Barr body test, and the PCR test, the IOC could not ascertain beyond a shadow of a doubt who was and was not genetically female" (Cavanaugh & Sykes, 2006, p. 80). The IOC abandoned mandatory sex testing of female athletes in 2000 during the Sydney Olympic Games, in part because of challenges to the scientific veracity of the tests and also due to a multitude of objections that were raised. By 2000, 24 of 29 international sports federations had abandoned routine gender-verification testing (Reeser, 2005).

In 2000, the IOC replaced mandatory testing with a policy that granted authority to medical experts at international events to arrange for the gender verification of an athlete's sex if it was called into question (Cavanaugh & Sykes,

2006; Ljungqvist & Genel, 2005). A medical team including an endocrinologist, a geneticist, a gynecologist, and a psychologist would determine the results of the "gender verification" test. According to Genel and Ljungqvist (2005), the abandonment of mandatory sex testing of female athletes was well received, and in the first several competitions, there were no objections to the new policy, nor was there a need to apply the policy.

While the IOC discontinued mandatory sex testing in the 2000 Olympic Games, they continued to retain the right to test athletes in cases deemed "suspicious," whereby the gender identity of an athlete was called into question (Buzuvis, 2010; Cavanaugh & Sykes, 2006; Wackwitz, 2003). Similar to the IOC's policy, the IAAF's Policy on Gender Verification (2006) no longer required "compulsory, standard or regular gender verification during IAAF sanctioned championships" (p. 2). Instead, according to the policy, a "gender issue" may arise due to a "challenge of an athlete or team" brought to the attention of authorities at an event, "suspicions" raised during the process of antidoping controls, or concerns expressed by the athlete or the athlete's national federation. This policy allowed for athletes with syndromes that are said to not confer an athletic advantage, including androgen insensitivity syndrome, gonadal dysgenesis, and Turner syndrome, to compete in female athletic competitions. Athletes with other conditions such as CAH, androgen-producing tumors, and polycystic ovary syndrome (POS) were also allowed to compete, according to the 2006 policy, even though the IAAF recognized that these "conditions may accord some advantages but nevertheless are acceptable" (p. 2). It should be noted that the 2006 Policy on Gender Verification was the policy in place when the international controversy surrounding Caster Semenya erupted.

The 2006 Policy on Gender Verification was replaced on May 1, 2011, by the IAAF's new policy on sex testing and sporting competition, titled Regulations Governing Eligibility of Females with Hyperandrogenism to Compete in Women's Competition. In the introduction, the policy states that the regulations are "predicated along the following principles," including "a respect for the very essence of the male and female classifications in Athletics" and "a respect for the fundamental notion of fairness of competition in Athletics" (IAAF, 2011, p. 1). According to this policy, female athletes with hyperandrogenism may compete in women's competitions as long as athletes notify the IAAF in advance and the IAAF medical manager determines, in consultation with an expert medical panel (established by the IAAF), that the athlete does not have a definitive unfair advantage. Also, as part of this new policy, the IAAF states that it would no longer use the terms *gender verification* or *gender policy* in its rules. There are also new procedures in place to ensure the confidentiality of the process. According to this policy, an expert medical panel may recommend that an athlete be able to compete in a woman's competition if she has androgen levels below the "normal male range" or if the female athlete has androgen levels within the normal male range but is "resistant such that she derives no *competitive advantage* from having androgen levels in the normal male range." (IAAF, 2011, p. 12; emphasis added). It should be noted that the IAAF medical manager has only to "take into account" the recommendation made by the expert medical panel (which under the new policy consists of experts in pediatrics, endocrinology, gynecology, obstetrics, genetics, and psychology). Although allowing individuals with hyperandrogenism appears to be inclusive of intersex conditions, there are concerns regarding the way in which athletes are compared with the average "normal values" (Camporesi & Maugeri, 2010). This concern recognizes that sport training changes the realm of the "normal" body, underscoring that there are biological factors that interact with environmental factors to shape the body.

Assumptions of Sex Testing: Sex as a Binary Category

In the following sections, we critically assess three major conceptual assumptions that undergird sex testing of female athletes. The first assumption of sex testing is that sex exists naturally as a dichotomous binary. In fact, prior to the late 20th century, technological constraints limited what could be known about sex. As such, scientists and medical professionals could not point to genes in the way we can today to define one's sex (Dreger, 1998). However, despite the fact that the technology now exists to allow us to determine the genetic components of sex, we echo the position of scholars who argued that this does not mean we have the "ultimate, necessary, for-all-time answer to what it means to be of a certain sex" (Dreger, 1998, p. 9). In writing about scientific attempts to definitively establish a binary classification of sex categories, Fausto-Sterling (2000) argued, "A body's sex is too complex. There is no either/or. Rather there are shades of difference" (p. 3). Indeed, the previous section illustrates how DSDs are but one example of these "shades of difference." Yet sport organizations continue to police the boundaries of sex through sex testing and the segregation of sports by sex, and the policies in place ostensibly are there to "ensure" that participants of men's competitions are male and women's competitions are female. Indeed, the IAAF's 2011 policy contains a key principle of maintaining "a respect for the very essence of the male and female classifications in Athletics" and thus illustrates how reaffirming the sex binary is central to sex testing policies.

The IOC's 2003 Stockholm Consensus illustrates how athletes that transverse the landscape of the sex/gender continuum are allowed to compete as long as the sex binary is resolutely (re)constituted and not challenged. It should be noted that the IOC allows for transsexual bodies that have received medical intervention (e.g., surgery, hormones) to participate in athletic competition, but bodies that are "naturally" of both sexes are deemed "unfair." Although the concern for governing bodies appears to be with the degree to which the "male" hormones of testosterone and androgen provide an "unfair advantage" to athletes in women's competitions (Vilain &Sánchez, 2012), the extent to which the IAAF and the IOC accommodate transsexual athletes and athletes with DSDs (the language they use in their policies and reports) illustrates how sport organizations are willing to embrace ambiguity in instances where ostensibly the IOC can monitor and classify participants as male or female (Sykes, 2006).

Assumptions of Sex Testing: Sport as a Level Playing Field

The second major assumption embedded in policies on sex testing / gender verification is the notion that sport is a level playing field (in other words, competitions should be determined through talent and hard work and thus athletes' superior performances are the result of individual talents and not any advantages other athletes may not have the ability to possess) and its corollary: that unfair advantages need to be policed to continue to ensure sport is a level playing field. In response to the gender-verification testing of Semenya published in the *Journal of Genetic Counseling*, Caplan (2010) wrote,

> If an athlete's gender is called into question, the task of scientists and physicians is to determine if genetics or biology has conferred an advantage upon the competitor that others in the gender group lack or could not obtain through training and practice. The question is not simply a matter of gonads, genes or hormones, but has biology or genetics conferred an unfair advantage on the athletes that others in the same class and competition lack. (p. 550)

We agree that whether one has an advantage in sport cannot be determined simply based on identifying various sex characteristics (e.g., gonads, genes, hormones) of the athlete. However, we contest the assumption that unfair advantages must be monitored to ensure that sport is a fair and level playing field for competitors. We make two central critiques regarding the assumption that sport is a level playing field: (a) sport as a level playing field is neither an organizational reality nor a possibility, given the historical and contemporary social, economic, and cultural arrangements of sport; and (b) the way that sport organizations police unfair advantages is not implemented consistently for all physical advantages, given that sport-governing bodies tolerate myriad physical advantages that are not available to nor attainable by all athletes.

Sport studies scholars have noted the ways in which sport is *not* a level playing field; rather, it is a site wherein broader forms of social inequality are accepted, tolerated, and ignored. The historic and contemporary structure and culture of sport institutions often reproduces hegemonic masculinity, racism, classism, gender inequalities, and nationalism (Messner, 2002; Sage, 1998). In Western societies, sporting institutions have been organizationally structured to benefit the interests of dominant groups (i.e., White, male, economically affluent; see Burstyn, 1999; Sage, 1998).

Historically, the rationale for sex testing in women's events was to prevent men who might "masquerade" as women in sport, which sport-governing bodies argue would prohibit a level playing field for the "real" (some use "unaffected") female athletes. Interestingly, the most frequently cited case used by sport-governing bodies to uphold the rationale for gender verification of female athletes occurred in the 1936 Berlin Olympics when Herman (Dora) Ratjen, a man, was forced by German officials to compete in the women's high-jump event disguised as a woman. Yet Ratjen placed fourth in the competition; all three medal winners were female competitors (Dickinson, Genel, Robinowitz, Turner, & Woods, 2002). While there are no further documented cases where sex testing revealed a male athlete knowingly masquerading as a woman to gain an unfair advantage in sport (Puffer, 2002; Ritchie, Reynard, & Lewis, 2008), there have been several high-profile examples of female athletes who were penalized by the gender verification system and were disqualified from competition and deemed ineligible. These female athletes were barred from competing in women's events (for a discussion of these cases, see Cahn, 1994; Cavanaugh & Sykes, 2006; Cole, 2000; Martinez-Patino et al., 2010).

If monitoring genetically conferred advantage to ensure a level playing field was the primary basis for ensuring fair play, as the IOC and the IAAF claim, athletes would not simply be tested for sex; sport organizations would also test for "performance enhancing genes that predispose them to be athletically superior" by improving muscle growth and efficiency as well as blood flow to skeletal muscles (Vilain & Sánchez, 2012). Sport-governing bodies would also test for other conditions that may predispose athletes to be athletically superior. For example, several basketball players have acromegaly, which is a condition responsible for excessive tallness, a clear advantage in basketball (Zaccone, 2010). Female volleyball players have been found to have Marfan syndrome, a disorder that contributes to their unusually tall height, an advantage in that sport. Endurance skier Eero Mäntyranta has primary familial and congenital polycythemia (PFCO), which causes high hemoglobin and increased oxygen capacity due to an inherited mutation in the erythropoietin receptor gene (EPOR; Genel, 2010).

Further illustrating the limitations of the claim that sport is a level playing field is how fairness is often defined by sport organizations and governing bodies. Fairness is understood as an adherence to the same rules (Buzuvis, 2010). "Unnatural" advantages, such as those gained from drug doping, violate standards of fairness in sport. However, Buzuvis (2010) argued that while unnaturally obtained advantages may violate standards of fairness, "fairness requires no such categorical limitation on naturally obtained advantages" (p. 39). There are naturally occurring variations in sex-related conditions, and in most if not all cases, these variations are unknown to the athlete until they are subjected to sex testing. Thus one could argue that intersex individuals, female athletes with varying levels of hormones, or athletes with a chromosomal makeup that does not conform to the sex binary have a naturally occurring genetic, chromosomal, or hormonal variation. Thus if Semenya did indeed have testosterone levels three times higher than the "average" woman (as many in the popular press claimed) and if this was due to natural variations in sex development and not doping (according to IAAF officials she tested negative for doping), then given the standards of fairness in sport, this is a "natural" variation that should be tolerated. The fact that female athletes were sex tested for these variations is particularly egregious, given that other "natural" variations and conditions, some of which confer advantages, are not monitored or deemed unfair by sport organizations.

Genetically or biologically conferred physical advantages are "unfair" to the same degree that various intersex conditions may be, yet sport organizations do not implement policies to test athletes for these variations, while they do so for those who do not fit into the dichotomous sex binary. At the same time, sport organizations do not view athletes with other types of genetic advantages as a threat to the so-called level playing field, even though researchers have found that athletes with these conditions benefit from clear physical advantages, which by the IOC/IAAF's standards would be construed as unfair. Thus as we have illustrated, the second key assumption that justifies the use of sex testing—it levels the playing field by eliminating unfair advantages—has not been consistently upheld when it comes to other naturally occurring genetic variations that predispose athletes to be "athletically superior." Furthermore, we have shown that sport is not a level playing field and have argued the claims that current policies are necessary to maintain "fairness" are contradictory (and later, we argue that these are discriminatory). Indeed, sport celebrates those individuals who exist on the extreme end of the biological, physical, and genetic spectrum of human diversity. Here we echo Vilain and Sánchez (2012), who argued that "attempting to create a 'level playing field' among people with unique biological profiles may be a futile endeavor" (pp. 198–199). The flaws in both the rationale and justification for sex testing policies raise a central question, which we return to in the conclusions, regarding the necessity or desirability of sex testing / gender verification policies.

Assumption of Sex Testing: Intersex Athletes Have an Unfair Advantage

If we accept the argument that a level playing field is desirable or possible (a point with which we disagree), then we ask why is it only *sex* that is tested while other physical advantages—which are also "naturally conferred"—are not monitored and policed. Here, the belief among sport-governing bodies such as the IOC and the IAAF, as well as some biomedical experts, is that to allow male athletes to participate with women at elite levels would prove unfair because the male competitor will win most, if not all, competitions given their physical superiority (Vilain, 2012). In this way, sport-governing bodies reaffirm the belief that categorically all male athletes are better at sports when compared to female athletes (Cahn, 1994; Cavanaugh & Sykes, 2006; Cole, 2000; Kane, 1995). However, "athletic prowess is not simply a matter of genetics or a matter of biological sex" (Zaccone, 2010, p. 397). In the United States, there is legal precedent that sex is not and cannot be a proxy for ability in athletics (McDonagh & Pappano, 2007). Yet the belief in the categorical physical superiority of male athletes and the physical inferiority of female athletes continues despite social science, biomedical research, and legal precedent that suggests otherwise (Dworkin & Cooky, 2012; Kane, 1995).

Given the overarching belief in natural male physical superiority and female inferiority, sex-testing policies target only female athletes. Despite the fact that sport requires powerful physical prowess, women are sex tested when they carry out an explosive athletic performance, have a high degree of musculature, or are perceived to be "too male." If it is found that their testosterone levels are greater than those of a "normal woman," this is said to confer unfair advantage to the other women in the field. Following the logic employed by sport-governing bodies, one question is:

Why are men not also tested for hormonal, muscular, endocrine, or other genetic advantages relative to other men? Here, one could also argue that these advantages are unfair, producing an unlevel playing field for some male athletes over other male athletes. If the need for sex testing resides in ensuring a level playing field, as sport-governing bodies and organizations claim, then why is there no inquiry or test to determine whether some men have testosterone that exceeds the "normal male range"? Biomedical scholars, including clinical geneticists, have posed similar questions for sport-governing bodies to consider: Should "male athletes with elevated levels of androgens be forced to take androgen inhibitors?" (Vilain & Sánchez, 2012, p. 198). Or should some men be prevented from participating in men's competitions, given that these athletes would have an "unfair advantage" over other male competitors who have lower levels of androgens?

The question as to why there is no parallel examination concerning what might make some men genetically or physiologically more competitive than other men has not been considered in the institution of sport. Indeed, from the vantage of sport organizations' policies on sex testing, there is no reason to believe that biology or genetics would confer an unfair advantage for some male athletes that other male athletes in the same competitive field lack. Instead, men's superior performances relative to other men are attributed to "natural talent," hard work, and dedication and are celebrated and embraced.

Given that sport organizations do not attempt to police the boundaries of biologically occurring advantages in men's sporting competitions and do not seem concerned with eliminating genetic outliers from men's sport events to level the playing field for men, this leads one to question why it is that women's sport is the only competitive context wherein sex is tested to determine a "naturally" occurring advantage. To put it another way:

> Taking an excess of testosterone is cheating. Producing an excess of testosterone is a genetic advantage, and there is nothing inherently wrong with that. Genetic advantages are the norm and not the exception in competitive sports. High-level competitive athletes are rife with individuals who are genetic outliers. (Hercher, 2010, p. 552)

Part of the reason why only athletes in women's sport competitions are tested for sex and why sex is the only "naturally occurring advantage" that is tested is this: For sport-governing bodies, sex testing is necessary because of the underlying belief that all biological males are stronger, bigger, faster, and thus superior athletes when compared to all biological women competing in the same sport. Hence sex testing legitimates sex segregation as necessary to "ensure a level playing field" in sport,

> whereby it seems intuitively obvious, given the physiological differences that exist between men and women, that athletes should compete against others of the same sex, unless otherwise specified by rule—for example, in co-educational contests—or in disciplines for which the physiological differences between men and women offer no competitive advantage or disadvantage. (Reeser, 2005, p. 695)

While biology and the need for ensuring fair play through sex segregation are often cited as the reasons for differences in women's and men's athletic performances, numerous sport and gender scholars have challenged this logic (Cahn, 1994; Cavanaugh & Sykes, 2006; Cole, 2000; Kane, 1995; Lenskyj, 1986; Ritchie, 2003; Ritchie et al., 2008). Historically, women have been purposefully excluded from competing with or against men. When women were given the opportunity and excelled against men in direct competition, they were subsequently banned from sport (for a discussion, see Dworkin & Cooky, 2012; Cahn, 1994).

Examples of women restricted from direct competition with men are abundant, particularly in the Olympics and international competitions. Women were not allowed to compete in marathon events in the United States until 1965, and it was not until the 1984 Olympics that the marathon was added to the women's Olympic Games events; medical experts deemed women too frail and vulnerable to reproductive problems should they compete in endurance events (Cahn, 1994; Vertinsky, 1994). Numerous contemporary examples of sex discrimination in sport also exist; for example, in 2010, despite protests, women's ski jumping was not added to the Olympics even though the numbers of women in the sport had risen dramatically (Travers, 2011). Thus assumptions of female inferiority and frailty frequently underlie the decision to keep sport sex segregated (Dworkin & Wachs, 2009; McDonagh & Pappano, 2007; Messner, 2002). Given that the logic of sport organizations and sport-governing bodies is undergirded by an assumption that women are inherently physically inferior to men, they view men and intersex athletes as individuals who should be prohibited from competing with women. This logic is viewed as eliminating any "unfair advantage" and is said to ensure that female athletes are able to participate in sport. And given that sports are sex segregated, this further justifies the necessity to police the boundaries of sex in women's sport.

Although it is believed that intersex athletes/female athletes with CAH or other DSDs may have an "unfair advantage" relative to other female athletes without DSDs (primarily as a result of the higher levels of androgens they possess), the research is inconclusive regarding what types of conditions confer or do not confer a so-called advantage and to what extent (Vilain &Sánchez, 2012). Some researchers have found that female athletes with CAH may be at a disadvantage in some sports—especially those that require height, such as basketball and volleyball. This is because women with CAH tend to be shorter (Wonkam, Fieggen, & Ramesar, 2010). There is also an issue with salt loss for individuals with CAH, which may be a disadvantage in some endurance events (Wonkam et al., 2010).

In this section, we have argued that principles of unfair advantage are not consistently applied in women's and men's sport. We have drawn upon available empirical research to challenge the notion that "real" (or "unaffected" or "normal") female athletes are categorically disadvantaged relative to male athletes and intersex female athletes.

Concluding Comments and Suggestions for Change

On July 6, 2010, the IAAF made the decision to reinstate Caster Semenya and to clear her for competitive sporting events. In a separate ruling on August 28, 2011, the IAAF decided to change its requirements for what qualifies as a women's world record in marathon road races. Specifically, the IAAF elected to ban women's marathon records if the woman attained the world record with a male pacer who ran with her at the time. The IAAF declared that the only world records that count are those from a "women's-only" event and that in "mixed-race" events (where men are a part of the race at the same time), a woman's world record would not be deemed a world record; instead, it would be classified as a "world's best." In fact, even though this policy was written in 2011, the IAAF maintained that it would go back to marathon world records attained by women from 2003 to 2011 and declare those records invalid. The reason? The IAAF claimed that women had an "unfair advantage" if a man was present, running with them in the field. The IAAF has not sought to make a parallel examination of the men's events to see if there are any pacers on the road that offer men the ability to pace themselves faster than they typically would run (producing an unfair advantage in the men's events). Here too, it is evident that sex segregation in sport and beliefs about male physical superiority and female inferiority are key factors undergirding the practice and ensuing policies. Rather than suggest that we can objectively determine how far women can go without the help of extra testosterone or male pacers who train with them, we suggest that many sportsmen and sportswomen have "unfair advantages." If a level playing field is desired (or even possible), then we posit sport-governing bodies and sport organizations should treat all genetic advantages and all pacing advantages equally. Following the logic employed by sport-governing bodies in their rationale to sex test female athletes, we argue that male athletes who have unusually high levels of endogenic testosterone or androgen levels that exceed the "normal male range" should also be prevented from participating in men's competitions or be required to take androgen inhibitors (Vilain & Sánchez, 2012). By the IOC's and IAAF's own standards, these athletes would have an "unfair advantage" over other male competitors who have lower levels of testosterone. While testing men for high levels of endogenous testosterone would implement the logic of fairness more consistently because it would equally apply the claim that certain levels of testosterone represent a definitive athletic advantage, this suggestion is not supported by empirical evidence in biomedical research. As Karkazis, Jordan-Young, Davis, and Camporesi (2012) discussed, "Despite the many assumptions about the relationship between testosterone and athletic advantage, there is no evidence showing that successful athletes had higher testosterone levels than less successful athletes" (p. 9). With regard to the use of pacers, male athletes who pace themselves with other male athletes or pacers and perform better given their presence should also have their world records invalidated. If genetic advantages or pacers are not treated equally within women's and men's sporting competition and only records in women's sports are revoked and only women are sex tested and disqualified from sport, these are evident cases of sex discrimination that should be pursued through appropriate legal channels.

These suggestions assume that we agree with the organization of sport as it currently exists. Other solutions are certainly possible. For example, rather than viewing sex segregation as necessary and "disorders of sex development" as a much-needed category that is used to "objectively" determine who is and is not a woman in sport, we argue the category of "sex" is not the only acceptable way to organize sport. Echoing Travers (2008), we argue that "all sports competitions should be based on the abilities of individuals who seek to play, not on stereotypical attributes" of sex (p. 93).

One thing is apparent: when "suspicious" female athletes are sex tested, the ambiguities of sex as a dichotomous category—and the real social processes involved in constituting and reconstituting what sex is—become exposed. Rather than leveling the playing field, sex testing in sport offers us the biological reality of a continuum of sex. Simultaneously, sex testing illustrates how sport organizations, scientists, athletes, and broader society adhere to notions of categorical difference and efforts to maintain sex dichotomies and sex segregation in sport. Such a policy not only interferes with the right to participate in sport but also bolsters the inequitable treatment of intersex and female athletes in sport.

As we have noted elsewhere, the voice of Caster Semenya was silenced in the aftermath of the 2009 Berlin World Championships (Cooky, Dycus, & Dworkin, 2012; Dworkin, Swarr, & Cooky, 2013). Indeed, in the hearings that were held to determine the IOC's and the IAAF's new policies, the voices of athletes who have been disqualified by the policies were excluded from the deliberations. Yet representatives of intersex communities argued that the policies were discriminatory (Viloria & Martinez-Patino, 2012). Echoing these representatives, including Hida P. Viloria and Maria Jose Martinez-Patino (Martinez-Patino is an athlete who was disqualified from participating in sport after "failing" a sex test) along with other scholars (Karkazis et al., 2012), we call for the abandonment of sex testing in sport. It is time for sport-governing bodies and organizations to cease justifying the discriminatory policy and practice of sex testing. Arguing that sport is a level playing field and that sex testing is about "respect" for male and female differences is highly dubious, as we have illustrated. We advocate the end of these discriminatory policies that violate the rights of some female athletes to compete in sport (Viloria & Martinez-Patino, 2012). This change is necessary not only to protect the rights of female athletes who may be intersex but also to ensure the rights of all female athletes to participate in sport that is free from discriminatory policies.

Questions for Reflection and Discussion

Why are sports sex segregated? How do notions of fairness and sport as level playing field shape our understandings of participation and who is eligible to participate in women's or men's events? How might desegregating sports lead to gender equality?

References

Athlete Caster Semenya free to compete. (2010, July 6). *BBC News*. Retrieved from http://news.bbc.co.uk/sport2/hi/athletics/8793668.stm

Blackless, M., Charuvastra, A., Derryk, A., Fausto-Sterling, A., Lauzanne, K., & Lee, E. (2000). How sexually dimorphic are we? Review and synthesis. *American Journal of Human Biology, 12*, 151–166.

Burstyn, V. (1999). *The rites of men: Manhood, politics, and the culture of sport.* Toronto, Canada: University of Toronto Press.

Buzuvis, E. E. (2010). Caster Semenya and the myth of a level playing field. *The Modern American, 6*, 1–7.

Cahn, S. (1994). *Coming on strong: Gender and sexuality in twentieth century women's sport.* New York, NY: Free Press.

Camporesi, S., & Maugeri, P. (2010). Caster Semenya: Sport, categories, and the creative role of ethics. *Journal of Medical Ethics, 36*, 378–379.

Caplan, A. L. (2010). Fairer sex: The ethics of determining gender for athletic eligibility: Commentary on "Beyond the Caster Semenya controversy: The case of the use of genetics for gender testing in sport." *Journal of Genetic Counseling, 19*, 549–550.

Cavanaugh, S. L., & Sykes, H. (2006). Transsexual bodies at the Olympics: The International Olympics Committee's policy on transsexual athletes at the 2004 Athens summer games. *Body and Society, 12*, 75–102.

Cole, C. L. (2000). One chromosome too many? In K. Schaffer & S. Smith (Eds.), *The Olympics at the millennium: Power, politics, and the game* (pp. 128–146). New Brunswick, NJ: Rutgers University Press.

Cooky, C., Dycus, R., & Dworkin, S. L. (2012). "What makes a woman a woman?" vs. "our first lady of sport": A comparative analysis of the United States and the South African media coverage of Caster Semenya. *Journal of Sport and Social Issues*. Advance online publication. doi:10.1177/0193723512447940

Coyle, E. F. (2005). Improved muscular efficiency displayed as Tour de France champion matures. *Journal of Applied Physiology, 98*, 2191–2196.

de la Chapelle, A. (1986). The use and misuse of sex chromatin screening for "gender verification" of female athletes. *Journal of the American Medical Association, 256*, 1920–1923.

Dickinson, B. D., Genel, M., Robinowitz, C. B., Turner, P. L., & Woods, G. L. (2002). Gender verification of female Olympic athletes. *Medicine and Science in Sports and Exercise, 34*, 1539–1542.

Dreger, A. (1998). *Hermaphrodites and the medical invention of sex.* Cambridge, MA: Harvard University Press.

Dworkin, S. L., & Cooky, C. (2012). Sport, sex segregation, and sex testing: Critical reflections on this unjust marriage. *American Journal of Bioethics, 12*(7), 21–23.

Dworkin, S. L., Swarr, A. L., & Cooky, C. (in press). Sex, gender, and racial (in)justice in sport: The case of South African track star Caster Semenya. *Feminist Studies.*

Dworkin, S. L., & Wachs, F. L. (2009). *Body panic: Gender, health, and the selling of fitness.* New York, NY: New York University Press.

Elias, L. J., Ljungqvist, A., Ferguson-Smith, M., Simpson, J. L., Genel, M., Carlson, A. S., et al. (2000). Gender verification of female athletes. *Genetics in Medicine, 2*, 249–254.

Fausto-Sterling, A. (2000). *Sexing the body: Gender politics and the construction of sexuality.* New York, NY: Basic Books.

Genel, M. (2010, October). *Sex and gender in sport: Fallacy of the level playing field.* Paper presented at the Third Congress of the European Academy of Paediatric Societies, Copenhagen, Denmark.

Genel, M., & Ljungqvist, A. (2005). Gender verification of female athletes. *Lancet, 366*, S41.

Hercher, L. (2010). Gender verification: A term whose time has come and gone. *Journal of Genetic Counseling, 19*, 551–553.

IAAF: Semenya decision in November. (2009, September 16). *ESPN.com*. Retrieved from http://sports.espn.go.com/oly/trackandfield/news/story?id/4464405

International Association of Athletics Federations. (2011, May). *IAAF Regulations governing eligibility of females with hyperandrogenism to compete in women's competition*. Retrieved from http://www.iaaf.org/mm/Document/AboutIAAF/Publications/05/98/78/20110430054216_httppostedfile_HARegulations%28Final%29Appendices-AMG-30.04.2011_24299.pdf

Kane, M. J. (1995). Resistance/transformation of the oppositional binary: Exposing sport as a continuum. *Journal of Sport and Social Issues, 19*, 191–218.

Karkazis, K. (2008). *Fixing sex: Intersex, medical authority, and lived experience*. Durham, NC: Duke University Press.

Karkazis, K., Jordan-Young, R., Davis, G., & Camporesi, S. (2012). Out of bounds? A critique of the new policies on hyperandrogenism in elite female athletes. *American Journal of Bioethics, 12*, 3–16.

Lenskyj, H. (1986). *Out of bounds: Women, sport, and sexuality*. Toronto, Canada: Women's Press.

Ljungqvist, A., & Genel, M. (2005). Transsexual athletes: When is competition fair? *Lancet, 366*, 42–43.

Ljungqvist, A., Martinez-Patino, M., Martinez-Vidal, A., Zagalaz, L., Diaz, P., & Mateos, C. (2006). The history and current policies on gender testing in elite athletes. *International SportMed Journal, 7*, 225–230.

Ljungqvist, A., & Simpson, J. L. (1992). Medical examination for health of all athletes replacing the need for gender verification in international sports: The International Amateur Athletic Federation Plan. *Journal of the American Medical Association, 267*, 850–852.

Martinez-Patino, M. J., Mateos-Padorno, C., Martinez-Vidal, A., Sanchez, A. M., Garcia, J. L., Diaz, M. P., et al. (2010). An approach to the biological, historical and psychological repercussions of gender verification in top level competitions. *Journal of Human Sport and Exercise, 5*, 307–321.

McDonagh, E., & Pappano, E. (2007). *Playing with the boys: Why separate is not equal in sports*. New York, NY: Oxford University Press.

Messner, M. A. (2002). *Taking the field: Women, men, and sports*. Minneapolis, MN: University of Minnesota Press.

Puffer, J. C. (2002). Commentary to accompany gender verification of female athletes. *Medicine and Science in Sports and Exercise, 34*, 1543.

Reeser, J. C. (2005). Gender identity in sport: Is the playing field level? *British Journal of Sports Medicine, 39*, 695–699.

Ritchie, I. (2003). Sex tested, gender verified: Controlling female sexuality in the age of containment. *Sport History Review, 34*, 80–98.

Ritchie, R., Reynard, J., & Lewis, T. (2008). Intersex and Olympic games. *Journal of the Royal Society of Medicine, 101*, 395–399.

Sage, G. (1998). *Power and ideology in American sport*. Champaign, IL: Human Kinetics.

Simpson, J. L., Ljungqvist, A., de la Chapelle, A., Ferguson-Smith, M. A., Genel, M., Carlson, A. S., et al. (1993). Gender verification in competitive sports. *Sports Medicine, 16*, 305–315.

Sykes, H. (2006). Transsexual and transgender policies in sport. *Women in Sport and Physical Activity, 15*, 3–13.

Travers, A. (2008). The sport nexus and gender injustice. *Studies in Social Justice, 2*, 79–101.

Travers, A. (2011). Women's ski jumping, the 2010 Olympic Games, and the deafening silence of sex segregation, whiteness, and wealth. *Journal of Sport and Social Issues, 35*, 126–145.

Vertinsky, P. (1994). Women, sport, and exercise in the 19th century. In V. Costa & S. Guthrie (Eds.), *Women and sport: Interdisciplinary perspectives* (pp. 63–82). Champaign, IL: Human Kinetics.

Vilain, E. (2012, June 18). Gender testing for athletes remains a tough call. *The New York Times*. Retrieved from http://www.nytimes.com/2012/06/18/sports/olympics/the-line-between-male-and-femaleathletes-how-to-decide.html?pagewanted/all

Vilain, E., & Sánchez, F. J. (2012). Reproductive endocrinology: Athletes' bodies, sexed bodies—Intersexuality in athletics. *Nature Reviews Endocrinology, 8*, 198–199.

Viloria, H. P., & Martinez-Patino, M. J. (2012). Reexamining rationales of "fairness": An athlete and insider's perspective on the new policies on hyperandrogenism in elite female athletes. *American Journal of Bioethics, 12*(7), 17–33.

Wackwitz, L. A. (2003). Verifying the myth: Olympic sex testing and the category "woman." *Women's Studies International, 26*, 553–560.

Wonkam, A., Fieggen, K., & Ramesar, R. (2010). Beyond the Caster Semenya controversy: The case of the use of genetics for gender testing in sport. *Journal of Genetic Counseling, 19*, 545–548.

Zaccone, L. (2010). Policing the policing of intersex bodies: Softening the lines in Title IX athletic programs. *Brooklyn Law Review, 76*, 385–438.

3

Gender Relations and Sport

• •

Local, National, Transnational

MICHAEL A. MESSNER

The prominent Australian sociologist Raewyn Connell has criticized the tendency of European and American scholars to focus only on what is happening in our own nations and local communities while ignoring knowledge emerging from the developing world, what is often known as "the global south." I am a sociologist who is as guilty as anyone of this sort of national chauvinism. Nearly all of my work has focused on the United States, with the occasional nod to North American neighbors Canada or Mexico. So when I was invited in 2012 to join a group of scholars at the University of Nevada, Reno Center for Basque Studies to discuss sport in global perspective, I took this as an opportunity to begin to challenge myself to think more broadly. I learned a good deal from others at the conference. And the paper I subsequently wrote applied one of Connell's key ideas about gender to the study of sport: that we should consider how relations of gender are organized in local, national and international contexts. My "local" case drew from my study of gender relations in youth sports in my own

Source: "Gender Relations and Sport: Local, National, Transnational," by M. A. Messner, 2014, in Mariann Vaczi (Ed.), *Playing fields: Power, practice, and passion in sport* (pp. 17–35), Reno, Nevada: Center for Basque Studies Press. Copyright 2013 by the Center for Basque Studies. Reprinted with permission.

town. The "national" case analyzes my experiences in participating in the contested politics of Title IX—the legal statute passed in the United States to ensure gender equality in public schools, including school sports. And the "international" case draws on recent research—including Cheryl Cooky's work that you will see elsewhere in this volume—on the controversies surrounding runner Caster Semenya, when global sport organizations struggled with the charge of whether "gender-verification tests" were fair to determine whether Semenya—or any other athlete, for that matter—is a "true woman." Each of these three cases revealed how limiting it is to even try to think about gender simply and categorically as being about boys and girls, men and women: Race, social class, national origin, and the recent emergence of transgender people complicate and enrich our understandings of gender relations in sport. This chapter illustrates too how putting the local, the national, and the transnational into play with each other, rather than treating them as separate levels of analysis, can challenge and deepen our understandings of each. Even a "local" study of one's own community, Connell has suggested, will be enriched if examined in light of national and transnational processes. This is certainly true of sport.

—Michael A. Messner

In this chapter, I explore how organized sport works as a constitutive element of current gender relations. To state the project this way requires a move away from a common "sociology of sport" perspective that focuses on relations *within* sport toward a "sport and society" perspective that explores the ways that sport articulates with strains, tensions, and shifting formations of gender in communities, the nation, and the world. Two conceptual frames are important here. First, when I write of *gender relations*, I am assuming a multidimensional analytic framework: gender as an important part of the symbolic realm of cultural meanings; gender as actively created through day-to-day interactional processes; and gender divisions of labor and power as a dynamic part of the structure of social institutions.[1] Second, drawing from Australian sociologist Raewyn Connell (1987), I explore the institutional structure of gender in three geographic registers: a local institutional gender regime; a national gender order (of the United States); and a location within the international gender order.

Whether at the level of local gender regimes or at that of national or international gender orders, these concepts never imply a fixity of gender relations. Rather, they are tools we can use to grasp the "state of play" of gender and power, oscillating between moments of crisis and change and hegemonic moments of relative stability and consensus. Moments of hegemonic stability in turn always create new strains and tensions that foster new possibilities for change, less often radical disruptions, more often contestations over what Connell (2011) calls the "steering" of gender relations—within a gender regime, between gender regimes, and within larger gender orders. It is my aim in this chapter to move from local to national to international registers of gender relations by looking first at a local study of youth sports, next at the national politics of Title IX in the United

States, and finally at the recent case of South African runner Caster Semenya's "gender-verification test" controversy, with the aim of illuminating some strains and tensions in the international gender order. I will argue that my local study suggests an emergent hegemonic moment of postfeminist "soft essentialism," while the national and international foci reveal some strains and tensions that inhere in this moment of gender formation, as well as the limitations of both a local ethnographic study and of an analysis that focuses primarily on gender.

Sport, Gender, and Society

Before moving to the body of this chapter, I will briefly reiterate an argument about how sport figures in U.S. historical gender relations. Following an early 20th-century burst of athleticism among girls and women that accompanied a powerful wave of feminism, a backlash against vigorous physical activity for women eliminated many women's sports and vastly marginalized those that remained. The resulting binary opposition of athletic males and nonathletic females helped to construct and naturalize a gendered public–domestic split in the mid-20th-century U.S.—a divide especially evident in the middle class—and a hierarchical ordering of gender that was premised on ideologies of male superiority. I have called this midcentury ideology "hard essentialism"—the shared belief that women and men are *naturally and categorically different* and should thus be sorted into different and unequal spheres that reflect their natures.[2]

The resurgence of a feminist movement in the 1970s led to a new burst of female athleticism, corresponding with (especially middle-class) women's more general move into public life. On one level, this dramatic growth of female athleticism served as a challenge to the ideology of hard essentialism. However, the particular institutional organization of sport differed from that of most other institutions that were undergoing sex-desegregation in the late 20th century. Unlike higher education, medicine, law, or politics, the integration of girls and women into sport was taking place within an almost entirely sex-segregated structure. Put simply, "equal opportunity" for girls and women in sport has been sought mostly within a "separate but equal" strategy, where male and female bodies, assumed to be naturally different, are sorted into separate binary categories. As equal opportunity is sought, difference is affirmed. Thus sport becomes a dynamic site for the simultaneous contestation and reproduction of gender equality and inequality, a "contested terrain" of gender relations (Hargreaves, 1986; Willis, 1983; Messner, 1988).

A Local Terrain of Contested Gender Relations

Between 1999 and 2007, I conducted a study of my local community's soccer, baseball, and softball youth sports programs. I was particularly interested in gender divisions of labor and power among adult volunteers (mostly parents), and in the course of the study, I became increasingly focused on how the division of labor and power in youth sport's gender regime (nearly all of the coaches were men and nearly all of the "team moms" were women) tended to articulate neatly with the gendered work and family relations in this professional-class and White-dominated[3] Los Angeles suburb. Much of the book that resulted from this study analyzes the adults' gender formation processes that result in sex segregation (Messner, 2009). Here, I briefly outline two interrelated parts of this process: First, the ways in which professional-class adults, through talk and actions, "gender" the boys and girls whom they are coaching; and second, the ways in which adults' gendering of kids reflects and naturalizes the gendered work-family divisions of labor and power in their own families, thus helping to construct the ascendant hegemony of "soft essentialism."

Youth sports coaches, including most of the small number of women coaches, tend to view and treat girls and boys in very different ways. Adults applaud their daughters' participation in sports, seeing it as healthy and empowering. When asked to talk about girls, adults often drop into a language of individual choice: they talk of their daughters' futures as realms of choice for which, they believe, sports participation is helping to prepare them. This new articulation of girls as flexible choosers is a remarkable sign of social change, vastly different from earlier generations who tended to view their daughters as destined for domesticity. In particular, it is a dramatic indicator of the success of liberal feminism. However, the limits of this language of choice for girls are revealed in the asymmetrical ways that adults talk about boys. Adults, simply put, are far less articulate when asked to talk about boys and gender. Ultimately, most adults meander to clichés about boys' supposed natural (testosterone-driven) aggression and emotional linearity (as opposed to the supposed emotional complexity of girls) and about boys' natural inclinations for sport in particular and public life in general. I call this shared view of girls as flexible choosers and boys as inflexible biologically driven creatures "soft essentialism." Similar to hard essentialism, soft essentialism is still premised on a belief in natural differences between boys and girls, but soft essentialism no longer posits this difference to be categorical—especially when it comes to girls, who are now viewed as flexible choosers who as adults will be expected to navigate across and between the challenges and demands of public and domestic life. This changed view of girls stands in stark contrast to a largely unreconstructed view of boys.

Soft essentialist ideology, projected onto children, takes on clearer meaning when we consider common patterns of gender relations in professional-class families. Mothers in these families are college educated, often holding graduate degrees, and have spent years building careers in medicine, law, finance, and other professions. On arrival of children in a family—especially second or third children—many of these mothers face a common dilemma—not so much a "biological pull to motherhood," as conservative pundits would have it, but the constraining experience of being stretched to the limits by the combination of inflexible workplaces, career-committed husbands who do minimal family labor, and expanding public expectations for mothers to involve themselves in the "third shift" of community and school-based work necessary for the concerted cultivation of their own children (Blair-Loy, 2003; Lareau, 2003; Stone, 2007). Thus challenged, some of these women decide to opt entirely out of their high-powered careers, while others change to less demanding (but lower pay and lower status) jobs. These women narrate their resulting shift in attention away from career and toward care of kids in the language of individual choice, inflected with a feminist sensibility.

In short, the gender regime of youth sports has undergone a huge transformation in the past 40 years. And there is evidence to support the contention that girls' dramatic movement into sports is correlated with health benefits and has fostered embodiments of a competitive professional-class habits (Miller, Sabo, Farrell, Barnes, & Melnick, 1999; Miller, Melnick, Barnes, Farrell, & Sabo, 2005).

However, the youth sports–based construction of girls as flexible choosers and boys as naturally destined for competition in public life plays a largely conservative and stabilizing role in the context of professional-class work-family gender regimes, where highly educated mothers exercise "choice" to opt out or scale back careers, while men continue largely to focus on their public careers. Gender inequalities that persist at the nexus of professional-class work and family gender regimes, rather than being viewed as sites of collective struggle for change, are narrated through soft essentialism as resulting from women's individual, even feminist-inspired choices. The ideology of soft essentialism, constructed in part within youth sports, helps to naturalize the inequalities that inhere in this moment of hegemonic, class-based gender relations.

An obvious limit of my local study of youth sports is my analytic foregrounding of gender. How might the intersecting gender regimes of youth sports, families, and work look through an intersectional analysis that extends beyond the gender/social class matrix at the center of my analysis? This question could be explored by attending more centrally to the experiences of marginalized people within the White, professional-class-dominated community that I studied, or by comparing youth sports in my community to, for instance, youth sports within adjacent working-class and predominantly Latina/o communities. Such a shift in empirical focus would likely reveal the ways in which concepts like "gender regimes" can obscure as much as they reveal. An intersectional analysis that attends as much to class and race relations might better view youth sports not as simply a "gender regime," but as a dynamic "inequality regime" that intersects with other institutional inequality regimes (Acker, 2006).

And though I do connect my analysis from the local youth sports gender regimes to local family and work gender regimes, such a study can be limited by its very locality unless it is connected to an analysis of the historical and macroinstitutional context in which it is embedded. In the next section of this chapter, I draw out the scope to think more about sport and the national gender order of the United States. And while there are many potential points of entry into an exploration of gender and sport on a national scale, I will limit my comments here to what the politics of Title IX can tell us about current strains and tensions in the national gender order.

Title IX, Sport, and the National Gender Order

Initiated in the United States in 1972 to ensure equal opportunities for boys and girls in educational institutions, Title IX has had a huge impact on sports, helping to usher in a dramatic and continuing surge of sports participation by girls and women in high schools and colleges (Acosta & Carpenter, 2012). In the terms discussed in the introduction of this chapter, Title IX can be seen as a largely successful legal and political effort at "steering" the gender regimes of schools and universities toward gender equity. This equity steering did not go unopposed; from the start, the patriarchal center of institutionalized U.S. sport, led by the football lobby, opposed Title IX, and over the years, many legal challenges to Title IX have been fought (see Brake, 2010; Suggs, 2005). For my purposes here, these conflicts illustrate the unevenness of gender reform within and between gender regimes. With gender regimes more deeply contested by feminism in the 1970s, education, politics, and the law clashed with the more stubbornly conservative and less vigorously contested gender regime of organized sports. Title IX can be seen as a political and legal means of steering the internal gender regime of sport toward consensus and continuity with the gender regime of education—and with that of the larger gender order.

Title IX politics came to a head at the national level in 2002 when the Bush administration called for a series of public hearings to assess the effects of Title IX. The subsequent regional meetings (I attended and testified at the one held in San Diego) revealed Title IX to be a lightning rod for backlash discourse but also—and even more so, as it turned out—a powerful rallying point for supporters of girls' and women's sport. Legal activist Nancy Solomon and I observed that the anti–Title IX discourse at the hearings tended to invoke a language of male victimization by the state, which was viewed as unfairly representing women's interests (Messner & Solomon, 2007). We argued that the language of bureaucratic victimization of individual men—especially as symbolized by the threatened male "walk-on"—was a strategy that seemed to find fertile ground among young White males who face a world destabilized by feminism, gay and lesbian liberation, the civil rights movement, and major shifts in the economy.

It is striking how anti–Title IX talk is one of the few places in national discourse about sport where men become at least potentially visible as gendered beings ("gender and sport" nearly always implies "women and sport"). But critics' stories veer decidedly away from any possible analysis of boys and men as a socially formed group with shared interests (much less shared privileges) in sport. Instead, the discourse of critics of Title IX consistently invokes the values of individualism by telling stories of individual men victimized by liberal state policies that promote the group interests of women. And this discourse rests its case on an essentialist foundation—individual men, the critics argue, are just naturally more interested in sports than are women. The critics agree that it's a good thing for girls and women to have the right to choose to play sports, but they implied that due to their different natures, boys and men will naturally be drawn to sports, whereas fewer girls and women will be.

The critics thus used the values of individualism to smuggle in an articulation of "men's interests" as collectively opposed to Title IX, but this strategy was limited by the actual complexity of men's interests. To be sure, there is a powerful centripetal pull, even for many marginalized boys and men, to the privilege and erotic power that lie at the center of male-dominated institutions like sport. However, under some conditions, some men disidentify with *and* even oppose institutionalized male privilege. It has become common to hear stories, for instance, of fathers who become overnight equity activists when they find suddenly that their daughters have been denied access to sport or have been offered substandard playing fields or unqualified coaches. In these cases, individual men clearly see their own interests as intertwined with the interests of their female family members.

Indeed, collective opposition to Title IX appears to have faded in recent years, and many would say that this is because of the popularity of Title IX and the widespread support for girls and women's sport participation, including substantial support from men. A 2007 national poll conducted by the National Women's Law Center found that of those who recognize what Title IX is, 82% support it. Two Women's Sports Foundation studies in 2008 and 2009 in Boston and San Antonio revealed that only half of those polled knew about Title IX, but the vast majority agreed with its goals. And a 2008 national survey found adults widely supportive of girls' athletic opportunities (Sabo & Veliz, 2008).

In addition to growing pro–Title IX public opinion, it is also likely that the very legal structure of Title IX has allowed for a smoothing of current tensions and for a movement toward a national consensus that stabilizes a hegemonic moment of gender formation. In a cogent analysis of the legal politics of Title IX, Deborah Brake (2010) demonstrates how Title IX strategically melds different (and in some ways, fundamentally contradictory) strands of feminist legal theory. On the one hand, Brake argues, Title IX is premised on the liberal feminist ideal of equal treatment for individuals based on merit. Under the law, individuals have the right to equal opportunities to participate in sport. However, this individualist focus in the law is continually in tension with the sex-segregated (and still unequal) collective structure of sport. The liberal feminist strand of Title IX, Brake explains, "strives for equal treatment of men and women without questioning the male-dominated structure of sports and. . . . the reasons men and women are differently situated in sport" (p. 9).

Counterbalancing the limits of liberal individualism is the strand of "difference feminism" also undergirding the legal theory of Title IX. Difference feminism, according to Brake, "embrace[s] and value[s] women's distinctive interests, needs, and experiences equally with those of men . . . [and] accommodates gender difference in sport by its allowance of sex-separate teams" (2010, p. 10). While helping to protect and extend the collective interests of girls and women, this aspect of Title IX also echoes the essentialism of 19th-century "social feminists" (Vertinsky, 1994). Premised on a presumed biologically based need to create and maintain a gendered boundary around girls' and women's sports, the law creates and protects a separate sphere within which female sport participation can grow and thrive while simultaneously risking—perhaps even ensuring—a marginalization of women's sports that stigmatizes female athletes as inferior and often in need of protection. The tension between these two strains of feminist theory is clear: Can individual girls and women ever have truly equal opportunities, resources, and treatment in an institution that is divided in binary terms according to an assumed-to-be-natural hierarchy of male–female bodily difference?[4]

Title IX, then, is an organically evolving law, its contradictory elements giving it a built-in flexibility that allows advocates to use the law as a tool to push for individual equal opportunity while simultaneously arguing that categorical sex difference creates a distinct group-based interest that must be protected and defended. The effectiveness of this melding of "equal treatment" with "difference accommodation" is evident, according to Brake (2010), in recent legal cases that have dealt with pregnancy among athletes (p. 171–177). National advocacy organizations like the Women's Sports Foundation tend to mirror this dual strategy of advocating for individual equal opportunity alongside a defense of women's group-based interests in maintaining different and separate sports (Heywood, 2007).

For my purposes here, I want to emphasize how Title IX's very strengths, and likely too its popularity, are grounded not so much in a revolutionary potential to disrupt gender relations but to the contrary, in the ways that its melding of equal opportunity and essential difference articulates neatly with the emergence of the professional-class ideology of soft essentialism. In particular, Title IX's emphasis on the individual rights of girls and women as flexible choosers tends to affirm professional-class beliefs in individual meritocracy while deflecting critical focus away from the ways that gendered institutions constrain those very choices. Simultaneously, the law's essentialist underpinnings then naturalize the unequally gendered outcomes of women's (apparently individual) choices. The inherent strains and tensions built into soft essentialism, I argued above, are (1) its tendency to smuggle in a White, professional-class-based ethic and to either render invisible and/or impose that ethic on class- and race-marginalized and subordinated others, and (2) to render boys and men as an undifferentiated, unexamined, and thus unreconstructed category. In the United States, much pro–Title IX advocacy discourse for girls and women in sport does just that. The liberal feminist individualism helps to construct an individual professional-class White subject, while difference feminism's essentialism helps to maintain boys and men as a naturalized and largely unmarked category. As scholars of masculinities and of Whiteness have shown, the invisibility of superordinate categories is often central to the reproduction of the privilege that adheres to these categories.

If politics involves the steering of the gender order, then what strategic steering directions might be implied by the current strains and tensions discussed above? I have argued elsewhere that to push the sport gender regime toward greater democratic egalitarianism would involve two strategies. First, while most advocates of girls' and women's sports are committed to the current institutional segregation of girls' and women's sports as necessary to ensure participation opportunities, many community activists are moving toward a more intersectional understanding of the interests of girls and women, creating sports programs targeted to the needs, for instance, of inner-city girls, girls of color, Muslim girls, or differently abled girls. Working creatively with this dynamic tension between the collective interests of girls, as protected under Title IX, and the interests of particular groups of girls who are not privileged by professional-class, White, or able-bodied status is one of the keys to pushing beyond the class-based individualist limits of Title IX as a strategy for social justice (Cooky, 2009).

Second, a national social-justice strategy would move toward a strategic degendering of boys' and men's sports. This would mean three things. First, this degendering would build a broad social recognition that boys, as much as girls, are socially gendered beings and not simply products of a sexed biological nature. Second, youth sports would be constructed as sites where adults could prepare boys to become flexible choosers who, like girls, need to develop the skill sets and emotional flexibilities that allow them to negotiate across and between the challenges of public and domestic realms of life (see Atkinson & Kehler, 2010). This would involve, in part, seeing youth sports as a place in which boys can expand (rather than contract) their emotional repertoires. Third, the homosocial boundaries of boys' and men's sports should be challenged, including, especially, by opening up coaching opportunities for women coaches and continuing the integration of girls into previously all-boys' sporting activities. Together, these strategies would push sport away from its current role as a professional-class gender comfort zone.

Using Title IX as a lens through which to view the current state of play of the U.S. national gender order extends our understanding beyond that of the local ethnographic study discussed in the first part of this chapter by connecting the national legal and political "steering" of gender relations to our understanding of local work–family youth sports gender regimes. I argue that we can see the ascendant class-based gender ideology of soft essentialism at both the local and the national level. At both levels, we can see the expansion of individual equal opportunity for girls as a major accomplishment of feminism (albeit one that disproportionately benefits girls from privileged backgrounds), while also seeing how persistent essentialist beliefs—however "soft" they may be—continue to construct and naturalize gender hierarchy, smuggle in class and race privilege under the guise of feminist progress, and leave boys and men as an unexamined and unreconstructed category.

A Transnational Moment of Gender Trouble

Gender and sport scholars in the United States have recently begun to develop a global focus in their theoretical frameworks and empirical analyses. Connell (2009) observes that imperialism and globalization have generated institutions—transnational corporations and markets, global media, the United Nations, NGOs—that are part of a world gender order. Such globalization processes are evident in sport to the extent that scholars can now begin to analyze sport as one site for the collision of national gender orders within a larger world gender order (Campbell, 2011; Miller, McKay, Lawrence, & Rowe, 2001). The case of South African runner Caster Semenya is one such transnational moment of collision for gender meanings and politics.

In 2009, 18-year-old South African runner Caster Semenya won the gold medal at the International Association of Athletics Federations (IAAF) World Championships in the 800 m run. Although the IAFF had previously joined other international sports governing bodies by doing away with mandatory "gender-verification tests," it was still the case that if and when competitors raised questions about an athlete's "true sex," a gender-verification test could be ordered. This occurred in the case of Semenya, setting off an international debate about human rights, "true womanhood," race, and the use of gender-verification testing.

I do not intend here to discuss the incipient scholarly literature on the politics of transgender or transsexual athletes.[5] Nor do I intend to tackle the very complicated task of understanding the full meanings of the Caster Semenya story, either within or outside of South Africa (to do so would risk oversimplification at best and a reinscription of an oppressive colonial gaze at worst). Instead, my goal is more modest: I simply want to use this case as an example of a transnational sporting event that makes questions of sex and gender salient and visible, thus revealing some strains and tensions within the international gender order. From this, I hope to gain insight into the limits of my analysis of local and national gender orders. Fortunately, other scholars have developed a sophisticated analysis of the meanings and nuances of the Semenya incident, and I draw here from two such current works (Cooky, Dycus, & Dworkin, 2013; Dworkin, Swarr, and Cooky, 2013).

An understanding of the transnational meanings of the Semenya incident begins with a sketch of the role of sport in the developing gender order of postapartheid South Africa. Jennifer Hargreaves conducted perhaps the first such overview. Gathered in 1995, shortly after the formal end of apartheid, Hargreaves's research in South Africa offers a glimpse into the development of sport within an emergent postcolonializing gender order. Hargreaves (2000) observes that sport in preapartheid South Africa was "a symbol and celebration of racial . . . superiority and White masculinity," and the immediate years following the end of apartheid were characterized by "piece-meal sport reforms . . . [that] systematically prioritized boys' and men's sports" (pp. 18, 28, 30). But by 1995, South African sport had also become a site of struggle for race and gender-justice: "Black women see sport as a channel for self-definition-simultaneously Afrocentric and feminist. Following years of subjugation under apartheid, their struggles in sport today are part of a wider quest for recognition and dignity; their successes reflect a radical independence and autonomy often absent in other areas of life. Sport is an important politico-cultural space for Black people" (p. 36).

A result of these struggles by the South African women's sports lobby was the development of national efforts to promote gender equity in sports, including the 1997–2000 establishment of a "Women in Sport South Africa" initiative within each province. Hargreaves observed that women's sports participation was becoming a visible pillar in the building of a postapartheid South African national identity. And—of central importance for my purposes here—unlike the White and professional-class values embedded in the promotion of women's sports in the United States, the development of women's sports in South Africa is intertwined with a state-sponsored movement to resist and transform White supremacy and colonial domination. The Caster Semenya event, a decade later, reveals the strains and tensions at the nexus between this national South African gender order and that of a transnational gender order dominated by the Global North.

Following Semenya's victorious run, the subsequent IAAF imposition of a gender-verification test on Semenya, along with the hand-wringing in the Euro-American sports media, can be seen as the Global North flexing its imperial muscle to impose Euro-American, binary conceptions of gender on a less powerful nation of the Global South. After all, the very organizational structure within which Semenya was competing was created by, and in the image of, the powers of the Global North. But such a simplistic one-way analysis risks reinscribing a colonial gaze, and—especially important for my purposes here—misses seeing the dialectical nature of such transnational events. As Connell (2009) argues, "The interaction of gender orders is not all one-way ... There is no question that the pressure of the metropole on the gender orders of the global periphery is much stronger than pressure the other ways. [However] we should not think of that as simple 'modernization' of gender. [Rather], the wider historical literature on gender and imperialism show turbulence in the process, and sometimes acute tension" (p. 128–129).

The Semenya incident reveals such turbulence and tensions at the intersection of North-South gender orders, which may provide opportunities for disruption and change not only transnationally but also possibly within the national gender orders of the Euro-American metropole.

First, this focus on a moment of transnational sporting "collision" reveals, even more than my local or national foci, the limits of a simple focus on gender relations. In particular, the Semenya case brings into stark relief the need for an intersectional analysis of gender with that of race and nation. Sociologists Cheryl Cooky, Ranissa Dycus, and Shari L. Dworkin (2013) conducted a systematic analysis of media coverage of the Semenya event, comparing South African print coverage of the story with coverage in the United States. In the U.S. coverage, the dominant media frame "centered on the 'medicalized' aspect of sex/gender ... among scientists and academics on whether or not 'sex tests' could identify and verify 'real' female athletes" (Cooky et al., 2013). In the South African press, the imposition of gender-verification testing on Semenya was not framed simply (or even primarily) as a violation of an individual human right, or even simply as a violation of "women's rights," but as a White, Euro-American insult to the integrity of South African identity. Semenya, for her South African advocates, was not so much seen as a champion of the rights of women or of transgender or intersexed people, but as "our girl," thus revealing the particular way that race and gender configure to construct the emergent postapartheid South African national identity.

I do not want to imply a romanticized view of South Africa (or anywhere else in the Global South) as a place where sex/gender binaries are less than meaningful or where gender fluidity is embraced. To the contrary, feminists in South Africa continue to organize around the strategic interests of women as a social category, fighting against stubborn legacies of institutionalized patriarchy in politics, the labor force, health care, and families, as well as struggling against various forms of violence against women (Dworkin, Colvin, Hatcher, & Peacock, 2012). And as Dworkin, Amanda Swarr, and Cooky (2013) point out, South African leaders have been no champions of human rights for transgender or gender-nonconforming people. But when South Africans witnessed scientific gender-verification tests being imposed on Caster Semenya by an institution representing the interests of the Global North, this conjured up recent historic parallels with oppressive medico-scientific practices during apartheid that subjected people to "race-verification tests." In response, it appears that the interests of asserting antiracist and anticolonial South African identity were best served not by engaging in debates about gender fluidity, but instead by embracing Semenya as "our girl" and denouncing as racist any questions about her gender. As such, the South African defense of Semenya affirms an antiracist, anticolonial construction of national identity, with women's sports as one pillar of this identity. Simultaneously, this defense reinforces, rather than challenges, an institutionalized gender binary in sport, thus erasing an opportunity to champion gender diversity and fluidity as part of an expanding human rights discourse (Cooky et al., 2013).

Second, the Semenya case reveals the limited scope of the concept of soft essentialism for thinking about contemporary gender relations in a global context. On the surface, we see in the Semenya case similarities with central aspects of soft essentialism—reaffirmations of binary sex categories; women's sports treated as a realm that requires "protection" (in this case, through gender-verification testing that aims to affirm a protective boundary around women athletes); and a silence surrounding boys and men as an unmarked, never sex tested, and thus naturalized superior sex category. But the North-South asymmetries in what the category of "women's sports" means, and in how these categories were strategically deployed, reveals some differences. While the sport agencies and mass media of the Global North attempted to impose their own institutionalized (and "science-based") essentialist and categorical male–female sport binaries, when we examine the meanings and strategies that emerge from South African groups, we see that these sex/gender binary categories were deployed not as a way of creating an individual professional-class "choosing" female subject (as in soft essentialist discourse), but rather as a collective form of resistance against White supremacy and control by the Global North.

In the Semenya case, gender categoricalism is reaffirmed in sport by the dominant discourse of both the Global North and the Global South, but it seems to be a very forced categoricalism, strained at both ends by Northern attempts to use science to force Semenya into one or the other sex category and by Southern discourse that insists on Semenya's femaleness by denying the veracity of gender-verification tests, thus erasing potential questions about gender fluidity and even muting the emergence of Semenya's own voice in the matter (Cooky et al., 2013).

Superimposing the concept of soft essentialism onto this transnational moment, then, risks adopting the standpoint of the Global North, thus doing violence to the intersecting interests at stake and the different ways these interests are played out in sport.

Conclusion

This chapter has been an exercise in examining sport and contemporary gender relations via three registers: a local gender regime, a national gender order, and a site that reveals some dynamics of a global gender order. This exercise is useful in two broad ways. First, it offers a means of expanding my own scholarly standpoint beyond the local or the national levels, thus potentially shifting or disrupting my domain assumptions. For those like myself who mostly conduct scholarly research on gender and sport within the Global North, attempting to look through a standpoint from the Global South hints at broader strategies for change within the metropole. When we observe sporting institutions dominated by the Global North in direct contact with those of the Global South, our assumptions about the momentary hegemonies within the U.S. national gender order and within local gender regimes can face some radical challenges. It is the very insularity of the U.S. scholars' work on gender and sport, my own included, that can lead us to falsely universalize concepts like "soft essentialism," and to assume, for instance (as I have seen in international discussions of gender and sport), that Title IX has some relevance and meaning to those outside the United States. A transnational focus illuminates the limits (without necessarily denying the local relevance) of local or national concepts and policies.

Second, a shift in geographic registers can help us to understand more deeply how the strains and tensions in local and national hegemonies are already intertwined with larger, transnational structures. I have argued that at the local level of a gender regime of youth sports in a professional-class, White-dominated U.S. community, we can see the emergence of an ideology of soft essentialism that reveals both the success and the limits of a professional-class-based individualist feminism. At the level of the national gender order of the United States, I argue, we can see this same soft essentialism at work in the legal and political "steering" of the gender regime of school sports. I have acknowledged that the successes of this steering at the local and national levels are impressive but also limited by the class-based liberal feminist focus on individual equal opportunity and by the ways that categorical gender discourse and sport policies render the gendering of boys and men as invisible.

Drawing our scope out from national to transnational further complicates the analysis of sport and contemporary gender relations. The controversy surrounding Caster Semenya raises many potential questions, fundamentally among them the question of "What is at stake in questions of gender equality in sport?" (with a tentative reply being, "Not always the same things in all situations and all places"). When and how are assertions of categorical sex difference oppressive? When and how can the categorical interests of girls and women be strategically invoked to press for greater equality and distributive justice? When and how might *other* categories (for example intersexed, race, or place) acutely reveal to us the extent to which "gender" itself is a limiting frame through which institutional sex segregation and naturalization of two supposedly dichotomous sexes is accomplished? And how does an intersectional analysis—especially one that goes beyond the trinity of local race, class, and gender—help us to understand the complexities and contradictions in pressing for categorical justice? For example, in asserting the rights of girls and women, when does Title IX in the United States erase the particular interests of girls and women marginalized by social class, race, or ethnicity or of people with differently gendered bodies? In South Africa or elsewhere, how might the deployment of women's sports as resistance against White supremacy and colonial domination also simultaneously render invisible the particular needs of differently gendered people who don't (or won't) fit into binary sex categories, however strategically they may be deployed? In other words, by shifting through these different regional registers, we can more clearly see the ways in which gender relations in sport express the complexities of intersectional inequalities and how "gender politics" can be a means of steering toward one aspect of social justice while steering away from another.

Questions for Reflection and Discussion

How are gender relations in local youth or community sports impacted by global changes, such as growing immigrant populations? How do national debates about gender equity in sport impact our local schools or colleges? How does our media immersion in high-profile elite sports events like the Olympic Games impact our understanding of gender relations in local and national sports?

Notes

1   I develop this three-tiered conceptual framework in Messner (2002).
2   I introduce the concepts of hard and soft essentialism in Messner (2009) and further develop the concepts in Messner (2011).
3   I emphasize "professional-class and white-*dominated*" here because in fact the community I studied evidenced considerable class and racial/ethnic diversity (for example, only 44% of the community is White). However, I argue that youth sports and other community activities are dominated in form, values, and visible leadership by an ascendant (predominantly white) professional class.
4   Most advocates of women's and girls' sports argue that such a separation is needed, while a few feminist critics argue that separate sports for girls and boys will always reproduce gender inequality. See, for instance, McDonagh and Pappano (2008).
5   For foundational works on this topic, see Birrell and Cole (1994), Sykes (2006), and Travers (2008).

68 • Michael A. Messner

References

Acker, J. (2006). Inequality regimes: Gender, class, and race in organizations. *Gender & Society, 20*(4), 441–464.

Acosta, R. V., & Carpenter, L. J. (2012). Women in intercollegiate sport: A longitudinal thirty-five-year update. Brooklyn College. Retrieved from http://www.acostacarpenter.org/

Atkinson, M., & Kehler, M. (2010). Boys, gyms, locker rooms and heterotopia. In M. Atkinson & M. Kehler (Eds.), *Boys' Bodies: Speaking the Unspoken*. New York, NY: Peter Lang.

Birrell, S., and Cole, C. L. (1994). Double fault: Renee Richards and the construction and naturalization of difference. In S. Birrell & C. L. Cole (Eds.), *Women, sport and culture* (pp. 373–397). Champaign, IL: Human Kinetics.

Blair-Loy, M. (2003). *Competing devotions: Career and family among women executives*. Cambridge, MA: Harvard University Press.

Brake, D. L. (2010). *Getting in the game: Title IX and the women's sports revolution*. New York, NY: New York University Press.

Campbell, R. (2011). Staging globalization for national projects: Global sport markets and elite athletic transnational labour in Qatar. *International Review for the Sociology of Sport, 46*(1), 45–60.

Connell, R. (1987). *Gender & Power*. Stanford, CA: Stanford University Press.

Connell, R. (2009). *Gender*. Cambridge, England: Polity Press.

Connell, R. (2011). Steering toward equality? How gender regimes change inside the state. In *Confronting equality: Gender, knowledge and global change*. Cambridge, England: Polity Press.

Cooky, C. (2009). "Girls just aren't interested": The social construction of interest in girls' sport. *Sociological Perspectives, 52*(2), 259–283.

Cooky, C, Dycus, R., & Dworkin, S. L. (2013). "What makes a woman a woman?" vs. "our first lady of sport": A comparative analysis of United States and South African media coverage of Caster Semenya. *Journal of Sport and Social Issues, 37*, 31–56.

Dworkin, S. L., Swarr, A. L., & Cooky, C. (2013). (In)Justice in sport: The treatment of South African track star Caster Semenya. *Feminist Studies, 39*(1), 40–69.

Dworkin, S. L., Colvin, C., Hatcher, A., & Peacock, D. (2012). Men's perceptions of women's rights and changing gender relations in South Africa: Lessons for working with men and boys in HIV and antiviolence programs. *Gender & Society, 26*(1), 97–120.

Hargreaves, J. (2000). *Heroines of sport: The politics of difference and identity*. London, England: Routledge.

Hargreaves, J. (1986). Where's the virtue? Where's the grace? A discussion of the social production of gender through sport. *Theory Culture and Society, 3*(1), 109–122.

Heywood, L. (2007). Producing girls: Empire, sport and the neoliberal body. In J. Hargreaves & P. Vertinsky (Eds.), *Physical culture, power and the body* (pp. 101–120). Abingdon, England: Routledge.

Lareau, A. (2003). *Unequal childhoods: Class, race, and family life*. Berkeley, CA: University of California Press.

McDonagh, E., & Pappano, L. (2008). *Playing with the boys: Why separate is not equal in sports*. New York, NY: Oxford University Press.

Messner, M. A. (1988). Sports and male domination: The female athlete as contested ideological terrain. *Sociology of Sport Journal, 5*, 197–211.

Messner, M. A. (2002). *Taking the field: Women, men and sports*. Minneapolis, MN: University of Minnesota Press.

Messner, M. A. (2009). *It's all for the kids: Gender, families, and youth sports*. Berkeley, CA: University of California Press.

Messner, M. A. (2011). Gender ideologies, youth sports, and the production of soft essentialism. *Sociology of Sport Journal, 28,* 151–170.

Messner, M. A., & Solomon, N. M. (2007). Social justice and men's interests: The case of Title IX. *Journal of Sport and Social Issues, 31*(2), 162–178.

Miller, K., Sabo, D., Farrell, M., Barnes, G., & Melnick, M. (1999). Sports, sexual activity, contraceptive use, and pregnancy among female and male high school students: Testing cultural resource theory. *Sociology of Sport Journal, 16,* 366–387.

Miller, K., Melnick, M., Barnes, G., Farrell, M., & Sabo, D. (2005). Untangling the links among athletic involvement, gender, race, and adolescent academic outcomes. *Sociology of Sport Journal, 22,* 178–193.

Miller, T., McKay, J., Lawrence, G., & Rowe, D. (2001). *Globalization and sport: Playing the world.* Thousand Oaks, CA: Sage.

National Women's Law Center. (2007). *Barriers to Fair Play.* Washington, DC: National Women's Law Center and the Mellman Group.

Sabo, D. F., & Veliz, P. (2008). *Youth sport in America.* East Meadow, NY: Women's Sports Foundation.

Stone, P. (2007). *Opting out: Why women really quit careers and head home.* Berkeley, CA: University of California Press.

Suggs, W. (2005). *A place on the team: The triumph and tragedy of Title IX.* Princeton, NJ: Princeton University Press.

Sykes, H. (2006). Transsexual and transgender politics in sport. *Women in Sport and Physical Activity Journal, 15,* 3–13.

Travers, A. (2008). The sport nexus and gender injustice. *Studies in Social Justice, 2,* 79–101.

Vertinsky, P. A. (1994). *The eternally wounded woman: Doctors and exercise in the late nineteenth century.* Urbana, IL: University of Illinois Press.

Willis, P. (1983). Women in sport in ideology. In J. Hargreaves (Ed.), *Sport, culture and ideology* (pp. 117–135). London, England: Routledge & Kegan Paul.

Women's Sports Foundation. (2008). *GoGirlGo! San Antonio 2008.* East Meadow, NY: Women's Sports Foundation.

Women's Sports Foundation. (2009). *GoGirlGo! Boston Post-test 2009.* East Meadow, NY: Women's Sports Foundation.

4

Women, Sports, and Activism

• • • • • • • • • • • • • • • • • • • •

CHERYL COOKY

As an undergraduate kinesiology major, even though I had never taken a course in women's or gender studies, I was interested in gender differences in sports and physical activity; in particular, I was committed to debunking myths about female physical frailty and as such used my course assignments in motor development, exercise physiology, and others to explore this topic. It was not until graduate school when I took courses on women, gender, and feminism that I learned the language to fully articulate my commitment to gender equity. Interestingly, despite having earned graduate concentrations in women's and gender studies in my masters and PhD programs, I took only one course on women and sports. As a faculty member, I held academic appointments in women's studies and continued to notice the absence of sport in these programs. The introductory women's studies textbooks I assigned in my classes rarely included discussions of sports, and when they were included, they were given only cursory treatment. And while topics like "women and work," "women and politics," and "women in society" were required courses situated centrally in the women's studies curriculum, "women and sports" was on occasion offered as a "elective." Moreover, the women's studies conferences I attended rarely had sessions on sports. This always struck me as an odd positioning of sports relative to field of women's and gender studies, particularly given that sport is one of the remaining, if not only, institutions in our society wherein sex/gender segregation is both legally enforced and culturally accepted. Recently I was invited to write a book chapter for a collection on U.S. women's social movement activism. Despite having too many other projects on my plate, I agreed to write the chapter mostly because I was excited that the editors had deemed sports as relevant to their collection and I wanted to take advantage of the opportunity to get sports on women's studies disciplinary radar, even though I wasn't quite confident what exactly I would write about. While issues like equal pay, access to education, rape and sexual assault, and reproductive rights seemed to figure centrally in the women's social movements of the 1960s and 1970s and have become so deeply engrained in the cultural imagery of women's movements, unbeknownst to the editors (thankfully), I was uncertain how I would find enough material to write an entire chapter on sport! After some thought, I realized this was an opportunity to explore some of these observations and my personal frustrations regarding the relationship of sports to women's studies, including the seeming absence of overt feminist activism in sports contexts and the marginalization of sports as central issue in women's social movements and academic feminism. Upon further research into the literature, I was pleased to discover the ways sports and physical activity figured in women's social movements throughout the 20th century and am encouraged by the recent examples of social activism and feminist activism in particular in the world of sports.

—Cheryl Cooky

Introduction

In the summer of 2015, during the lead-up to the women's World Cup, a quadrennial sports event that captures the attention of American soccer fans and nonfans alike and generates more media coverage for women's soccer in two weeks than the previous four years combined, several high-profile soccer players, including Abby Wambach, pursued a lawsuit against FIFA (International Federation of Football Associations) when it was announced that the World Cup tournament games would be played on artificial turf instead of natural grass. According to the lawsuit, players expressed concerns regarding the higher potential for injury and claimed that artificial turf is less forgiving than natural grass. In addition, artificial turf is a different surface than natural grass, and playing on artificial turf changes how balls travel and bounce. The overarching complaint, though, was gender equity. The men's World Cup tournament is always played on natural grass, leading a journalist at *The Atlantic* to refer to the lawsuit as challenging "The Grass Ceiling" (Dellinger, 2015). This, along with several other incidents, including the FIFA president's comments on U.S. player Alex Morgan's physical appearance and attractiveness, directed news media coverage of the World Cup to issues of gender inequality in women's soccer.

Despite this and other persisting inequalities in women's sports, a journalist at *The Atlantic* writing about the World Cup posed the following question: "Female athletes have historically received very little attention from activists and advocates for gender equality. Why?" (Martens, 2015). Unlike other gender inequalities that have generated highly visible social movements in the United States, such as women's suffrage, reproductive rights, pay equity, sexual assault and violence, gender equality in sports has not produced the same passion, attention, concern, and mobilization among U.S. feminist activists, despite the fact that many of the gender inequalities in wider society—like pay equity, sexual assault and violence, and lack of women in leadership positions—are manifested in sports contexts.

In her book *Getting in the Game: Title IX and the Women's Sports Revolution*, legal scholar Deborah Brake (2010) suggests that we should not be surprised that sport has not garnered the same attention and concern as other feminist projects. She writes,

> Emphasizing the significance of sport and justifying it as an important subject for feminist attention require believing in the potential for women's bodies to become a source of positive identity and individual empowerment. They also require overcoming any feminist ambivalence about sport and its role in society. Skeptics might view sport as such a thoroughly masculinized institution, celebrating brute force and the physical domination of others, that there is little left to salvage for women. Throw in Western culture's disparagement of physical pursuits in favor of rationality, and feminism's prioritizing of the pursuit of equality for women in the workplace and political and civic arenas seems predictable, if not inevitable. (p. 4)

Moreover, sports have not played a significant role in what constitutes the "canon" of feminist writings on activism and is often overlooked in feminist collections, women's studies textbooks, and anthologies. Given the relationship between feminist theory and praxis and the development of academic feminism from women's social movements, this is to be expected. As Sabo and Ward (2006) explain,

> On U.S. campuses, there was not much connection between academic feminists and women sports proponents, and the distancing went in both directions. Historically, the generation of second-wave academic feminists had little or no personal athletic experience in their cultural backgrounds. They were part of the pre-Title IX generation of women, for whom shooting hoops, throwing elbows, and sweating buckets were as alien as boardroom banter. In addition, those women who *were* involved with sports during the 1970s and 1980s (e.g., as athletes, administrators, and coaches) often resisted being associated with any form of feminism. Nor did they line up to take women's studies courses. To be labeled a "feminist" in the masculine and homophobic culture of sport could have drawn unfriendly fire from colleagues and those in power. (p. 3–4)

This is not to suggest that sport is of little concern to mainstream feminism. Activism and advocacy in sports certainly does exist, as this chapter will illustrate. Instead, how this activism and advocacy are manifested in sports, how they are articulated, and thus how they are academically investigated and understood may differ from other popular issues of women's social movements because of these important contextual factors. As such, this chapter draws upon the scholarship in feminist sport studies to focus on three issues related to women's activism in sports: sports as a site for women's advocacy and activism, sports as a site for female empowerment, and female athleticism as cultural iconography in discursive articulations of feminist activism and women's empowerment. The chapter concludes with insights on the potential for intersections between women's sports advocacy and feminist activism in women's sports at the turn of the 21st century and offers possible directions for future research.

Women's Advocacy, Activism, and Sport

Similar to other social institutions, women's advocacy and activism in the realm of sport has historically centered on efforts toward participatory inclusion, with the implicit assumption that inclusion will lead to cultural acceptance. This section provides a brief overview regarding the mass entry of women into American sports in the 20th century and the relationship between women's sports advocacy and struggles for inclusion with broader gender relations and women's movements.

At the turn of the 20th century, major shifts in the economic structure in the United States led to massive changes in social life (e.g., industrialization, urbanization, mass immigration) altering the structures of work and family life (Burstyn, 1999). As men's labor increasingly moved from the family and home to the public sphere, men were absent from daily family life, often for extended periods of time. Boys were no longer socialized by fathers or male relatives; instead, mothers and female educators were the primary socializing agents of boys. Moreover, the first wave of the feminist movement began in the mid-1800s and gained momentum at the turn of the 20th century.

The surge of feminism at the time culminated in the passage of the Nineteenth Amendment in 1920, establishing women's constitutional right to vote. Sport and physical activity played an important symbolic role in the U.S. suffrage movement. In her article "The Physical Is Political: Women's Suffrage, Pilgrim Hikes, and the Public Sphere," feminist sport historian Jamie Shultz observed that during the first several decades of the 20th century, women engaged in various physical activities such as swimming, hiking, and scaling mountains to draw attention to the women's suffrage movement and "spectacularized suffrage by positioning their bodies in the public sphere" (2010, p. 1133). Shultz notes that these pilgrim hikes also served as an important visual challenge to the myth of female frailty, which had been used to argue against women's right to vote and to justify their disenfranchisement.

The first-wave feminist movement and the new political rights shifted gender relations, and alongside these changes, the "first wave of athletic feminism" swelled

(Twin, 1979, as cited in Messner, 2002). Young women were enrolling in colleges and had access to participation in sports. White affluent women were participating in lawn tennis and bicycling as leisure activities. Moreover, female athletes challenged Victorian notions of femininity and women's "natural" frailty and became household names (Messner, 2002). For example, in 1926 Gertrude Ederle swam the English Channel and broke the men's record. In doing so, she subverted the prevailing gender ideologies that positioned women as frail and weak.

These societal changes, both within and outside of sports, produced a crisis in gender norms, expectations, and ideologies; dominant notions of masculinity and femininity became highly contested (Burstyn, 1999). To address this gender crisis, at the turn of the 20th century, homosocial organizations, such as the Boy Scouts and the Young Men's Christian Association (YMCA), and youth sport organizations, such as Little League Baseball, were established to socialize boys and young men into masculine roles in order to combat the presumably negative influences of an increasingly feminized social world (Cahn, 1994; Messner, 1995). The role of sports in socializing boys and men into hegemonic masculinity would set the stage for ongoing battles for women's inclusion into the institution of sport throughout the 20th century. The legacies of this history continue in the contemporary landscape of women's sports.

By the 1920s, women's athleticism and the growing popularity of women's participation in physical activity and sport encountered a backlash from educators, medical doctors, and others, who feared women's participation in sports would create "mannish" women. Given that sports were upheld as the site wherein boys would become men, many asked what impact girls and women's participation would have, and more important, what women's participation would mean for gender relations if girls and women celebrated physicality, dominance, prowess, and competition. Within colleges and universities, many female physical educators feared the corrupting influences for women of the male model of sport, including competition and commercialization, and they wanted to maintain control over women's sports. They also resisted young women's participation in competitive sport out of concern that competitive participation would masculinize female students. Thus most female physical educators held the belief that women should not emulate men's sport, but instead should build alternative models of sport believed to be "more humane and liberating" for women (Hargreaves, 1994, p. 31). Female physical educators advocated for a separatist model of sports, whereby young women would be shielded from the aggression, toughness, and primitiveness of the male sports model, thus liberating young women from the damaging influences of men and masculinity (Hargreaves, 1994, p. 31).

Female physical educators embraced physical fitness, calisthenics, and less vigorous sports pursuits, believing that mild physical activity could help girls and women by restoring a balance of energy in girls' and women's bodies. The "fixed energy" theory held currency among medical professionals at the time. According to this theory, women and men had a finite degree of energy and, as such, women should conserve as much energy as possible by avoiding physical exertion, work, and education (Hargreaves, 1994). If women engaged in athletic pursuits, they would lack energy for menstruation, reproduction, and childbirth. Given that female physical educators needed women to be physically active (otherwise their jobs would be obsolete), female physical educators advocated for limited female physicality within the context of noncompetitive sports, asserting that moderate physical activity could restore energy to the body, provide a balance between physical and mental energy, and thus would not pose a threat to young women's reproductive capacities (Hargreaves, 1994). Most female physical educators, however, agreed that women's participation in competitive sport was not desirable; they feared young women would be subject to the "masculinizing" effects of competitive sport participation (Cahn, 1994; Hargreaves, 1994).

Female physical educators at White colleges were concerned not only with the potential masculinizing effects of competitive sport participation, but also with male control over women's sport (Cahn, 1994; Hargreaves, 1994). This led to a division between female physical educators who wished to maintain the control over girls' and women's participation in sport by the male-controlled Amateur Athletic Union (AAU). The AAU is a nonprofit volunteer organization dedicated to the development and promotion of amateur sports and offers sports for boys and girls, men, and women. At the turn of the 20th century, as sports were emerging and developing in educational contexts (e.g., college sports) and within the national sports system (e.g., Olympic Games, other international events), the AAU was a powerful organization for the development of athletes, many of whom would later become prominent college and Olympic athletes. As Cahn (1994) explains, "female professionals [physical educators] were worried that male promoters would make a sexual spectacle of the female athlete, forcing her to reveal and overexert her body in the interest of commercial profit and male entertainment" (p. 25). The wider public concerns regarding (White, upper- and middle-class) young women's participation in vigorous and strenuous activities, as well as concerns that competition would lead to a morally impure women's game, contributed to the establishment of Play Days in the 1920s. The goal of Play Days was "a sport for every girl, and every girl for a sport." According to the organizers of Chicago Girl's Athletic City-Wide Play Day, the purpose was to "give an outlet for the natural and cultivated 'love of play' that exists in many girls" (Duncan and Cardiff, 1929, p. 82).

Conversely, working-class women, immigrant women, and women of color, who through their class and race were not subject to the cultural expectations of the "Cult of True Womanhood" (Smith-Rosenberg, 1985), experienced less resistance and fewer gendered barriers in their opportunity to participate in competitive organized sports. Women who occupied marginalized social locations often found their participation in competitive leagues encouraged and supported. Black women's sport participation was supported by communities and by Black female physical educators, as their participation created visibility for the larger civil rights movement and was not seen as antithetical to cultural notions of Black womanhood (Cahn, 1994; Hines Gissendander, 1994). For example, in contrast to their White counterparts, Black colleges and universities supported and endorsed intercollegiate competitive sport for Black women, particularly in the sports of basketball and track and field (Hines Gissendander, 1994). Many White women had abandoned track and field in the 1920s and 1930s, a sport that had declined in popularity as a result of negative media coverage and organized efforts to remove the sport for women in schools and international competitions (such as the Olympics). This exodus of White women from track and field left open opportunities for Black women's participation in the sport (Cahn, 1994). Working-class women, many of whom were employed in factories, experienced opportunities to participate in the industrial sports leagues. Women workers viewed participation in the industrial sports leagues as necessary for the broader struggle for workplace equality (Cahn, 1994). Many working-class and immigrant young women (and men) also had the opportunity to participate in sports through the Playground Movement of America. Founded in 1906, the Playground Movement established sports programs for boys and girls in urban areas as an alternative to the dangers of the streets and to assimilate immigrant youth into dominant American values (Cahn, 1994). Moreover, many working-class girls participated in sports in settlement houses, YWCAs (Young Women's Christian Association), playgrounds, and in some cases public schools (Cahn, 1994).

During the mid-20th century, female physical educators and other opponents of women's competition had successfully marginalized women's competitive sports into select women's universities and high schools or in sports leagues like the All American Girls' Baseball League (AAGBL). The AAGBL emerged during World War II in response to men's deployment overseas but was quickly disbanded several years after the end of the war. In allowing young women to engage in marginalized sport, both female physical educators and organizers of women's popular sports had to assuage the wider societal fears of "mannishness" among female athletes. Yet each group addressed those fears using different strategies (Cahn, 1994). The female physical educators promoted a wholesome image of girls and women who play sports and structured physical activity to highlight women participants' adherence to conventional femininity. Conversely, the mostly male organizers of popular competitive women's sports chose instead to market female athletes' (hetero)sexual appeal (Cahn, 1994; Messner, 2002). Even today, the representational imagery of female athletes as either the "girl next door" or the "sexy cover girl" continues to permeate popular imagery, in large part due to homophobia in women's sports and concerns regarding the gender identity (i.e., masculinization, sex testing) of female athletes (Cooky, Dycus, & Dworkin, 2013; Cooky & LaVoi, 2012).

Play Days remained popular until the 1950s and 1960s among physical education teachers who often discouraged female participation in varsity intercollegiate athletics (Festle, 1996). White female physical educators' desire to contain women's sport participation extended somewhat to interscholastic sports as well. Many high schools that once offered certain sports for girls—in many cases, basketball—began to cut programs by the 1910s and 1920s in order to provide more money in their budgets to fund boys' sports programs (Cahn, 1994). The elimination of interscholastic sports for girls, however, was not universal. Black colleges and industrial schools sponsored interscholastic athletics in the 1920s and 1930s (Cahn, 1994). Moreover, Black female physical educators strongly supported girls' and women's participation in interscholastic and intercollegiate sports competition. For Black female physical educators, women's participation in sport did not pose a threat to their femininity, nor did Black female physical educators hold the same fears as their White counterparts that sports competition would "masculinize" women (Cahn, 1994). This was in part due to the ways in which Black women have historically been excluded from dominant definitions of femininity and womanhood. Moreover, Black women's athletic participation was symbolically tied to larger societal struggles for civil rights, and Black women's participation was thus embraced within communities, as well as in educational institutions.

The second wave of feminism in the United States emerged in the 1960s and corresponded with several other social movements, including the civil rights movement, the gay liberation movement, and the antiwar movement, among others. While diverse in its scope and orientation, one facet of the second-wave movement was concerned with the participatory inclusion of women in the institutions of work, politics, and education. According to legal scholar Deborah Brake (2010), Title IX emerged out of these social movements and was precipitated by women's rights advocates' concerns regarding the discrimination faced by girls and women in education. Title IX was originally drafted by adding "sex" in place of race to the language of Title VII of the 1964 Civil Rights Act, which bans discrimination on the basis of race in federally funded programs, including education (Brake, 2010).

These efforts were successful, and in 1972 Title IX of the Educational Amendments passed. Title IX states, "No person in the United States shall, on the basis of sex, be excluded from participation in, be denied the benefits of, or be subjected to discrimination under any education program or activity receiving Federal financial assistance." While Title IX applied to any educational program or activity with the expressed objective to help increase girls and women's acceptance into higher education and in particular medical school and law school, the impact of Title IX on athletics was undeniable. The second wave of feminism that led to the passage of Title IX enabled and facilitated the second wave of female athleticism, characterized by the significant increase in opportunities for girls and women's sport participation during the 1970s and 1980s. The impact of Title IX continues today. For example, female high school sport participation increased from 294,015 in 1971–1972 to 3,287,735 in 2014–2015 (National Federation of State High School Associations, 2014–2015). Moreover, according to data compiled by the National Collegiate Athletics Association (NCAA), the major governing body that oversees college athletics, female college participation has dramatically increased since Title IX, with 205,120 women participating in college athletics in 2013–2014. Based on these numbers, girls and women comprise nearly 40% of all interscholastic and intercollegiate sport participants (Cooky & LaVoi, 2012).

Yet despite Title IX's impact on participation opportunities, not all girls and women have benefited equally from Title IX. For example, at the collegiate level, African American women typically do not have the same opportunities as White women. This is in part because the fastest growing women's sports on most college campuses are golf, soccer, lacrosse, and rowing, sports that require significant economic investment, space, and facilities—resources that are lacking in the schools where many racial minorities attend (Suggs, 2005). Moreover, researchers have found that in urban communities where resources are scarce, what little resources that do exist are directed to urban boys' sports participation. Girls in urban communities have lower participation rates than urban boys and suburban boys and girls (Sabo & Veliz, 2008). More generally, girls in urban communities, immigrant girls, and girls with physical disabilities have lower participation rates in organized sports, which impacts opportunities to play in high school and college (Sabo & Veliz, 2008).

Since Title IX's passage and the success of women's sports advocates' efforts toward increased and improved girls and women's sports participation, the overall progression has been accompanied by backlash, including conservative attacks against Title IX along with resistance by schools and universities to comply with the law (for more on the legal challenges and rulings on Title IX, see Hogshead-Makar & Zimbalist, 2007; McDonough & Pappano, 2009; and Brake, 2010). For example, in the first decade of the 2000s, the Bush administration made several attempts to weaken the impact of the law. Dennis Hassert, then U.S. House of Representatives Speaker and former wrestling coach, was at the helm of the "anti–Title IX" movement in the early 2000s and held particular influence with the Bush administration. Hassert blamed Title IX for cuts to men's sports, in particular men's wrestling. In 2002, the U.S. Department of Education established the Commission on Opportunity in Athletics, whose purpose was to review the current standards for measuring equal opportunity in sport under Title IX and to make recommendations for changes to the law. The Commission's focus was to address the effect of Title IX on men's opportunities, specifically the "unintended consequences" of Title IX on men's sports. According to conservatives, this included the removal of men's sports and the decline in opportunities for boys and men.

Yet neither the removal nor decline of male sports is supported by empirical data on participation rates. For example, in 2011 the Women's Sports Foundation published a report outlining the persistent "gender gap" in sports participation, with women continuing to lag behind men (Sabo & Veliz, 2011). The Women's Sports Foundation is the premier women's sports advocacy organization in the United States, founded in 1974 by tennis legend, founder of the Women's Tennis Association, and "Battle of the Sexes" (discussed later in the chapter) champion Billie Jean King. The Women's Sports Foundation has been the leader in women's sports advocacy for over 40 years, providing financial support for female athletes, empirically driven advocacy for gender equality in sports, and advocacy and activism for Title IX. This organization, in particular, has provided education and awareness of the law regarding women and sports, as well as recognition and acknowledgment of female athletes' leadership potential and achievements.

Although activists work to create opportunities for women in sport, feminists and women's sports advocates still feared that the Department of Education's creation of the Commission on Opportunities in Athletics would be a step toward the eventual erosion of Title IX. Fortunately, members of the Commission included Donna de Varona and Julie Foudy, both Olympic gold medalists with ties to the Women's Sports Foundation. Foudy and de Varona wrote a minority report highly critical of the Commission's recommendations (Brake,

2010). While these efforts were successful in preventing the Commission's recommendations from being enacted, the Bush administration would continue its efforts to weaken Title IX.

In 2005, the Office of Civil Rights issued a "Dear Colleague" letter that provided additional clarification regarding Title IX's three-prong test. The three-prong test, not written in the original legislation but included later in the 1979 Athletics Policy Interpretation, is used to determine whether or not a school is in compliance with Title IX. Schools must meet only one of the following three prongs to be considered in compliance:

> Prong One: Participation opportunities for male and female students are provided in numbers substantially proportionate to their respective enrollments.
> Prong Two: The school can show a history and continuing practice of program expansion that is demonstrably responsive to the developing interest and abilities of the members of that sex.
> Prong Three: The school can demonstrate that the present program fully and effectively accommodates the *interests* and abilities of the members of that sex. (as cited in Zimbalist, 2007, p. 284, emphasis in original)

The "Dear Colleague" letter was particularly controversial in that the Office of Civil Rights (the office within the Department of Education responsible for Title IX oversight) would accept the use of e-mail "interest surveys" sent to students to be the *sole* determinant of their interest level in sports. In other words, schools and universities would no longer have to demonstrate that the distribution of athletic opportunities was proportional to the overall student population, the most rigorous test of compliance and one that was most commonly used in court cases brought forth by female athletes. Moreover, the design of the surveys was critiqued by feminists and women's advocacy organizations for flaws in the methodology. For example, universities were allowed to interpret nonresponses as an indicator of no interest, which women's sports advocates faulted as a problematic assumption (Sabo & Grant, 2007). Additionally, women's sports advocates pointed out that this approach neglected consideration of the ways in which women's participation rates in sport had dramatically increased since the passage of Title IX and did not consider that interest is shaped by access to opportunity (Zimbalist, 2007). Studies show that interest in sports is socially constructed and shaped by social factors, including historical discriminatory practices as well as gender ideologies and cultural beliefs about the "natural differences" between boys and girls (Cooky, 2009).

At the time of the distribution of the "Dear Colleague" letter, the NCAA's participation data indicated that gender equity was still an issue in collegiate athletics but not for the lack of opportunity for men to participate. Women represented 54% of the student population, yet only 43% of athletic opportunities went to female athletes and only 38% of athletic department operating funds were devoted to women's athletics (Zimbalist, 2007). Moreover, the total number of male athletes in collegiate sports had increased by 38,482 from 2002 to

2011, while the number of female athletes increased by 32,662 (Schultz, 2014), refuting conservative claims that Title IX was harming men's sports by taking away opportunities from male athletes. Weighing in on the controversy, Myles Brand, then president of the NCAA, argued, "Title IX is not broken and it does not need to be fixed. Rather, it needs to be supported, enforced, and allowed to finish the job it was designed to do—provide equal opportunities for athletics participation without gender bias" (Brand, 2003).

Despite the support of the NCAA, the empirical evidence suggesting persisting inequalities, and the efforts of women's sports advocates, many people continue to believe that girls and women have ample opportunities to participate in sports. Thus they believe that any inequality is the result of individual choice, not discrimination or lack of access to opportunity (Gavora, 2002). They argue, therefore, that Title IX is no longer necessary. Indeed, this is what the Bush administration and other conservatives have based their arguments upon: Title IX is no longer needed, and in fact, it is doing more harm than good. Yet as feminist scholars Messner and Solomon (2007; see also Cooky, 2009) argue, merely asking girls and women if they are interested in sport erases the complex dynamics of history, ideology, culture, and structure that shape girls' experiences and their interest in sport participation. Gender essentialism frequently permeates the backlash with conservatives and "power feminists" like Jessica Gavora, arguing that Title IX harms men's sports and takes away opportunities from boys and men (for a review of the power feminist argument, see Gavora, 2002). This is a claim that has been empirically disproven, in particular by research produced by the Women's Sports Foundation. Boys and men's participation in sport has increased alongside girls and women's such that a "gender gap" in sports participation continues today (Sabo & Veliz, 2011).

While women's sports advocates were successful in defending Title IX against the myriad threats posed at the turn of the 21st century, Title IX compliance continues to be a challenge for most schools and universities. Women's advocacy groups, however, continue to play an important role in pressing for greater compliance. In November 2010, the National Women's Law Center filed a complaint against the Chicago Public School system and 11 other school districts for discrimination against girls in high school athletics. According to the complaint, the Chicago Public School districts had double-digit participation gaps, placing them out of compliance with Title IX. The Chicago Public School system and the other school districts identified in the complaint are not alone. According to the American Association of University Women, the National Women's Law Center, and other women's advocacy groups, most schools are not in compliance with Title IX, and even when schools are compliant, this is often achieved through the use of questionable measures.

In April 2011, the *New York Times* published a shocking series of articles examining the deceptive practices, known as "roster management." The *Times* revealed that universities engage in roster management to demonstrate compliance with prong one of Title IX. These practices ranged from listing female students on team rosters who never suit up for competition, let alone actually play, to counting one female track and field athlete as three (for indoor, outdoor, and cross-country) while not counting male track and field athletes similarly, to counting as female athletes those male athletes who participate on women's teams or male students who practice with women's teams (Thomas, 2011).

Despite the backlash and conservative challenges to Title IX and the continued challenges to ensure compliance with the law, broader societal changes in gender relations, alongside increased opportunities created by Title IX, produce today a context wherein competition among girls and women is culturally accepted and celebrated (Heywood & Dworkin, 2003). Thus the debates surrounding the potentially corruptive nature of competitive sports no longer plague female sports (to the extent that they did in the early days of girls' and women's sports). Moreover, unlike women during the first and second waves of female athleticism, because of Title IX, women and girls of the third wave of female athleticism (the period post–Title IX) assume they no longer have to advocate for the right to play sport. Sport is no longer reserved for an elite group of highly skilled girls and women but appears as a "normal part of girls' and women's everyday lives" (Heywood & Dworkin, 2003, p. xx).

Sports as a Site for Female Empowerment

Sport has been positioned both within popular culture and in the sport studies literature as a potential source of empowerment of girls and women (Cooky, 2010; Blinde, Taub, & Han, 1993; Heywood & Dworkin, 2003). Some scholars question how empowerment is conceptualized and ask critical questions regarding sports' potential to both empower and disempower women (Bradshaw, 2002). Others, however, assert the importance of women's participation in a social institution that has been traditionally male-dominated, male-controlled, and male-identified, an institution that, until recently, upholds men's physical (and thereby social, political, and economic) superiority. Women's participation in the institution disrupts gendered power relations. As such, women's sport participation is understood by feminist sport studies scholars as an important challenge to the ideological construction of both hegemonic masculinity and emphasized femininity (see Connell, 1987) and as dichotomous and linked to sex category (Kane, 1995; Messner, 1988). In this way, sports empower girls and women by challenging the discursive as well as the material realities upon which their oppression, subordination, and marginalization are based.

One way in which sport participation empowers girls and women is through its impact on the lived realities of girls and women. This research has consistently found that sport participation and physical activity have positive impact on the social, psychological, and physical well-being of girls and women (President's Council on Physical Fitness and Sports, 1997; Staurowsky et al., 2015; Tucker Center, 2007). Girls' participation in sport and physical activity is positively correlated with a number of desirable outcomes, including lower rates of obesity, teen pregnancy, and breast cancer incidence. Girls' participation is also linked to positive psychosocial outcomes, such as higher levels of self-esteem and positive body image, as well as a lower incidence of depression and suicide. Moreover, sport participation is linked to higher levels of academic achievement and performance in high school girls.

Equipped with these findings, women's sports advocates develop extracurricular programs designed to improve girls' lives through physical activity and sport (Rauscher & Cooky, 2016) and use the empirical findings discussed in the preceding as evidence in their advocacy and fundraising efforts. Girl-only sport and physical activity programs have grown tremendously since the 1990s. Girls on the Run; the Women's Sports Foundation's GoGirlGo! program; and Sporting Chance, offered through Girls Inc., operate in hundreds of cities across the United States. The Women's Sports Foundation's GoGirlGo! has reached almost one million girls since its inception in 2001. Girls on the Run currently serves close to 130,000 girls annually in more than 200 cities. These programs use sport and physical activity as the context to teach girls life skills—such as teamwork, confidence, and leadership—that are transferrable to other domains and that ultimately foster optimal healthy development (for a review, see Rauscher & Cooky, 2016). These organizations typically identify as "girl-serving" or "women-centered" rather than as explicitly feminist, and as such, these efforts are "feminist by default," rather than as the result of conscious or implicit feminist activism (for a discussion, see Sabo & Ward, 2006). While women's sports advocacy groups are reluctant to label their efforts as "feminist," Sabo and Ward (2006) note that, similarly, mainstream feminism and many feminist organizations have not explicitly engaged in issues pertaining to gender equality in sports. Instead, if sports are a consideration in feminist activist efforts, mainstream feminists tend to focus on the symbolic significance of female athletes and their representational meaning for the broader feminist movement and seem less concerned with engaging in feminist activism for equality for female athletes.

The following section discusses how female athleticism has served as an important cultural iconography, symbolic of the gains achieved by the women's movement, as well as women's position as empowered subjects.

Female Athleticism as Cultural Iconography

Throughout the modern history of American sports, individual female athletes and sporting practices have played an important role in the cultural imagery of women's movements and feminist activism. One of the most illustrative examples of this role is the tennis match between Billie Jean King and Bobby Riggs in 1973, titled the "Battle of the Sexes." The match was broadcast on television and was watched by an estimated 50 million viewers in the United States. Billie Jean King won the match in a dominant fashion. As the first matchup between a male and female athlete to be widely broadcast on television, King's win symbolically put to rest those Victorian myths regarding female frailty and male physical superiority. It also was significant given that the Battle of the Sexes match occurred at the height of the second-wave feminist movement and thus became symbolic of the broader struggles for women's liberation and women's equality. The Battle of the Sexes was considered a victory not only for King, but also for women's sports and women's liberation.

Yet a divide exists, as many female athletes and women's sports advocates do not publicly identify as feminists or do not always visibly participate in women's movements beyond the context of sports. As Brake (2010) explains,

> Many, and perhaps most, female athletes do not self-identify as feminists and do not perceive themselves as signing onto a feminist agenda when they play sports. Women's sports advocates work at the periphery of the feminist movement, and many of the athletes and fans who benefit from their work show little interest in broader feminist projects. The reasons for this divide are complicated, but surely it is influenced by the cultural contradictions triggered by women's participation in a traditionally masculine endeavor such as sport. If playing sports—especially playing masculine sports and playing them well—threatens to compromise women's culturally valued femininity, disavowing feminism can help women athletes reclaim a more acceptable feminine identity. (p. 4)

While there have been important debates regarding the importance of identifying as "feminist" generally, feminist scholars note how the term itself (and the broader movement) produces its own exclusions (hooks, 2000; Mohanty, 2003). For example, the marginalization of women of color and lesbian/queer women in the women's movements has been investigated by researchers (see Reger, 2014). In sport, the lack of visibility of female athletes who have identified with the women's movement and/or feminism or who have been outspoken on issues of gender inequality is perplexing, given the celebration of female athletes and women's sports as symbolic of the gains of the women's movement. As discussed earlier, the "Battle of the Sexes" and King's defeat of Bobby Riggs performed an important symbolic function, demonstrating that the sexes were indeed equal; if a woman could beat a man in sport, then women deserve equal pay for equal work and access to opportunity in education, politics, and the workplace. Thus the "Battle of the Sexes" helped challenge the ideological justifications for women's role as second-class citizens. The fact that the tennis match was called the "Battle of the Sexes" is itself indicative of the significance of King's win. The "Battle of the Sexes" was more than a tennis match, and King herself knew the significance of that moment for the broader women's movement. "I thought it would set us back 50 years if I didn't win that match," she said. "It would ruin the women's tour and affect all women's self-esteem" (as quoted in Schwartz, n.d.).

There are other examples of female athletes who achieved significance both on the court and off and who served as symbolic icons of women's empowerment: Babe Didrikson, Althea Gibson, Sheryl Swoops, the 1999 U.S. Women's World Cup soccer team (in particular, Mia Hamm), Serena Williams, Rhonda Rousey, to name a few athletes whose images of physicality, intensity, strength, and competitive spirit seemingly pose a serious threat to the last male preserve. Yet while these athletes signify and symbolize the principles, gains, and goals of feminism, very few, if any, of these athletes identify either implicitly or explicitly with feminism or feminist activism.

Simultaneously, however, contemporary cultural iconography of female athletes as empowered subjects and feminist icons emerged in the 1990s (Cooky, 2010; Heywood & Dworkin, 2003). This historical moment marked the rise of third-wave feminism and "girl power." Within the realm of sports in the third wave of female athleticism, female athletes were often held as representatives of girl power (see Cooky, 2010), and advertising imagery borrowed from female athleticism as imagery of women's empowerment (see Heywood & Dworkin, 2003). For example, in 1999, the U.S. women's national soccer team won the World Cup and was heralded as the real life manifestation of girl power. The World Cup win also came to symbolize the achievements of the second-wave feminist movement, and the players were referred to by both media accounts and the players themselves, including Julie Foudy, as "Title IX babies" (Cooky, 2010). Moreover, representations of the team served as visual illustration of the popular discourse of girl power prevalent in third-wave feminism. For example, Brandi Chastain, whose sports bra–clad body was featured, after the 1999 USA Women's soccer team won the World Cup, on the cover of *Newsweek* (along with the announcement that "Girls Rule!"), was a significant representative of girl empowerment at the turn of the 21st century (Cooky, 2010). During the 1990s, a host of commercials and advertising campaigns featured female athletes and women's sports, appealing to girls' and young women's sense of empowerment. Images of the female athletes as empowered and empowering replaced the "mannish" athlete stereotype from earlier eras. Female athletes, according to third-wave feminist and weightlifting enthusiast Leslie Heywood (1998), were "heterosexy" and feminine, yet strong and able to "kick some ass" (p. 205). Heywood describes this "new" image of the female athlete drawing on what volleyball player Gabby Reese referred to as the "power chick":

> We don't have to reject our bodies because today "girl" doesn't mean little wuss, woman doesn't mean doormat, giving up all your time and dreams for other people. We can have muscles now and ostensibly those muscles will stand for power, self-determination, presence and place in the world. (p. 205)

As an embodiment of girl power, female athletes—understood as the "power chick"—send girls the message that second-wave feminist proscriptions to foster equality, such as Title IX, are no longer needed or desired in the postfeminist moment (Griffin, 2004; see also Cooky, 2010). For Heywood, this was not a contradiction or a step back for feminist principles but a forward progression of the women's movement, a rearticulation of feminism at a historical moment when women's struggles for equality have changed. As such, the female athlete could represent feminism to a new generation of girls.

Conversely, other feminist sport studies scholars argue that the imagery of female athletes, particularly as circulated through advertising, situates female athletes as commodities and female athleticism not as a form of women's empowerment, but as commodified feminism (Cole & Hribar, 1995). As such, feminists are compelled to consider critically the context in which these images circulate when assessing the potential for empowerment (beyond being empowered to participate in consumer culture). Cole and Hribar (1995) argue that the ostensibly empowering images put forth, for instance, in Nike advertisements cannot be read simply as empowering given that Nike is also attempting to seduce women to consume. Moreover, as Heywood and Dworkin (2003) argue, "Despite its triumphant, inspirational rhetoric, the affirmative model Nike and others offer is no magic pill that does away with the reality of inequitable conditions in a single stroke" (p. 38).

Yet female athleticism as cultural iconography, particularly as representative of girl power and an articulation of third-wave feminism, undeniably challenges stereotypical notions of what it means to be a (White, middle-class) girl or woman at the beginning of the 21st century, as well as gender ideologies about female strength and physicality. Moreover, images of girls and women "just doing it"—but "just doing it" in a traditionally male-dominated institution constructed in part to uphold hegemonic masculinity and male domination—can be an important source of empowerment for girls and women (Heywood & Dworkin, 2003; Messner, 2002). The cultural iconography of female athletes is an important challenge to the historical exclusion of women and has been influential in ushering in a third wave of female athleticism wherein girls and women no longer must advocate for participatory inclusion but often feel entitled to opportunity and expect equality (Cooky, 2010).

Conclusion

Feminist activism and advocacy may not be readily apparent in women's sports given the seeming divide between feminism and women's sports advocates. This chapter has offered insights into the dis/connections between mainstream feminism, female athletes, and women's sports advocacy. Women's social movements both emerged from and contributed to important social changes in gender relations and gendered power dynamics in U.S. society, including women's sports. Similarly, women's sports and female athletes played a role in serving as powerful vehicles for and symbols of gender equality and women's empowerment in the wider culture. Moreover, there are linkages between the major women's social movements, often referred to as "waves" in the U.S. context, and the advocacy efforts on behalf of women's sports. Each "wave" of feminism has been accompanied by a "wave" of female athleticism. This chapter has centered on three issues related to women's activism in sports: sports as a site for women's advocacy and activism, sports as a site for female empowerment, and female athleticism as cultural iconography in discursive articulations of feminist activism and women's empowerment.

While revising this chapter in the spring of 2016, the U.S. women's national soccer team once again was in the national news media spotlight, this time as the result of several players filing a wage discrimination lawsuit against the sport's governing body, USA Soccer. According to the complaint, the U.S. national women's team is paid less than their male counterparts despite having the same work requirements. Moreover, the women's team outperforms the team on a number of indicators. For example, the U.S. women's team has a record eight consecutive appearances in the World Cup, including three World Cup wins and four Olympic championships, compared to the men's national team's quarterfinal appearance in 2002. According to the suit, in 2015 the women's national team generated $20 million in revenue for USA Soccer, while the men's national team ran a deficit of $2 million.

Unlike their 1999 Women's World Cup counterparts, who were heralded as champions of girl power and celebrated as exemplars of the positive impact of Title IX, today's U.S. women's national team members are drawing much-needed attention to the continued inequalities faced by girls and women in sports (Cooky, 2016). Yet surprisingly or, given what I have discussed in this chapter, not so surprisingly, feminism and feminist activists are seemingly absent from the news media coverage. While female athletes have advocated for equal pay in sports, from Billie Jean King's brave and successful attempt in the 1970s to circumvent wage discrimination by founding her own professional tennis association (the Women's Tennis Association) and tour (the Virginia Slims tour) to Venus Williams's advocacy for equal prize money in Wimbledon in the 1990s and 2000s, the continued challenges to gender inequality in sports are important for mainstream feminist struggles for equality.

Yet in the early years of the 21st century, sport continues to operate as a form of "stealth feminism." For Heywood and Dworkin, sport as stealth feminism refers to the ways in which sports are "an arena where feminist questions emerge, where feminist principles and goals can be articulated, and where feminist strategies for change achieved all without an explicit declaration of those questions, principles, goals, or achievements as feminist" (2003, p. 50). As Heywood and Dworkin explain, stealth feminism "draws attention to key feminist issues and goals without provoking the kneejerk social stigma attached to the word *feminist*, which has been so maligned and discredited in the popular imagination" (2003, p. 51, emphasis in original). Although the culture of acceptance of feminism—or at least of popular feminism (a version of feminism articulated in and through popular cultural artifacts such as Sheryl Sandberg's *Lean In*, Beyoncé's music and videos, Emma Watson's "HeforShe" United Nations speech and campaign)—has clearly shifted within the U.S. context since Heywood and Dworkin (2003) were writing about the female athlete as cultural icon, stealth feminism continues to apply when considering how very few female athletes have situated themselves among the contemporary articulations of popular feminism, despite the seemingly activist/advocacy efforts by female athletes to address gender inequality in sports.

Moreover, this stealth feminism may explain and/or contribute to the void between feminists and female athletes. Consider how very few, if any, prominent feminist activists have spoken publicly in support of the U.S. women's national soccer team's wage discrimination suit (or in other advocacy efforts for wage/prize equality for female athletes) or other issues pertaining to inequality in sports. Heywood and Dworkin note, "For if female athletes needed feminism in the 70s to get them the resources they needed to play, today—in the context of what happened to feminism in the 90s—the situation is reversed. Now feminism—second wave, third wave, liberal, and radical—needs female athletes" (2003, p. 51). Female athletes and women's sports can help advance feminist agendas such as equality (as we see with the USWNT wage discrimination lawsuit), self-esteem for girls and women, and expanded fluidity of gender roles (Heywood and Dworkin, 2003). Similarly, female athletes need feminism, given the continued disparities in resources between men's and women's sports despite the gains in participatory inclusion as the result of the passage of Title IX in 1972.

Although female athletes and women's sports serve a powerful role in advocating for women's empowerment, as well as provide important iconography and symbolic representation of feminism, it is important in the early years of the 21st century that both mainstream feminism and academic feminism consider sports as a central object of inquiry and a central focus for advocacy and activism. There appears to be little intersection or dialogue between the social movements literature and the sport studies literature. Although hundreds of studies have been published on women's sports drawing upon feminist theoretical and methodological perspectives, little of this research, and particularly that from the social sciences, explicitly engages in questions regarding activism generally or feminist activism specifically in women's sports. Thus future research is needed that examines women's sports from a social movements perspective. Basic questions should be addressed. Who have been the main actors? What have been their organizational forms? How have they mobilized and framed their issues? And under what conditions have they succeeded? While much has been written about the historical development of women's sports in the United States, fewer studies have been published that empirically examine the role sports played within the broader feminist movements (Schultz, 2010 is one exception). More research is needed in this regard. Given this chapter's focus, another important area of inquiry is an examination of key stakeholders in women's sports advocacy and in women's social movements to the divide and disconnect between the two groups. An exploration may reveal more direct connections than previously understood in the feminist sport studies literatures and social movement literatures and could shed light on the processes by which these groups operate independently of one another.

Questions for Reflection and Discussion

Why do you think sports as a topic of focus and inquiry are not central in women's or gender studies? Why do you think gender equality in sports has not played a more significant role in mainstream women's social movements and organizing? With the recent examples of activism in sports (e.g., the U.S. women's national soccer team's fight for equal pay), do you think we will see more attention given to sports as an important site for feminist activism?

References

Blinde, E. M., Taub, D. E., & Han, L. (1993). Sport participation and women's personal empowerment: Experiences of the college athlete. *Journal of Sport and Social Issues, 17*(1), 47–60.

Bradshaw, A. (2002). Empowerment and sport feminism: A critical analysis. *International Sport Studies, 24*, 5–31.

Brake, D. L. (2010). *Getting in the game: Title IX and the women's sports revolution.* New York, NY: New York University Press.

Brand, M. (2003, April 28). Title IX seminar keynote address [Electronic Version]. Retrieved from http://www.ncaa.org/gender_equity/general_info/20030428speech.html

Burstyn, V. (1999). *The rights of men: Manhood, politics and the culture of sport.* Toronto, Canada: University of Toronto Press.

Cahn, S. (1994). *Coming on strong: Gender and sexuality in twentieth century women's sport.* New York, NY: Free Press.

Cole, C. L., & Hribar, A. (1995). Celebrity feminism: Nike style Post-Fordism, transcendence, and consumer power. *Sociology of Sport Journal, 12*(4), 347–369.

Connell, R. W. (1987). *Gender and Power.* Cambridge, England: Polity Press.

Cooky, C. (2009). "Girls just aren't interested": The social construction of interest in girls' sport. *Sociological Perspectives, 52*, 259–284.

Cooky, C. (2010). Do girls rule?: Understanding popular culture images of "Girl Power!" and sport. In S. Spickard Prettyman & B. Lampman (Eds.), *Learning culture through sports: Perspectives on society and organized sports* (pp. 210–226). Lanham, MD: Rowman & Littlefield.

Cooky, C. (2016, June 17). Striking goals for pay and prize parity in sport. *The Society Pages.* Retrieved from https://thesocietypages.org/papers/pay-and-prize-parity-in-soccer/

Cooky, C., Dycus, R., & Dworkin, S. L. (2013). "What makes a woman a woman?" vs. "our first lady of sport": A comparative analysis of United States and South African media coverage of Caster Semenya. *Journal of Sport and Social Issues, 37*, 31–56.

Cooky, C., & LaVoi, N. M. (2012). The unfinished revolution in women's sport. *Contexts: Understanding People in Their Social Worlds, 11*, 42–46.

Dellinger, H. (2015, July 5). The grass ceiling: How to conquer inequality in soccer. *The Atlantic.* Retrieved from http://www.theatlantic.com/entertainment/archive/2015/07/womens-soccer-world-cup-fifa-lawsuit/397592/

Duncan, M. M., & Cundiff, V. P. (1929). *Play days for girls and women.* New York, NY: A. S. Barnes & Co.

Festle, M. J. (1996). *Playing nice: Politics and apologies in women's sports.* New York, NY: Columbia University Press.

Gavora, J. (2002). *Tilting the playing field: Schools, sports, sex and Title IX.* San Francisco, CA: Encounter Books.

Griffin, C. (2004). Good girls, bad girls: Anglocentrism and diversity in the constitution of contemporary girlhood. In A. Harris (Ed.), *All about the girl: Culture, power and identity* (pp. 29–44). New York: Routledge.

Hargreaves, J. (1994). *Sporting females: Critical issues in the history and sociology of women's sports.* London, England: Routledge.

Heywood, L. (1998). All-American girls: Jock chic, body image and sports. In O. Edut (Ed.), *Adios Barbie: Young Women Write about Body Image and Identity* (pp. 201–210). Seattle, WA: Seal Press.

Heywood, L., & Dworkin, S. L. (2003). *Built to win: The female athlete as cultural icon.* Minneapolis, MN: University of Minnesota Press.

Hines Gissendander, C. (1994). African-American women and competitive sport, 1920–1960. In S. Birrell & C. L. Cole (Eds.), *Women, Sport and Culture* (pp. 81–92). Champaign, IL: Human Kinetics.

Hogshead-Makar, N., & Zimbalist, A. (2007). *Equal Play: Title IX and Social Change.* Philadelphia, PA: Temple University Press.

hooks, b. (2000). *Feminist theory: From margin to center* (2nd ed.). Brooklyn, NY: South End Press.

Kane, M. J. (1995). Resistance/transformation of the oppositional binary: Exposing sport as a continuum. *Journal of Sport and Social Issues, 19*, 191–218.

Martens, M. (2015, June 5). Women's soccer is a feminist issue. *The Atlantic*. Retrieved from http://www.theatlantic.com/entertainment/archive/2015/06/womens-soccer-is-a -feminist-issue/394865/

McDonough, E., & Pappano, L. (2009). *Playing with the boys: Why separate is not equal in sports*. New York, NY: Oxford University Press.

Messner, M. A. (1995). *Power at play: Sports and the problem of masculinity*. Boston, MA: Beacon Press.

Messner, M. A. (1988). Sports and male domination: The female athlete as contested ideo-logical terrain. *Sociology of Sport Journal, 5*, 197–211.

Messner, M. A. (2002). *Taking the field: Women, men and sports*. Minneapolis, MN: Univer-sity of Minnesota Press.

Messner, M. A., & Solomon, N. M. (2007). Social justice and men's interests: The case of Title IX. *Journal of Sport and Social Issues, 31*(2), 162–178.

Mohanty, C. (2003). *Feminism without borders: Decolonizing theory, practicing solidarity*. Durham, NC: Duke University Press.

National Federation of State High School Associations. Participation data. Retrieved from http://www.nfhs.org/ParticipationStatics/PDF/2014-15_Participation_Survey_Results .pdf

Rauscher, L., & Cooky, C. (2016). "Ready for anything the world gives her"?: A critical look at sports-based positive youth development for girls. *Sex Roles, 74*, 288–298. doi:10.1007/ s11199-014-0400-x

Reger, J. (Ed.). (2005). *Different wavelengths: Studies of the contemporary women's movement*. New York, NY: Routledge.

Sabo, D., & Grant, C. (2007). Limitations of the Department of Education's on-line survey method for measuring athletic interest and ability on U.S.A. campuses. In *Wherefore Art Thou Feminisms?: Feminist Activism, Academic Feminisms, and Women's Sports Advocacy*, D. Sabo & J. V. Ward (Eds.), *The Scholar and Feminist Online, 4*(3) The Barnard Center for Research on Women. Retrieved from http://www.barnard.edu/sfonline

Sabo, D., & Veliz, P. (2008). Go out and play: Youth sports in America. In N. Hogshead-Makar & A. Zimbalist (Eds.), *Equal Play: Title IX and Social Change* (pp. 276–282). Philadelphia, PA: Temple University Press.

Sabo, D., & Veliz, P. (2011). *Progress without equity: The provision of high school athletic opportunity in the United States, by Gender 1993–94 through 2005–06*. East Meadow, NY: Women's Sports Foundation.

Schultz, J. (2010). The physical is political: Women's suffrage, pilgrim hikes, and the public sphere. *International Journal of the History of Sport, 27*, 1133–1153.

Schultz, J. (2014). *Qualifying times: Points of change in U.S. women's sport*. Champaign, IL: University of Illinois Press.

Schwartz, L. (n.d.) Billie Jean won for all women. Retrieved from https://espn.go.com/ sportscentury/features/00016060.html

Smith Rosenberg, C. (1985). *Disorderly conduct: Visions of gender in Victorian America*. New York, NY: Oxford University Press.

Staurowsky, E. J., DeSousa, M. J., Miller, K. E., Sabo, D., Shakib, S., Theberge, N., Veliz, P., Weaver, A., & Williams, N. (2015). *Her life depends on it III: Sport, physical activity, and the health and well-being of American girls and women*. East Meadow, NY: Women's Sports Foundation.

Suggs, W. (2005). *A place on the team: The triumph and tragedy of Title IX*. Princeton, NJ: Princeton University Press.

Thomas, K. (2011, April 25). College teams, relying on deception, undermine gender equity.

The New York Times. Retrieved from http://www.nytimes.com/2011/04/26/sports/26titleix.html?_r=0

Zimbalist, A. (2007). Bush administration uses stealth tactics to subvert Title IX. In N. Hogshead-Makar & A. Zimbalist (Eds.), *Equal Play: Title IX and Social Change* (pp. 283–285). Philadelphia, PA: Temple University Press.

Part II

Sport as Gendered Practice

• •

5

Barbie Girls versus Sea Monsters

● ●

Children Constructing Gender

MICHAEL A. MESSNER

Sometimes, sociologists discover our best ideas right under our noses. Being a "participant observer" in the everyday lives of my two sons when they were youngsters provided me with some fascinating sociological observations. This article is based not on a systematic research study, but rather on a serendipitous observation I made at the opening ceremony of my then 6-year-old son Sasha's soccer season. When I saw a team of boys and team of girls having a brief and hilarious conflict over a huge Barbie doll and observed the response of the kids' parents, it brought out the gender sociologist in me. The fact that most of the adults around me apparently found pleasure in interpreting this moment as evidence of natural differences between boys and girls led me to an examination of how the social context had shaped this moment, making this kind of highly gendered interaction between boys and girls possible. I used this moment of gender construction to explore the utility of a tri-level theoretical analysis. Most obvious to me initially was that an interactionist perspective was useful in describing how the children and the parents actively

Source: "Barbie girls versus sea monsters: Children constructing gender," by M. A. Messner, 2000, *Gender & Society, 14*(6), pp. 765–784, doi:10.1177/089124300014006004. Copyright 2000 by Sociologists for Women in Society. Reprinted with permission of Sage Publications.

"do" or "perform" gender. But I also wanted to explore how institutional context (in this case, a sex-segregated youth sports league) and familiar cultural symbols (gendered team names and especially Barbie) create contexts that shape the possibilities of group interactions. Gender, this perspective suggests, is not simply something that individuals "have"—like the color of our eyes—rather, it is actively constructed by groups within institutional and cultural contexts that are themselves organized by gender and saturated with gender meanings.

—Michael A. Messner

In the past decade, studies of children and gender have moved toward greater levels of depth and sophistication (e.g., Jordan and Cowan, 1995; McGuffy & Rich, 1999; Thorne, 1993). In her groundbreaking work on children and gender, Thorne (1993) argued that previous theoretical frameworks, although helpful, were limited: The top-down (adult-to-child) approach of socialization theories tended to ignore the extent to which children are active agents in the creation of their worlds—often in direct or partial opposition to values or "roles" to which adult teachers or parents are attempting to socialize them. Developmental theories also had their limits due to their tendency to ignore group and contextual factors while overemphasizing "the constitution and unfolding of *individuals* as boys or girls" (Thorne, 1993, p. 4). In her study of grade school children, Thorne demonstrated a dynamic approach that examined the ways in which children actively construct gender in specific social contexts of the classroom and the playground. Working from emergent theories of performativity, Thorne developed the concept of "gender play" to analyze the social processes through which children construct gender. Her level of analysis was not the individual but "*group life*—with social relations, the organization and meanings of social situations, the collective practices through which children and adults create and recreate gender in their daily interactions" (Thorne, 1993, p. 4).

A key insight from Thorne's research is the extent to which gender varies in salience from situation to situation. Sometimes, children engage in "relaxed, cross sex play"; other times—for instance, on the playground during boys' ritual invasions of girls' spaces and games—gender boundaries between boys and girls are activated in ways that variously threaten or (more often) reinforce and clarify these boundaries. However, these varying moments of gender salience are not free-floating; they occur in social contexts, such as schools, in which gender is formally and informally built into the division of labor, power structure, rules, and values (Connell, 1987).

The purpose of this article is to use an observation of a highly salient gendered moment of group life among 4- and 5-year-old children as a point of departure for exploring the conditions under which gender boundaries become activated and enforced. I was privy to this moment as I observed my 5-year-old son's first season (including weekly games and practices) in organized soccer. Unlike the long-term, systematic ethnographic studies of children conducted by Thorne (1993) or Adler and Adler (1998), this article takes one moment as its point of departure. I do not present this moment as somehow "representative" of what happened throughout the season; instead, I examine this as an example of what Hochschild (1994) calls "magnified moments," which are "episodes of heightened importance, either epiphanies, moments of intense glee or unusual insight, or moments in which things go intensely but meaningfully wrong. In either case, the moment stands out; it is metaphorically rich, unusually elaborate and often echoes [later]" (p. 4). A magnified moment in daily life offers a window into the social construction of reality. It presents researchers with an opportunity to excavate gendered meanings and processes through an analysis of institutional and cultural contexts. The single empirical observation that serves as the point of departure for this article was made during a morning. Immediately after the event, I recorded my observations with detailed notes. I later slightly revised the notes after developing the photographs that I took at the event.

I will first describe the observation—an incident that occurred as a boys' 4- and 5-year-old soccer team waited next to a girls' 4- and 5-year-old soccer team for the beginning of the community's American Youth Soccer Organization (AYSO) season's opening ceremony. I will then examine this moment using three levels of analysis.

The interactional level: How do children "do gender," and what are the contributions and limits of theories of performativity in understanding these interactions?

The level of structural context: How does the gender regime, particularly the larger organizational level of formal sex segregation of AYSO, and the concrete, momentary situation of the opening ceremony provide a context that variously constrains and enables the children's interactions?

The level of cultural symbol: How does the children's shared immersion in popular culture (and their differently gendered locations in this immersion) provide symbolic resources for the creation, in this situation, of apparently categorical differences between the boys and the girls?

Although I will discuss these three levels of analysis separately, I hope to demonstrate that interaction, structural context, and culture are simultaneous and mutually intertwined processes, none of which supersedes the others.

Barbie Girls versus Sea Monsters

It is a warm, sunny Saturday morning. Summer is coming to a close, and schools will soon reopen. As in many communities, this time of year in this small, middle- and professional-class suburb of Los Angeles is marked by the beginning of another soccer season. This morning, 156 teams with approximately 1,850 players ranging from 4 to 17 years old, along with another 2,000 to 3,000 parents, siblings, friends, and community dignitaries, have gathered at the local high school football and track facility for the annual AYSO opening ceremonies. Parents and children wander around the perimeter of the track to find the assigned station for their respective teams. The coaches muster their teams and chat with parents. Eventually, each team will march around the track behind their new team banner as they are announced over the loudspeaker system and are applauded by the crowd. For now though, and for the next 45 min to an hour, the kids, coaches, and parents must stand, mill around, talk, and kill time as they await the beginning of the ceremony.

The Sea Monsters is a team of 4- and 5-year-old boys. Later this day, they will play their first-ever soccer game. A few of the boys already know each other from preschool, but most are still getting acquainted. They are wearing their new uniforms for the first time. Like other teams, they were assigned team colors—in this case, green and blue—and asked to choose their team name at their first team meeting, which occurred a week ago. Although they preferred "Blue Sharks," they found that the name was already taken by another team and settled on "Sea Monsters." A grandmother of one of the boys created the spiffy team banner, which was awarded a prize this morning. As they wait for the ceremony to begin, the boys inspect and then proudly pose for pictures in front of their new award-winning team banner. The parents stand a few feet away—some taking pictures, some just watching. The parents are also getting to know each other, and the common currency of topics is just how darned cute our kids look and will they start these ceremonies soon before another boy has to be escorted to the bathroom?

Queued up one group away from the Sea Monsters is a team of 4- and 5-year-old girls in green-and-white uniforms. They too will play their first game later today, but for now, they are awaiting the beginning of the opening ceremony. They have chosen the name "Barbie Girls," and they also have a spiffy new team banner. But the girls are pretty much ignoring their banner, for they have created another more powerful symbol around which to rally. In fact, they are the only team among the 156 marching today with a team float—a red Radio Flyer wagon base, on which sits a Sony boom box playing music and a 3-foot-plus-tall Barbie doll on a rotating pedestal. Barbie is dressed in the team colors—indeed, she sports a custom-made green-and-white cheerleader-style outfit with the Barbie Girls' names written on the skirt. Her normally all-blonde hair has been streaked with Barbie-Girl green and features a green bow with white polka dots. Several of the girls on the team also have supplemented their uniforms with green bows in their hair.

The volume on the boom box nudges up, and four or five girls begin to sing a Barbie song. Barbie is now slowly rotating on her pedestal, and as the girls sing more gleefully and more loudly, some of them begin to hold hands and walk around the float in sync with Barbie's rotation. Other same-aged girls from other teams are drawn to the celebration and, eventually, perhaps a dozen girls are singing the Barbie song. The girls are intensely focused on Barbie, on the music, and on their mutual pleasure.

As the Sea Monsters mill around their banner, some of them begin to notice and then begin to watch and listen as the Barbie Girls rally around their float. At first, the boys are watching as individuals, seemingly unaware of each other's shared interest. Some of them stand with arms at their sides, slack-jawed, as though passively watching a television show. I notice slight smiles on a couple of their faces, as though they are drawn to the Barbie Girls' celebratory fun. Then with side-glances, some of the boys begin to notice each other's attention on the Barbie Girls. Their faces begin to show signs of distaste. One of them yells out, "NO BARBIE!" Suddenly, they all begin to move—jumping up and down, nudging, and bumping one other—and join into a group chant: "NO BARBIE! NO BARBIE! NO BARBIE!" They now appear to be every bit as gleeful as the girls as they laugh, yell, and chant against the Barbie Girls.

The parents watch the whole scene with rapt attention. Smiles light up the faces of the adults as our glances sweep back and forth from the sweetly celebrating Barbie Girls to the aggressively protesting Sea Monsters. "They are SO different!" exclaims one smiling mother approvingly. A male coach offers a more in-depth analysis: "When I was in college," he says, "I took these classes from professors who showed us research that showed that boys and girls are the same. I believed it until I had my own kids and saw how different they are." "Yeah," another dad responds, "Just look at them! They are so different!"

The girls, meanwhile, show no evidence that they hear, see, or are even aware of the presence of the boys who are now so loudly proclaiming their opposition to the Barbie Girls' songs and totem. They continue to sing, dance, laugh, and rally around the Barbie for a few more minutes before they are called to reassemble in their groups for the beginning of the parade.

After the parade, the teams reassemble on the infield of the track but now in a less organized manner. The Sea Monsters once again find themselves in the general vicinity of the Barbie Girls and take up the "NO BARBIE!" chant again. Perhaps put out by the lack of response to their chant, they begin to dash in twos and threes, invading the girls' space and yelling menacingly. With this, the Barbie Girls have little choice but to recognize the presence of the boys—some look puzzled and shrink back, some engage the boys and chase them off. The chasing seems only to incite more excitement among the boys. Finally, parents intervene and defuse the situation, leading their children off to their cars, homes, and eventually to their soccer games.

The Performance of Gender

In the past decade, especially since the publication of Judith Butler's highly influential *Gender Trouble* (1990), it has become increasingly fashionable among academic feminists to think of gender not as some "thing" that one "has" (or not) but rather as situationally constructed through the performances of active agents. The idea of gender as performance analytically foregrounds the agency of individuals in the construction of gender, thus highlighting the situational fluidity of gender: here, conservative and reproductive, there, transgressive and disruptive. Surely the Barbie Girls versus Sea Monsters scene described above can be fruitfully analyzed as a moment of crosscutting and mutually constitutive gender performances: The girls—at least at first glance—appear to be performing (for each other?) a conventional 4- to 5-year-old version of emphasized femininity. At least on the surface, there appears to be nothing terribly transgressive here. They are just "being girls" together. The boys initially are unwittingly constituted as an audience for the girls' performance but quickly begin to perform (for each other?—for the girls, too?) a masculinity that constructs itself in opposition to Barbie and to the girls as not feminine. They aggressively confront—first through loud verbal chanting, eventually through bodily invasions—the girls' ritual space of emphasized femininity, apparently with the intention of disrupting its upsetting influence. The adults are simultaneously constituted as an adoring audience for their children's performances and as parents who perform for each other by sharing and mutually affirming their experience-based narratives concerning the natural differences between boys and girls.

In this scene, we see children performing gender in ways that constitute themselves as two separate, opposed groups (boys vs. girls) and parents performing gender in ways that give the stamp of adult approval to the children's performances of difference while constructing their own ideological narrative that naturalizes this categorical difference. In other words, the parents do not seem to read the children's performances of gender as social constructions of gender. Instead, they interpret them as the inevitable unfolding of natural, internal differences between the sexes. That this moment occurred when it did and where it did is explicable but not entirely with a theory of performativity. As Walters (1999) argues,

> The performance of gender is never a simple voluntary act. . . . Theories of gender as play and performance need to be intimately and systematically connected with the power of gender (really, the power of male power) to constrain, control, violate, and configure. Too often, mere lip service is given to the specific historical, social, and political configurations that make certain conditions possible and others constrained. (p. 250)

Indeed, feminist sociologists operating from the traditions of symbolic interactionism and/or Goffmanian dramaturgical analysis have anticipated the recent interest in looking at gender as a dynamic performance. As early as 1978, Kessler and McKenna developed a sophisticated analysis of gender as an everyday, practical accomplishment of people's interactions. Nearly a decade later, West and Zimmerman (1987) argued that in people's everyday interactions, they were "doing gender" and, in so doing, they were constructing masculine dominance and feminine deference. As these ideas have been taken up in sociology, their tendencies toward a celebration of the "freedom" of agents to transgress and reshape the fluid boundaries of gender have been put into play with theories of social structure (e.g., Lorber, 1994; Risman, 1998). In these accounts, gender is viewed as enacted or created through everyday interactions but crucially, as Walters suggested above, within "specific historical, social, and political configurations" that constrain or enable certain interactions.

The parents' response to the Barbie Girls versus Sea Monsters performance suggests one of the main limits and dangers of theories of performativity. Lacking an analysis of structural and cultural context, performances of gender can all too easily be interpreted as free agents' acting out the inevitable surface manifestations of a natural inner essence of sex difference. An examination of structural and cultural contexts, though, reveals that there was nothing inevitable about the girls' choice of Barbie as their totem, nor in the boys' response to it.

The Structure of Gender

In the entire subsequent season of weekly games and practices, I never once saw adults point to a moment in which boy and girl soccer players were doing the *same* thing and exclaim to each other, "Look at them! They are *so similar!*" The actual similarity of the boys and the girls, evidenced by nearly all of the kids' routine actions throughout a soccer season—playing the game, crying over a skinned knee, scrambling enthusiastically for their snacks after the games, spacing out on a bird or a flower instead of listening to the coach at practice—is a key to understanding the salience of the Barbie Girls versus Sea Monsters moment for gender relations. In the face of a multitude of moments that speak to similarity, it was this anomalous Barbie Girls versus Sea Monsters moment—where the boundaries of gender were so clearly enacted—that the adults seized to affirm their commitment to difference. It is the kind of moment—to use Lorber's (1994) phrase—where "believing is seeing," where we selectively "see" aspects of social reality that tell us a truth that we prefer to believe, such as the belief in categorical sex difference (p. 37). No matter that our eyes do not see evidence of this truth most of the rest of the time.

In fact, it was not so easy for adults to actually "see" the empirical reality of sex similarity in everyday observations of soccer throughout the season. That is due to one overdetermining factor: an institutional context that is characterized by informally structured sex segregation among the parent coaches and team managers and by formally structured sex segregation among the children. The structural analysis developed here is indebted to Acker's (1990) observation that organizations, even while appearing "gender neutral," tend to reflect, recreate, and naturalize a hierarchical ordering of gender. Following Connell's (1987) method of structural analysis, I will examine the "gender regime"—that is, the current "state of play of sexual politics"—within the local AYSO organization by conducting a "structural inventory" of the formal and informal sexual divisions of labor and power (p. 98–99).[1]

Adult Divisions of Labor and Power

There was a clear—although not absolute—sexual division of labor and power among the adult volunteers in the AYSO organization. The board of directors consisted of 21 men and 9 women, with the top two positions—commissioner and assistant commissioner—held by men. Among the league's head coaches, 133 were men and 23 were women. The division among the league's assistant coaches was similarly skewed. Each team also had a team manager who was responsible for organizing snacks, making reminder calls about games and practices, organizing team parties and the end-of-the-year present for the coach. The vast majority of team managers were women. A common slippage in the language of coaches and parents revealed the ideological assumptions underlying this position: I often noticed people describe a team manager as the "team mom." In short, as Table 5.1 shows, the vast majority of the time, the formal authority of the head coach and assistant coach was in the hands of a man, while the backup support role of team manager was in the hands of a woman.

These data illustrate Connell's (1987, p. 97) assertion that sexual divisions of labor are interwoven with, and mutually supportive of, divisions of power and authority among women and men. They also suggest how people's choices to volunteer for certain positions are shaped and constrained by previous institutional practices. There is no formal AYSO rule that men must be the leaders, women the supportive followers. And there are, after all, *some* women coaches and *some* men team managers.[2] So it may appear that the division of labor among adult volunteers simply manifests an accumulation of individual choices and preferences. When analyzed structurally, though, individual men's apparently free choices to volunteer disproportionately for coaching jobs, alongside individual women's apparently free choices to volunteer disproportionately for team manager jobs, can be seen as a logical collective result of the ways that the institutional structure of sport has differentially constrained and enabled women's and men's previous options and experiences (Messner, 1992). Since boys and men have had far more opportunities to play organized sports and thus to gain skills and knowledge, it subsequently appears rational for adult men to serve in positions of knowledgeable authority, with women serving in a support capacity (Boyle & McKay, 1995). Structure—in this case, the historically constituted division of labor and power in sport—constrains current practice. In turn, structure becomes an object of practice, as the choices and actions of today's parents recreate divisions of labor and power similar to those that they experienced in their youth.

The Children: Formal Sex Segregation

As adult authority patterns are informally structured along gendered lines, the children's leagues are formally segregated by AYSO along lines of age and sex. In each age group, there are separate boys' and girls' leagues. The AYSO in this community included 87 boys' teams and 69 girls' teams. Although the 4- to 5-year-old boys often played their games on a field that was contiguous with games being played by 4- to 5-year-old girls, there was never a formal opportunity for cross-sex play. Thus both the girls' and the boys' teams could conceivably proceed through an entire season of games and practices in entirely homosocial contexts.[3] In the all-male contexts that I observed throughout the season, gender never appeared to be overtly salient among the children, coaches, or parents. It is against this backdrop that I might suggest a working hypothesis about structure and the variable salience of gender: The formal sex segregation of children does not, in and of itself, make gender overtly salient. In fact, when children are absolutely segregated with no opportunity for cross-sex interactions, gender may appear to disappear as an overtly salient organizing principle. However, when formally sex-segregated children are placed into immediately contiguous locations, such as during the opening ceremony, highly charged gendered

Table 5.1. Adult Volunteers as Coaches and Team Managers by Gender

	Head Coaches	Assistant Coaches	Team Managers
Women (%)	15	21	86
Men (%)	85	79	14

NOTE: (N = 156 teams).

interactions between the groups (including invasions and other kinds of border work) become more possible.

Although it might appear to some that formal sex segregation in children's sports is a natural fact, it has not always been so for the youngest age groups in AYSO. As recently as 1995, when my older son signed up to play as a 5-year-old, I had been told that he would play in a coed league. But when he arrived to his first practice and I saw that he was on an all-boys team, I was told by the coach that AYSO had decided this year to begin sex segregating all age groups because "during half-times and practices, the boys and girls tend to separate into separate groups. So the league thought it would be better for team unity if we split the boys and girls into separate leagues." I suggested to some coaches that a similar dynamic among racial ethnic groups (say, Latino kids and White kids clustering as separate groups during halftimes) would not similarly result in a decision to create racially segregated leagues. That this comment appeared to fall on deaf ears illustrates the extent to which many adults' belief in the need for sex segregation—at least in the context of sport—is grounded in a mutually agreed upon notion of boys' and girls' "separate worlds," perhaps based in ideologies of natural sex difference.

The gender regime of AYSO, then, is structured by formal and informal sexual divisions of labor and power. This social structure sets ranges, limits, and possibilities for the children's and parents' interactions and performances of gender, but it does not determine them. Put another way, the formal and informal gender regime of AYSO made the Barbie Girls versus Sea Monsters moment possible, but it did not make it inevitable. It was the agency of the children and the parents within that structure that made the moment happen. But why did this moment take on the symbolic forms that it did? How and why do the girls, boys, and parents construct and derive meanings from this moment, and how can we interpret these meanings? These questions are best grappled within in the realm of cultural analysis.

The Culture of Gender

The difference between what is "structural" and what is "cultural" is not clear-cut. For instance, the AYSO assignment of team colors and choice of team names (cultural symbols) seem to follow logically from, and in turn reinforce, the sex segregation of the leagues (social structure). These cultural symbols such as team colors, uniforms, songs, team names, and banners often carried encoded gendered meanings that were then available to be taken up by the children in ways that constructed (or potentially contested) gender divisions and boundaries.

Team Names

Each team was issued two team colors. It is notable that across the various age groups, several girls' teams were issued pink uniforms—a color commonly recognized as encoding feminine meanings—while no boys' teams were issued pink uniforms. Children, in consultation with their coaches, were asked to choose their own team names and were encouraged to use their assigned team colors as cues to the theme of the team name (e.g., among the boys, the "Red Flashes," the "Green Pythons," and the blue-and-green "Sea Monsters"). When I analyzed the team names of the 156 teams by age group and by sex, three categories emerged:

1. Sweet names: These are cutesy team names that communicate small stature, cuteness, and/or vulnerability. These kinds of names would most likely be widely read as encoded with feminine meanings (e.g., "Blue Butterflies," "Beanie Babes," "Sunflowers," "Pink Flamingos," and "Barbie Girls").

2. Neutral or paradoxical names: Neutral names are team names that carry no obvious gendered meaning (e.g., "Blue and Green Lizards," "Team Flubber," "Galaxy," "Blue Ice"). Paradoxical names are girls' team names that carry mixed (simultaneously vulnerable *and* powerful) messages (e.g., "Pink Panthers," "Flower Power," "Little Tigers").

3. Power names: These are team names that invoke images of unambiguous strength, aggression, and raw power (e.g., "Shooting Stars," "Killer Whales," "Shark Attack," "Raptor Attack," and "Sea Monsters").

As Table 5.2 illustrates, across all age groups of boys, there was only one team name coded as a sweet name—"The Smurfs," in the 10- to 11-year-old league. Across all age categories, the boys were far more likely to choose a power name than anything else, and this was nowhere more true than in the youngest age groups, where 35 of 40 (87%) of boys' teams in the four-to-five and six-to-seven age groups took on power names. A different pattern appears in the girls' team name choices, especially among the youngest girls. Only two of the twelve 4- to 5-year-old girls' teams chose power names, while five chose sweet names and five chose neutral/paradoxical names. At ages six to seven, the numbers begin to tip toward the boys' numbers but still remain different, with half of the girls' teams now choosing power names. In the middle and older girls' groups, the sweet names all but disappear, with power names dominating but still a higher proportion of neutral/paradoxical names than among boys in those age groups.

Barbie Narrative versus Warrior Narrative

How do we make sense of the obviously powerful spark that Barbie provided in the opening ceremony scene described above? Barbie is likely one of the most immediately identifiable symbols of femininity in the world. More

Table 5.2. Team Names by Age Groups and Gender

	4-5		6-7		8-13		14-17		Total	
	n	%	n	%	n	%	n	%	n	%
Girls										
Sweet names	5	42	3	17	2	7	0	0	10	15
Neutral/ paradoxical	5	42	6	33	7	25	5	45	23	32
Power names	2	17	9	50	19	68	6	55	36	52
Boys										
Sweet names	0	0	0	0	1	4	0	0	1	1
Neutral/ paradoxical	1	7	4	15	4	12	4	31	12	15
Power names	13	93	22	85	29	85	9	69	73	82

conservatively oriented parents tend to happily buy Barbie dolls for their daughters while perhaps deflecting their sons' interest in Barbie toward more sex-appropriate "action toys." Feminist parents, on the other hand, have often expressed open contempt—or at least uncomfortable ambivalence—toward Barbie. This is because both conservative and feminist parents see dominant cultural meanings of emphasized femininity as condensed in Barbie and assume that these meanings will be imitated by their daughters. Recent developments in cultural studies, though, should warn us against simplistic readings of Barbie as simply conveying hegemonic messages about gender to unwitting children (Attfield, 1996; Seiter, 1995). In addition to critically analyzing the cultural values (or "preferred meanings") that may be encoded in Barbie or other children's toys, feminist scholars of cultural studies point to the necessity of examining "reception, pleasure, and agency," and especially "the fullness of reception contexts" (Walters, 1999, p. 246). The Barbie Girls versus Sea Monsters moment can be analyzed as a "reception context," in which differently situated boys, girls, and parents variously used Barbie to construct pleasurable intergroup bonds, as well as boundaries between groups.

Barbie is plastic both in form and in terms of cultural meanings children and adults create around her (Rogers, 1999). It is not that there are not hegemonic meanings encoded in Barbie: Since its introduction in 1959, Mattel has been successful in selling millions[4] of this doll that "was recognized as a model of ideal teenhood" (Rand, 1998, p. 383) and was "an icon—perhaps *the* icon—of true white womanhood and femininity" (DuCille, 1994, p. 50). However, Rand (1998) argues that "we condescend to children when we analyze Barbie's content and then presume that it passes untransformed into their minds, where, dwelling beneath the control of consciousness or counterargument, it generates self-image, feelings, and other ideological constructs." In fact, people who are situated differently (by age, gender, sexual orientation, social class, race/ ethnicity, and national origin) tend to consume and construct meanings around Barbie variously. For instance, some adult women (including many feminists) tell retrospective stories of having rejected (or even mutilated) their Barbies in favor of boys' toys, and some adult lesbians tell stories of transforming Barbie "into an object of dyke desire" (Rand, 1998, p. 386).

Mattel, in fact, clearly strategizes its marketing of Barbie not around the imposition of a singular notion of what a girl or woman should be but around "hegemonic discourse strategies" that attempt to incorporate consumers' range of possible interpretations and criticisms of the limits of Barbie. For instance, the recent marketing of "multicultural Barbie" features dolls with different skin colors and culturally coded wardrobes (DuCille, 1994). This strategy broadens the Barbie market, deflects potential criticism of racism, but still "does not boot blond, white Barbie from center stage" (Rand, 1998, p. 391). Similarly, Mattel's marketing of Barbie (since the 1970s) as a career woman raises issues concerning the feminist critique of Barbie's supposedly negative effect on girls. When the AAUW recently criticized Barbie, adult collectors defended Barbie, asserting that "Barbie, in fact, is a wonderful role model for women. She has been a veterinarian, an astronaut, and a soldier—and even before real women had a chance to enter such occupations" (Spigel, forthcoming). And when the magazine *Barbie Bazaar* ran a cover photo of its new "Gulf War Barbie," it served "as a reminder of Mattel's marketing slogan: 'We Girls Can Do Anything'" (Spigel, forthcoming). The following year, Mattel unveiled its "Presidential Candidate Barbie" with the statement, "It is time for a woman president, and Barbie had the credentials for the job." Spigel observes that these liberal feminist messages of empowerment for girls run—apparently unambiguously—alongside a continued unspoken understanding that Barbie must be beautiful, with an ultraskinny waist and long, thin legs that taper to feet that appear deformed so that they may fit (only?) into high heels.[5] "Mattel does not mind equating beauty with intellect. In fact, so long as the 11½ inch Barbie body remains intact, Mattel is willing to accessorize her with a number of fashionable perspectives—including feminism itself" (Spigel, forthcoming).

It is this apparently paradoxical encoding of the all-too-familiar oppressive bodily requirements of feminine beauty alongside the career woman role modeling and empowering message that "we girls can do anything" that may inform how and why the Barbie Girls appropriated Barbie as their team symbol. Emphasized femininity—Connell's (1987) term for the current form of femininity that articulates with hegemonic masculinity—as many second-wave feminists have experienced and criticized it, has been characterized by girls' and women's embodiments of oppressive conceptions of feminine beauty that symbolize and reify a thoroughly disempowered stance vis-à-vis men. To many second-wave feminists, Barbie seemed to symbolize all that was oppressive about this femininity—the bodily self-surveillance, accompanying eating disorders, slavery to the dictates of the fashion industry, and compulsory heterosexuality. But Rogers (1999) suggests that rather than representing an unambiguous image of emphasized femininity, perhaps Barbie represents a more paradoxical image of "emphatic femininity" that takes feminine appearances and demeanor to unsustainable extremes. Nothing about Barbie ever looks masculine, even when she is on the police force. . . . Consistently, Barbie manages impressions so as to come across as a proper feminine creature even when she crosses boundaries usually dividing women from men. Barbie the firefighter is in no danger, then, of being seen as "one of the boys." Kids know that; parents and teachers know that; Mattel designers know that too. (p. 14)

Recent third-wave feminist theory sheds light on the different sensibilities of younger generations of girls and women concerning their willingness to display and play with this apparently paradoxical relationship between bodily experience (including "feminine" displays) and public empowerment. In third-wave feminist texts, displays of feminine physical attractiveness and empowerment are not viewed as mutually exclusive or necessarily opposed realities but as lived (if often paradoxical) aspects of the same reality (Heywood & Drake, 1997). This embracing of the paradoxes of post-second-wave femininity is manifested in many punk, or Riot Grrrl, subcultures (Klein, 1997) and in popular culture in the resounding late 1990s success of the Spice Girls' mantra, "Girl Power." This generational expression of "girl power" may today be part of "the pleasures of girl culture that Barbie stands for" (Spigel, forthcoming). Indeed, as the Barbie Girls rallied around Barbie, their obvious pleasure did not appear to be based on a celebration of quiet passivity (as feminist parents might fear). Rather, it was a statement that they—the Barbie Girls—were here in this public space. They were not silenced by the boys' oppositional chanting. To the contrary, they ignored the boys, who seemed irrelevant to their celebration. And when the boys later physically invaded their space, some of the girls responded by chasing the boys off. In short, when I pay attention to what the girls *did* (rather than imposing on the situation what I *think* Barbie "should" mean to the girls), I see a public moment of celebratory "girl power."

And this may give us better basis from which to analyze the boys' oppositional response. First, the boys may have been responding to the threat of displacement they may have felt while viewing the girls' moment of celebratory girl power. Second, the boys may simultaneously have been responding to the fears of feminine pollution that Barbie had come to symbolize to them. But why might Barbie symbolize feminine pollution to little boys? A brief example from my older son is instructive. When he was about three, following a fun day of play with the 5-year-old girl next door, he enthusiastically asked me to buy him a Barbie like hers. He was gleeful when I took him to the store and bought him one. When we arrived home, his feet had barely hit the pavement getting out of the car before an 8-year-old neighbor boy laughed at and ridiculed him: "A *Barbie*? Don't you know that Barbie is a *girl's toy*?" No amount of parental intervention could counter this devastating peer-induced injunction against boys playing with Barbie. My son's pleasurable desire for Barbie appeared almost overnight to transform itself into shame and rejection. The doll ended up at the bottom of a heap of toys in the closet, and my son soon became infatuated, along with other boys in his preschool, with Ninja Turtles and Power Rangers.

Research indicates that there is widespread agreement as to which toys are appropriate for one sex and polluting, dangerous, or inappropriate for the other sex. When Campenni (1999) asked adults to rate the gender appropriateness of children's toys, the toys considered most appropriate to girls were those pertaining to domestic tasks, beauty enhancement, or child rearing. Of the 206 toys rated, Barbie was rated second only to Makeup Kit as a female-only toy. Toys considered most appropriate to boys were those pertaining to sports gear (football gear was the most masculine-rated toy, while boxing gloves were third), vehicles, action figures (G. I. Joe was rated second only to football gear), and other war-related toys. This research on parents' gender stereotyping of toys reflects similar findings in research on children's toy preferences (Bradbard, 1985; Robinson & Morris, 1986). Children tend to avoid cross-sex toys, with boys' avoidance of feminine-coded toys appearing to be stronger than girls' avoidance of masculine-coded toys (Etaugh & Liss, 1992). Moreover, preschool-age boys who perceive their fathers to be opposed to cross-gender-typed play are more likely than girls or other boys to think that it is "bad" for boys to play with toys that are labeled as "for girls" (Raag & Rackliff, 1998).

By kindergarten, most boys appear to have learned—through experiences similar to my son's, where other male persons police the boundaries of gender-appropriate play and fantasy, and/or by watching the clearly gendered messages of television advertising—that Barbie dolls are not appropriate toys for boys (Rogers, 1999, p. 30). To avoid ridicule, they learn to hide their desire for Barbie, through denial and oppositional/pollution discourse and/or through sublimation of their desire for Barbie into play with male-appropriate "action figures" (Pope, Olivarda, Gruber, & Borowiecki, 1999). In their study of a kindergarten classroom, Jordan and Cowan (1995) identified "warrior narratives . . . that assume that violence is legitimate and justified when it occurs within a struggle between good and evil" to be the most commonly agreed upon currency for boys' fantasy play (p. 728). They observe that the boys seem commonly to adapt story lines that they have seen on television. Popular culture—film, video, computer games, television, and comic books—provides boys with a seemingly endless stream of Good Guys versus Bad Guys characters and stories—from cowboy movies, Superman, and Spiderman to Ninja Turtles, Star Wars, and Pokémon—that are available for the boys to appropriate as the raw materials for the construction of their own warrior play.

In the kindergarten that Jordan and Cowan studied, the boys initially attempted to import their warrior narratives into the domestic setting of the "Doll Corner." Teachers eventually drove the boys' warrior play outdoors, while the Doll Corner was used by the girls for the "appropriate" domestic play for which it was originally intended. Jordan and Cowan argue that kindergarten teachers' outlawing of boys' warrior narratives inside the classroom contributed to boys' defining schools as a feminine environment, to which they responded with a resistant, underground continuation of masculine warrior play. Eventually though, boys who acquiesce and successfully sublimate warrior play into fantasy or sport are more successful in constructing what Connell (1989) calls "a masculinity organized around themes of rationality and responsibility [that is] closely connected with the 'certification' function of the upper levels of the education system and to a key form of masculinity among professionals" (p. 291).

In contrast to the "rational/professional" masculinity constructed in schools, the institution of sport historically constructs hegemonic masculinity as *bodily superiority* over femininity and nonathletic masculinities (Messner, 1992). Here, warrior narratives are allowed to publicly thrive—indeed, are openly celebrated (witness, for instance, the commentary of a televised NFL [National Football League] football game or especially the spectacle of televised professional wrestling). Preschool boys and kindergartners seem already to know this, easily adopting aggressively competitive team names and us-versus-them attitudes. By contrast, many of the youngest girls appear to take two or three years in organized soccer before they adopt or partially accommodate themselves to aggressively competitive discourse, indicated by the 10-year-old girls' shifting away from the use of sweet names toward more power names. In short, where the gender regime of preschool and grade school may be experienced as an environment in which mostly women leaders enforce rules that are hostile to masculine fantasy play and physicality, the gender regime of sport is experienced as a place where masculine styles and values of physicality, aggression, and competition are enforced and celebrated by mostly male coaches.

A cultural analysis suggests that the boys' and the girls' previous immersion in differently gendered cultural experiences shaped the likelihood that they would derive and construct different meanings from Barbie—the girls through pleasurable and symbolically empowering identification with "girl power" narratives and the boys through oppositional fears of feminine pollution (and fears of displacement by girl power?) and with aggressively verbal, and eventually physical, invasions of the girls' ritual space. The boys' collective response thus constituted them differently *as boys* in opposition to the girls' constitution of themselves *as girls*. An individual girl or boy, in this moment, who may have felt an inclination to dissent from the dominant feelings of the group (say, the Latina Barbie Girl who, her mother later told me, did not want the group to be identified with Barbie or a boy whose immediate inner response to the Barbie Girls' joyful celebration might be to join in) is most likely silenced into complicity in this powerful moment of border work.

What meanings did this highly gendered moment carry for the boys' and girls' teams in the ensuing soccer season? Although I did not observe the Barbie Girls after the opening ceremony, I did continue to observe the Sea Monsters' weekly practices and games. During the boys' ensuing season, gender never reached this "magnified" level of salience again—indeed, gender was rarely raised verbally or performed overtly by the boys. On two occasions, though, I observed the coach jokingly chiding the boys during practice that "if you don't watch out, I'm going to get the Barbie Girls here to play against you!" This warning was followed by gleeful screams of agony and fear and nervous hopping around and hugging by some of the boys. Normally, though, in this sex-segregated, all-male context, if boundaries were invoked, they were not boundaries between boys and girls but boundaries between the Sea Monsters and other boys' teams or sometimes age boundaries between the Sea Monsters and a small group of dads and older brothers who would engage them in a mock scrimmage during practice. But it was also evident that when the coach was having trouble getting the boys to act together as a group, his strategic and humorous invocation of the dreaded Barbie Girls once again served symbolically to affirm their group status. They were a team. They were the boys.

Conclusion

The overarching goal of this article has been to take one empirical observation from everyday life and demonstrate how a multilevel (interactionist, structural, cultural) analysis might reveal various layers of meaning that give insight into the everyday social construction of gender. This article builds on observations made by Thorne (1993) concerning ways to approach sociological analyses of children's worlds. The most fruitful approach is not to ask why boys and girls are so different but rather to ask how and under what conditions boys and girls constitute themselves as separate, oppositional groups. Sociologists need not debate whether gender is "there"—clearly, gender is always already there, built as it is into the structures, situations, culture, and consciousness of children and adults. The key issue is under what conditions gender is activated as a salient organizing principle in social life and under what conditions it may be less salient. These are important questions, especially since the social organization of categorical gender difference has always been so clearly tied to gender hierarchy (Acker, 1990; Lorber, 1994). In the Barbie Girls versus Sea Monsters moment, the performance of gendered boundaries and the construction of boys' and girls' groups as categorically different occurred in the context of a situation systematically structured by sex segregation, sparked by the imposing presence of a shared cultural symbol that is saturated with gendered meanings, and actively supported and applauded by adults who basked in the pleasure of difference, reaffirmed.[6]

I have suggested that a useful approach to the study of such "how" and "under what conditions" questions is to employ multiple levels of analysis. At the most general level, this project supports the following working propositions.

Interactionist theoretical frameworks that emphasize the ways that social agents "perform" or "do" gender are most useful in describing how groups of people actively create (or at times disrupt) the boundaries that delineate seemingly categorical differences between male persons and female persons. In this case, we saw how the children and the parents interactively performed gender in a way that constructed an apparently natural boundary between the two separate worlds of the girls and the boys.

Structural theoretical frameworks that emphasize the ways that gender is built into institutions through hierarchical sexual divisions of labor are most useful in explaining under what conditions social agents mobilize variously to disrupt or to affirm gender differences and inequalities. In this case, we saw how the sexual division of labor among parent volunteers (grounded in their own histories in the gender regime of sport), the formal sex segregation of the children's leagues, and the structured context of the opening ceremony created conditions for possible interactions between girls' teams and boys' teams.

Cultural theoretical perspectives that examine how popular symbols that are injected into circulation by the culture industry are variously taken up by differently situated people are most useful in analyzing how the meanings of cultural symbols in a given institutional context might trigger or be taken up by social agents and used as resources to reproduce, disrupt, or contest binary conceptions of sex difference and gendered relations of power. In this case, we saw how a girls' team appropriated a large Barbie around which to construct a pleasurable and empowering sense of group identity and how the boys' team responded with aggressive denunciations of Barbie and invasions.

Utilizing any one of the above theoretical perspectives by itself will lead to a limited, even distorted, analysis of the social construction of gender. Together, they can illuminate the complex, multileveled architecture of the social construction of gender in everyday life. For heuristic reasons, I have falsely separated structure, interaction, and culture. In fact, we need to explore their constant interrelationships, continuities, and contradictions. For instance, we cannot understand the boys' aggressive denunciations and invasions of the girls' space and the eventual clarification of categorical boundaries between the girls and the boys without first understanding how these boys and girls have already internalized 4 or 5 years of "gendering" experiences that have shaped their interactional tendencies and how they are already immersed in a culture of gendered symbols, including Barbie and sports media imagery. Although "only" preschoolers, they are already skilled in collectively taking up symbols from popular culture as resources to be used in their own group dynamics—building individual and group identities, sharing the pleasures of play, clarifying boundaries between in-group and out-group members, and constructing hierarchies in their worlds.

Furthermore, we cannot understand the reason that the girls first chose "Barbie Girls" as their team name without first understanding the fact that a particular institutional structure of AYSO soccer preexisted the girls' entrée into the league. The informal sexual division of labor among adults, and the formal sex segregation of children's teams, is a preexisting gender regime that constrains and enables the ways that the children enact gender relations and construct identities. One concrete manifestation of this constraining nature of sex-segregated teams is the choice of team names. It is reasonable to speculate that if the 4- and 5-year-old children were still sex integrated, as in the pre-1995 era, no team would have chosen "Barbie Girls" as its team name, with Barbie as its symbol. In other words, the formal sex segregation created the conditions under which the girls were enabled—perhaps encouraged—to choose a "sweet" team name that is widely read as encoding feminine meanings. The eventual interactions between the boys and the girls were made possible—although by no means fully determined—by the structure of the gender regime and by the cultural resources that the children variously drew on.

On the other hand, the gendered division of labor in youth soccer is not seamless, static, or immune to resistance. One of the few woman head coaches, a very active athlete in her own right, told me that she is "challenging the sexism" in AYSO by becoming the head of her son's league. As post–Title IX women increasingly become mothers and as media images of competent, heroic female athletes become more a part of the cultural landscape for children, the gender regimes of children's sports may be increasingly challenged (Dworkin & Messner, 1999). Put another way, the dramatically shifting opportunity structure and cultural imagery of post–Title IX sports have created opportunities for new kinds of interactions, which will inevitably challenge and further shift institutional structures. Social structures simultaneously constrain and enable, while agency is simultaneously reproductive and resistant.

Questions for Reflection and Discussion

The observation that this chapter is based on took place nearly two decades ago. Would such scenes still be common in youth sports? Why or why not? Can you think of other examples of daily life when gender boundaries are "activated" and gender difference becomes highly salient? Can you think of other examples when gender boundaries blur or evaporate and dichotomous gender differences become less salient or even irrelevant? How and when might it be useful to deploy the three levels of gender analysis—interactional, structural, and symbolic—to understand the gender dynamics at work in everyday life outside of youth sports?

Notes

1   Most of the structural inventory presented here is from a content analysis of the 1998–1999 regional American Youth Soccer Organization (AYSO) yearbook, which features photos and names of all of the teams, coaches, and managers. I counted the number of adult men and women occupying various positions. In the three cases where the sex category of a name was not immediately obvious (e.g., Rene or Terry) and in the five cases where simply a last name was listed, I did not count it. I also used the AYSO yearbook for my analysis of the children's team names. To check for reliability, another sociologist independently read and coded the list of team names. There was disagreement on how to categorize only 2 of the 156 team names.

2   The existence of some women coaches and some men team managers in this AYSO organization manifests a less extreme sexual division of labor than that of the same community's Little League Baseball organization, in which there are proportionally far fewer women coaches. Similarly, Saltzman Chafetz and Kotarba's (1999) study of parental labor in support of Little League baseball in a middle-class Houston community revealed an apparently absolute sexual division of labor, where nearly all of the supportive "activities off the field were conducted by the women in the total absence of men, while activities on the field were conducted by men and boys in the absence of women" (p. 52). Perhaps youth soccer, because of its more recent (mostly post–Title IX) history in the United States, is a more contested gender regime than the more patriarchally entrenched youth sports like Little League Baseball or youth football.

3   The 4- and 5-year-old kids' games and practices were absolutely homosocial in terms of the kids due to the formal structural sex segregation. However, 8 of the 12 girls' teams at this age level had male coaches, and 2 of the 14 boys' teams had female coaches.

4   By 1994, more than 800 million Barbies had been sold worldwide. More than $1 billion was spent on Barbies and accessories in 1992 alone. Two Barbie dolls were purchased every second in 1994, half of which were sold in the United States (DuCille, 1994, p. 49).

5   Rogers (1999) notes that if one extrapolates Barbie's bodily proportions to "real woman ones," she would be "33-18-31.5 and stand five feet nine inches tall, with fully half of her height accounted for by her 'shapely legs'" (p. 23).

6   My trilevel analysis of structure, interaction, and culture may not be fully adequate to plumb the emotional depths of the magnified Barbie Girls versus Sea Monsters moment. Although it is beyond the purview of this article, an adequate rendering of the depths of pleasure and revulsion, attachment and separation, and commitment to ideologies of categorical sex difference may involve the integration of a fourth level of analysis: gender at the level of personality (Chodorow, 1999). Object relations theory has fallen out of vogue in feminist sociology in recent years, but as Williams (1993) has argued, it might be most useful in revealing the mostly hidden social power of gender to shape people's unconscious predispositions to various structural contexts, cultural symbols, and interactional moments.

References

Acker, J. (1990). Hierarchies, jobs, bodies: A theory of gendered organizations. *Gender & Society, 4*, 139–158.

Adler, P. A., & Adler, P. (1998). *Peer power: Preadolescent culture and identity.* New Brunswick, NJ: Rutgers University Press.

Attfield, J. (1996). Barbie and Action Man: Adult toys for girls and boys, 1959–93. In P. Kirkham (Ed.), *The gendered object* (pp. 80–89). Manchester, England: Manchester University Press.

Boyle, M., & McKay, J. (1995). "You leave your troubles at the gate": A case study of the exploitation of older women's labor and "leisure" in sport. *Gender & Society, 9*, 556–576.

Bradbard, M. (1985). Sex differences in adults' gifts and children's toy requests. *Journal of Genetic Psychology, 145*, 283–284.

Butler, J. (1990). *Gender trouble: Feminism and the subversion of identity.* New York, NY: Routledge.

Campenni, C. E. (1999). Gender stereotyping of children's toys: A comparison of parents and nonparents. *Sex Roles, 40*, 121–138.

Chodorow, N. J. (1999). *The power of feelings: Personal meanings in psychoanalysis, gender, and culture.* New Haven, CT: Yale University Press.

Connell, R. W. (1987). *Gender and power.* Stanford, CA: Stanford University Press.

Connell, R. W. (1989). Cool guys, swots and wimps: The interplay of masculinity and education. *Oxford Review of Education, 15*, 291–303.

DuCille, A. (1994). Dyes and dolls: Multicultural Barbie and the merchandising of difference. *Differences: A Journal of Cultural Studies, 6*, 46–68.

Dworkin, S. L., & Messner, M. A. (1999). Just do . . . what?: Sport, bodies, gender. In M. Marx Ferree, J. Lorber, & B. B. Hess (Eds.), *Revisioning gender* (pp. 341–361). Thousand Oaks, CA: Sage.

Etaugh, C., & Liss, M. B. (1992). Home, school, and playroom: Training grounds for adult gender roles. *Sex Roles, 26*, 129–147.

Heywood, L., & Drake, J. (Eds.). (1997). *Third wave agenda: Being feminist, doing feminism.* Minneapolis, MN: University of Minnesota Press.

Hochschild, A. R. (1994). The commercial spirit of intimate life and the abduction of feminism: Signs from women's advice books. *Theory, Culture & Society, 11*, 1–24.

Jordan, E., & Cowan, A. (1995). Warrior narratives in the kindergarten classroom: Renegotiating the social contract? *Gender & Society, 9*, 727–743.

Kessler, S. J., & McKenna, W. (1978). *Gender: An ethnomethodological approach*. New York, NY: John Wiley.

Klein, M. (1997). Duality and redefinition: Young feminism and the alternative music community. In L. Heywood & J. Drake (Eds.), *Third wave agenda: Being feminist, doing feminism* (pp. 207–225). Minneapolis, MN: University of Minnesota Press.

Lorber, J. (1994). *Paradoxes of gender*. New Haven, CT: Yale University Press.

McGuffy, C. S., & Rich, B. L. (1999). Playing in the gender transgression zone: Race, class and hegemonic masculinity in middle childhood. *Gender & Society, 13*, 608–627.

Messner, M. A. (1992). *Power at play: Sports and the problem of masculinity*. Boston, MA: Beacon Press.

Pope, H. G., Jr., Olivarda, R., Gruber, A., & Borowiecki, J. (1999). Evolving ideals of male body image as seen through action toys. *International Journal of Eating Disorders, 26*, 65–72.

Raag, T., & Rackliff, C. L. (1998). Preschoolers' awareness of social expectations of gender: Relationships to toy choices. *Sex Roles, 38*, 685–700.

Rand, E. (1998). Older heads on younger bodies. In H. Jenkins (Ed.), *The children's culture reader* (pp. 382–393). New York, NY: New York University Press.

Risman, B. (1998). *Gender vertigo: American families in transition*. New Haven, CT: Yale University Press.

Robinson, C. C., & Morris, J. T. (1986). The gender-stereotyped nature of Christmas toys received by 36-, 48-, and 60-month-old children: A comparison between nonrequested vs. requested toys. *Sex Roles, 15*, 21–32.

Rogers, M. F. (1999). *Barbie culture*. Thousand Oaks, CA: Sage.

Saltzman Chafetz, J., & Kotarba, J. A. (1999). Little League mothers and the reproduction of gender. In J. Coakley & P. Donnelly (Eds.), *Inside sports* (pp. 46–54). London, England: Routledge.

Seiter, E. (1995). *Sold separately: Parents and children in consumer culture*. New Brunswick, NJ: Rutgers University Press.

Spigel, L. (Forthcoming). Barbies without Ken: Femininity, feminism, and the art-culture system. In L. Spigel (Ed.), *Sitting room only: Television, consumer culture and the suburban home*. Durham, NC: Duke University Press.

Thorne, B. (1993). *Gender play: Girls and boys in school*. New Brunswick, NJ: Rutgers University Press.

Walters, S. D. (1999). Sex, text, and context: (In) between feminism and cultural studies. In M. M. Ferree, J. Lorber, & B. B. Hess (Eds.), *Revisioning gender* (pp. 222–257). Thousand Oaks, CA: Sage.

West, C., & Zimmerman, D. H. (1987). Doing gender. *Gender & Society, 1*, 125–151.

Williams, C. (1993). Psychoanalytic theory and the sociology of gender. In P. England (Ed.), *Theory on gender, gender on theory* (pp. 131–149). New York, NY: Aldine.

6

"Girls Just Aren't Interested"

• •

The Social Construction of Interest in Girls' Sport

CHERYL COOKY

I entered into graduate school in the mid-1990s interested in girls' participation in sports and, in particular, the ways in which sports had, or had not, changed since I was a girl playing sports in junior high and high school in the mid to late 1980s. I was struck by the cultural acceptance and celebration of female athletes and female physicality within popular discourses and specifically Girl Power discourses that seemed ubiquitous at the time. This cultural celebration was in stark contrast not only to my experience growing up, wherein girls who played sports were tomboys at best or "chicks with dicks" at worst, but what I imagined was the experience of girls in low-income urban communities, who are predominantly girls of color and immigrant girls. I wondered, What type of access do girls in low-income communities have to sport? If so, what were those opportunities like, and how did girls come to understand themselves as female athletes? This chapter is based on my dissertation research,

Source: "'Girls just aren't interested': The social construction of interest in girls' sport," by C. Cooky, 2009, *Sociological Perspectives, 52*(2), pp. 259–284, doi:10.1525/sop.2009.52.2.259. Copyright 2009 by Pacific Sociological Association. Reprinted with permission of Sage Publications.

a participant observation study of recreational sports programs designed to increase opportunities for low-income urban girls in the Los Angeles metropolitan region. This study is a qualitative investigation into two recreational parks and the sports programs offered to girls. I spent many hours "in the field" observing the girls and the programs, attending practices and games as well as team picture days, end-of-the-season award ceremonies, and other events. As is common in qualitative research, the questions that a researcher may have when they begin a study often shift once they become immersed in the field. In this case, I had originally planned to talk to girls about what it meant for them to be a female athlete and whether and how this corresponded with wider cultural discourses of female physicality and athleticism. Instead, I found myself drawn to the ways in which the beliefs of the adult organizers were shaping the implementation of the sports program itself. Cultural beliefs regarding girls' interest in sports emerged from my field notes as quite salient to understanding the girls' experiences in that context. Influenced by the work of Michael Messner (see chapter 8), who was my dissertation advisor at the time, I turned the analytical lens toward an investigation of how girls' interest in sport is socially constructed at the levels of structure, culture, and interaction. The main findings from this research reveal the ways in which gendered cultural beliefs and ideologies shape how sports programs are designed and implemented, as well as how adults interact with girl athletes. The findings also demonstrate that cultural beliefs and ideologies are not accepted wholesale, and in fact individuals have agency to reproduce or transform gender relations.

—Cheryl Cooky

Girls just aren't interested in sport.
—Coach Andre, Centerville Girls Play
Los Angeles (GPLA)

A dominant American ideology posits that creating new structures of opportunity or expanding existing structures so that they are inclusive of minorities will increase the number of unrepresented groups in those structures. This ideology, frequently reproduced in girls' sport (Cooky & McDonald, 2005; Shakib & Dunbar, 2002), echoes the tenets of liberal political philosophy. However, increased structures of opportunity do not necessarily lead to an increased acceptance of minorities among dominant groups (Bonilla-Silva, 2003; Messner, 2002). Where this strategy fails is in its inability to alter persisting sexist and/or racist ideologies that often serve to legitimate institutional discrimination (Bonilla-Silva, 2003).

Sport has been, and continues to be, a contested terrain wherein real and symbolic boundaries have been drawn to limit access for racial minorities, women, gays and lesbians, and other disadvantaged members of society (Dworkin & Messner, 2002). Historically, girls and women have encountered resistance to their participation (Cahn, 1994; Hargreaves, 1994). Resistance against women's presence in sport continues today as a result of sport's historical foundation to teach boys and men hegemonic masculinity during a time when their lives were becoming increasingly "feminized"—an outcome of the dramatic changes in work, family, and leisure during the 20th century (Burstyn, 1999). For example, in their research on male and female high school sport participation, Shakib and Dunbar (2002) found that high school students viewed girls' basketball as "less than" boys' basketball and that girls' basketball had lower social value, even though the girls' team ranked higher than the boys' team at this particular high school. Based on these findings, the authors rightfully question the potential for girls' sport participation to challenge the gender order (Shakib & Dunbar, 2002).

As a result of the significant increase in the number of women and girls participating in sports over the past 37 years, it is now a commonly held belief that girls and women have ample opportunities to participate in sport and, consequently, that girls and women who do not participate choose to do so because they simply lack interest in sport. While statistics demonstrate that girls are participating in sport in greater numbers than ever before (Carpenter & Acosta, 2005), there are still many girls who do not participate because of limited opportunities, structural barriers, and gender ideologies (Messner, 2002). As Messner (2002) argues, despite the growth of women's sports in recent years, there remains a "contested, but still powerful 'center' of sport" (p. xx). This sport center continues to be constructed by and for men (Messner, 2002). In this chapter, I argue that in order to assess the degree to which structures of opportunity have impacted gender equality, researchers must not simply consider the inclusion of girls and women into the structure of sport but must more importantly consider *how* women and girls are included in those structures.

Girls' participation in the institution of sport is of significant concern for sociologists, feminists, educators, and girl advocacy groups, such as Girls Inc. and Girl Scouts of America. This is because girls' sport participation is linked to positive social outcomes—for example, improved academic performance and self-esteem. Sport can also empower girls. Indeed, youth sport groups such as the Afghan Youth Sport Exchange encourage Afghani girls to play sport in order to empower their lives and to challenge the oppressive gender proscriptions of the Taliban regime. Moreover, in the United States, the naturalization of gender difference has historically served as a justification for gendered inequality in access and opportunity (Hargreaves, 1994). Sport, as a bodily performance, is one of the few remaining social institutions in our society where the ostensibly natural differences between men and women are reproduced (Dowling, 2000). Thus girls' and women's participation in sport can potentially be empowering because it challenges the very foundations upon which gender inequality is based (Messner, 2002). An understanding of the social structure of sport and the social processes that occur in that social institution with respect to girls' participation has implications not only for those who study sport but also for sociologists concerned with social equality and social change, for feminists concerned with gender equality, and for educators and advocates who wish to improve the lives of girls.

Access to sport opportunities is necessary for young girls to participate. However, many young girls, especially girls of color and girls from low-income communities, have limited sport opportunities (Sabo, Miller, Melnick, & Heywood, 2004). This lack of opportunity is based on a number of factors, including lack of transportation to and from sport activities; lack of funds to pay for equipment and registration fees; lack of organizations that provide sport to girls in urban communities; lack of space and facilities in urban communities; societal gender roles, which often confine girls to the home or limit their mobility outside the home; and societal ideologies that conflate athleticism with masculinity (Sabo et al., 2004). In their summary of current research on physical activity and sport in the lives of American girls, Sabo et al. note that a significant barrier to girls' full participation in sport is the sociocultural assumption that *girls "naturally" lack interest in sport* (Sabo et al., 2004, emphasis added). For girls of color, because of race, gender, and class inequalities, the essentialist assumption that girls "just aren't interested" in sport serves as an additional constraint.

Sport is a primary site for the study of classic sociological and feminist concerns regarding agency and structural constraint (Dworkin & Messner, 2002). As a significant social and cultural institution, sport allows sociologists to uncover the ways in which ostensibly "objective" understandings of gender differences are socially constructed through the complex array of dynamics between structures, cultural ideologies, and agency. More broadly, this article will explore the social processes by which interest is socially constructed, specifically how cultural ideologies shape social structure, how formal and informal social structures can enable and constrain social actors, and how social actors enact various forms of agency that can be either reproductive of, or resistant to, social structure and constraint. Qualitative analysis of a girls' sport program for low-income minority girls reveals the complex dynamic between structure and culture that socially constructs girls' interest in sport in everyday social interactions. Based on participant observations and interviews, girls' interest in sport is constructed, contextualized, and understood through this complex interplay of structure, agency, and culture. Thus this study sheds light on the structural dynamics in sport, which will provide researchers, advocates, and educators with a thorough understanding of the potential and limitations of liberal strategies to bring about social change.

Structure and Agency in Sport

Theoretical debates regarding the relationship between structure and agency have been central to the discipline of sociology since its inception. Giddens's theories of structuration provide linkages between structure and agency such that there is a recursive relationship rather than a unidirectional cause-and-effect dynamic (Gieryn, 2000). Most sociologists today recognize the need to consider structure, culture, and agency in our understandings of social life (Hays, 1994; Messner, 2002). Indeed, debates regarding the primacy of structure or agency in sociological theory are rendered insignificant when one considers how individuals constitute and are constituted by social structure (Gieryn, 2000). Fine (1992) argued for the importance of moving beyond binary theoretical discussions of structure or agency to link structure and agency in interactionist theories—what he calls "synthetic interaction." Fine writes,

> I suggest that we can make interactional sense of agents and their structures by recognizing that people act in situations on the basis of the meanings that previous contexts of behavior have provided. These contexts are shaped by structural forces, and, as a consequence, structures are embedded in the meanings that contexts generate. (p. 101)

In other words, structures do not exist outside of human interaction, nor do individuals act outside of structural forces and institutions (Giddens, 1984; Hays, 1994; Messner, 2002). Instead, structures are constituted through ongoing collective social action, while the experiences of social actors are constituted through structures of opportunity and constraint (Connell, 1987; Hays, 1994).

Giddens (1984) recognized how power is integral in understanding the relationship between structure and agency. He argued that "dialectic of control" exists where all individuals have some degree of power, given that they are able to transform, change, or alter the circumstances in which they find themselves (Sugden & Tomlinson, 2002). Even subordinate groups have some degree of agency to counter dominant groups (Giddens, 1984). On the surface, it may appear that Giddens suggests agency is always transformative or resistant. However, as Hays (1994) argues, agency can also be reproductive of social structures. Therefore, it is useful to conceptualize agency along a continuum that ranges from transformative or resistant to reproductive of social structures.

Methods and Methodology

As part of a larger research project, I conducted fieldwork on the Girls Play Los Angeles (GPLA) recreation sport program for one sport season at two different Los Angeles recreation centers. Field observations at each recreation center began in January 2004 and ended in April 2004, the end of the sport season (fieldwork was conducted concurrently at both centers). The GPLA program offered basketball in the winter/spring and softball in the summer. The fieldwork focused primarily on the basketball season.

In December 2003, I met with the Director of Gender Equity, who is responsible for the oversight of the GPLA program, to discuss my research and to receive permission to conduct observations of the program. The Director of Gender Equity chose each center to "provide an adequate representation of the GPLA program." Throughout the article, I refer to the two centers by the pseudonyms "Fairview" and "Centerville." At the Fairview recreation center, I observed three basketball teams of 8 to 10 girls. Of the three Fairview teams I observed, two held practice once a week for one hour. The other team held practice once a week for two hours. Each team had a competitive game scheduled once a week for one hour. I spent at least 60 hours at the Fairview GPLA (the actual number of hours is higher than this estimate because I also conducted observations before and after games and practices, as well as other GPLA events). Most of the girls on the Fairview GPLA teams were Latina; several were first generation. The race of the participants in the GPLA program was determined based on last names, informal conversations with the girls and their parents, and in some cases, the girls' own racial and ethnic identification.

At the Centerville recreation center, I observed three basketball teams in order to mirror the Fairview sample. Several teams were omitted from selection based on their practice schedules because they overlapped with the Fairview schedule. Of the three Centerville GPLA teams chosen, two of the teams had practice twice a week for an hour. The other team had practice four times a week for an hour. Each team also played approximately two games a week. Each game was an hour in length. I spent approximately 100 hours observing the Centerville GPLA program. Most of the girls at the Centerville GPLA were Latina (similar to Fairview). However, there were several White, Asian/Pacific Islander, and South Asian/Indian girls in the league. For reasons to be discussed later, most of the observations of the Centerville recreation center are from the games, rather than both games and practices.

In addition to fieldwork, I conducted open-ended, semistructured interviews with 13 girls (11 from Fairview, 2 from Centerville) at the end of the season about their sport experiences (for a detailed analysis of the interviews, see Cooky, 2006). While an equal number of girls were recruited from both sites, there was a low response rate at the Centerville site. This was due to several factors, including the girls' inconsistent attendance at practice and games, which made scheduling interviews difficult; the eventual high dropout rate in the program; girls' failure to show up to scheduled interviews, and the last-minute cancellation of practices by coaches and staff, which negatively impacted my ability to establish trust and rapport with the girls.

Each girl was asked questions on her sport background, why she chose to participate in the GPLA program, her likes and dislikes of the program and of sport, her thoughts on and experiences in the program and with sport, and her thoughts on how the program might be changed or improved. Other interviews were conducted with the Director of Gender Equity for Los Angeles Parks and Recreation regarding the GPLA program, the senior staff attorney at the California Women's Law Center regarding the *Baca v. City of Los Angeles* case, the site directors at Centerville and Fairview about their park and GPLA programs, and two coaches at Fairview regarding their experiences and coaching philosophies. Informal discussions with coaches, girls, and parents were also included in field notes and subsequently analyzed.

Fieldwork and interviews were collected and analyzed using qualitative research methodology (Denzin & Lincoln, 2003). While qualitative methods have multiple traditions, contemporary qualitative methods emphasize that social understandings, experiences, and structures are socially constructed (Denzin & Lincoln, 2003). Comparing two parks located in two different geographical locations (Centerville and Fairview) and studying the GPLA program, the experiences of coaches, girl participants, and program administrators was not done to provide a "comparative wedge" (Gieryn, 2000). Instead, studying two sites highlights the ways knowledge of the social world is constructed through social interactions and shaped by wider social structures.

The "sociology of accounts" is a useful theoretical and methodological concept that sociologists can employ in qualitative research to understand how individuals experience and identify with meanings and their social world (Orbach, 1997). Emerging out of Goffman's dramaturgical analysis, accounts are ways individuals socially construct their performance of self. According to Orbach (1997), for scholars who are interested in narratives or accounts, there is not an "objective reality" that can be studied through research methods. Instead, the narratives themselves become "real" as presented to the researcher. The sociology of accounts allows narrative scholars to "highlight the idea that subjective explanations develop and evolve in the context of cultural and social factors" (Orbach, 1997, p. 467). The sociology of accounts is also relevant to this study, for it emphasizes the importance of culture in individuals' construction of narratives and the way that culture may serve as a constraint to individual behavior (Orbach, 1997). Given this study's focus on structure, culture, and agency, the sociology of accounts is a useful lens through which to analyze interviews and observations. Based on field notes and interviews, girls' interest in sport is socially constructed but becomes understood by social actors as part of an "objective reality" through the social contexts and places in which girls' sports occur.

Originally, my goal was to study the social construction of gender and the ways adolescent girls negotiated femininity in recreational sport contexts. With qualitative methods, research objectives are data driven. An emergent theme from my observations was not how girls negotiated gender but rather the ways in which seemingly "objective" realities were socially constructed through the complex processes of interactions between structure, agency, and culture. It was these differences in the everyday interactions, despite the same formal structure of the program, that led me to explore how place becomes space in ways that enable and constrain girls' interest in sport (Gieryn, 2000). Thus considerations of place as space allow researchers to examine the dynamic, recursive relationship between structure and agency.

Baca v. City of Los Angeles: Can Girls Play in L.A.?

In 1998, five years prior to the start of my fieldwork, the California Women's Law Center worked with the American Civil Liberties Union to represent the West Valley Girls' Softball League in a case against the City of Los Angeles, *Baca v. City of Los Angeles*. The plaintiffs sued the City of Los Angeles, contending the city did not comply with California's Equal Protection Clause and had violated the civil rights of girls by denying the team equal access to the city-owned ball fields, which were dominated by male teams. *Baca v. City of Los Angeles* was settled out of court in 1999. As part of this settlement, the Los Angeles Department of Recreation and Parks was required to implement a girls-only sports league. This league was called "Girls Play Los Angeles" (GPLA), a year-round, gender-specific sports league program for "at-risk" girls, ages 13 to 15. According to the Director of Gender Equity for the Los Angeles Department of Recreation and Parks (a position also required as part of the settlement), the department defined "at-risk" girls as those from low-income families who live in particular residential communities in the Los Angeles metropolitan area. Although it was never explicitly stated what girls were "at-risk" for, based on conversations with staff, coaches, and participants, girls were understood to be "at-risk" for teen sex, pregnancy, and gang involvement. Another factor that girls were "at-risk" for was early dropout from sport. While boys' and girls' sport and physical activity participation decreases once they reach adolescence (Dwyer et al., 2006), the dropout rate for girls is almost six times that of boys (Garrett, 2004). Girls in this age group (13 to 15), particularly Latina girls (Denner & Dunbar, 2004; Jamieson, 2005), struggle with the pressure to conform to dominant notions of femininity that often conflict with sport participation (Malcolm, 2003). The GPLA program addressed these risk factors by targeting the program to girls transitioning into adolescence.

Sport and physical activity have been, and continue to be, viewed as a panacea for girls' physical and psychosocial problems. Research has found positive correlations between (some) girls' sport participation and academic performance (Miller, Melnick, Barnes, Farrell, & Sabo, 2005; Videon, 2002), self-esteem (Tracy & Erkut, 2002), and body image (Crissey & Honea, 2006). Research has also found a negative correlation between sport participation and the risk of teen pregnancy (Miller, Sabo, Farrell, Barnes, & Melnick, 1999). This body of research provided empirical support for women's sport advocates, who vociferously fought for Title IX and for continued support of girls' sport programs. During the 1990s, many school and recreation sport programs were developed to increase opportunities for girls to play sport, given the correlation between sport participation and prosocial outcomes.

The discussion of the broader context from which the GPLA program emerged illustrates how cultural ideologies impacted the origination of the GPLA program. Ideologies of individualism and liberal discourses of equality reinforce the belief that girls have the right to participate in sport and that social institutions are obligated to create structures of opportunity for girls to participate. These ideologies and discourses also provide a social context for which the girls and parents of the West Valley Girls' Softball League felt entitled and within their legal rights to pursue more equitable treatment for girl athletes. In addition, ideologies of gender equity shaped the formal structure of the GPLA program. The program is based on the notion that all girls, regardless of race or class background, should have access to sport opportunities. Research in the social sciences linking sport participation with increased levels of self-esteem, academic performance, decreased sexual activity, and other socially valued characteristics contributed to a cultural understanding that sport is good for the overall health and well-being of girls. Thus girls' participation in sport should be socially supported and encouraged (Messner, 2002).

Just Let Them Play: Title IX 37 Years Later

Title IX states, "No person in the United States shall, on the basis of sex, be excluded from participation in, be denied the benefits of, or be subjected to discrimination under any education program or activity receiving Federal financial assistance." This legislation, passed 37 years ago, continues to be credited for the significant strides toward gender equity in sport. Unfortunately, the significant changes in women's sports have created a commonsense cultural belief that girls and women now have ample opportunities to participate. Although structures of opportunity in women's sport exist more so than at any point in history, the Women's Sports Foundation (2007) estimates that 80% of universities and colleges are not in compliance with Title IX. Moreover, in popular culture, the sport experiences of White middle-class girls and women have come to serve as the representation of all girls and women. This representation obscures the complex ways in which race, class, and gender intersect to constitute girls' sport experiences and opportunities (Cooky, in press). The argument that "Title IX has passed and opportunities have increased; therefore Title IX is no longer necessary" is analogous to the argument that "Affirmative action has passed and women and minorities are now in colleges and the workplace; therefore affirmative action legislation is no longer necessary." Yet as sociologists consistently find, the gender wage gap continues, sexual harassment is still an issue in many workplaces, and women and minorities continue to be underrepresented in management and overrepresented in entry-level positions.

As with affirmative action legislation, throughout Title IX's history, conservatives have challenged the law and debated on how universities should prove compliance (Dworkin & Messner, 2002). Within the law, one way to prove compliance is by demonstrating that a given university's athletic program meets the interests of the underrepresented sex. The most recent controversy (as of May 2007) centers on the use of e-mail interest surveys to measure female students' interest in intercollegiate athletics. Many believe that if college women are not participating in sport, it is because they are not interested (Gavora, 2002). However, as Messner and Solomon (2007) argue, merely asking girls and women if they are interested in sport erases the complex dynamics of history, ideology, culture, and structure that shape girls' experiences and their interest in sport participation.

While Title IX does not apply to recreational sport programs, only educational institutions that receive federal funding, it has an indirect impact on recreational programs by shaping cultural ideologies of girls' and women's right to play sport and by reproducing ideologies of gender equality. In the post–Title IX era (here the "post" is used chronologically and not to suggest Title IX is no longer necessary), girls and women playing sport permeate our cultural imagery and challenge conventional gender ideologies that conflate femininity with weakness, frailty, submissiveness, and passivity (Dowling, 2000; Messner, 2002). The female athlete as a "cultural icon" expands cultural notions of femininity and female athleticism and may positively impact girls' participation in sport by providing girls with female athletic role models (Heywood & Dworkin,

2003). Despite contemporary American culture's embracing of female athletic competition, hegemonic ideologies of individualism, meritocracy, and competition, which are reproduced in sport (Garrett, 2004; Sage, 1998), reinforce the dominant belief that interest in sport stems from individually based desire or motivation. In the following sections, I discuss how discourses of interest in sport, as shaped by wider debates and controversies, were incorporated into the formal and informal structures of the GPLA program.

How Do We Know If Girls Are Interested?

Through my research, it became apparent that Title IX and ideologies of gender equality impacted the formal structure of the GPLA program. The Director of Gender Equity emphasized that Los Angeles was the only city to keep track of recreational sport participation rates by gender. This was done to ensure equal opportunities for both boys and girls. In *Baca v. City of Los Angeles*, the City Council stated that the "Raise the Bar" program (of which GPLA is a part) should increase the participation of girls in recreational youth sports by a minimum of 10% after year one (1999) and a minimum of 25% after year two (2000). The report also cautioned that eventually girls' participation rates would plateau.

In response, the Los Angeles Department of Recreation and Parks conducted its own "interest survey" with boys ($n = 247$) and girls ($n = 294$), ages 6 to 15, at local middle schools, high schools, and recreation centers. The survey included three questions that asked respondents how often they went to recreation centers; whether they registered for an activity at the recreation center; and when they came to the park, what activities they were most interested in overall. When I spoke to the director and the "Youth Sports Czar," their interpretations of the findings were that girls were not interested in sport. More boys, whether they were surveyed either at a school (44% of boys vs. 21% of girls) or at a recreation center (67% of boys vs. 47% of girls), reported sport as their main interest. Because girls in both groups reported a lower level of interest in playing sports, the administrators interpreted the data as evidence that girls were just not as interested in sport. When discussing their interpretations, the administrators admitted they had limited knowledge of statistics and were looking to hire someone with expertise in statistical analysis but were limited by their budget. Thus their interpretations were constrained by a lack of knowledge and resources.

If we consider the context in which the surveys were administered, important observations can be made regarding the social construction of interest. Both girls and boys surveyed at the parks reported higher levels of interest in sport compared to their counterparts surveyed at school. The administrators interpreted the data as evidence that categorically *all* girls are not as interested in sport as *all* boys are. Yet the surveys could also be interpreted as demonstrating that *some* girls (those surveyed at the park) are more interested in sport than other girls (at the school) and *some* boys (those surveyed at the park) are more interested in sport than other boys (at the school). This illustrates how structures of opportunity construct girls' interest in sport. Girls at the schools composed the group least likely to report interest in sport, possibly because they were the least likely to have experience in and exposure to sport programs. Indeed, many of the girls I interviewed mentioned that a number of boys' sports teams were offered at their middle school, while there were few, if any, sports offered for girls.

The Department's use of interest surveys to determine the level of interest in sport among girls sheds light on how interest in sport is socially constructed through the structurally reproductive agency of the park administrators. The use of the "interest survey" demonstrates how discourses regarding gender equality and Title IX shape the social construction of girls' interest in sport. It also points to the ways that gender difference is socially constructed through objective measures.

Making Space a Place: Organizational Practices at GPLA

When sociologists conduct qualitative research, space is an inherent part of the research context (Gieryn, 2000). However, Gieryn makes an important conceptual distinction between space and place. He notes that, unlike space, place is not the physical geography in which social life occurs. The places of our research are not just the backdrop; rather, they are an "agentic player in the game" (Gieryn, 2000, p. 466). Physical spaces become "place" when space is rendered with individuals' "interpretations, representations, and identifications" of that physical space (Gieryn, 2000). Following Gieryn's theoretical conceptualization of "place," the GPLA program becomes place as the program is constructed through actors' interpretations of girls' interest in sport. The structure of the GPLA program took shape through the everyday social interactions at the centers where the program was offered to girls. In the sections below, I discuss how the GPLA program is constituted through the meanings ascribed to the actions that occur in and through the centers. Girls' interest in sport was socially constructed through three main organizational practices: the scheduling of games and practices, the marketing of the program and recruitment of girl participants, and the organization of awards ceremonies and "outside" events. These organizational practices illustrate how the informal structure and the agency enacted to construct the informal structure played a significant role in enabling girls' interest in sport.

The Fairview GPLA Program: Enabling Girls' Interest in Sport

Scheduling of Practice and Games: Together, on Time

The scheduling of games and practices can enable or constrain girls' interest in sport. A consistent and reliable schedule of practices and games was crucial to participation, as girls relied on parents or other caregivers for transportation to and from the park. If games and practices were scheduled during a parent's typical work hours or during times when girls may have other responsibilities (such as taking care of younger siblings), girls would be less likely to attend and thus less likely to develop an interest in sport. Scheduling was also important in the construction of interest because girls had familial and school responsibilities that impacted their ability to play. In addition, the surrounding neighborhoods were not deemed safe for young girls, so scheduling of games and practices late in the evenings served as a barrier to girls' participation. For girls who were already "at-risk" of dropping out of sport and/or who did not typically play sport (as was true for most girls in the GPLA program), desirable and consistent scheduling of games enabled their participation.

At Fairview, practices for all three teams were held on Friday evenings between 6 p.m. and 8 p.m. Games were scheduled on Sunday afternoons. The Fairview center's practices and games were consistently held at their scheduled time. Coaches always attended practices and games, except for one game when a coach did not show up because he "wrote down the wrong start time on [his] calendar." He arrived at the gym just as the GPLA game had ended. Despite his absence, another volunteer coach was available to coach the team. The majority of girls regularly attended practices and games. There were some girls who missed a practice or game. However, they typically informed the coach in advance of their absence. On those occasions, girls were absent because of family obligations, birthday parties, quinceañeras, or family vacations. Only one girl, out of approximately 30, dropped out of the program. According to some of the girls interviewed, she dropped out because her father would not allow her to play. He feared she would get hurt when another girl at the park (not in the GPLA program) threatened to beat her up. The rest of the girls regularly attended games and practices and finished the entire season.

Parents at the Fairview GPLA program also attended practices and games, which was one way that parents demonstrated their support of, and interest in, their daughter's participation. Indeed, when I asked girls if their parents supported their participation, and if so how, all of the girls interviewed responded that their parents supported their participation. Every girl said they knew this because their parent(s) attended games and practices and cheered for them during the game. Yvette (all names are pseudonyms) said her parents support her playing because they come to her games, "and when I win or lost [sic], they would tell me, 'Good job, you can do it next time.'" Liz discussed the importance of parents enabling their daughter's sport participation. "They bring me to all the practices, which helps me a lot 'cause if not, I couldn't come."

When asked why girls might not play sport, 8 of the 13 girls interviewed (PBJ, Rosa, Caroline, Jessica, Laurie, Jamie, Diane, and Isabel) mentioned parents as a significant factor in whether girls play sport (other responses included physical disabilities or girls not wanting to play). Jessica (Fairview) thought girls might not play sport because "they live far and their parents don't have time to drive them or they don't care what they want." Isabel (Fairview) explains, "They [parents] don't like sports or they don't like their girls playing sports. There's a lot of parents that just think that it's not good for their girls to play sports."

Recruitment and Marketing: Girls Play Here

The second way coaches and staff constructed girls' interest in sport was through recruitment and marketing. It is apparent that marketing and publicizing the program was especially important for girls who typically do not participate in sport. Girls' interest in sport would be negatively impacted if girls were not made aware that a low-cost recreational sport program existed in their neighborhood. Recruiting girls in school or as they walked home from school enabled girls' interest in sport. Conversely, in the absence of marketing and recruitment, the potential to develop girls' interest in sport was constrained.

At the level of the formal structure of the program, the City of Los Angeles's Raise the Bar initiative required the individual park district sites to market the GPLA program in several ways: by hanging "GPLA: Girls Play Here" banners outside the facilities, by displaying a girls-only bulletin board, by including the Raise the Bar motto ("Achieving Gender Equity through a Continuous Commitment to Girls and Women in Sports") on all brochures and flyers distributed to the public, and by promoting girls' sports to the media. Although this was mandated in the formal structure of the GPLA program, adult organizers' agency shaped the implementation of the informal structure of the program.

Fairview displayed its GPLA banners on every outside wall of the main building. People who attended the park for other activities or passersby could see the banners from the street and from other areas of the park. Inside the gymnasium, a girls-only poster board included information about the GPLA program, practice and game schedules, and pictures cut from magazines of professional female basketball, soccer, gymnastics, and track and field athletes. The board also included magazine clippings of inspirational quotes. The quotes celebrated female athletic participation. The site director asked if I could bring in posters from my university's women's sport teams, which were later posted on the board. At Fairview, every practice schedule, game schedule, and all other materials printed for GPLA, including reminders for team picture day and off-site events like a field trip to a Los Angeles Angels of Anaheim game, included the Raise the Bar motto.

Jennifer, the Fairview center director, articulated a strong commitment to the GPLA program and to increasing the number of girls who participate. Besides the mandated marketing of the program, site directors and staff were responsible for the recruitment of new girls to the program. In order to increase participation, Jennifer told me she recruited girls from the neighborhood and actively approached girls who came to the park. Indeed, Caroline mentioned in her interview that she found out about GPLA from Jennifer. Jennifer approached girls hanging out at the park and told girls about the park activities, the GPLA program, and other sports that were offered to girls. She also recruited players from several neighboring middle schools by sending staff to talk to girls about the GPLA program. Fairview mailed out flyers to the families who had children participating in other recreation center activities.

In her interview, Jennifer highlighted the importance of getting girls involved in sport, citing the benefits girls receive when they participate—for example, increased self-esteem and a decreased chance of getting involved in gangs or getting pregnant. She mentioned that some of the girls at the park were known to date gang members. She thought informing them of the GPLA program might prevent them from "getting into trouble." Jennifer's accounts (Orbach, 1997) are informed by gender ideologies that position sport as a key site for the empowerment of young girls (Cooky, in press). Her accounts are also informed by social science research that links sport participation to addressing the social problems of "at-risk" youth.

Jennifer articulated that girls' sport participation could improve the lives of girls. Her accounts of her commitment to girls' sport participation were embodied in the structurally transformative organizational practices implemented in Fairview's GPLA program. This empirical finding is evidence that researchers must recognize the ways in which structure and agency intersect at the level of social interactions. It is also of use for those in public policy to demonstrate the importance of transformative agency in structures designed to address forms of social inequality and access to opportunity.

Awards Ceremonies and Noncompetitive Events: Celebrating Girls' Sport

The third way that adult organizers of the GPLA program constructed interest in sport was in the organization of the end-of-the-season award ceremony and the opportunity, or lack thereof, to participate in other noncompetitive events. Noncompetitive events were activities that were open to girls who registered for the GPLA program that did not involve girls' sport participation. At Fairview, this included a team photo shoot and a trip to a Los Angeles Angels of Anaheim baseball game. In the previous season, the Fairview GPLA girls went to a University of Southern California women's basketball game. These events fostered interest in the GPLA program and women's sports, celebrated the girls' achievements, and awarded the girls' participation. They also provided opportunities for girls to get to know one another outside the program. These events were especially important for the many girls whose first exposure to sport was the GPLA program. Adult organizers developed and enabled girls' interest in sport by exposing them to other sports.

Jennifer said she had planned the award ceremony in advance and contacted parents to coordinate which families would bring what type of food. She also told me she allocated funds in her budget to supply drinks and cake to everyone, as well as for decorations. The day of the ceremony, Jennifer decorated the entire gym with colorful streamers and balloons. Tables were covered with colored paper tablecloths and every team had food on its table. The girls invited me to their table, and their parents offered food to everyone, passing plates of rice, enchiladas, and tamales. Rather than joining their parents in the traditional home-cooked dishes, the girls instead chose to eat Pizza Hut pizza and KFC chicken and wings. While we ate, Jennifer went to each table, offering refills of juice and soda. She also cut slices of cake and personally made certain everyone received a piece. Turntables and speakers were rented for the event. One of the coaches, Hector, spun records after the awards were announced. The girls danced with each other to the latest hip-hop songs. A few girls even performed choreographed routines for the crowd. Everyone watched the dance performances and cheered with claps, whistles, hoots, and hollers.

Toward the end of the season, Jennifer organized a "team picture day." All the girls in the GPLA league were scheduled to have their pictures taken by a professional photographer with their teammates and coaches. Girls could also choose to have an individual photo taken. During the awards ceremony, each girl took home a frame with her team photo and individual photo. The team photo day brought the girls together and gave value to their experience in the program. Girls appreciated the award ceremony and said they proudly displayed their trophies in their bedrooms. Jennifer was responsible for hiring the photographer and contacting the parents and coaches. She also coordinated the event to ensure that each team had its picture taken and that enough girls were available that day for a team photo.

The Centerville GPLA: Constraining Girls' Interest in Sport

I opened the discussion of the analysis on Fairview, given the richer data that emerged from observations at that site. It is my contention that the "lack of data" gleaned from the Centerville site is in itself evidence of the constraints imposed upon girls' interest in sport. Despite my spending almost twice as many hours at the Centerville site, I had fewer field notes to analyze. I frequently left Centerville with little to no observations. As I discuss below, practices and games at Centerville were often canceled, relocated, or rescheduled without much notice. Coaches frequently missed games and practices. Many girls either attended events sporadically or dropped out of the program. At the beginning of the season, approximately 60 girls enrolled. Only 20 girls attended the championship game. About half of those girls went to the award ceremony.

At one point during the season, I asked Coach Andre, who was a basketball coach and staff member of the Centerville center, why more girls did not come to games and practices. He responded, "Girls just aren't interested in sport." He contrasted the Centerville GPLA program with the number of boys who participated in the Centerville boys' basketball league. Coach Andre understood the difference between the dwindling participation rates in the GPLA program and the high rates in the boys' junior league (approximately the same age range as the GPLA program, 13 to 16) through natural differences in boys' and girls' interest in sport. The low enrollment frustrated Coach Andre to the point where he suggested that Centerville "not bother having a GPLA program next year."

In the process of telling a colleague, Charles (also a sociologist), about my research, I discovered he grew up near the Centerville site and spent most of his youth playing recreational sports there. I asked if he would participate in an informal interview to discuss his experiences and observations of Centerville and the GPLA program. At the time I was conducting my fieldwork, he was coaching one of the boys' basketball teams. When I shared some of my initial observations, he said, like GPLA, the boys' junior leagues also suffered from low enrollment. In his experience, coaches typically attributed the low enrollment in the junior boys' league to the myriad interests competing for teenage boys' time, such as cars, work, and girls. Yet Charles said he never heard the same explanations for the low enrollment in the Centerville GPLA program. Instead, according to Charles, many coaches believed that girls did not participate because "girls just aren't interested." Charles's accounts may be surprising to some, especially given the ways that female athletes are represented in popular culture and the media. In this "post–Title IX" moment when girl athletes and girls' sports are openly embraced in a market-driven culture (Cooky, in press), when Nike tells girls to "just do it," and the female athlete is a "cultural icon" (Heywood & Dworkin, 2003), it may seem antiquated to suggest that people continue to embrace the conventional gender ideologies that link athleticism with masculinity (Burstyn, 1999). Yet this was confirmed by my observations and conversations I had with the Centerville coaches and staff, along with Charles's accounts of Centerville.

Scheduling of Games and Practices: "They (Don't) Pay to Play"

The Centerville GPLA program had what women's sport advocates would consider an undesirable scheduling of practices and games. According to a senior staff attorney at the California Women's Law Center, scheduling is a common form of gender discrimination in sport. Girls' teams typically receive the least desirable time spots to practice and play, while the boys' teams receive the most desirable time slots. At Centerville, the GPLA games were scheduled at 7:30 and 8:30 p.m. on school nights and at 7 and 8 p.m. on Fridays and Saturdays. The boys' games were held earlier in the evenings at 5 and 6 p.m. At the Centerville site, the boys' league end-of-the-season trophy ceremony was scheduled at 7 p.m., immediately after the boys' championship game. The GPLA league's ceremony was at 8 p.m.

While it may appear that the later start times are more desirable given the long work day of many families, for the girls of the Centerville GPLA program, the late schedule time constrained girls from attending the games. One reason was that the neighborhood was deemed unsafe at night. PBJ was one of two girls from the Centerville site I interviewed. When asked about the "bad things" about the Centerville GPLA program, she replied, "I have to walk to the park every day 'cause my mom and dad are working. My parents are a little worried about me going by myself. I try to stay on the streets with the signal lights where there's lots of people going by." Moreover, many of the late games took place during weeknights when many girls had curfew for the next school day. A game that started at 8:30 p.m. would not end until 9:30 p.m. Although I did not interview parents in the study, part of the interview with Isabel (Fairview) highlights the importance of the scheduling of practices. She explains, "My dad . . . doesn't like it 'cause we have to practice late. He's worried about us." Isabel participated in the Fairview program, where the practices were held much earlier in the evening (6 p.m. versus 8:30 p.m.). It is reasonable to assume that other parents had similar reservations with the late scheduling at the Centerville site.

Another way girls' participation and interest was constrained was in the unreliable and unpredictable scheduling of games and practices. Often, staff would cancel practices and/or games without advance notice due to the lack of participants or an absent coach. Most coaches at both sites were unpaid volunteers, young men who worked and/or attended college. Since the coaches were frequently absent for games, at times either Coach Andre or the site director,

Tiffany, would substitute. Despite not having any coaching experience or formal knowledge of how to play basketball, I was asked to substitute coach twice during the Centerville's GPLA season.

Girls' interest in sport was also constrained at Centerville because of the staff's relocation of practices to the middle school as a result of schedule conflicts. This happened frequently and prevented the girls from regularly attending practices and games. Often, girls were not informed in advance of the cancellation or relocation. One day I arrived for practice surprised to find there were no girls at the gym.

Instead, a team from the boys' league was practicing. Confused, I asked at the front desk and the staff employee said the GPLA practice had been relocated to the middle school to accommodate the boys' practice. As I walked toward my car to drive to the middle school, I noticed a girl in the GPLA program getting dropped off. She ran inside the building as the car drove away. She never showed up later that day for practice.

On another occasion, the Centerville center site director, Tiffany, inadvertently scheduled a minors' league game (a league for girls ages 8 to 10 whose parents pay the full registration fee of $65) in the same time slot as a GPLA game. The mistake was not noticed until minutes before the game. Girls from both the minors' teams and the GPLA teams had congregated in the stands and outside the gymnasium waiting for the boys' game to end. Tiffany made the decision to cancel the GPLA game. Many GPLA players showed up to the game in uniform and ready to play. They were quite upset when they found out that the game was canceled and the minors' teams would play instead. Several of the girls had been dropped off by their parents and now had to wait an hour to be picked up. As we stood outside the gym, many girls expressed their anger and frustration, telling me, "It isn't fair!" They explained that since they were older, they should be allowed to play. Upon hearing the news of the canceled game, Angelica, one of the GPLA players, exclaimed, "Big girls should go first! We should get a petition that says that!"

Upon subsequent informal conversations with the Centerville coaches and staff, I learned why the GPLA game was canceled: "They [the minors and major leagues] pay to play," Tiffany explained. The parents of the 8- to 10-year-old girls pay a significant amount of money for their girls to play. One main objective of the GPLA program is to increase sport opportunities for girls in low-income communities who would otherwise not participate in sport. While girls who resided in the same communities and participated in non-GPLA sports leagues at the Los Angeles Parks and Recreation centers pay anywhere from $65 to $120 to register for one sport, girls eligible for the GPLA program pay only $10. This fee includes the cost of registration, a uniform (jersey and shorts), and a trophy at the end of the season for all GPLA participants.

In their accounts (Orbach, 1997) of girls' lack of interest in sport, the Centerville staff said that since the minor and major league parents have more invested in the game, the younger girls should be given priority in scheduling. At several points during the season, the Centerville coaches and staff explained the lack of participation in the GPLA league as a result of the low registration fee. In response to the low attendance rate, one coach reasoned that if the older girls who participated in the GPLA league had to pay $65 to participate, their parents would make sure they went to games and practices. During my first visit to the Centerville center, both Tiffany and Coach Andre stated that because the girls get a uniform regardless of their participation, many girls sign up to get a pair of shorts and a jersey. According to Tiffany, this "is cheaper than you would pay for a pair of shorts and jersey at Sports Chalet" (a discount retail sports store). Coach Andre's frustration was rooted in his desire to get girls participating in basketball. His team was the only team that held practices four times a week. However, he combined his minor girls' (8 to 10 years old) team practice with his GPLA girls' (13 to 15 years old) practice. This inadvertently constrained, rather than enabled, girls' participation. I heard several girls on GPLA teams say they did not like playing with "little girls."

For the Centerville coaches and staff, there was "empirical evidence" to suggest that their accounts were an accurate assessment of girls' lack of interest in sport. At Centerville, there were higher attendance rates for the major and minor girls' leagues at both practices and games. In addition, more parents attended games and practices for the major and minor leagues. There were approximately 30 to 40 people in the stands for the girls' major and minor league games I attended and only about 20 to 25 in the stands at the GPLA games. The majority of people in the stands were GPLA participants who had finished a game or were waiting for a game to begin.

Recruitment and Marketing: "Lost Causes"

The Centerville site displayed the GPLA banner inside the gymnasium, which could only be viewed by those who were already at the center. It was only until the middle of the season that the banner was moved outdoors above the main entrance. The girls-only poster board was constructed simply and decorated sparsely. Practice and game schedules were stapled to the board and were surrounded by construction paper stars with the team names of the GPLA, major, and minor girls' league written in black marker. The Raise the Bar motto was not included on practice or game schedules.

I had informal conversations with Coach Andre regarding recruitment. He said he went to the middle schools in the area to recruit 10- to 12-year-old girls. I asked if he ever went to the high schools to recruit, given that the GPLA program is for girls 13 to 15. He flatly responded, "No." He explained, "If they aren't already involved in basketball by high school, it is difficult to get them interested in the program." Coach Andre said most of the girls in the GPLA program are "lost causes." "They get interested in boys and then they don't want to play sports. They don't have the motivation." Instead, he explained that he recruits the younger girls from the major and minor leagues. He thought this would be a more effective way of recruiting.

Awards Ceremonies and Outside Events: Separate but Not Equal

At the Centerville site, the only noncompetitive event was the end-of-the-season award ceremony. The GPLA award ceremony was scheduled for the same time as the girls' minor and major leagues' award ceremony. After the games, several of the girls went home and returned dressed in fashionable jeans and sweaters, wearing makeup, and had their hair styled. Some of the girls remained at the Centerville center after the game. They hung out with friends or watched the next game until the ceremony began. In the auditorium adjacent to the gym, there were several folding tables that were decorated by the parents of the girls in the major and minor leagues. These tables had streamers, brightly colored paper tablecloths, and balloons and were covered with food, treats, cakes, and cookies. One table had an ice cream cake from Baskin Robbins. A mother stood over the cake, cutting pieces for girls who were clamoring to get a slice. Another table had several boxes of KFC, while the adjacent table was covered with pizzas from Domino's. Girls from the major and minor leagues laughed and giggled with one another or talked animatedly with parents about the championship game they just played. All the chairs were full. Parents had even pulled chairs from other tables to accommodate all of the players, friends, siblings, and parents in attendance.

The minor and major leagues' tables were in stark contrast to the tables where the GPLA girls sat. Most girls from GPLA did not attend the award ceremony. The GPLA girls were sparsely distributed at their tables, with only several girls from a team sitting at a table. A few girls came with their parents and several were with friends, but most had arrived alone. The tables were not decorated, nor had the girls brought food. Tiffany provided drinks and snacks for all the girls. I stood next to her while she prepared snacks and opened two-liter soda bottles. She said she was upset that none of the GPLA girls had bought their own food to share. Visibly frustrated, she told me this had been a problem in the past. As the GPLA girls stood in line, she instructed that they were limited to one Twinkie, a handful of chips, and one drink. While we were waiting for the award ceremony to begin, the girls sat in silence, eating quietly. The GPLA girls left shortly after they received their awards. The minor and major league girls stayed well after the awards were distributed, celebrating with family and friends.

Coach Andre, Tiffany, and other adult organizers articulated that girls were just not interested in sport. Their accounts of girls' sport participation were embodied in the structurally reproductive organizational practices implemented in Centerview's GPLA program. This empirical finding is evidence that researchers must recognize the ways in which agency is not only freedom from constraint but also freedom to constrain. In other words, agency can be reproductive of structural constraints and inequalities. Discussed in more detail below, these findings are of import to those in public policy because they illustrate how reproductive agency can be a constraint when enacted in structures designed to address forms of social inequality and access to opportunity.

Girls' Experiences in the GPLA Program: "It's Not All about Winning"

The reasons girls participated in the GPLA program differed from what some of the coaches and staff thought their reasons were. In many cases, coaches and staff at the Centerville site applied what Coakley (2006) refers to as the "performance model" of sport to girls' participation. In the performance model of sport, demonstrating interest in sport is predicated on dedication, hard work, competition, desire to win at any cost, intensity, and an aggressive pursuit of athletic superiority as demonstrated through winning. When girls did not live up to these standards, the Centerville coaches and staff interpreted this as a lack of interest. One Centerville coach, frustrated that his team "refused" to play zone defense, decided to quit near the end of the season and did not attend his team's championship game. I spoke with Sabrina, one of the girls on the team about Coach Jose's absence. She explained that the reason the girls did not play zone was because most of them did not know how, either because they had not attended enough practices or because this was a skill they had yet to master.

From the interviews with girls and informal discussions, girls *were* interested in playing sport. For the girls of this study, the reasons and desires for participating did not coincide with the hegemonic definition of interest in sport. Rather, their reasons for participating centered on what Coakley (2006) refers to as the "participation-model" of sport. The participation-model of sport emphasizes participation for play, enjoyment, connections to others, and competing *with* someone, rather than *against* someone.

Most of the girls interviewed registered for the program to be with friends, not necessarily to learn how to play the game of basketball or to win. Lizbeth, from the Centerville GPLA program, told me she was very competitive when she played basketball for her high school team. However, when asked about the bad things about the Centerville GPLA program, Lizbeth felt that some people take it too seriously: "It's just a game. Some people care about winning so much that they forget how to have fun. It's not all about winning." Lizbeth understood that the GPLA program should embody the participation-model of sport. Although she constructed her "self" as a very competitive person, she participated in GPLA to "have fun."

The reasons girls participate in the GPLA program reflects the participation-model, wherein sport provides an opportunity to connect with others and to foster relationships. In the girls' accounts, many said they enrolled in the program because either a friend or family member encouraged them to join. Ana (Fairview) said, "It's fun to be around people that you meet and stuff and you try to get to know them and you play with them . . . and it's fun 'cause you get to do something that you like to do." Rosa (Fairview) said she got involved in sports because "my friends told me to get into sports." For Rosa what makes playing sports fun is "you get to be with your friends." When asked what she would do if there was no GPLA, Ana said, "I'd be at home doing nothing." Besides her motivation to play sports because she likes to "exercise and work," Lizbeth (Centerville) plays sports "to keep me busy and like not to be bored at home. You know, you're bored at home and you could be doing something good and probably getting better (at basketball)." For these girls, having fun was based not on competition or winning but on meeting new girls, spending time with friends, and getting out of the house.

Most of the girls in the program did not seem to mind too much if their team won or lost. If a team won a game, the girls would cheer and celebrate, but quickly the "high" wore off. Regardless of whether a team won or lost, the girls typically ran to the bench to get snacks and juice; talked about what they were going to do next; found their parents, family members, or friends in the stands; and headed home. Girls often celebrated individual accomplishments on the court rather than team wins. During a game at Fairview where the "slaughter rule" had been imposed (the rule states that if the point differential is more than 20, the scoreboard goes to 0–0 and score is no longer kept for the remainder of the game), Isabel and Trina cheered for their teammate Diane. Diane had struggled all season with her shooting. After her shot went successfully through the hoop, all three girls cheered and celebrated, despite the team losing by more than 20 points. When they returned to the bench, they celebrated their teammate's individual improvement.

In the girls' accounts, the reasons the girls said they participated in the program, what they thought was fun about the program, and the experiences through which they derived a sense of accomplishment and enjoyment were more reflective of the principles of the "participation-model" of sport. This was also in line with the formal structure of the GPLA program, in which participation was given priority and winning and competition was deemphasized. This finding illustrates how the social construction of interest was coconstructed among the girls. The girls of this study are interested in sport but in ways that challenge hegemonic sport structures.

Conclusions and Implications

Theoretical Implications

The findings of this study illustrate how structures, as they are embodied through the everyday interactions of their participants, simultaneously constrain certain *forms* of agency while enabling others. The research presents empirical data to demonstrate the ways in which agency is both reproductive of social structures as well as resistant to those very same structures. The study's findings point to the importance of social theories that simultaneously engage in multiple levels of analysis. The findings also expose the limitations of binary theoretical frameworks (e.g., structure versus agency) or conceptualizations of core theoretical concepts (e.g., agency as freedom from constraint). Building upon classical and contemporary theoretical frameworks on structure and agency, this study empirically advances the theoretical argument that dynamic interactions exist between structure, culture, and agency. It illustrates the importance of theories of structuration to assist in our understanding of social life, social interactions, and social meanings (Giddens, 1984). The relationship between structure and agency is not binary (Fine, 1992; Gieryn, 2000), nor does structure solely operate as a constraint to agency. The empirical evidence presented demonstrates that agency is simultaneously constrained and enabled by social structures, while social structures are reproduced and transformed through individual and collective agency in the context of social interactions.

Implications for Conceptual Understandings of Gender and Social Construction

In applying the sociology of accounts (Orbach, 1997), the research demonstrates how social realities are constructed through the complex process of interactions between structure, culture, and agency. As Orbach (1997) notes, accounts often reflect culturally normative explanations. Although each GPLA program differed in whether it was transformative (Fairview) or reproductive (Centerville) of broader forms of structural gender inequality, the adult organizers at both sites engaged in accounts that reflected "culturally embedded normative explanations" (Orbach, 1997, p. 455). In doing so, each site either enabled or constrained girls' interest in sport. This illustrates the power of individual and collective agency in shaping social interactions.

The Director of Gender Equity and the "Youth Sports Czar" socially constructed an account of girls' sport that reflected the normative explanation that girls do not have the same level of interest as boys. The accounts of the adult organizers at the Fairview GPLA program reflected the cultural discourses regarding sport as a site for empowerment of girls. They incorporated the formal structural philosophy of the program (which was also informed by cultural discourses) to advocate for girls in sport. The adult organizers at the Centerville program engaged in cultural discourses that positioned girls' sport participation in conflict with girls' "natural" interests. This account of the GPLA program is also constructed in a social context wherein adult organizers encounter difficulty enabling interest in sport, given the predominance of the "if you build it, they will come" philosophy that drives societal understandings of social inequality. The adult organizers at both leagues were given resources to address one structural barrier to girls' participation in sport (lack of opportunity due to access and money), but they lacked resources to address the myriad structural constraints that operate in their own lives and in the lives of the girls the program targets.

The sociology of accounts cautions against assuming that what people say about the meanings they ascribe to their social experiences and interactions is valid. Instead, as researchers we should question why a group represents others in a particular way and in doing so represents itself (Orbach, 1997). When considering the organization and implementation of girls' recreation sport programs, fieldwork and interviews highlight the ways in which girls and adult organizers coconstructed interest in sport. Researchers should consider how accounts cocreate and construct social interactions and understandings of social life in ways that manifest as natural or as common sense.

Promises and Limitations of Liberal Strategies to Address Inequality

The major emergent theme from my observations was the stark contrast between two seemingly similar centers. At Fairview, the adult organizers expressed commitment to girls' sport and accepted cultural ideologies that sport was a site for girls' equality and empowerment. At Fairview, adult agency was transformative of sport structures that had previously constrained girls' experiences at the Los Angeles recreation centers (as evidenced in the *Baca v. City of Los Angeles* case). Fairview represented the informal structural embodiment of the philosophical principles of the GPLA program (as constructed in the formal structure of the GPLA program). At Fairview, the transformative agency of the adults and the rejection of the belief that "girls just aren't interested in sport" helped to give life to everyday social practices wherein girls' sport experiences were enabled. The adult organizers and coaches valued the GPLA program and recognized the importance of the program in the lives of the girl participants.

At Centerville, GPLA girls' lack of participation, sporadic attendance, and high dropout rate served to coconstruct the gender ideology that "girls just aren't interested in sport." The informal structure at the Centerville site was emblematic of a larger problem that had plagued the Los Angeles Department of Recreation and Parks in the past: the unequal allocation of resources. Although the formal structure of the GPLA program had opened opportunities for girls to play sport with its low fees and accessibility to all girls regardless of skill or talent, the informal structure of the program, as enacted through the collective agency of adult organizers, constrained girls' participation.

While Title IX, civil rights legislation, and other forms of legislation are necessary for girls to assert their right to participate in sport and in other social institutions such as education and work, this study illustrates the importance of considering how structural opportunities become embodied through agency as enacted through social interactions. While the girls in the Centerville GPLA program, because of the complex social dynamics between culture and structure, did drop out or attend sporadically, this is not evidence to support the elimination of the GPLA program, nor is it evidence that girls "just aren't interested in sport." Instead, the success of the Fairview program sheds light on the importance of adult organizers and organizational practices for socially constructing experiences in sport. The adult organizers socially construct narratives. These narratives then become a part of an "objective reality" that frames subsequent agency, which for the Fairview program was resistant/transformative but for the Centerville program was reproductive of broader forms of gender inequality. Thus the social construction of interest is the process by which social actors' understandings of their social worlds come to inform their perceptions of the groups with which they interact.

The everyday organizational practices that served to reproduce structures of inequality point to the limitations of liberal strategies to increase opportunities for girls to play sport. Simply put, if you build it, they might not want to come. It is not enough to expand structures of opportunities and allocate resources. The findings illustrate the importance of agency in the implementation of sport programs. When adult agency is reproductive, as at the Centerville GPLA program, girls' interest is constrained; when adult agency is transformative, as at the Fairview GPLA program, girls' interest is enabled.

Implications for Social Change and Public Policy

The study provides empirical evidence to support the argument that increasing structures of opportunity alone is not enough to achieve equality. This is because structures are imbued with meaning in part by the agency of the participants within those structures. In addition, structure is intricately linked with ideology, and ideology shapes the ways in which social actors interpret and make sense of their worlds. Ideological interpretations then influence how we come to "see" and experience our social worlds (Lorber, 1994).

This study also exemplifies issues that transcend sport that have relevance to other institutions where similar issues and dynamics occur. As one example, Title IX prohibits sex discrimination in educational institutions that receive federal funding. While Title IX has had a significant impact on interscholastic and intercollegiate sport, it applies to other educational programs as well. According to an article in the *New York Times*, Congress ordered agencies to begin Title IX compliance reviews in 2006 (Tierney, 2008). Universities are also under investigation for discriminating against women in science. The National Science Foundation, as well as other governmental agencies, has established programs to investigate discrimination in physics, engineering, and other science disciplines (Tierney, 2008). Critics against the "Title Nining" of university science departments argue that the gender gap in science is the result of differences in men's and women's *interest* in science, rather than any institutional or structural form of discrimination. Research on gender inequality and science, engineering, and technology suggests that "equal opportunities politics" has been unsuccessful in addressing the "structures of gendered disadvantage" (Phipps, 2007).

The results and findings of this study may have broader implications to those working for positive social change in other social institutions such as race- and class-based efforts to eliminate educational inequalities and affirmative action programs to address gender and race inequality in the workplace and in the science disciplines. Public policy is one step in the direction of addressing the problem of social inequality. However, strategies for broad-based change must also consider the power of agency to be both structurally transformative as well as structurally reproductive as influenced by cultural ideologies.

Questions for Reflection and Discussion

While this study focused on girls' sports, in what ways are cultural beliefs about boys' interest in sport participation also socially constructed? What are some current examples of how girls and women continue to face the belief that they are "just not interested in sports"? What lessons can we learn from this study in regard to providing opportunities for urban girls to play sports? If you were to conduct this study today, what do you think you would find?

Acknowledgments

The author would like to thank Michael A. Messner, PhD, Stephan R. Walk, PhD, Sarah Banet-Weiser, PhD, Sharon Hays, PhD, and the anonymous reviewers of *Sociological Perspectives* for their insightful comments and critique; a special thanks to the girls of the GPLA program for sharing their lives. The John Haynes and Dora Haynes Dissertation Fellowship and the Women's Sports Foundation each partially funded this research.

References

Bonilla-Silva, E. (2003). *Racism without racists: Color-blind racism and the persistence of racial inequality in the United States*. Lanham, MD: Rowman & Littlefield Publishers.

Burstyn, V. (1999). *The rights of men: Manhood, politics and the culture of sport*. Toronto, Canada: University of Toronto Press.

Cahn, S. (1994). *Coming on strong: Gender and sexuality in twentieth century women's sport*. New York, NY: Free Press.

Carpenter, L. J., & Acosta, R. V. (2005). *Title IX*. Champaign, IL: Human Kinetics Publishers.

Coakley, J. J. (2006). *Sports in Society: Issues and Controversies* (9th ed.). New York, NY: McGraw-Hill Publications.

Connell, R. W. (1987). *Gender and power*. Stanford, CA: Stanford University Press.

Cooky, C. (2006). Getting girls in the game: A qualitative analysis of girls' sport programs. *Dissertations Abstracts International, 61*, 10A.

Cooky, C. (2010). Do girls rule?: Understanding popular culture images of "Girl Power!" and sport. In S. Spickard Prettyman & B. Lampman (Eds.), *Learning culture through sports: Perspectives on society and organized sports* (pp. 210–226). Lanham, MD: Rowman & Littlefield.

Cooky, C., & McDonald, M. G. (2005). "If you let me play": Young girls' insider-other narratives of sport. *Sociology of Sport Journal, 22*, 158–177.

Crissey, S. R., & Honea, J. C. (2006). The relationship between athletic participation and perceptions of body size and weight control in adolescent girls: The role of sport type. *Sociology of Sport Journal, 23*, 248–272.

Denner, J., & Dunbar, N. (2004). Negotiating femininity: Power and strategies of Mexican-American girls. *Sex Roles: A Journal of Research, 50*, 301–315.

Denzin, N. K., & Lincoln, Y. S. (2003). *The landscape of qualitative research: Theories and issues* (2nd ed.). Thousand Oaks, CA: Sage.

Dowling, C. (2000). *The frailty myth: Women approaching physical equality*. New York, NY: Random House.

Dworkin, S. L., & Messner, M. A. (2002). Introduction: Gender relations and sport. *Sociological Perspectives, 45*, 347–352.

Dwyer, J. J. M., Allison, K. R., Goldenberg, E. R., Fein, A. J., Yoshida, K. K., & Boutilier, M. A. (2006). Adolescent girls' perceived barriers to participation in physical activity. *Adolescence, 41*, 76–89.

Fine, G. A. (1992). Agency, structure and comparative contexts: Toward a synthetic interactionism. *Symbolic Interactionism, 15*, 87–107.

Garrett, R. (2004). Negotiating a physical identity: Girls, bodies and physical education. *Sport, Education and Society, 9*, 223–237.

Gavora, J. (2002). *Titling the playing field: Schools, sports, sex and Title IX*. San Francisco, CA: Encounter Books.

Giddens, A. (1984). *The constitution of society: Outline of the theory of structuration*. Berkeley, CA: University of California Press.

Gieryn, T. F. (2000). A space for place in sociology. *Annual Review of Sociology, 26*, 463–496.

Hargreaves, J. (1994). *Sporting females: Critical issues in the history and sociology of women's sports*. London, England: Routledge.

Hays, S. (1994). Structure and agency and the sticky problems of culture. *Sociological Theory, 12*, 57–72.

Heywood, L., & Dworkin, S. L. (2003). *Built to win: The female athlete as cultural icon*. Minneapolis, MN: University of Minnesota Press.

Jamieson, K. M. (2005). "All my hopes and dreams": Families, schools, and subjectivities in collegiate softball. *Journal of Sport and Social Issues, 29*, 133–147.

Lorber, J. (1994). *Paradoxes of gender.* New Haven, CT: Yale University Press.

Malcolm, N. L. (2003). Constructing female athleticism: A study of girls' recreational softball. *American Behavioral Scientist, 46*, 1387–1404.

Messner, M. A. (2002). *Taking the field: Women, men and sports.* Minneapolis, MN: University of Minnesota Press.

Messner, M. A., & Solomon, N. M. (2007). Social justice and men's interests: The case of Title IX. *Journal of Sport and Social Issues, 31*(2), 162–178.

Miller, K. E., Melnick, M. J., Barnes, G. M., Farrell, M. P., & Sabo, D. (2005). Understanding the links among athletic involvement, gender, race and adolescent academic outcomes. *Sociology of Sport Journal, 22*, 178–193.

Miller, K. E., Sabo, D., Farrell, M. P., Barnes, G. M., & Melnick, M. J. (1999). Sports, sexual behavior, contraceptive use, and pregnancy among female and male high school students: Testing cultural resource theory. *Sociology of Sport Journal, 16*, 366–387.

Orbach, T. L. (1997). People's accounts count: The sociology of accounts. *Annual Review of Sociology, 23*, 455–478.

Phipps, A. (2007). Re-inscribing gender binaries: Deconstructing the dominant discourse around women's equality in science, engineering and technology. *The Sociological Review, 55*, 768–787.

Sabo, D., Miller, K. E., Melnick, M. J., & Heywood, L. (2004). *Her life depends on it: Sport, physical activity and the health and well-being of American girls.* East Meadow, NY: Women's Sports Foundation.

Sage, G. (1998). *Power and ideology in American sport: A critical perspective* (2nd ed.). Champaign, IL: Human Kinetics Publishers.

Shakib, S., & Dunbar, M. D. (2002). The social construction of female and male high school basketball participation: Reproducing the gender order through a two-tiered sporting institution. *Sociological Perspectives, 45*(4), 353–378.

Sugden, J., & Tomlinson, A. (2002). Theory and method for a critical sociology of sport. In J. Sugden & A. Tomlinson (Eds.), *Power Games: A Critical Sociology of Sport* (pp. 3–22). London, England: Routledge.

Tierney, J. (2008, August 20). A new frontier for science: Title IX. *The New York Times.* Retrieved from http://www.nytimes.com/2008/07/15/science/15tier.html

Tracy, A. J., & Erkut, S. (2002). Gender and race patterns in the pathways from sport participation to self-esteem. *Sociological Perspectives, 45*, 445–466.

Videon, T. M. (2002). Who plays and who benefits: Gender, interscholastic athletics and academic outcomes. *Sociological Perspectives, 45*, 415–444.

Women's Sports Foundation. (2007, June 1). *Issues & action: Title IX compliance FAQs.* Retrieved from http://www.womenssportsfoundation.org/cgi-bin/iowa/issues/expert _results.html

7

Ready for Anything the World Gives Her?

• •

A Critical Look at Sports-Based Positive Youth Development for Girls

LAUREN RAUSCHER AND

CHERYL COOKY

This chapter developed from a collaboration with a colleague and friend, Lauren Rauscher. She and I have similar research interests related to girls' participation in sports. As a part of that research, we both found ourselves working with nonprofit organizations dedicated to expanding and improving opportunities to play. I was a graduate student when I did this work, and I struggled with tensions and, to a certain extent, a translational gap that I perceived between the critical feminist theories I had learned in my coursework and the realities of delivering sports programming to girls in urban communities. Indeed, it is much easier to address barriers like "access" by providing girls transportation via a school bus with a volunteer driver than it is to address barriers related to institutionalized sexism, entrenched poverty, or systematic racism—all of which are very real factors that present seemingly insurmountable barriers to girls' access and opportunities in sports. I felt conflicted about my presence in these nonprofit spaces, as it felt like I had the "solutions" to the problems girls faced (based on my knowledge of feminist sociological theories), or at the very least, it seemed that I knew the "real" reasons why girls were not able to participate in sports and the programs seemed unable to address those "real" reasons or deliver on the solutions. These dilemmas seem always present, albeit in the background, influencing and shaping but never fully addressed or acknowledged. After listening to a conference presentation Rauscher delivered to the Society for the Study of Social Problems, I realized how much our perspectives and experiences overlapped and suggested that we collaborate. This chapter features one of those collaborations. We would chat on the phone about our observations, experiences, and shared desire to see the lives of girls improved. We each appreciated the barriers to delivering quality sports programming to girls. We saw many limitations to the conventional approaches. This chapter is our attempt to offer a feminist sociological critique regarding youth development programs. As we discuss in this chapter, often these programs focus on the individual girl and her immediate context to the neglect of larger institutional and cultural factors that that also shape her life. On the one hand, many sports-based youth development programs hope to improve the lives of girls through sports, yet on the other, programs are not always designed or equipped to address the social and political context in which girls reside. This chapter is an attempt to bring to light these factors and to encourage research on developing, designing, and implementing programs to utilize a "transformative" social justice approach to youth sports development.

—Cheryl Cooky

Introduction

Girl-centered sport and physical activity programs that are grounded in a positive youth development approach have grown tremendously in the United States since the mid-1990s. These programs use sport and physical activity as the context to teach girls life skills—such as confidence and leadership—that are believed to be transferrable to other domains and ultimately foster optimal, healthy development (Holt & Neely, 2011; Perkins & Noam, 2007; Weiss, 2008, 2011; Weiss, Kipp, & Bolter, 2012a). Girls on the Run, the Women's Sports Foundation's GoGirlGo! curricula, and Sporting Chance through Girls Inc. (n.d.) operate in hundreds of cities across the United States. Other programs are city specific, such as PowerPlay in New York City (PowerPlay NYC., n.d.), Girls in the Game in Chicago (Girls in the Game, n.d.), and Girls Row Boston (Community Rowing, Rowing for all, n.d.). Girls are participating in these programs in record numbers. GoGirlGo! has reached almost one million girls since its inception in 2001 (Women's Sports Foundation, n.d.); Girls on the Run began in 1996 and now serves close to 130,000 girls annually in more than 200 cities (Girls on the Run, n.d.); and hundreds of girls participate in local programs each year.

While research on the efficacy of sports-based positive youth development is limited (Tucker Center for Research, 2007; Weiss, 2011), recent studies suggest that some programs in the United States are achieving success (Weiss et al., 2012a; Gabriel, Debate, High, & Racine, 2011). Evaluation research conducted in the United States demonstrates that participation in sport-based positive youth development programs improves girls' body esteem and self-worth and that youth use interpersonal and self-management tools learned through sport in other domains (Ciccomascolo & Grossi, 2008; Debate, Gabriel, Zwald, Huberty, & Zhang, 2009; Frelich, Patterson, & Romack, 2005; Kater, Rohwer, & Londre, 2002; Waldron, 2007; Warner, Dixon, & Schumann, 2009; Weiss et al., 2012).

Our assessment of the literature and programming efforts also highlights a significant gap in the theoretical assumptions of girl-centered, sport-based positive youth development. This gap raises the question of how instrumental these programs can be in promoting optimal development for girls, so that girls can "take charge of their lives" (Girls on the Run of Puget Sound, n.d., para. 1) and "define the future on their own terms" (Girls on the Run, n.d., para. 1). We argue that absent from the positive youth development approach and youth sport psychology is a focus on the complexity of sport and physical activity, particularly within a critical gendered context. The emphasis on individual girls and their immediate social contexts (e.g., coaches, families, and peers) is not surprising given the developmental psychology origins of sport-based positive youth development (Holt & Neely, 2011; Weiss, 2008). A feminist perspective, however, allows a broader lens to situate girls' lives and to mobilize social action necessary for the broad-based changes that many programs wish to achieve.

In this paper, we respond to calls for a multidisciplinary approach to sport-based positive youth development (Weiss, 2008), by adding a feminist sociological perspective (Taft, 2010; Coakley, 2011). We wish to expand how sport-based positive youth development is conceptualized and implemented so that girls may be positively impacted on both individual and collective levels. We argue that a feminist sociological lens enables one to see how the current approach to sport-based positive youth development for girls in the United States presents a paradox: Sport participation and physical activity can improve girls' lives along numerous psychosocial dimensions, yet without meaningful attention to the social and political context of gender and girls' lives in particular, sport-based positive youth development programs risk unwittingly maintaining the gender status quo. We discuss three specific critiques to illustrate this paradox: (1) the emphasis on the individual and the immediate context of girls' lives masks larger systems of inequality and privilege, (2) the use of postfeminism narratives—such as Girl Power—suggest that girls live in a world beyond sexism, and (3) the focus on reducing the childhood "obesity epidemic" through fitness contributes to harmful fat phobic messages for girls (Campos, Saguy, Ernsberger, Oliver, & Gaesser, 2006). We close with recommendations for scholars and practitioners. Our goal is for future programs to build on their existing strengths to make a more meaningful impact on girls' lives that address the cultural and structural, as well as individual and interpersonal, factors.

Girls' Sport and Sports-Based Positive Youth Development

In the 1990s and 2000s, there was a dramatic growth in feminist research on girls and women in sport in the United States. This was driven, in part, by the increased sport participation made possible by Title IX. (Title IX of the Education Amendments of 1972 states that "No person in the United States shall, on the basis of sex, be excluded from participation in, be denied the benefits of, or be subjected to discrimination under any educational program or activity receiving Federal financial assistance" [Title IX, 20 U.S.C. §1681 et seq.].) In contemporary U.S. culture, girls' sport participation has become more culturally accepted and celebrated despite persisting gendered ideologies that continue to reaffirm sports as a male preserve and maintain broader structural inequalities in girls and women's sport (Cooky, 2010; Heywood & Dworkin, 2003; Messner, 2002; Cooky & LaVoi, 2012; Sabo & Veliz, 2011). While sports in the United States continues to be male-dominated, male-identified, and male-controlled (Coakley, 2009), research conducted on U.S. sport consistently finds that participation in sport and physical activity has a positive impact on the social, psychological, and physical well-being of girls and women (Staurowsky et al., 2009; President's Council on Physical Fitness and Sports, 1997; Tucker Center for Research, 2007). More specifically, U.S.-based research demonstrates sport and physical activity is positively correlated with improvements to girls' cardiovascular endurance, bone density, and immune system functioning (Phillips, 1998), and lower breast cancer incidence in adulthood (Lagerros, Hsieh, & Hsieh, 2004). Girls' participation is also linked to positive psychosocial outcomes such as higher levels of self-esteem, positive body image (Crissey & Honea, 2006; Huang, Norman, Zabinski, Calfas, & Patrick, 2007), as well as a lower incidence of depression (Raudsepp & Neissaar, 2012; Boone & Leadbeater, 2006), teen pregnancy (Miller, Barnes, Melnick, Sabo, & Farrell, 2002), and suicide (Sabo, Miller, Melnick, Farrell, & Barnes, 2005). Moreover, sport participation in the United States is correlated with higher levels of academic achievement and performance in high school girls (Troutman & Dufur, 2007). Equipped with these research findings, girl advocates developed extracurricular programs designed to improve girls' lives through physical activity and sport.

Sport-based positive youth development is part of the larger positive youth development approach, informing many extracurricular programs, that has gained momentum over the past 20 years in the United States (Holt & Neely, 2011). Positive youth development is a strengths-based model whereby programs and policies focus on building adolescents' psychological, social, and cognitive competencies to promote optimal development and provide youth with the skills necessary to become healthy, contributing adults (Benson, Scales, Hamilton, & Semsa, 2006; Larson, 2000; Lerner, Almerigi, Theokas, & Lerner, 2005; Roth & Brooks-Gunn, 2003; Wilson-Simmons, 2007). This approach to youth development views adolescents as full of potential and capacities rather than from the deficit model that dominated youth development work during most of the 20th century (Sukarieh & Tannock, 2011). Sports-based positive youth development uses sport and physical activity as the context through which youth learn life skills and competencies—including motor skills and physical competencies—that can be transferred to other domains outside of sport (Petitpas, Cornelius, Van Raalte, & Jones, 2005; Perkins & Noam, 2007; Weiss et al., 2012a; Weiss, 2011; Weiss, Stuntz, Bhalla, Bolter, & Price, 2012b). By building and/or strengthening these competencies and developmental assets, youth should become healthy, engaged citizens who are less likely to participate in risky behaviors.

Positive youth development objectives are conceptualized in a variety of ways. For example, Lerner's (2004) 5 Cs include competence, character, confidence, connection, and caring; a sixth C—contribution to community—occurs subsequently if the first five C's are achieved. Benson (2003) specifies 40 internal assets (e.g., commitment to learning, positive identity, decision making, caring, responsibility, healthy lifestyle) and external assets (e.g., positive peer influences, service to others) necessary for youth to develop into healthy, productive, thriving adults.

To achieve these objectives and overall goals, the structure of positive youth development programming is key (Roth & Brooks-Gunn, 2003; Weiss, 2011; Weiss et al., 2012a, 2012b), particularly when the context is sport and physical activity, which can also foster skills and attitudes antithetical to positive youth development, such aggression, violence, cheating, and the like (Coakley, 2011; Holt & Neely, 2011). Program structure must be deliberate "to create a setting of developmentally intentional learning experiences" (Perkins & Noam, 2007, p. 77). More specifically, proponents of positive youth development argue that structured activity and learning must occur in a safe, empowering environment that fosters leadership development and that involves supportive relationships with both adults and peers (Roth & Brooks-Gunn, 2003; Weiss et al., 2012a, 2012b). Sport-based positive youth development in particular focuses on the importance of positive and informative coach feedback, meaningful peer interactions, supportive parental involvement, and a mastery-oriented motivational climate (Weiss & Wiese-Bjornstal, 2009; Weiss et al., 2012a, 2012b).

Developmental psychology and sport psychology provide the foundations for sport-based positive youth development (Holt & Neely, 2011; Weiss, 2008), and in turn, these theoretical assumptions set the parameters for organizational missions and programmatic aims, goals, and successful outcomes. "A developmental theoretical orientation is defined as one that seeks to describe and explain psychosocial and behavioral changes over time within individuals (intraindividual change) and differences and similarities in such changes among individuals (interindividual differences)" (Weiss, 2008, p. 435). As such, measurable outcomes of how sport and physical activity impact youth development focus namely on self-esteem, perceptions of competence, motivation, moral development, social relationships, leadership, resilience, substance use, body image, fitness, and motor skills (for reviews, see Coakley, 2011; Holt & Neely, 2011; and Weiss, 2008).

Although positive youth development programs formally recognize that building competencies should, in turn, lower the incidence of youth engaged in risk behaviors, many programs have informally operated on the philosophy that sports programming itself can reduce risky behaviors and protect girls from the social problems they may encounter in their communities, such as gang activity and teen pregnancy (Coakley, 2011; Cooky, 2009). This illustrates the distinction between what Sukarieh and Tannock (2011) refer to as the "old" 20th-century model of youth development and the "new" one of the 21st century: Instead of focusing on "at risk" populations, the "new" positive youth development model emphasizes the benefits of building strengths for *all* youth (for further discussion, see Sukarieh and Tannock, 2011). For example, according to Girls in the Game's website (Girls in the Game, n.d.) and annual reports, the language of the program is girl-centered, helping girls make healthy decisions with respect to nutrition, education, and other personal factors (such as self-esteem). Many of these programs (e.g., Girls in the Game, Chicago and the Women's Sports Foundation's Go Girl Go! curricula) have demonstrated both anecdotal and evidence-based successes (Warner et al., 2009) and represent an improvement over programs that relied solely upon sport to create positive social change and reduce "at risk" behavior (Coakley, 2011). Research also demonstrates the critical role adult organizers play in translating the philosophical elements of a program regarding how and under what conditions actual life skills are taught to the girl participants (Cooky, 2009). Therefore, regardless of whether a program operates under the "old" model of positive youth development or the "new," efficacy is always shaped in and through the agency of those responsible for program organization and delivery as well as the structural and cultural contexts that both enable and constrain those individuals.

Without question, these programmatic aims and competencies are important for girls, given the empirical evidence from the United States demonstrating that girls are more likely than boys to report lower self-esteem, particularly as they enter middle school and high school (AAUW, 1994), be unhappy with their bodies (Lowes & Tiggemann, 2003; Smolak & Levine, 2001), experience sexual harassment at school (Hill & Kearl, 2011), and trail behind boys in youth sport, particularly for low-income girls in urban areas (Sabo & Veliz, 2008). Without explicit attention to the ways in which broad social, cultural, economic, and political systems shape girlhood and girls' lives, the conclusion reached is that girls themselves must be changed rather than underlying systems that create and maintain gendered experiences and gender inequality (Brown, 2001).

Masking Systems of Inequality That Shape Girls' Lives

Drawing from an ecological model of development, positive youth development addresses how the context in which youth live impacts their development (Roth & Brooks-Gunn, 2003). According to human ecology theory, development occurs through interactions between individuals and various environmental systems embedded in one's communities and society, such as family, peers, religion, school, cultural beliefs, norms, and sociohistoric events (Bronfenbrenner, 1974). While Bronfenbrenner's theory includes the role that macrolevel systems, such as the social and cultural environment, have in shaping human development, today's positive youth development approach focuses primarily on youth's immediate context. The immediate context includes a child's family, friends, peers, school, and, in some cases, her neighborhood, to address the whole child as well as the structure of the programs themselves (Perkins & Noam, 2007). Given the research on how relationships among youth, their coaches, peers, and families shape children's sport experiences, sports-based positive youth development programs, scholars, and practitioners emphasize these specific relationships to optimize the positive assets that can come from participating in sport and physical activity (Weiss et al., 2012a, 2012b).

Yet girls in the United States and elsewhere grow up in a world marked by institutionalized sexism. And many girls live with the additional hardships of poverty, racism, heterosexism, disability, and physical/sexual/emotional abuse. Garbarino (1995) refers to these systemic forms of oppression as social toxins because they threaten well-being and damage the process of healthy development. While the "old" model of youth development that focused on "at-risk" youth acknowledged the role that poverty, family violence, and abuse played in the lives of young people (Sukarieh & Tannock, 2011), the recent shift to a strengths-based approach, grounded in resiliency theory, conceptualizes all youth as "assets," making it easier to ignore larger social issues and structural conditions (Coakley, 2011; Ginwright, 2006; Ginwright & Cammarota, 2002; Sukarieh & Tannock, 2011).

Indeed, many girl-centered, sports-based youth development programs obscure the way that gender is a social and political system that structures girls' lives. These programs do not directly address how gender intersects with other systems—such as race, ethnicity, social class, and sexuality—that create systems of disadvantage for some girls and privilege for others. Notably, as Ginwright (2006) succinctly argues, "one of the most significant challenges facing the youth development field is its capacity to confront questions of social inequality" (p. 41). As such, "we are left with an over-romanticized, problem-free view of youth" (Ginwright & Cammarota, 2002, p. 84). This view leaves girls without tools to understand the underlying sources of tensions and challenges they may face. Thus girls—and adults who want to support them—are likely to see themselves both as the problem and the solution.

While part of this shift can be attributed to the dominance of developmental psychology in the realm of sport-based positive youth development programs (Weiss, 2008), one cannot underestimate the hegemony of neoliberalism in the United States (and elsewhere) as an important contextual factor undergirding both programmatic philosophies and the very existence of the programs themselves. Shifting the burden of addressing the lives of girls from the state to the private sector (albeit often through nonprofit organizations funded extensively through corporations engaging in corporate social responsibility and cause-related marketing) illustrates how programs are enmeshed in a larger economic and political context. The discursive contexts in which these programs operate are imbued with neoliberal ideology, which emphasizes personal responsibility, individual-level empowerment, freedom from government intervention and support, preparing youth for the formal labor market, and consumerism (Chawansky, 2012; Coakley, 2011; Heywood, 2007; Sukarieh & Tannock, 2011).

Most sports-based positive youth development programs, particularly in the United States, envision girls' civic identities through this neoliberal lens, relying on psychological understandings of girls' problems while viewing the public sphere as a source of threat to girls—an unsafe space that stands in contrast to the so-called safe and secure spaces created in girls-only programs (Taft, 2010). Brown (2001) cautions,

> Without the opportunity and capacity to examine our own histories of bias, women—with the best of intentions—may mistakenly enact the role of cheer-leader: enthusiastically encouraging girls to be confident, courageous, and bold but leading them into hostile territory without preparing them well for the consequences they may face. (p. 4)

In contrast, a transformative approach to positive youth development engages girls in a sociological analysis of their lives, encourages girls to get involved with social change projects, and promotes girls' authority in the public sphere (Taft, 2010). This is similar to Ginwright's (2006) notion of a social justice-oriented positive youth development, where building a social and political consciousness is key to youth development. This is particularly important for girls whose everyday experiences are structured by institutionalized sexism and other forms of oppression (Brown, 2001; Ginwright, 2006). A critical consciousness enables girls to understand how external systemic forces and their immediate surroundings shape their opportunities, barriers, and experiences. Furthermore, it can equip girls with the tools to collectively make changes in their communities and in their culture.

Living in a World beyond Sexism: Postfeminism and Girls

In the United States, the idea that sport can be used to channel girls into pro-social behaviors is not new, and thus contemporary sport-based youth development programs must be situated within this larger sociohistorical context. Since the late 19th and early 20th centuries in the United States, sport has been understood as an important institution in developing the social, moral, and physical well-being of youth (Cahn, 1994). The philosophy of today's sport-based youth development programs for girls mirrors that of the Play Days of a century past. According to a how-to manual written during the 1920s on creating a successful Play Day program, sports for girls should be about equal opportunity, increased access to opportunities for all girls, teamwork, and sportsmanship (Duncan & Cundiff, 1929). Play Days were about extending sports to all girls, not just the most skilled. The authors of the manual advised that, "strenuous games requiring previous training, highly organized play and more than average athletic ability are not fundamentally sound in a Play Day program" (Duncan & Cundiff, 1929, p. 5). Rather, Play Days were seen as an ideal space to instill sportsmanship, the spirit of play, and teamwork. With the leadership and guidance of adult supervisors, girls would experience an environment that fostered health, physical efficiency, and the development of good citizenship. In this way, the Play Days and contemporary sport programs for girls both utilize sport to promote positive character development among youth.

Although similar in their objectives and goals, there are key distinctions between the Play Days and the girl-centered, sports-based positive youth development programs of the early 21st century. The Play Days were in part a backlash response to the first wave of female athleticism (turn of the 20th century in the United States, wherein mass numbers of women gained access to organized sports and physical activity in either educational settings or work-based sports leagues). Play Days emerged as a clear response against the competitive and so-called masculinizing effects of female participation in sport. The adult organizers of Play Days took a protectionist stance toward young female participants, using Play Days to shield girls from what were perceived to be the more dangerous aspects of sport, particularly competition and strenuous physicality. In replacement of competitive sport, adult organizers offered a different version deemed more palatable for young women yet would still provide the physical and social benefits of sport.

The sports-based positive youth development programs of the 21st century emerged not as a backlash to a wave of female athleticism (i.e., the second wave, post-Title IX), but as part of the larger cultural Girl Power movement, wherein girls' physicality was celebrated and encouraged and female athleticism was positioned as a "cultural icon" (Cooky, 2010; Heywood & Dworkin, 2003). Moreover, adult organizers of sports-based positive youth development no longer have the same concerns regarding the "masculinization" of girls and women who participate in sport. In contrast to girls' sport participation at the turn of the 20th century, sport now appears as a "normal part of girls' and women's everyday lives" (Heywood & Dworkin, 2003, p. xx).

Girl power refers to the cultural moment/movement in which the empowerment of girls in all realms of society, including sport, is embraced and celebrated. The most notable representatives of girl power were the all-girl pop group the Spice Girls, whose version of girl power, while empowering on an individual level and celebratory of girls' strengths, ultimately contained antifeminist messages, presenting girl power as a "non-political, non-threatening alternative to feminism" (Taft, 2004, p. 70). On the surface, girl power appeared empowering, yet it constructed barriers to both girls' activism in general and girls' engagement with feminist politics in particular (Cooky, 2010). Rather, empowerment was achieved primarily through consuming popular culture rather than through equal pay for equal work or the right to birth control (Cooky, 2010; Banet-Weiser, 2004). As such, feminist scholars locate girl power as part of a postfeminist historical and cultural context. Postfeminism refers to the notion that feminism made an impact; girls and women are now equal to boys and men, and thus political activism for gender equality is no longer needed (Taft, 2004). Kinser (2004) explains, "The only thing post feminism has to do with authentic feminism (. . .) is to contradict it at every turn while disguising this agenda, to perpetuate the falsehood that the need for feminist change is outdated" (p. 124). As such, there is no longer the need for girls and women to challenge male-dominance in any political way (Griffin, 2004).

Girl Power discourses were not limited to popular music and media; they also informed the U.S. government's public policy in the aptly named "Girl Power!" campaign. The purpose of this campaign (instituted in 1998 by Donna Shalala, Secretary of the Department of Health and Human Services, in conjunction with then President Clinton's President's Council on Physical Fitness and Sports) was to "encourage and empower girls to make the most of their lives" (United States Department of Health and Human Services, 1998). Health officials, educators, feminists, and girl advocates such as the Girl Scouts of America sought to empower girls by promoting sport and physical ability in order to boost girls' self-esteem, launching after-school programs to improve the lives of young girls, and working with girls in collaborative, community-based projects.

Given this context, it is not surprising that youth development programs with an expressed goal to improve girls lives were shaped by discursive narratives wherein girls' deficits included low self-esteem and body image and that sports-based positive youth development programs were informed by the research demonstrating a positive relationship between girls' sport participation and improvements in self-esteem and other social, psychological, and health benefits (Orenstein, 1994; Pipher, 1994; President's Council on Physical Fitness, 1997). At the same time, the Girl Power postfeminist narrative that girls can do anything is inherently problematic, especially when considering the goals and objectives of many sports-based youth development programs. Postfeminism emerged within a specific sociopolitical moment of neoliberalism, and conversely neoliberal discourse enables and sustains a postfeminist discursive culture. As Gonick, Renold, Ringrose, and Weems (2009) observe, neoliberal and postfeminism are connected in that "the effects of neo-liberal discourses individualize and de-politicize and have enabled post feminist discourses to thrive, since the individualizing, fragmenting logic works to destabilize collective movements like feminism" (p. 2). Thus the contemporary neoliberal, postfeminist context creates a paradox for girls in that depoliticized forms of agency are exercised within the constraints of gender difference (Gonick et al., 2009). In other words, the individualism of Girl Power in the mid-1990s positioned girls as individual agents responsible for their own lives despite the very real structures constraining girls. Moreover, since the mid-1990s, definitions of empowerment for girls and women have undergone rearticulations wherein empowerment is located within public and overt expressions of sexuality rather than within physicality, strength, and athleticism (Levy, 2005). In other words, at the turn of the 21st century, girl empowerment is intricately aligned with hypersexuality and "strip culture" more so than with sport and athleticism (Cooky, 2010; Levy, 2005). Girl-centered, sports-based positive youth development programs often are ill equipped, unable, or unwilling to address this cultural reality.

The "Obesity Epidemic" in Positive Youth Development: Producing Fitness or Fat Phobia?

Sports-based positive youth development programs in the United States emphasize the importance of building physical competencies alongside psychological and social competencies. According to the U.S. President's Council on Physical Fitness and Sports, motor and sport-specific skills; physical fitness; knowledge about physical activities, sports, and games; physiological competencies; and physical health are inextricably linked to the overall healthy development of youth within the positive youth development framework (Weiss & Wiese-Bjornstal, 2009). The physical health and bodies of youth are particularly appealing to many public health officials, child advocates, educators, and policy makers given the discourse and alarm about childhood obesity. Research on inactivity among American youth (Eaton et al., 2007), their body mass index (Ogden, Flegal, Carroll, & Johnson, 2002), and decreases in physical education requirements (Lee, Burgeson, Fulton, & Spain, 2007) have provided the foundation for countless public and private initiatives for intervention programs that link physical activity, nutrition, and weight.

On a national scale, initiatives such as "Let's Move!" (Let's Move!, n.d.), the Presidential Youth Fitness Program (n.d.), and the National Football League's "Play 60" (American Heart Association, n.d.) encourage American youth to make healthy choices about nutrition, increase their physical activity, and instill lifelong healthy habits. Obesity prevention underpins most of these initiatives despite scientific debate about the validity of an "epidemic" and dispute about the direct linkages between fatness and disease (Campos et al., 2006). While some initiatives are explicit in their mission to fight childhood obesity directly (Let'sMove!, n.d.), others implicate obesity in more indirect ways by positioning their mission of overall health against the backdrop of obesity statistics and an accompanying list of long-term risks and economic costs (American Heart Association, n.d.). They all, however, share a preoccupation with fat, and a major goal of these initiatives is a reduction of fatness and fat bodies. As such, these goals reflect the current context of healthism, a paradigm that equates thinness with health and fatness with disease and illness, which is the product of morally irresponsible individuals (Crawford, 1980; Lupton, 1995).

Given the pervasive attention to fat (Saguy, 2013) and the available funding, especially in the United States, to fight it, it is not surprising that many sports-based positive youth development programs wish to increase youth fitness and physical activity in an effort to reduce childhood obesity (directly or indirectly). Indeed, many positive youth development programs rely on outside funding to sustain programming, and in the last 5 years, 80% of nonprofit organizations and community-based programs reported significant fiscal stress in light of the economic recession; 40% reported that the stress was severe (Salamon, Geller, & Spence, 2009). While funding for youth sports and arts declined during this period in the United States, more grant dollars have been available for organizations whose programming helps reduce childhood obesity through increased physical activity from sources such as the U.S. Department of Agriculture, National Institute of Health, General Mills

Foundation, and the Robert Wood Johnson Foundation (Gillibrand, 2013). These efforts also dovetail with larger cultural discourses in the United States that fitness is linked to empowerment, especially for girls and women.

Wright, O'Flynn, & Macdonald (2006) warn however that health promotion specialists should "be cognizant of the ways that messages about health, about obesity, and about physical activity are taken up by young people" (p. 716). Qualitative research that probes the meaning of health, fitness, and healthy eating among young people finds that the meaning of fitness for girls and young women is inextricably linked to their body shape and size. Young women in Wright et al.'s (2006) study talked about "maintaining a balance of food and exercise to achieve a slim body shape" (p. 711), and they linked food to losing weight rather than its nutritional content. Similarly, Chapman (1999) found that women have replaced the term "dieting" to describe their control of food consumption, replacing it with "healthy eating," even though the outcome of weight control is the same. And Rauscher, Kauer, and Wilson (2013) found that preteen girls who said that being "fit" best described "strong and healthy" girls used language such as being toned and having four or six pack muscles, terms reflective of external bodily attributes.

These findings reflect the larger social and cultural construction of fitness (Dworkin & Wachs, 2009) whereby the logic has shifted from sport to aesthetic fitness, which emphasizes appearance over physical practices or measures of performance (Dworkin & Wachs, 2009). "Looking good is central to the 'empowering' solutions" (p. 157). Moreover, the meaning of fitness is gendered. For girls and women, being "fit" means achieving the athletic aesthetic, today's hegemonic feminine body ideal where women are ultrathin, curvaceous, and toned (but not too muscular), and they have flat stomachs, large breasts, and virtually no fat (George, 2005; Krane, Choi, Baird, Aimar, & Kauer, 2004; Markula, 1995). Attempts to achieve these unattainable ideals require constant body surveillance and disciplinary bodily practices, which also reflect moral citizenship and an investment in consumerism (Dworkin & Wachs, 2009).

Girls are inundated with messages about this body ideal; they are bombarded with both a culture of ultrathinness and fat phobia (Rauscher et al., 2013). Girls internalize these messages and "fat talk" from mothers (McCabe et al., 2007; Nichter, 2002), health care professionals (Teachman & Brownell, 2001), peers (Brownell, Schwartz, Puhl, Henderson, & Harris, 2009), and media (Klein & Shiffman, 2006; Levin & Kilbourne, 2009). As such, 40% of elementary-age girls report dissatisfaction with their body size (Smolak & Levine, 2001), and even younger girls, at 5 and 6 years old, want to diet and be thinner (Lowes & Tiggemann, 2003). In response, some girls engage in harmful dieting practices, excessive exercise, and disordered eating (Hesse-Biber, Leavy, Quinn, & Zoino, 2006; Levine & Murnen, 2009). Thus without a critical analysis of fitness, health, and weight, sports-based positive youth development for girls risks reproducing gendered bodily ideals that are detrimental to them (Rauscher et al., 2013).

Conclusion and Recommendations

In this paper, we have offered a feminist sociological perspective on sports-based positive youth development (Coakley, 2011; Taft, 2010; Weiss, 2008). We have argued that while sport participation can improve girls' lives along numerous physical, psychological, and social dimensions, sports-based positive youth development programs can also unwittingly reproduce the gender status quo in absence of meaningful attention to the social and political context of gender and girls' lives. We outlined three specific critiques to support our claim: (1) an emphasis on the individual and the immediate context of girls' lives masks larger systems of inequality and privilege, (2) the use of postfeminism narratives—such as Girl Power—suggests that girls live in a world beyond sexism, and (3) a focus on reducing the childhood "obesity epidemic" through fitness contributes to harmful fat phobic messages for girls (Campos et al., 2006). Each of these critiques is reflective of the theoretical origins of positive youth development as well as larger political and cultural contexts in which organizations, schools, and public policies operate—namely, neoliberalism, postfeminism, and healthism. We believe that by incorporating a feminist sociological perspective, sports-based positive youth development programs for girls are ideally situated to expand on their existing strengths by attending to the structural and cultural dimensions of girls' lives alongside their individual and interpersonal lives. Below, we offer insights from two critical youth development experts who model various ways to incorporate such changes, both of whom emphasize bolstering girls' critical consciousness and collective action to understand and challenge the environments that are stressful and destructive to their well-being.

First, Ginwright's pivotal work on youth development provides an excellent theoretical foundation from which girl-centered, sports-based positive youth development can benefit. Ginwright and colleagues argue that a social justice approach to youth development is key for groups whose life experiences, well-being, and overall development are influenced by complex structural systems, such as racism, sexism, and poverty (Ginwright & Cammarota, 2002; Ginwright, 2006). A social justice approach,

> examines the processes by which urban youth contest, challenge, respond, and negotiate the use and misuse of power in their lives. . . . [It] acknowledges social contexts and highlights the capacity for youth to respond to community problems and heal from the psycho/social wounds of hostile urban environments. (Ginwright & Cammarota, 2002, p. 87)

More specifically, a social justice model analyzes power within social relationships, emphasizes identity, promotes systemic change, encourages collective action, and embraces youth culture (Ginwright & James, 2002). Encouraging youth to identify oppressive systems that shape their lives is necessary for them (and adult organizers) to understand the experiences, opportunities, barriers, and choices youth make, thus creating a more "complete model" of positive youth development (Ginwright & Cammarota, 2002, p. 87). While Ginwright's work focuses primarily on urban African American youth, we see the applicability of his approach to girls, all of whom experience institutionalized sexism and many of whom experience the intersections of sexism, racism, poverty, and systemic violence (Kirshner & Ginwright, 2012).

Second, the girl development scholar and cofounder of the nonprofit Hardy Girls Healthy Women (HGHW) in Maine encourages girl advocates to move beyond "the purely psychological" aspects of girls lives (e.g., self-esteem and depression) and instead cultivate girls' hardiness zones (Brown, 2001, p. 1). The concept of hardiness shares many objectives of the current positive youth development movement, such as making choices in difficult circumstances, having positive connections with others, and bolstering girls' sense of purpose. It also explicitly engages the larger social and cultural world in which girls live so that girls can identify their stresses and challenges in that larger context and so that they learn tools for mobilization rather that defeat in the midst of sexism, classism, and racism (Brown, 2001).

Similar to Ginwright, Brown (2001) argues that it is necessary for girls to identify and understand systemic, institutionalized sexism, racism, and classism so that they can engage those systems and transform them. As a result, approaching girl development from a hardiness perspective allows practitioners to see different issues and concerns (in addition to their peer and family relationships) that are necessary for girls to thrive. Hardy Girls, Healthy Women (HGHW), a nonprofit organization devoted to girls' health and well-being in Maine, reflects this approach:

> We believe that it is not the girls, but rather the culture in which they live that is in need of repair. . . . We see girls not as the sum of any particular pathology (self-cutting, disordered eating, drug use) or struggle (body image, self-esteem, early sexual activity), but as whole beings living within and affected by a variety of social systems. With increased control in their lives, greater challenge from adults, and closer commitment to their communities, girls *will* and *do* thrive. (Hardy Girls Healthy Women, n.d., para 2–4)

We understand that nonprofit organizations and community-based programs operate within very real constraints that shape the extent to which they are able or willing to modify their visions, missions, and programming. Given these constraints, sports-based positive youth development scholars and practitioners can still make small changes to engage the larger context of girls' lives for optimal development, such as partnering with feminist organizations that directly address oppressive systems in girls' lives. In absence of programs that address the persisting forms of inequality and social injustice experienced by young girls, any significant, meaningful change beyond the interpersonal or interactional level is questionable (Gabriel et al., 2011; Warner et al., 2009; Weiss et al., 2012a, 2012b). We recognize that sports-based positive youth development programs alone will not be able to eradicate structural and cultural systems of oppression we have identified in this paper. Rather, it is our intent to illustrate the ways in which many programs rely on and unwittingly reproduce neoliberalism, postfeminism, and healthism—often to the detriment of improving girls' lives. Given the shared goals of empowering girls and young women, girl advocates, activists, and scholars must recognize and work toward the abolishment of these oppressive structures and cultural discourses. Empowering girls while leaving these structures intact simply equips girls to remain blind to the context of social injustice and retains the gender status quo that limits their potential.

Questions for Reflection and Discussion

What is a transformative social justice approach to sports-based youth development, and what are some concrete ways one could design and deliver a girls sports program using such an approach? Why do most programs use a psychological rather than a sociological approach to addressing and improving girls' lives? How do neoliberalism, postfeminism, and healthism shape the current sports programming for girls? What are some ways programs can avoid these-isms? Why is this important?

References

American Association of University Women (AAUW). (1994). *Shortchanging girls, shortchanging America*. Washington, DC: American Association of University Women.

American Heart Association. (n.d.). NFL Play 60 Challenge. Retrieved from http://www .heart.org/HEARTORG/Educator/FortheClassroom/NFLPlay60Challenge/NFL -PLAY-60-Challenge-Page_UCM_304278_Article.jsp

Banet-Weiser, S. (2004). Girls Rule!: Gender, feminism and Nickelodeon. *Critical Studies in Media Communication, 21,* 119–139. doi:10.1080/07393180410001688038

Benson, P. L. (2003). Developmental assets and asset-building community: Conceptual and empirical foundations. In R. M. Lerner & P. L. Benson (Eds.), *Developmental assets and asset-building communities: Implications for research, policy, and practice* (pp. 19–43). Norwell, MA: Kluwer.

Benson, P. L., Scales, P. C., Hamilton, S. F., & Semsa, A., Jr. (2006). Positive youth development: Theory, research, and applications. In W. Damon & R. M. Lerner (Eds.), *Handbook of child psychology: Theoretical models of human development* (6th ed., Vol. 1, pp. 894–941). Hoboken, NJ: Wiley.

Boone, E. M., & Leadbeater, B. J. (2006). Game on: Diminishing risks for depressive symptoms in early adolescence through positive involvement in team sports. *Journal of Research on Adolescence, 16,* 79–90. doi:10.1111/j.1532-7795.2006.00122.x

Bronfenbrenner, U. (1974). Developmental research, public policy, and the ecology of childhood. *Child Development, 45,* 1–5. doi:10.2307/1127743

Brown, L. M. (2001, June). Cultivating hardiness zones for adolescent girls in Maine. Keynote address at Girls' Health Summit, Rockport, ME.

Brownell, K. D., Schwartz, M. B., Puhl, R. M., Henderson, K. E., & Harris, J. L. (2009). The need for bold action to prevent adolescent obesity. *Journal of Adolescent Health, 45,* S8–S17. doi:10.1016/j.jadohealth.2009.03.004

Cahn, S. (1994). *Coming on strong: Gender and sexuality in twentieth century women's sport.* New York, NY: Free Press.

Campos, P., Saguy, A., Ernsberger, P., Oliver, E., & Gaesser, G. (2006). The epidemiology of overweight and obesity: Public health crisis or moral panic? *International Journal of Epidemiology, 35*, 55–60. doi:10.1093/ije/dyi254

Chapman, G. (1999). From "dieting" to "healthy" eating: An exploration of shifting constructions of eating for weight control. In J. Sobal & D. Maurer (Eds.), *Interpreting weight: The social management of fatness and thinness* (pp. 73–87). New York: Walter de Gruyter, Inc.

Chawansky, M. (2012). Good girls play sports: International inspiration and the construction of girlhood. *Feminist Media Studies, 12*, 473–478. doi:10.1080/14680777.2012.698095

Ciccomascolo, L. E., & Grossi, L. M. (2008). The effect of an 8-week educational curriculum and physical activity program on attitudes toward physical activity and body image of urban adolescent girls. *Women in Sport & Physical Activity Journal, 17*, 17–23. Retrieved from http://hhs.uncg.edu/wordpress/pagwspa/wspaj/

Coakley, J. (2011). Youth sports: What counts as positive development? *Journal of Sport and Social Issues, 35*, 306–324. doi:10.1177/0193723511417311

Coakley, J. (2009). *Sports in society: Issues and controversies* (10th ed.). New York, NY: McGraw-Hill.

Community Rowing, Rowing for all. (n.d.). Girls row Boston. Retrieved from https://www.communityrowing.org/outreach/girls-rowboston/

Cooky, C., & LaVoi, N. M. (2012). Playing but losing women's sports after Title IX. *Contexts: Understanding people in their social worlds, 11*, 42–46. doi:10.1177/1536504212436495

Cooky, C. (2010). Do girls rule?: Understanding popular culture images of "Girl Power!" and sport. In S. Spickard Prettyman & B. Lampman (Eds.), *Learning culture through sports: Perspectives on society and organized sports* (pp. 210–226). Lanham, MD: Rowman & Littlefield.

Cooky, C. (2009). "Girls just aren't interested": The social construction of interest in girls' sport. *Sociological Perspectives, 52*, 259–284. doi:10.1525/sop.2009.52.2.259

Crawford, R. (1980). Healthism and the medicalization of everyday life. *International Journal of Health Services, 10*, 365–388. doi:10.2190/3H2H-3XJN-3KAY-G9NY

Crissey, S. R., & Honea, J. C. (2006). The relationship between athletic participation and perceptions of body size and weight control in adolescent girls: The role of sport type. *Sociology of Sport Journal, 23*, 248–272. Retrieved from http://journals.humankinetics.com/ssj

Debate, R. D., Gabriel, K. P., Zwald, M., Huberty, J., & Zhang, Y. (2009). Changes in psychosocial factors and physical activity frequency among third-to eighth-grade girls who participated in a developmentally focused youth sport program: A preliminary study. *Journal of School Health, 79*, 474–484. doi:10.1111/j.1746-1561.2009.00433.x

Duncan, M. M., & Cundiff, V. P. (1929). *Play days for girls and women.* New York, NY: A. S. Barnes & Co.

Dworkin, S. L., & Wachs, F. L. (2009). *Body panic: Gender, health, and the selling of fitness.* New York, NY: New York University Press.

Eaton, D. K., Kann, L., Kinchen, S., Shanklin, S., Ross, J., Hawkins, J., & Wechsler, H. (2008). Youth risk behavior surveillance–United States, 2007. *Morbidity and mortality weekly report. Surveillance summaries, 57*(4), 1–131. Retrieved from http://origin.glb.cdc.gov/mmwr/preview/mmwrhtml/ss5704a1.htm

Frelich, S. G., Patterson, D. L., & Romack, J. L. (2005). Enhancing self-concept through physical activity: The GoGirlGo! project in an economically disadvantaged minority female population. *Research Quarterly for Exercise and Sport, 76*, A99–A100. doi:10.1080/02701367.2005.10599272

Gabriel, K. K. P., Debate, R. D., High, R., & Racine, E. F. (2011). Girls on the run: A quasi-experimental evaluation of a developmentally focused youth sport program. *Journal of*

Physical Activity and Health, 8, S285-S294. Retrieved from http://journals.humankinetics.com/jpah-supplements

Garbarino, J. (1995). *Raising children in a socially toxic environment.* San Francisco, CA: Jossey-Bass Publishers.

George, M. (2005). Making sense of muscle: The body experiences of collegiate women athletes. *Sociological Inquiry, 75,* 317–345. doi:10.1111/j.1475-682X.2005.00125.x

Gillibrand, K. E. (2013). *A Guide to funding opportunities for obesity prevention and access to nutritious foods: How to navigate the funding process.* Washington, DC: United States Senate.

Ginwright, S., & James, T. (2002). From assets to agents of change: Social justice, organizing, and youth development. *New Directions for Youth Development, 96,* 27–46. doi:10.1002/yd.25

Ginwright, S., & James, T. (2002). From assets to agents of change: Social justice, organizing, and youth development. *New Directions for Youth Development, 96,* 27–46. doi:10.1002/yd.25

Ginwright, S. (2006). Racial justice through resistance: Important dimensions of youth development for African Americans. *National Civic Review, 95,* 41–46. doi:10.1002/ncr.130

Girls Inc. (n.d.). Girls Inc. Sporting Chance. Retrieved from http://www.girlsinc.org/resources/programs/girls-inc-sporting-chance.html

Girls in the Game. (n.d.). Sport-Health-Leadership-Life. Retrieved from https://www.girlsinthegame.org/content/index.asp?s=482&t=Our-Programs

Girls on the Run. (n.d.). What we do. Retrieved from http://www.girlsontherun.org/Who-We-Are/Our-History

Girls on the Run of Puget Sound. (n.d.). What we do. Retrieved from http://girlsrun.org/our-program/our-approach/

Gonick, M., Renold, E., Ringrose, J., & Weems, L. (2009). Rethinking agency and resistance: What comes after girl power? *Girlhood Studies, 2,* 1–9. doi:10.3167/ghs.2009.020202

Griffin, C. (2004). Good girls, bad girls: Anglocentrism and diversity in the constitution of contemporary girlhood. In A. Harris (Ed.), *All about the girl: Culture, power and identity* (pp. 29–44). New York, NY: Routledge.

Hardy Girls Healthy Women. (n.d.). About Us. Retrieved from http://www.hghw.org/content/about-us

Hesse-Biber, S., Leavy, P., Quinn, C. E., & Zoino, J. (2006). The mass-marketing of disordered eating and eating disorders: The social psychology of women, thinness, and culture. *Women's Studies International Forum, 29,* 208–224. doi:10.1016/j.wsif.2006.03.007

Heywood, L. (2007). Producing girls: Empire, sport and the neoliberal body. In J. Hargreaves & P. Vertinsky (Eds.), *Physical culture, power and the body* (pp. 101–120). Abingdon, England: Routledge.

Heywood, L., & Dworkin, S. L. (2003). *Built to win: The female athlete as cultural icon.* Minneapolis, MN: University of Minnesota Press.

Hill, C. H., & Kearl, H. (2011). *Crossing the line: Sexual harassment at school.* Washington, DC: American Association of University Women.

Holt, N. L., & Neely, K. C. (2011). Positive youth development through sport: A review. *Revista de Iberoamericana de Psicologia del Ejercico y Deporte, 6,* 299–316. Retrieved from http://www.redalyc.org/articulo.oa?id=311126249009

Huang, J. S., Norman, G. J., Zabinski, M. F., Calfas, K., & Patrick, K. (2007). Body image and self-esteem among adolescents undergoing an intervention targeting dietary and physical activity behaviors. *Journal of Adolescent Health, 40,* 245–251. doi:10.1016/j.jadohealth.2006.09.026

Kater, K. J., Rohwer, J., & Londre, K. (2002). Evaluation of an upper elementary school program to prevent body image, eating, and weight concerns. *Journal of School Health, 72*, 199–204. doi:10.1111/j.1746-1561.2002.tb06546.x

Kinser, A. E. (2004). Negotiating spaces for/through Third Wave feminism. *National Womens Studies Association Journal, 16*(3), 125–153. Retrieved from https://muse.jhu.edu/login?auth-0&type=summary&url=/journals/nwsa_journal/v016/16.3kinser.html

Klein, H., & Shiffman, K. S. (2006). Messages about physical attractiveness in animated cartoons. *Body Image, 3*, 353–363. doi:10.1016/j.bodyim.2006.08.001

Krane, V., Choi, P., Baird, S., Aimar, C., & Kauer, K. (2004). Living the paradox: Female athletes negotiate femininity and muscularity. *Sex Roles, 50*, 315–329. doi:10.1023/B:SERS.0000018888.48437.4f

Kirshner, B., & Ginwright, S. (2012). Youth organizing as a developmental context for African American and Latino adolescents. *Child Development Perspectives, 6*, 288–294. doi:10.1111/j.1750-8606.2012.00243.x

Lagerros, Y. T., Hsieh, S. F., & Hsieh, C. C. (2004). Physical activity in adolescence and young adulthood and breast cancer risk: A quantitative review. *European Journal of Cancer Prevention, 13*, 5–12. doi:10.1097/00008469-200402000-00002

Larson, R. W. (2000). Toward a psychology of positive youth development. *The American Psychologist, 55*, 170–183. doi:10.1037/0003066X.55.1.170

Lee, S. M., Burgeson, C. R., Fulton, J. E., & Spain, C. G. (2007). Physical education and physical activity: Results from the school health policies and programs study 2006. *Journal of School Health, 77*, 435–463. doi:10.1111/j.1746-1561.2007.00229.x

Lerner, R. M. (2004). *Liberty: Thriving and civic engagement among American youth.* Thousand Oaks, CA: Sage.

Lerner, R. M., Almerigi, J. B., Theokas, C., & Lerner, J. V. (2005). Positive youth development: A view of the issues. *The Journal of Early Adolescence, 25*, 10–16. doi:10.1177/0272431604273211

Let's Move! (n.d.) Learn the facts: About Let's Move! Retrieved from http://www.letsmove.gov/learn-facts/epidemic-childhood-obesity

Levin, D. E., & Kilbourne, J. (2009). *So sexy so soon: The new sexualized childhood and what parents can do to protect their kids.* New York, NY: Ballantine Books.

Levine, M. P., & Murnen, S. K. (2009). Everybody knows that mass media are/are not [pick one] a cause of eating disorders: A critical review of evidence for a causal link between media, negative body image, and disordered eating. *Journal of Social and Clinical Psychology, 28*, 9–42. doi:10.1521/jscp.2009.28.1.9

Levy, A. (2005). *Female chauvinist pigs: Women and the rise of raunch culture.* New York, NY: Free Press.

Lowes, J., & Tiggemann, M. (2003). Body dissatisfaction, dieting awareness, and the impact of parental influence in young children. *British Journal of Health Psychology, 8*, 135–147. doi:10.1348/135910703321649123

Lupton, D. (1995). *The imperative of health: Public health and the regulated body.* London, England: Sage.

Markula, P. (1995). Firm but shapely, fit but sexy, strong but thin: The post-modern aerobicizing female bodies. *Sociology of Sport Journal, 12*, 424–453. Retrieved from http://journals.humankinetics.com/ssj

McCabe, M. P., Ricciardelli, L. A., Stanford, J., Holt, K., Keegan, S., & Miller, L. (2007). Where is all the pressure coming from? Messages from mothers and teachers about preschool children's appearance, diet, and exercise. *European Eating Disorders Review, 15*, 221–230. doi:10.1002/erv.717

Messner, M. A. (2002). *Taking the field: Women, men and sports*. Minneapolis, MN: University of Minnesota Press.

Miller, K. E., Barnes, G. M., Melnick, M. J., Sabo, D., & Farrell, M. P. (2002). Gender and racial/ethnic differences in predicting adolescent sexual risk: Athletic participation versus exercise. *Journal of Health and Social Behavior, 43*, 436–450. doi:10.2307/3090236

Nichter, M. (2002). *Fat talk: What girls and their parents say about dieting*. Cambridge, MA: Harvard University Press.

Ogden, C., Flegal, K. M., Carroll, M. S., & Johnson, C. L. (2002). Prevalence and trends in overweight among US children and adolescents, 1999–2000. *JAMA, 288*, 1728–1732. doi:10.1001/jama.2014.732

Orenstein, P. (1994). *School girls: Young women, self-esteem, and the confidence gap*. New York, NY: Anchor Books.

Perkins, D. F., & Noam, G. G. (2007). Characteristics of sports-based youth development programs. *New Directions for Youth Development, 115*, 75–84. doi:10.1002/yd.224

Petitpas, A. J., Cornelius, A. E., Van Raalte, J. L., & Jones, T. (2005). A framework for planning youth sport programs that foster psychosocial development. *The Sport Psychologist, 19*, 63–80.

Phillips, L. (1998). *The girls report: What we know & what we need to know about growing up female*. New York, NY: The National Council for Research on Women.

Pipher, M. (1994). *Reviving Ophelia: Saving the selves of adolescent girls*. New York, NY: Ballantine.

PowerPlay NYC. (n.d.). About. Retrieved from http://powerplaynyc.org/?page_id=64

Presidential Youth Fitness Program. (n.d.). About. Retrieved from http://www.pyfp.org/about/index.shtml

President's Council on Physical Fitness and Sports. (1997). *Physical activity & sport in the lives of girls: Physical & mental health dimensions from an interdisciplinary approach*. Minneapolis, MN: University of Minnesota, Tucker Center for Research on Girls & Women in Sport.

Raudsepp, L., & Neissaar, I. (2012). Brief report: Relationships between physical activity and depressive symptoms in adolescent girls. *Journal of Adolescence, 35*, 1399–1402. doi:10.1016/j.adolescence.2012.04.003

Rauscher, L., Kauer, K., & Wilson, B. D. M. (2013). The healthy body paradox: Organizational and interactional influences on preadolescent girls' body image in Los Angeles. *Gender & Society, 27*, 208–230. doi:10.1177/0891243212472054

Roth, J., & Brooks-Gunn, J. (2003). Youth development programs: Risk, prevention, and policy. *Journal of Adolescent Health, 32*, 170–182. doi:10.1016/j.adolescence.2012.04.003

Sabo, D., Miller, K. E., Melnick, M. J., Farrell, M. P., & Barnes, G. M. (2005). High school athletic participation and adolescent suicide: A nationwide study. *International Review for the Sociology of Sport, 40*, 5–23. doi:10.1177/1012690205052160

Sabo, D., & Veliz, P. (2011). *Progress without equity: The provision of high school athletic opportunity in the United States, by Gender 1993–94 through 2005–06*. East Meadow, NY: Women's Sports Foundation.

Sabo, D., & Veliz, P. (2008). *Go out and play: Sport and American families*. East Meadow, NY: Women's Sports Foundation.

Saguy, A. (2013). *What's wrong with fat?* New York, NY: Oxford University Press.

Salamon, L. M., Geller, S. L., & Spence, K. L. (2009, June 29). *Impact of the 2007–09 economic recession on nonprofit organizations. Listening Post project communique No. 14*. Baltimore, MD: The Johns Hopkins Center for Civil Society Studies.

Smolak, L., & Levine, M. P. (2001). Body image in children. In J. K. Thompson & L. Smolak

(Eds.), *Body image, eating disorders, and obesity in youth: Assessment, prevention, and treatment* (pp. 41–66). Washington, DC: American Psychological Association.

Staurowsky, E. J., DeSousa, M. J., Ducher, G., Gentner, N., Miller, K. E., Shakib, S., Theberge, N., & Williams, N. (2009). *Her life depends on it II: Sport, physical activity and the health and well-being of girls and women.* East Meadow, NY: Women's Sports Foundation.

Sukarieh, M., & Tannock, S. (2011). The positivity imperative: A critical look at the "new" youth development movement. *Journal of Youth Studies, 14,* 675–691. doi:10.1080/13676261.2011.571663

Taft, J. K. (2004). Girl power politics: Pop-culture barriers and organizational resistance. In A. Harris (Ed.), *All about the girl: Culture, power and identity* (pp. 69–78). New York, NY: Routledge.

Taft, J. (2010). Girlhood in action: Contemporary U.S. girls organizations and the public sphere. *Girlhood Studies, 3,* 11–29. doi:10.3167/ghs.2010.030202

Teachman, B. A., & Brownell, K. D. (2001). Implicit anti-fat bias among health professionals: Is anyone immune? *International Journal of Obesity, 25,* 1525–1531. doi:10.1038/sj.ijo.0801745

Title IX of the Education Amendments of 1972 (discrimination based on sex), 20 U.S.C.A. §§ 1681–1688 (West Supp. 2006).

Troutman, K. P., & Dufur, M. K. (2007). From high school jocks to college grads: Assessing the long-term effects of high school sport participation on females' educational attainment. *Youth & Society, 38,* 433–462. doi:10.1177/0044118X06290651

Tucker Center for Research on Girls & Women in Sport. (2007). *Developing physically active girls: An evidenced-based multidisciplinary approach.* Minneapolis, MN: University of Minnesota.

United States Department of Health and Human Services. (1998, December). Girl Power Campaign. Retrieved from http://www.girlpower.gov

Waldron, J. J. (2007). Influence of involvement in the girls on track program on self-perceptions of early adolescent girls. *Research Quarterly for Exercise and Sport, 78,* 520–531. doi:10.1080/02701367.2007.10599451

Warner, S., Dixon, M. A., & Schumann, C. (2009). Enhancing girls' physical activity and self-image: A case study of the GoGirlGo program. *Women in Sport & Physical Activity Journal, 18*(1), 28–41. Retrieved from http://hhs.uncg.edu/wordpress/pagwspa/wspaj/

Weiss, M. R. (2008). Field of dreams: Sport as a context for youth development. *Research Quarterly for Exercise and Sport, 79,* 434–449. doi:10.1080/02701367.2008.10599510

Weiss, M. R., & Wiese-Bjornstal, D. M. (2009). *Promoting positive youth development through physical activity.* Washington, DC: President's Council on Physical Fitness & Sports.

Weiss, M. R. (2011). Teach the children well: A holistic approach to developing psychosocial and behavioral competencies through physical education. *Quest, 63,* 55–65. doi:10.1080/00336297.2011.10483663

Weiss, M. R., Kipp, L. E., & Bolter, N. D. (2012a). Training for life: Optimizing positive youth development through sport and physical activity. In S. M. Murphy (Ed.), *The Oxford handbook of sport and performance psychology* (pp. 448–475). New York, NY: Oxford University Press.

Weiss, M. R., Stuntz, C. P., Bhalla, J. A., Bolter, N. D., & Price, M. S. (2012b). "More than a game": Impact of The First Tee life skills programme on positive youth development: Project introduction and year 1 findings. *Qualitative Research in Sport, Exercise, and Health, 5,* 1–31. doi:10.1080/2159676X.2012.712997

Wilson-Simmons, R. (2007). *Positive youth development: An examination of the field.* Princeton, NJ: Robert Wood Johnson Foundation.

Women's Sports Foundation. (n.d.). About GoGirlGo! Retrieved from http://www
.womenssportsfoundation.org/home/programs/gogirlgo/about-gogirlgo

Wright, J., O'Flynn, G., & Macdonald, D. (2006). Being fit and looking healthy: Young
women's and men's constructions of health and fitness. *Sex Roles, 54*, 707–716. doi:10
.1007/s11199-006-9036-9

8

Separating the Men from the Moms

● ●

The Making of Adult Gender
Segregation in Youth Sports

MICHAEL A. MESSNER AND

SUZEL BOZADA-DEAS

After I wrote the "Barbie Girls versus Sea Monsters" article (see chapter 5 in this book), I got more and more interested in the ways in which adults—mostly mothers and fathers—participated in their kids' youth sports. With then graduate student Suzel Bozada-Deas, I began a study of my local town's American Youth Soccer Organization (AYSO) and Little League Baseball leagues, with the aim of better understanding how it came to be that nearly all of the coaches were men and nearly all of the women who volunteered to help became "team moms." I observed several years of soccer, baseball, and softball games, practices, team meetings, and team parties, and Suzel and I conducted interviews with coaches and managers. What became most interesting to me is how gendered assumptions (for instance,

Source: "Separating the men from the moms: The making of adult gender segregation in youth sports," by M. A. Messner, 2009, *Gender & Society, 23*(1), pp. 49–71, doi:10.1177/0891243208327363. Copyright 2009 by Sociologists for Women in Society. Reprinted with permission of Sage Publications.

"coach" being so commonly identified as a male occupation), as well as routine infor-
mal interactions channeled most women away from coaching, even those who had
lots of athletic experience. I also found it fascinating how the ways that most parents
saw this gender division of labor as "natural," or at least as a product of "individual
choice," tended to reflect these same sorts of gender divisions in their work and fam-
ily lives. It fascinated me how adults tended to view their own work-family gen-
der divisions (like fathers working more hours at their jobs after the arrival of kids
and mothers reducing their time in the paid labor force to become more involved at
home and in the community) as a result of "personal choice" and how they tended
to project these values on to their children in the form of ideologies that I call "soft
essentialism" (introduced in this book in chapter 1). Through this study, I came to
see how youth sports is intimately connected to uneven change in gender relations in
people's everyday lives as workers and as family members.

—Michael A. Messner

In volunteer work, just as in many families and workplaces, gender divisions are pervasive and persistent. Women are often expected to do the work of caring for others' emotions and daily needs. Women's volunteer labor is routinely devalued in much the same ways that housework and childcare are devalued in the home and women's clerical and other support work is devalued in the professions (Hook, 2004). Similarly, men tend to do the instrumental work of public leadership, just as they do in the family and the workplace, and their informal work is valued accordingly.

This article examines the social construction of adult gender divisions of labor in a community volunteer activity, youth sports. A few scholars have examined women's invisible labor in sports (Boyle & McKay, 1995). In her study of a Little League Baseball league, Grasmuck (2005) estimates that the 111 league administrators, head coaches, and assistant coaches (mostly men) contribute a total of 33,330 hours of volunteer labor in a season—an average of about 300 hours per person. Much of the work women do in youth sports is behind-the-scenes support that is less visible than coaching (Thompson, 1999). In a study of Little League Baseball in Texas, Chafetz and Kotarba (1999) observed that "team mothers" in this "upper middle class, 'Yuppie' Texas community" do gender in ways that result in "the re-creation and strengthening of the community's collective identity as a place where, among other things, women are primarily mothers to their sons" (pp. 48–49). As yet, no study has focused on how this gender divide among adults in youth sports happens. How do most men become coaches, while most women become "team moms"? How do adult gender divisions of labor in youth sports connect with commonsense notions about divisions between women and men in families and workplaces? This is important: Millions of children play community-based youth sports every year, and these athletic activities are a key part of the daily lives of many families. It is also important for scholars of gender—studying segregation in this context can reveal much about how gender divisions are created and sustained in the course of everyday life.

Coaches and "Team Moms"

In 1995, when we (the first author, Mike, and his family) arrived at our 6-year-old son's first soccer practice, we were delighted to learn that his coach was a woman. Coach Karen, a mother in her mid-30s, had grown up playing lots of sports. She was tall, confident, and athletic, and the kids responded well to her leadership. It seemed to be a new and different world than the one we grew up in. But during the next decade, as our two sons played a few more seasons of soccer, two years of youth basketball, and more than decade of baseball, they never had another woman head coach. It was not that women were not contributing to the kids' teams. All of the "team parents" (often called "team moms")—parent volunteers who did the behind-the-scenes work of phone-calling, organizing weekly snack schedules and team parties, collecting money for gifts for the coaches, and so on—were women. And occasionally, a team had a woman assistant coach. But women head coaches were few and far between.

In 1999, we started keeping track of the numbers of women and men head coaches in Roseville's[1] annual American Youth Soccer Organization (AYSO) and Little League Baseball/Softball (LLB/S) yearbooks we received at the end of each season. The yearbooks revealed that from 1999 to 2007, only 13.4% of 1,490 AYSO teams had women head coaches. The numbers were even lower for Little League Baseball and Softball; only 5.9% of 538 teams were managed by women. In both AYSO and LLB/S, women coaches were clustered in the younger kids' teams (ages five to eight) and in coaching girls. Boys—and especially boys older than age 10—almost never had women coaches. These low numbers are surprising for several reasons. First, unlike during the 1950s and 1960s when there were almost no opportunities for girls to play sports, today millions of girls participate in organized soccer, baseball, softball, basketball, and other sports. With this demographic shift in youth sports, we expected that the gender division of labor among parents would have shifted as well. Second, today's mothers in the United States came of age during and after the 1972 institution of Title IX and are part of the generation that ignited the booming growth of female athletic participation. We wondered how it happened that these women did not make a neat transition from their own active sports participation into coaching their own kids. Third, women in Roseville outnumber men significantly in every volunteer activity having to do with kids, such as the Parent and Teacher Association (PTA), Scouts, and school special events. Coaching youth sports is the great exception to this rule. Sport has changed over the past 30 years from a world set up almost exclusively by and for boys and men to one that is moving substantially (although incompletely) toward gender equity (Messner, 2002). Yet men dominate the very public on-field volunteer leadership positions in community youth sports.

This article is part of a larger study of gender in adult volunteering in two youth sports programs in a small independent suburb of Los Angeles that we call

Roseville. Both of the sports leagues are local affiliates of massive national and international organizations. LLB/S and AYSO offer an interesting contrast in youth sports organizations, especially with respect to gender. Little League Baseball began in 1938 and for its first 36 years was an organization set up exclusively for boys. When forced against its will by a court decision in 1974 to include girls, Little League responded by creating a separate softball league into which girls continue to be tracked. Today, LLB/S is an organization that boasts 2.7 million child participants worldwide, 2.1 million of them in the United States. There are 176,786 teams in the program, 153,422 of them in baseball and 23,364 in softball. Little League stays afloat through the labor of approximately one million volunteers.

When AYSO started in 1964, it was exclusively for boys, but by 1971, girls' teams had been introduced. Thus over the years, the vast majority of people who have participated in AYSO have experienced it as an organization set up for boys *and* girls. AYSO remains today mostly a U.S. organization, with more than 650,000 players on more than 50,000 teams. The national AYSO office employs 50 paid staff members, but like LLB/S, AYSO is an organization largely driven by the labor of volunteers, with roughly 250,000 volunteer coaches, team parents, and referees.

The differently gendered history of these two organizations offers hints as to the origins of the differences we see; there are more women head coaches in soccer than in baseball. Connell (1987) argues that every social institution—including the economy, the military, schools, families, or sport—has a "gender regime," which is defined as the current state of play of gender relations in the institution. We can begin to understand an institution's gender regime by measuring and analyzing the gender divisions of labor and power in the organization (i.e., what kinds of jobs are done by women and men, who has the authority, etc.). The idea that a gender regime is characterized by a "state of play" is a way to get beyond static measurements that result from a quick snapshot of an organizational pyramid and understanding instead that organizations are always being created by people's actions and discourse (Britton, 2000). These actions often result in an organizational inertia that reproduces gender divisions and hierarchies; however, organizations are also subject to gradual—or occasionally even rapid—change.

Institutional gender regimes are connected with other gender regimes. Put another way, people in their daily lives routinely move in, out, and across different gender regimes—families, workplaces, schools, places of worship, and community activities such as youth sports. Their actions within a particular gender regime—for instance, the choice to volunteer to coach a youth soccer team—and the meanings they construct around these actions are constrained and enabled by their positions, responsibilities, and experiences in other institutional contexts. We will show how individual decisions to coach or to serve as team parents occur largely through nonreflexive, patterned interactions that are infused with an ascendant gender ideology that we call "soft essentialism." These interactions occur at the nexus of the three gender regimes of community youth sports, families, and workplaces.

Research Methods

The low numbers of women coaches in Roseville AYSO and LLB/S and the fact that nearly all of the team parents are women gave us a statistical picture of persistent gender segregation. But simply trotting out these numbers couldn't tell us *how* this picture is drawn. We wanted to understand the current state of play of the adult gender regime of youth sports, so we developed a study based on the following question: What are the social processes that sustain this gender segregation? And by extension, we wanted to explore another question: What is happening that might serve to destabilize and possibly change this gender segregation? In other words, are there ways to see and understand the internal mechanisms—the face-to-face interactions as well as the meaning-making processes—that constitute the "state of play" of the gender regime of community youth sports?

Questions about social processes—how people, in their routine daily interactions, reproduce (and occasionally challenge) patterned social relations—are best addressed using a combination of qualitative methods. Between 2003 and 2007, we systematically explored the gender dynamics of volunteer coaches in Roseville by deploying several methods of data collection. First, we conducted a content analysis of nine years (1999–2007) of Roseville's AYSO and LLB/S yearbooks (magazine-length documents compiled annually by the leagues, containing team photos as well as names and photos of coaches and managers). The yearbook data on the numbers and placement of women and men coaches provides the statistical backdrop for our study of the social processes of gender and coaching that we summarized above.

Second, we conducted field observations of numerous girls' and boys' soccer, baseball, and softball practices and games. We participated in clinics that were set up to train soccer and baseball coaches and a clinic to train soccer referees. We observed annual baseball and softball tryouts, a managers' baseball "draft," and several annual opening ceremonies for AYSO and LLB/S.

Third, Mike conducted several seasons of participant observation—as a volunteer assistant coach or as scorekeeper—of his son's Little League Baseball teams, ranging from 6- and 7-year old coed T-ball teams to 13- and 14-year-old boys' baseball teams. These positions gave him observational vantage points near the coaches from which he could jot down short notes that he would later develop into longer field notes. Mike's "insider" role as a community member and a father of kids in these sports leagues allowed him easy access. He always informed the coaches of his sons' teams that he was doing a study, but like many who conduct participant observation, it seemed that his role as researcher was frequently "forgotten" by others and that he was most often seen as a father, an assistant coach, or a scorekeeper.

Fourth, we conducted 50 in-depth interviews with women and men volunteers—mostly head soccer coaches and baseball or softball managers of both boys' and girls' teams but also a small number of assistant coaches and team parents. The interviewees were selected through a snowball sampling method. All but three of those interviewed were parents of children playing in the

Roseville soccer, baseball, or softball leagues. Although there were far more men coaches than women coaches from whom to choose, we purposely interviewed roughly equal numbers of women (24) and men (26) coaches. Two of the women coaches were single with no children, one was a divorced single mother, one was a mother living with her female partner, and the rest were mothers living with a male spouse. One of the men coaches was single with no children, two were divorced fathers, and the rest were fathers living with a female spouse. Most of the men interviewed were in their 40s, with an average age of 45. The women were, on average, 39 years old. Nearly all of the interviewees were college educated, living in professional-class families. They self-identified ethnically as 68% White, 18% Hispanic, 4% Asian American, and 10% biracial or other. This ethnic breakdown of our interviewees reflects roughly the apparent ethnic composition of coaches in the annual yearbooks. However, since Whites are only 44% and Asian Americans are 27% of the population of Roseville, it is apparent that Whites are overrepresented as coaches and Asian Americans are underrepresented (Roseville is 16% Hispanic).

We conducted the first three interviews together. Suzel then conducted 38 of the subsequent interviews, while Mike did nine. Mike used his insider status as a member of the community and as a parent of kids who had played in the local youth sports leagues to establish trust and rapport with interviewees. No doubt his status as a White male college professor with a deep background in sports also gave him instant credibility with some interviewees. Suzel, by contrast, was an outsider in most ways. She was a Latina graduate student, not a resident of Roseville, and her own two daughters did not play local youth sports. Moreover, she had almost no sports background. Suzel closed the social distance with her interviewees by enrolling in a coaching clinic and a refereeing clinic and by observing several practices and games to better understand the role that coaches play with the kids. In the interviews, Suzel judiciously used her knowledge from these clinics and her observations of practices and games to ask knowledgeable questions and sharp follow-up probes. This strategy created rapport, and it also allowed Suzel to demonstrate knowledge of sports and coaching, thus bridging what might otherwise have been a credibility gap between her and some of those with deep athletic experience and knowledge. At times, Suzel used her outsider status as a benefit, asking naïve questions about the particularities of Roseville that might have sounded disingenuous coming from an insider.

The Coaches' Stories

When we asked a longtime Little League Softball manager why he thinks most head coaches are men while nearly all team parents are women, he said with a shrug, "They give opportunities to everybody to manage or coach, and it just so happens that no women volunteer, you know?" This man's statement was typical of head coaches and league officials who generally offered up explanations grounded in individual choice: Faced with equal opportunities to volunteer, men just *choose* to be coaches, while women *choose* to be team parents.

But our research shows that the gendered division of labor among men and women volunteers in youth coaching results not simply from an accumulation of individual choices; rather, it is produced through a profoundly *social* process. We will first draw from our interviews with head coaches to illustrate how gender divisions of labor among adult volunteers in youth sports are shaped by gendered language and belief systems and are seen by many coaches as natural extensions of gendered divisions of labor in families and workplaces. We next draw observations from our field notes to illustrate how everyday interactions within the gendered organizational context of youth sports shapes peoples' choices about men's and women's roles as coaches or team parents. Our main focus here will be on reproductive agency—the patterns of action that reproduce the gender division of labor. But we will also discuss moments of resistance and disruption that create possibilities for change.

Gendered Pipelines

When we asked coaches to describe how they had decided to become coaches, most spoke of having first served as assistant coaches—sometimes for just one season, sometimes for several seasons—before moving into head coaching positions. Drawing from language used by those who study gender in occupations, we can describe the assistant coach position as an essential part of the "pipeline" to the head coach position (England, 2006). One of the reasons for this is obvious: Many parents—women and men—believe that as a head coach, they will be under tremendous critical scrutiny by other parents in the community. Without previous youth coaching experience, many lack the confidence that they feel they need to take on such a public leadership task. A year or two of assistant coaching affords one the experience and builds the confidence that can lead to the conclusion that "I can do that" and the decision to take on the responsibility of a head coaching position.

But the pipeline from assistant coaches to head coaches does not operate in a purely individual voluntarist manner. A male longtime Little League manager and a member of the league's governing board gave us a glimpse of how the pipeline works when there is a shortage of volunteers:

> One time we had 10 teams and only like six or seven applicants that wanted to be strictly manager. So you kinda eyeball the yearbook from the year before, maybe a couple of years [before], and see if the same dad is still listed as a[n assistant] coach, and maybe now it's time he wants his own team. So you make a lot of phone calls. You might make 20 phone calls and hopefully you are going to get two or three guys that say, "Yes, I'll be a manager."

The assistant coach position is a key part of the pipeline to head coaching positions both because it makes people more confident about volunteering to be a head coach and, as the quote above illustrates, because it gives them visibility in ways that make them more likely to be actively recruited by the league to be a head coach. To understand how it is that most head coaches are men, we need to understand how the pipeline operates—how it is that, at the entry level, women's and men's choices to become assistant coaches and/or team parents are constrained or enabled by the social context.

Recruiting Dads and Moms to Help

There is a lot of work involved in organizing a successful youth soccer, baseball, or softball season. A head coach needs help from two, three, even four other parents who will serve as assistant coaches during practices and games. Parents also have to take responsibility for numerous support tasks like organizing snacks, making team banners, working in the snack bar during games, collecting donations for year-end gifts for the coaches, and organizing team events and year-end parties. In AYSO, parents also serve as volunteer referees. When we asked head coaches how they determined who would help them with these assistant coaching and other support tasks, a very common storyline developed: The coach would call a beginning-of-the-season team meeting, sometimes preceded by a letter or e-mail to parents, and ask for volunteers. Nearly always, they ended up with dads volunteering to help as assistant coaches and moms volunteering to be team parents. A woman soccer coach told a typical story:

> At the beginning of the season I sent a little introductory letter [that said] I really badly need an assistant coach and referee and a "team mom." You know anyone that is keen on that, let's talk about it at the first practice. And this year one guy picked up the phone and said, "Please, can I be your assistant coach?" And I spoke to another one of the mums who I happen to know through school and she said, "Oh, I can do the team mum if you find someone to help me." And by the first practice, they'd already discussed it and it was up and running.

We can see from this coach's statement how the assistant coach and team parent positions are sometimes informally set up even before the first team meeting and how a coach's assumption that the team parent will be a "team *mom*" might make it more likely that women end up in these positions. But even coaches—such as the woman soccer coach quoted below—who try to emphasize that team parent is not necessarily a woman's job find that only women end up volunteering:

> Before the season started, we had a team meeting and I let the parents know that I would need a team parent and I strongly stressed *parent*, because I don't think it should always be a mother. But we did end up with the mom doing it and she assigns snacks and stuff like that.

None of the head coaches we interviewed said that they currently had a man as the team parent. Four coaches recalled that they had once had a man as a team parent (although one of these four coaches said, "Now that I think about it, that guy actually volunteered his wife do it"). When we asked if they had ever had a team parent who was a man, nearly all of the coaches said never. Many of them laughed at the very thought. A woman soccer coach exclaimed with a chuckle, "I just can't imagine! I wonder if they've *ever* had a 'team mom' who's a dad. I don't know [laughs]." A man soccer coach stammered his way through his response, punctuating his words with sarcastic laughter: "Ha! In fact, that whole concept—I don't think I've ever *heard* of a team dad [laughs]. Uh—there *is* no team dad, I've never heard of a team dad. But I don't know why that would be." A few coaches, such as the following woman softball coach, resorted to family metaphors to explain why they think there are few if any men volunteering to be team parents: "Oh, it's always a mom [laughs]. 'Team mom.' That's why it's called 'team *mom*.' You know, the coach is a male. And the mom—I mean, that's the *housekeeping*—you know: Assign the snack."

There are gendered assumptions in the language commonly linked to certain professions, so much so that often, when the person holding the position is in the statistical minority, people attach a modifier, such as *male* nurse, *male* secretary, *female* judge, *female* doctor. Or *female* head coach. Over and over, in interviews with coaches, during team meetings, and in interactions during games, practices, and team parties, we noticed this gendered language. Most obvious was the frequent slippage from official term *team parent* to commonly used term *team mom*. But we also noticed that a man coach was normally just called a coach, while a woman coach was often gender marked as a woman coach. As feminist linguists have shown, language is a powerful element of social life—it not only reflects social realities such as gender divisions of labor, it also helps to construct our notions of what is normal and what is an aberration (Thorne, Kramarae, & Henley, 1983). One statement from a woman soccer coach, "I wonder if they've *ever* had a 'team mom' who's a dad," illustrates how gendered language makes the idea of a man team parent seem incongruous, even laughable. In youth sports, this gendered language supports the notion that a team is structured very much like a traditional heterosexual family: The head coach—nearly always a man—is the leader and the public face of the team; the team parent—nearly always a woman—is working behind the scenes, doing support work; assistant coaches—mostly men, but including the occasional woman—help the coach on the field during practices and games.

Teams are even talked about sometimes as "families," and while we never heard a head coach referred to as a team's "dad," we did often and consistently hear the team parent referred to as the "team mom." This gendered language, drawn from family relations, gives us some good initial hints as to how coach and team parent roles remain so gender segregated. In their study of self-managing teams, which was intended to break down gender divisions in workplaces, Ollilainen and Calasanti (2007) show how team members' use of family metaphors serves to maintain the salience of gender and thus helps to reproduce a gendered division of labor. Similarly, in youth sports contexts, gendered language structures people's conversations in ways that shape and constrain their actions. Is a man who volunteers to be a team parent now a "team mom"?

Gender Ideology and Work/Family Analogies

When we asked the coaches to consider why it is nearly always women who volunteer to be the team parent, many seemed never to have considered this question before. Some of the men coaches seemed especially befuddled and appeared to assume that women's team-parenting work is a result of an almost "natural" decision on the part of the woman. Some men, such as the following soccer coach, made sense of this volunteer division of labor by referring to the ways that it reflected divisions of labor in men's own families and in their community: "In this area we have a lot of stay-at-home moms, so it seems to kind of fall to them to take over those roles." Similarly, a man baseball coach whose wife served as the team parent explained, "I think it's because they probably do it at home. You know, I mean my wife—even though she can't really commit the time to coach, I don't think she would *want* to coach—uh, she's very good with that [team parent] stuff." A man soccer coach explained the gender divisions of youth sports teams in terms of people's comfort with a nostalgic notion of a "traditional family":

> That's sort of the classical family, you know, it's like the Donna Reed family is AYSO, right?... They have these assigned gender roles... and people in Roseville, probably all over the United States, they're fairly comfortable with them, right? It's, uh, maybe insidious, maybe not, [but] framed in the sort of traditional family role of dad, mom, kids.... people are going to be comfortable with that.

Another man baseball coach broadened the explanation, drawing connections to divisions of labor in his workplace:

> It's kinda like in business. I work in real estate, and most of your deal makers that are out there on the front lines, so to speak, making the deals, doing the shuckin' and jivin', doing the selling, are men. It's a very Good Ol' Boys network on the real estate brokerage side. There are a ton a females who are on the property management side, because it's *housekeeping*, it's *managing*, it's like running the *household*, it's behind the scenes, it's like cooking in the kitchen—[laughs]—I mean, I hate to say that, but it's that kind of role that's secondary. Coach is out in the front leading the squad, mom sitting behind making sure that the snacks are in order and all that. You know—just the way it is.

Having a male coach and a "team mom" just seemed normal to this man—"You know, just the way it is"—because it seemed to flow naturally from divisions of labor in his household and in his workplace—gendered divisions of labor that have the "the Good Ol' Boys" operating publicly as the leaders "on the front lines... shuckin' and jivin'," while the women are offering support "behind the scenes... like cooking in the kitchen." Echoing this view, a man soccer coach said, "I hate to use the analogy, but it's like a secretary: You got a boss and you've got a secretary, and I think that's where most of the opportunities for women to be active in the sports is, as the secretary."

When explaining why it is that team parents are almost exclusively women, a small number of women coaches also seemed to see it in essentialist terms—like most of the men coaches saw it.

Many women coaches, however, saw the gendering of the team parent position as a problem and made sense of its persistence, as did many of the men, by referring to the ways that it reflects family- and work-related divisions of labor. But several of the women coaches added an additional dimension to their explanations by focusing on why they think the men don't or won't consider doing team parent work. A woman soccer coach said, "I think it's because the dads want to be involved with the action. And they are not interested in doing paperwork and collecting money for photos or whatever it is. They are not interested in doing that sort of stuff." Another woman soccer coach extended this point: "I think it's probably, well, identity, which is probably why not many men do it. You know, they think that is a woman's job, like secretary or nurse or, you know." In short, many of the women coaches were cognizant of the ways that the team parent job was viewed by men, like all "women's work," as nonmasculine and thus undesirable. A woman Little League coach found it ironically funny that her husband, in fact, does most of the cooking and housework at home but will not take on the role of team parent for his daughter's team. When asked if changing the name to "team dad" might get more men to volunteer, she replied with a sigh,

> I don't know. I wish my husband would be a team dad because he's just very much more domesticated than I am [laughs]. You know, "Bring all the snacks, honey, hook us up," you know. I think there's a lot of men out there, but they don't want to be perceived as being domesticated.

This coach's comment illustrates how—even for a man who does a substantial amount of the family labor at home—publicly taking on a job that is defined as "feminine" threatens to saddle him with a "domesticated" public image that would be embarrassing or even humiliating. In sum, most coaches—both women and men—believe that men become coaches and women become team parents largely because these public roles fit with their domestic proclivities and skills. But the women add an important dimension to this explanation: Women do the team parent work because it has to be done . . . and because they know that the men will not do it.

Finding a "Team Mom"

The interview data gave us a window into how people make sense of decisions that they have made as youth sports volunteers and provided insights into how gendered language and beliefs about men's and women's work and family roles help to shape these decisions. Yet asking people to explain how (and especially why) things such as gendered divisions of labor persist is not by itself the most reliable basis for building an explanation. Rather, watching *how* things happen gives us a deeper understanding of the social construction of gender (Thorne,

1993). Our observations from team meetings and early season practices reveal deeper social processes at work—processes that shaped people's apparently individual decisions to volunteer for assistant coach or team parent positions. This excerpt from field notes from the first team meeting of a boys' baseball team illustrates how men's apparent resistance to even consider taking on the team parent position ultimately leaves the job in the hands of a woman (who might also have been reluctant to do it):

> *Coach Bill stands facing the parents, as we sit in the grandstands. He doesn't ask for volunteers for assistant coaches; instead, he announces that he has "invited" two of the fathers "who probably know more about baseball than I do" to serve as his assistants. He then asks for someone to volunteer as the "team mom." He adds, "Now, 'team mom' is not a gendered job: it can be done by a mom or a dad. But we really need a 'team mom.'" Nobody volunteers immediately. One mom sitting near me mutters to another mom, "I've done this two years in a row, and I'm not gonna do it this year." Coach Bill goes on to ask for a volunteer for scorekeeper. Meanwhile, two other moms have been whispering, and one of them suddenly bursts out with "Okay! She's volunteered to be 'team mom!'" People applaud. The volunteer seems a bit sheepish; her body-language suggests someone who has just reluctantly agreed to do something. But she affirms that, yes, she'll do it.*

This first practice of the year is often the moment at which the division of labor—who will be the assistant coaches, who will be the team parent—is publicly solidified. In this case, the men assistant coaches had been selected before the meeting by the head coach, but it apparently took some cajoling from a mother during the team meeting to convince another mother to volunteer to be the "team mom." We observed two occasions when a woman who did not volunteer was drafted by the head coach to be the "team mom." In one case, the reluctant volunteer was clearly more oriented toward assistant coaching, as the following composite story from field notes from the beginning of the season of a 7-year-old boys' baseball team illustrates:

> *At the first practice, Coach George takes charge, asks for volunteers. I tell him that I am happy to help out at practice and games and that he should just let me know what he'd like me to do. He appoints me Assistant Coach. This happens with another dad, too. We get team hats. Elena, a mother, offers to help out in any way she can. She's appointed "co-team mom" (the coach's wife is the other 'team mom'). She shrugs and says okay, fine. Unlike most 'team moms', Elena continues to attend all practices. At the fifth practice, Coach George is pitching batting practice to the kids; I'm assigned to first base, the other dad is working with the catcher. Elena (the 'team mom') is standing alone on the sidelines, idly tossing a ball up in the air to herself. Coach George's son suddenly has to pee, so as George hustles the boy off to the bathroom, Elena jumps in and starts pitching. She's good, it turns out, and can groove the pitch right where the kids want it. (By contrast, George has recently been*

plunking the kids with wild pitches.) Things move along well. At one point, when
Coach George has returned from the bathroom, with Elena still pitching to the kids,
a boy picks up a ball near second base and doesn't know what to do with it. Coach
George yells at the kid: "Throw it! Throw it to the 'team mom!'" The kid, confused,
says, "Where is she?" I say, "The pitcher, throw it to the pitcher." Coach George says,
"Yeah, the 'team mom.'"

A couple of years later, we interviewed Elena and asked her how it was that
she became a team parent and continued in that capacity for five straight years.
Her response illuminated the informal constraints that channel many women
away from coaching and toward being team parents:

> The first year, when [my son] was in kindergarten, he was on a T-ball team, and
> I volunteered to be manager, and of course the league didn't choose me, but they
> did allow me to be assistant coach. And I was so excited, and [laughs] of course I
> showed up in heels for the first practice, because it was right after work, and the
> coach looked at me, and I informed him that "I'm your new assistant." And he
> looked at me—and I don't know if *distraught* is the correct word, but he seemed
> slightly *disappointed*, and he went out of his way to ask the parents who were
> there watching their children if there was anyone who wanted to volunteer, even
> though I was there. So there was this male who did kind of rise to the occasion,
> and so that was the end. He demoted me without informing me of his decision
> [laughs]—I was *really* enthused, because [my son] was in kindergarten, so I
> *really* wanted to be coach—or assistant coach at least—and it didn't happen. So
> after that I didn't feel comfortable to volunteer to coach. I just thought, okay,
> then I can do "team mom."

As this story illustrates, women who have the background, skills, and desire
to work as on-field assistant coaches are sometimes assigned by head coaches
to be "team moms." Some baseball teams even have a niche for such moms: A
"dugout coach" (or "dugout mom") is usually a mom who may help out with on-
field instruction during practices, but on game days, she is assigned the "indoors"
space of the dugout, where it is her responsibility to keep track of the lineup
and to be sure that the boy who is on deck (next up to bat) is ready with his
batting gloves and helmet on. The dugout coach also—especially with younger
kids' teams—might be assigned to keep kids focused on the game, to keep equipment orderly, to help with occasional first aid, and to help see that the dugout
is cleaned of empty water bottles and snack containers after the game is over.
In short, the baseball, softball, and soccer fields on which the children play are
gendered spaces (Dworkin, 2001; Montez de Oca, 2005). The playing field is
the public space where the (usually male) coach exerts his authority and com-
mand. The dugout is like the home—a place of domestic safety from which one
emerges to do one's job. Work happens in the indoor space of the dugout, but it
is like family labor, behind-the-scenes, supporting the "real" work of leadership
that is done on the field.

Challenges and Resistance

The head coach's common assumption that fathers will volunteer to be assistant coaches and mothers to be "team moms" creates a context that powerfully channels men and women in these directions. Backed by these commonsense understandings of gendered divisions of labor, most men and women just "go with the flow" of this channeling process. Their choices and actions help to reproduce the existing gendered patterns of the organization. But some do not; some choose to swim against the tide. A mother who had several seasons of experience as a head soccer coach described the first team meeting for her youngest child's team:

> At our first team meeting, the coach announced, "I'm looking for a couple of you to help me out as assistant coaches," and he looked directly at the men, and *only* at the men. None of them volunteered. And it was really amazing because he didn't even *look* at me or at any of the other women. So after the meeting, I went up to him and said, "Hey, I've coached soccer for like 10 seasons; I can help you out, okay?" And he agreed, so I'm the assistant coach for him.

This first team meeting is an example of a normal gendered interaction that, if it had gone unchallenged, would have reproduced the usual gender divisions of labor on the team. It is likely that many women in these situations notice the ways that men are, to adopt Martin's (2001) term, informally (and probably unconsciously) "mobilizing masculinities" in ways that reproduce men's positions of centrality. But this woman's 10 years of coaching experience gave her the confidence and the athletic "capital" that allowed her not only to see and understand but also to challenge the very gendered selection process that was taking place at this meeting. Most mothers do not have this background, and when faced with this sort of moment, they go with the flow.

On another occasion, as the following composite story from field notes describes, Mike observed a highly athletic and coaching-inclined woman assertively use her abilities in a way that initially *seemed* to transcend the gender segregation process, only to be relegated symbolically at season's end to the position of "team mom":

> *A new baseball season, the first team meeting of the year; a slew of dads volunteer to be assistant coaches. Coach George combs the women for a "team mom" and gets some resistance; at first, nobody will do it, but then he finds a volunteer. At the first few practices, few assistant coaches actually show up. Isabel, a mom, clearly is into baseball, very knowledgeable and athletic, and takes the field. She pitches to the kids, gives them good advice. On the day when George is passing out forms for assistant coaches to sign, he hands her one too. She accepts it, in a matter-of-fact way. Isabel continues to attend practices, working with the kids on the field.*
>
> *Though few dads show up for many of the practices, there never seems to be a shortage of dads to serve as assistant coaches at the games. At one game, Coach George invites Isabel to coach third base, but beyond that, she is never included in an on-field coaching role during a game.*

> *End of season, team party. Coach George hands out awards to all the kids. He hands out gift certificates to all the assistant coaches but does not include Isabel. Then he hands out gift certificates to the "team moms," and includes Isabel, even though I don't recall her doing any team parent tasks. She had clearly been acting as an assistant coach all season long.*

This story illustrates how, on one hand, a woman volunteer can informally circumvent the sorting process that pushes her toward the "team mom" role by persistently showing up to practices and assertively doing the work of a coach. As Thorne (1993) points out, individual incidences of gender crossing are often handled informally in ways that affirm, rather than challenge, gender boundaries: An individual girl who joins the boys' game gets defined "as a token, a kind of 'fictive boy,' not unlike many women tokens in predominantly men settings, whose presence does little to challenge the existing arrangements" (p. 133). Similarly, Isabel's successful "crossing" led to her becoming accepted as an assistant coach during practices but rarely recognized as a "real" coach during games. She was a kind of "token" or "fictive" coach whose gender transgression was probably unknown to the many adults who never attended practices. So in the final moment of the season, when adults and children alike were being publicly recognized for their contributions to the team, she was labeled and rewarded for being a "team mom," reaffirming gender boundaries.

A few coaches whom we interviewed consciously attempted to resist or change this gendered sorting system. Some of the women coaches, especially, saw it as a problem that the team parent job was always done by a woman. A woman softball coach was concerned that the "team mom" amounted to negative role-modeling for kids and fed into the disrespect that women coaches experienced:

> The kids think that the moms should just be "team moms." Which means that they don't take the mothers seriously, and I think that's a bad thing. I mean it's a *bad thing*. I think that's a lack of respect to women, to mothers.

Another woman Little League coach said that most team parents are women because too many people assume

> that's all the women are good for. I think that's what the mentality is. I made it very clear to our parents that it did not have to be a mother, that it could be a father and that I encourage any dad out there that had time to do what team parents are supposed to do, to sign up and do it. But it didn't happen.

Such coaches find that simply degendering the language by calling this role *team parent* and even stressing that this is not a gendered job is unlikely to yield men volunteers. So what some women coaches do is simply refuse to have a team parent. A woman soccer coach said, "I do it all. I don't have a team parent." Another said, "I think in general, compared to the men who coach, I do more of that [team parent work]." This resistance by women coaches is understandable, especially from those who see the phenomenon of "team mom" as contributing to a climate of disrespect for women coaches. However, this form of resistance ends up creating extra work for women coaches—work that most men coaches relegate to a "team mom."

The very few occasions when a father does volunteer—or is recruited by the coach—to be the team parent are moments of gender "crossing" that hold the potential to disrupt the normal operation of the gender category sorting process. But ironically, a team parent who is a man can also reinforce gender stereotypes. One man soccer coach told me that the previous season, a father had volunteered to be the team parent, but that

> he was a disaster [laughs]. He didn't do *anything*, you know, and what little he did it was late; it was ineffective assistance. He didn't come, he didn't make phone calls, I mean he was just like a black hole. And so that—that was an unfortunate disaster. This year it's a woman again.

The idea that a man volunteered—and then failed miserably to do the team parent job—may serve ultimately to reinforce the taken-for-granted assumption that women are naturally better suited to do this kind of work.

The Devaluation of Women's Invisible Labor

The Roseville "team moms" we observed were similar to those studied by Chafetz and Kotarba (1999) in terms of their education, professional-class status, and family structure. The Texasville and Roseville "team moms" are doing the same kinds of activities, simultaneously contributing to the "concerted cultivation" of their own children while helping to enhance the social cohesion of the team, the league, and the community (Lareau, 2003).

Despite the importance of the work team parents are doing, it is not often recognized as equivalent to the work done by coaches. Of course, the team parent typically puts in far fewer hours of labor than does the head coach. However, in some cases, the team parents put in more time than some assistant coaches (dads, for instance, whose work schedules don't allow them to get to many practices but who can be seen on the field during a Saturday game, coaching third base). Yet the team parent's work remains largely invisible, and coaches sometimes talk about team parents' contributions as trivial or unimportant. Several coaches, when asked about the team parent job, disparaged it as "not very hard to do," "an easy job." But our interviews suggest that the women team parents are often doing this job as one of many community volunteer jobs, while most of the men who coach are engaged in this and only this volunteer activity. A field note from a boys' baseball game illustrates this:

> *It is the second to last game of the season. During the first inning, Dora, the "team mom," shows up and immediately starts circulating among the parents in the stands,*

talking and handing out a flier. The flier announces the "year end party," to be held in a couple of weeks. She announces that she will supply ice cream and other makings for sundaes. Everyone else can just bring some drinks. She also announces (and it's on the flier) that she's collecting $20 from each family to pay for a "thank you gift . . . for all their hard work" for the head coach and for each of the three assistant coaches (all men). People start shelling out money, and Dora starts a list of who has donated. By the start of the next inning, she announces that she's got to go, saying "I have a Webelos [Cub Scouts] parents meeting." She's obviously multitasking as a parent volunteer. By the fourth inning, near the end of the game, she is back, collecting more money, and informing parents on details concerning the party and the upcoming playoffs. Finally, during the last inning, she sits and watches the end of the game with the rest of us.

Dora, like other "team moms," is doing work before, during, and after the game—making fliers, communicating with parents, collecting money, keeping lists and records, organizing parties, and making sure everyone knows the schedule of upcoming events. And she is sandwiching this work around other volunteer activities with another youth organization. This kind of labor keeps organizations running, and it helps to create and sustain the kind of vibrant community "for the kids" that people imagine when they move to a town like Roseville (Daniels, 1985).

Sorting and Soft Essentialism

In this article, we have revealed the workings of a gender-category sorting process that reflects the interactional "doing" of gender discussed by West and Zimmerman (1987). Through this sorting process, the vast majority of women volunteers are channeled into a team parent position, and the vast majority of men volunteers become coaches. To say that people are "sorted" is not to deny their active agency in this process. Rather, it is to underline that organizations are characterized by self-perpetuating "inequality regimes" (Acker, 2006). What people often think of as "free individual choices" are actually choices that are shaped by social contexts. We have shown how women's choices to become team parents are constrained by the fact that few, if any, men will volunteer to do this less visible and less honored job. Women's choices are enabled by their being actively recruited—"volunteered"—by head coaches or by other parents to become the "team mom." Moreover, men's choices to volunteer as assistant coaches and not as team parents are shaped by the gendered assumptions of head coaches, enacted through active recruiting and informal interactions at the initial team meeting.

This gender category sorting system is at the heart of the current state of play of the gender regime of adult volunteer work in youth sports in Roseville. There are several ways we can see the sorting system at work. First, our research points to the role of gendered language and meanings in this process. The term *coach* and the term *team mom* are saturated with gendered assumptions that are consistent with most people's universe of meanings. These gendered meanings mesh with—and mutually reinforce—the conventional gendered divisions of labor and power in the organization in ways that make decisions to "go with the flow" appear natural. Second, we have shown how having women do the background support work while men do the visible leadership work on the team is also made to appear natural to the extent that it reiterates the gender divisions of labor that many parents experience in their families and in their workplaces. Roseville is a diverse community that is dominated culturally by White, professional-class families, who—partly through the language and practice of youth sports—create a culturally hegemonic (though not a numerical majority) family form in which educated mothers have "opted out" of professional careers to engage in community volunteer work and "intensive mothering" of their own children (Hays, 1996; Stone, 2007).

The women we interviewed who had opted out of professional careers narrated their decisions to do so in language of personal choice rather than constraint. The husbands of these women say that they support their wives' choices. This language of (women's) personal choice also saturates coaches' discussions of why women become "team moms." By contrast, when people talk about men, they are far less likely to do so using a language of choice. Men seem to end up in public careers or as youth sports coaches as a matter of destiny. Grounded in the strains and tensions of contemporary professional-class work–family life, this discourse on gender recasts feminist beliefs in a woman's "right to choose" as her responsibility to straddle work and family life, while the man continues "naturally" to be viewed as the main family breadwinner. We call this ascendant gender ideology "soft essentialism." Youth sports are a powerful institution in which children are initiated into a gender-segregated world with its attendant ideology of soft essentialism (Messner, forthcoming).

In the past, sport tended to construct a categorical "hard" essentialism—boys and men, it was believed, were naturally suited to the aggressive, competitive world of sport, while girls and women were not. Today, with girls' and women's massive influx into sport, these kinds of categorical assumptions of natural difference can no longer stand up to even the most cursory examination. Soft essentialism, as an ascendant professional-class gender ideology, frames sport as a realm in which girls are empowered to exercise individual choice (rehearsing choices they will later face in straddling the demands of careers and family labor) while continuing to view boys as naturally hardwired to play sports (and ultimately, to have public careers). Girls are viewed as flexibly facing a future of choices, boys as inflexible, facing a linear path toward public careers. Soft essentialism, in short, initiates kids into an adult world that has been only partially transformed by feminism, where many of the burdens of bridging and balancing work and family strains are still primarily on women's shoulders. Men coaches and "team moms" symbolize and exemplify these tensions.

Time after time, we heard leaders of leagues and some women coaches say that the league leadership works hard to recruit more women coaches but just cannot get them to volunteer. The *formal agency* here is to "recruit more women coaches." But what Martin (2001) calls the *informal practicing of gender* (revealed most clearly in our field note vignettes) amounts to a collective and (mostly) nonreflexive sorting system that, at the entry level, puts most women and men on separate paths. Martin's work has been foundational in showing how gender works in organizations in informal, nonreflexive ways that rely on peoples' "tacit knowledge" about gender. In particular, she points out "how and why well-intentioned, 'good people' practise gender in ways that do harm" (Martin, 2006, p. 255).

Our study shows a similar lack of "bad guys" engaged in overt acts of sexism and discrimination. Instead, we see a systemic reproduction of gender categorization, created nonreflexively by "well intentioned, good people." The mechanisms of this nonreflexive informal practicing of gender are made to seem normal through their congruence with the "tacit knowledge" of soft essentialism that is itself embedded in hegemonic professional-class family and workplace gender divisions of labor. The fact that soft essentialism emerges from the intersections of these different social contexts means that any attempt to move toward greater equality for women and men in youth sports presupposes simultaneous movements toward equality in workplaces and families.

Questions for Reflection and Discussion

What can we learn from the experiences of women coaches in youth sports about occupational "pipelines" in other traditionally male-dominated fields, like science and technology professions or the military? What is the importance of gendered language (like "team moms") in helping to shape gender relations in daily life? How might women's and men's belief that gender divisions of labor result from their "individual choices" serve to obscure institutional, interactional, and symbolic factors that differently constrain or enable women's and men's choices? What can we learn from the actions and strategies of women coaches and other pioneers who cross or attempt to eliminate gender boundaries?

Note

1   Roseville is a pseudonym for the town we studied. All names of people interviewed or observed for this study are also pseudonyms.

References

Acker, J. (2006). Inequality regimes: Gender, class, and race in organizations. *Gender & Society, 20*(4), 441–464.

Boyle, M., & McKay, J. (1995). "You leave your troubles at the gate": A case study of the exploitation of older women's labor and "leisure" in sport. *Gender & Society, 9*, 556–576.

Britton, D. (2000). The epistemology of the gendered organization. *Gender & Society, 14*, 418–434.

Connell, R. W. (1987). *Gender and power.* Stanford, CA: Stanford University Press.

Daniels, A. K. (1985). Invisible work. *Social Problems, 34*, 363–374.

Dworkin, S. L. (2001). Holding back: Negotiating a glass ceiling on women's muscular strength. *Sociological Perspectives, 44*(3), 333–350.

England, P. (2006). Toward gender equality: Progress and bottlenecks. In F. D. Blau, M. C. Brinton, & D. B. Grusky (Eds.), *The declining significance of gender?* New York, NY: Russell Sage.

Grasmuck, S. (2005). *Protecting home: Class, race, and masculinity in boys' baseball.* New Brunswick, NJ: Rutgers University Press.

Hays, S. (1996). *The cultural contradictions of motherhood.* New Haven, CT: Yale University Press.

Hook, J. L. (2004). Reconsidering the division of household labor: Incorporating volunteer work and informal support. *Journal of Marriage and Family, 66*, 101–117.

Lareau, A. (2003). *Unequal childhoods: Class, race, and family life.* Berkeley, CA: University of California Press.

Martin, P. Y. (2001). Mobilizing masculinities: Women's experiences of men at work. *Organization, 8*, 587–618.

Martin, P. Y. (2006). Practicing gender at work: Further thoughts on reflexivity. *Gender, Work and Organization, 13*, 254–276.

Messner, M. A. (2002). *Taking the field: Women, men and sports.* Minneapolis, MN: University of Minnesota Press.

Messner, M. A. Forthcoming. *It's all for the kids: Gender, families and youth sports.* Berkeley, CA: University of California Press.

Montez de Oca, J. (2005). As our muscles get softer, our missile race becomes harder: Cultural citizenship and the "muscle gap." *Journal of Historical Sociology, 18*, 145–171.

Ollilainen, M., & Calasanti, T. (2007). Metaphors at work: Maintaining the salience of gender in self-managing teams. *Gender & Society, 21*, 5–27.

Saltzman Chafetz, J., & Kotarba, J. A. (1999). Little League mothers and the reproduction of gender. In J. Coakley & P. Donnelly (Eds.), *Inside sports* (pp. 46–54). London, England: Routledge.

Stone, P. (2007). *Opting out: Why women really quit careers and head home.* Berkeley, CA: University of California Press.

Thompson, S. (1999). The game begins at home: Women's labor in the service of sport. In J. Coakley & P. Donnelly (Eds.), *Inside sports.* London, England: Routledge.

Thorne, B. (1993). *Gender play: Girls and boys in school.* New Brunswick, NJ: Rutgers University Press.

Thorne, B., Kramarae, C., & Henley, N. (1983). *Language, gender and society.* Rowley, MA: Newbury House.

West, C., & Zimmerman, D. H. (1987). Doing gender. *Gender & Society, 1*, 125–151.

9

Gender and Sport Participation in Montenegro

••••••••••••••••••••••

CHERYL COOKY, MARKO BEGOVIC,

DON SABO, CAROLE A. OGLESBY,

AND MARJ SNYDER

Typically as researchers, we have a specific idea for a study that we systematically plan and implement. Every now and then, however, a research idea "falls into your lap." This was the case with the research presented in this chapter. I first met Don Sabo, one of the coauthors on this paper, at an academic conference nearly two decades ago. I was a graduate student presenting a paper I had written for a statistics course. In the paper, I challenged some of the results of one of Sabo's research articles. Lucky for me, Sabo was quite forgiving of my young bravado and we became close colleagues, in part because of shared interest and advocacy for girls' and women's sports participation. Don Sabo was also the research director for the Women's Sports Foundation, which is the premier nonprofit organization in the United States founded by Billie

Source: "Gender and sport participation in Montenegro," by C. Cooky, M. Begovic, D. Sabo, C. A. Oglesby, & M. Snyder, 2014, *International Review for the Sociology of Sport, 51*(8), pp. 917–939, doi:10.1177/1012690214559109. Copyright 2014 by the Authors. Reprinted with permission of Sage Publications.

Jean King dedicated to gender equality in women's sports. As the research director, he produced a number of important reports that assisted the Women's Sports Foundation in their efforts to advocate for gender equality in sports. When the Women's Sports Foundation received a call from a representative from a Montenegrin NGO seeking assistance for a nationwide assessment of girls' and women's participation in sport, according to Sabo, he responded, "We need to get Cooky on this!" and the rest is history. In all seriousness, as a junior assistant professor, I was quite flattered and appreciative of the opportunity to partner with the Women's Sports Foundation. I believe I learned more on this project than any other during my career. Part of the project entailed my travel to Montenegro to visit with key government officials, female athletes, and coaches in women's sports. I met with representatives of the Montenegrin Olympic Committee, the Ministry of Education and Sports, and the Ministry of Human and Minority Rights, among other political figures and sports delegates. The United Nations Development Program, a partner on the project, organized a press conference, and the results from the study were discussed in the evening news and in the major newspapers. It was quite an experience to meet with my Montenegrin collaborator, Marko Begovic, and to be able to meet with such powerful and influential individuals who were highly invested in developing women's sports. I had never traveled outside the United States, other than to Canada, and certainly had never been to a country where English was not an official language! Of course, the language and cultural barrier was at times quite difficult to navigate, yet the "love for the sport" that Montenegrin female athletes attributed to their participation certainly needed no translation. As a feminist scholar who is highly invested in improving and enhancing opportunities for girls' and women's sports, it was an invaluable experience to see firsthand the impact of the research on advocacy efforts in the country. I still keep in touch with my Montenegrin collaborator and friend, Marko, and I am always pleased to hear the latest developments or achievements for girls' and women's sports in his country.

—Cheryl Cooky

Introduction

Researchers in the United States and elsewhere have found that girls and women's participation in sport is linked to a number of positive outcomes, including a decreased likelihood for breast cancer and osteoporosis in adulthood, decreased incidence of smoking or illicit drug use, improved educational outcomes and academic performance, and decreased likelihood of depression, suicide, and risky sexual behaviors during teenage years (Staurowsky et al., 2009; Tucker Center for Research, 2007). Girls' sport participation in the United States also has been associated with family satisfaction and improved quality of life for girls (Sabo & Veliz, 2008). Systematic summaries of extant research in the United States conclude that girls and women who participate in sport benefit from a number of positive psychological outcomes including increased levels of self-esteem and confidence (Tucker Center for Research, 2007; United Nations, 2007), and socially, girls and women experience empowerment through their sport participation (Division, 2007). Participation in specific sports has also been associated with educational achievement among both girls and boys (Sabo & Veliz, 2013).

Although sport can provide many benefits, girls and women in many countries, including the Global North, face a number of different obstacles that can limit their interest and participation in sport. These barriers vary in terms of their complexity and potential to be remedied and can range from a lack of proper clothing and equipment to cultural stereotypes or decreased opportunities that result from war and political conflict. For example, cultural stereotypes play a role in many countries, channeling girls and women into specific sports. These sports are often less culturally valued than the sports men typically play, resulting in fewer resources for female athletes, less prize money and lower salaries than men's sports (Division, 2007). Women from certain cultural backgrounds may also encounter barriers to their participation based on cultural beliefs. For example, certain Muslim women in Egypt, depending on their interpretation of the Koran, see sport and physical activity as in conflict with their religious beliefs (Walseth & Fasting, 2003). In Afghanistan, the political climate and the cultural beliefs of the Taliban have proved a significant barrier to participation in sport, particularly girls and women's participation in sport. Moreover, economic factors play a role. For example, researchers in the United Kingdom have found that women who work in what they termed "routine" or "semi-routine" jobs like care assistants, shop assistants, and cleaners had lower levels of participation in physical activity and sport than women who worked in professional or managerial roles (UK Sport, 2006).

At the same time, researchers note the ways that girls and women's sport participation can be encouraged and facilitated. For example, a nongovernmental organization (NGO) in Zambia provides proper clothing so that girls can play football (Division, 2007). The Afghan Women's Network helps to create opportunities for girls and women to participate in sport and physical activity. In the United States, Title IX (governmental legislation prohibiting discrimination on the basis of sex) has had a tremendous impact on increasing the levels of participation of girls and women in high school and collegiate sports (Carpenter & Acosta, 2004). Nonprofit organizations design and deliver programs specifically to address the needs of girls, and in particular the needs of low-income, minority girls (Cooky, 2009). Advocacy groups, NGOs and other organizations throughout the world are working on behalf of girls and women to increase participation and to improve upon those opportunities. The majority of the published research on gender and sport, appearing in higher profile journals, focuses on Western/Global North and/or developed countries (Brady, 2011). Certainly, little is known about the current context of girls and women's sport in Montenegro. The purpose of this study was to conduct the first evidence-based research assessing the current status of girls and women's sport participation in Montenegro at all institutional levels. The research identifies who plays organized sport in Montenegro and the factors (family, education, economic, gender stereotypes, and so on) that contribute to, or that limit, girls and women's participation in sport. The goals of the study were to determine the numbers of girls and women participating in sport as compared to boys and men in similar categories, to identify why girls and women do or do not participate in sport, and to examine perceived sport experiences of female athletes and of those who work in professional roles (coach, medical staff, manager, delegate, and so on) in female athletics.

As research in the United States has shown, sport provides many benefits (see Staurowsky et al., 2009; Tucker Center for Research, 2007). If the same is true for girls and women in Montenegro, then there are important implications for women in sport in Montenegro. Increasing the number of girls and women participating in sport—and improving the quality of their sport experiences—can have a number of societal benefits to the development of Montenegro in the 21st century, including improved academic performance, the enhancement of physical and psychological health, and the social advancement of girls and women. Gender equity at all levels and in all institutions can promote human development and human capital in this newly transitioning society. The findings generated by this study may also serve as a benchmark for future monitoring and assessments of gender and sport participation in Montenegro. This research may also help researchers in the United States and elsewhere to understand the similarities and differences in the trends of women's sport participation.

The purpose of the first wave of the study (Wave I) was to conduct a baseline assessment of opportunities and funding among men's and women's sports in Montenegro to determine any gender disparities in participation. This information provided the overall trends in sport participation in Montenegro to determine the extent of gender equality or inequality in the country and to identify any gendered patterns in participation, such as differences in participation rates regionally, by profession (coach, medical staff, manager, etc.), or by sport. The purpose of the second wave of the study (Wave II) was to determine the factors that may serve as barriers to participation for girls and women, as well as to identify the factors that facilitate girls and women's involvement in sport. The overall objective of the study was to assess, both quantitatively and qualitatively, female sport participation in Montenegro to determine patterns of gender equality or inequality, to identify key facilitators and barriers, to develop evidence-based strategies for increasing women's sport participation, and to inform the development of gender-specific sports policies and legislation.

At the time of the study, Montenegro lacked the systemic, institutional, and individual capacity to produce and maintain adequate baseline statistical data in many developing fields, and sports were no exception. There has been no systemic effort on a national level to collect and maintain the gender-related data in sports, which could then be used to inform policy development and implementation. For the first time, this study produces the relevant information needed not only for research, but for policy. We hope the findings generated by this study will serve as a benchmark for future monitoring of gender equality and assessments of gender and sport participation in Montenegro. This research also yields insights on the similarities and differences in the trends of female sport participation in transitioning societies.

Gender Inequality in Montenegro

Since 2006, when the Montenegrin Parliament declared independence, Montenegro has experienced an impressive economic growth averaging an annual rate of 8% (up until early 2009 when the effects of the global economic crisis began to have an impact) and an upward trend in human development indicators. Nonetheless, these two factors have been accompanied by a rise in gender inequality. In Montenegro, women do not have equal opportunity or institutional conditions to contribute effectively to social, cultural, economic, and political development in ways that might allow them to benefit from that very development (Montenegro Department of Gender Equality, 2007). The wider regional economic and political instability and the ensuing political and military crisis of the 1990s only further exacerbated the situation, which contributed to a significant deterioration in the overall position of women in the Montenegrin society. Here we draw upon the data available at the time of the study to accurately reflect gender relations. Within the realm of politics, although 51.8% of the population in Montenegro is female, women held only 11% of all seats in the Montenegrin Parliament and only 7% of all seats in local parliaments. Of a total of 17 ministers, only one was a woman, and similarly only one out of 21 mayors was a woman. The extent of women's participation in business is similarly sparse. An estimated 39.5% of all employees were women yet only 7.2% perform managerial tasks, and only 1% were business owners (Montenegro Department of Gender Equality, 2007). Only 6% of women owned cars and only 8% owned or coowned homes and/or apartments. In terms of domestic violence, civic sector research showed that every third woman in Montenegro is a victim of physical violence. In 2008, the rate of reported cases of domestic violence increased by 7.8% (European Union, 2008), as had the number of murders committed as the culmination of long-term family violence. These statistics may actually underestimate the actual incidence of domestic violence, as women are often unlikely to report such cases, particularly given the lack of support networks and resources for abused women. The data on education revealed a similar picture in terms of gender inequality. While the overall literacy rates in Montenegro were quite high, the number of illiterate women was four times higher than the number of illiterate men; 4.2% versus 0.8% (Statistical Office of Montenegro, 2010). Additionally, men achieved higher levels of education. The gender disparity in educational attainment increased with advanced level degrees; for example, whereas 50.7% of men and 49.3% of women completed masters' degree programs, 78.5% of doctoral degrees were awarded to men, compared to 21.4% awarded to women (Statistical Office of Montenegro, 2010).

Overall, the national outlook of gender inequality was reflected regionally. However, there were some disparities among the three main regions (north, south, and central) in terms of economics and social resources. Moreover,

Montenegro is ethnically diverse and economic disparities vary among those ethnic groups. In the north of Montenegro, which is the most economically underdeveloped region and is traditionally more conservative, relative to the south and central regions, only 30% of women were employed compared to a 45% employment rate for women living in the south or central regions of Montenegro (Montenegro Department of Gender Equity, 2007).

Women in Montenegro experience discrimination with respect to income, career promotion, professional development, and participation in strategic decision-making. There is a general consensus that a first step forward in addressing this situation is to improve institutional mechanisms for enforcement of gender sensitive policies (e.g., the Ministry for Human and Minority Rights) that would eliminate cultural and gender biases in national strategic frameworks and to mainstream gender awareness into all relevant programs and policies nationwide. Sport plays a very important role in Montenegrin national identity, especially during times where economic crises exacerbate the gap between classes with potential negative impacts on the vulnerable population, given it is a transitioning society and a relatively new nation-state. Ensuring higher participation of women in all social, political, and economic institutions, including sport, will contribute to the overall level of human development and stability in Montenegro.

Methodology

Background of the Study

The Montenegro Olympic Committee and a Montenegrin NGO called Inovativnost partnered with the Women's Sports Foundation (USA) to assess gender and participation rates in Montenegro. The second author worked for Inovativnost at the time of the study and contacted the Women's Sports Foundation to assess interest in establishing a research partnership. The last author was the research director for the Women's Sports Foundation and identified researchers in the United States with an expertise on women's sport participation (first, third, and fourth authors) to design and assist the Montenegrin partners in the design, implementation, and analysis. This study is a unique, multicultural collaboration between scholars, researchers, and advocates from NGOs, nonprofit organizations, and universities in Montenegro and in the United States.

At the time of the study, Montenegro lacked systemic institutional and individual capacity to produce and maintain statistical databases in many fields, including sports. There had been no sustained effort on a national level to collect and maintain gender-related sports participation data to inform policy development and implementation. Thus this study represents the first evidence-based investigation into gender and sport participation in Montenegro.

The research design combined descriptive statistics with focus groups in order to describe and analyze participation rates (in part to establish baseline data that could then be used to track trends in participation rates over time) as well as barriers and facilitators to sport participation to better understand the contemporary context of sport participation.

Wave I: Quantitative Assessment of Gender and Participation

According to Montenegrin law (Law.on.Sport, article.87-Official Gazette [36/11]), the National Sport Federations (an umbrella group of each sport) are required to keep a registrar of the people within their club or association. Clubs and associations submit this information to the National Sport Federation for their sport. Members of the Montenegrin research team requested these registrars from the seven most popular sports in Montenegro (football [soccer], volleyball, basketball, water polo, handball, judo, and track and field) and received completed surveys from the associations and clubs from six of the seven sports (water polo provided only partial data and was thus excluded from our analysis). As such, we have complete data for each of the sports associations and sport clubs from the 21 municipalities, thus providing a representative sample of sports participation in Montenegro. Considering that the research was conducted in summer 2010, when many athletes are changing clubs, the data was collected at the end of the 2009–2010 sports season.

Descriptive statistics were generated from raw data solicited by the sport associations (data on referees, medical staff, and delegates) and sports clubs (data on coaches, managerial staff, and athletes) for each of the 21 municipalities within the country at the end of the 2009–2010 sports season. We assessed the number of clubs within each of the seven sports identified to determine the geographical distribution of sports opportunities, gender differences in participation rates, and the distribution of men and women as athletes, managerial staff, coaches, medical staff, referees, and delegates. There had been no systemic effort on a national level to collect and maintain the gender related data in sports to inform policy development and implementation. This study seeks to address that gap.

Wave II: Qualitative Assessment of Gender and Sport Participation

In December 2010 and January 2011, the second author in collaboration with Montenegrin professors with expertise in focus group methodology conducted a total of 10 semistructured focus groups. Two focus groups, comprised of six to nine female athletes, were conducted in each of the three geographical regions (North: 13 participants; Central: 17 participants, and South: 14 participants) for a total of six focus groups with 44 female athletes. Female athletes were recruited through the Montenegro Olympic Committee. Focus groups were heterogeneous in terms of sport-type as female athletes from various sports participated in a given focus group in order to create diversity in experiences. Focus groups were homogenous in terms of gender and geographic location (two focus groups with female athletes from the north region, for example). We wished to explore how athletes got involved in sport and to identify the facilitators that enable their participation and the barriers they, and other women in Montenegro, confront. We also asked female athletes their thoughts on addressing barriers to girls and women's participation and what suggestions they had for increasing and improving female sport participation in Montenegro.

We also conducted focus groups with sports professionals who work in women's sports. Sports professionals are individuals who are hired by the sports clubs or associations and are not athletes (i.e., coaches, managerial staff, medical staff, delegates). Two focus groups were conducted with female professionals and two focus groups were conducted with male professionals. Eleven female professionals participated in two focus groups (one group had five participants, one group had six) and eight male professionals participated in two focus groups (four participants in each focus group) for a total of four focus groups with 19 women's sports professionals. Women's sports professionals (male or female) were recruited through the Montenegro Olympic Committee. To enhance openness, focus groups were homogenous in terms of gender but were heterogeneous in terms of type of sport and professional role (coach, delegate, medical staff, etc.). We wished to explore the dearth of women in decision-making positions in sports clubs and associations (as was determined through the descriptive statistics from Wave I) as well as to examine their perceptions regarding the trends in participation rates (Wave I) and facilitators and barriers to female athletic sport participation. As with our female athlete focus group, we asked women's sports professionals their thoughts on addressing barriers to girls and women's participation and what suggestions they had for increasing and improving female sport participation in Montenegro.

Focus groups were conducted either at a university in Montenegro, a local high school, the Montenegro Olympic Committee building, or similar public spaces. All focus group participants signed a consent form and completed a demographic questionnaire (name, sport, and years played for athletes; years with the team and years in professional role for the professionals). The focus group moderator also verbally explained the rights of the participants. Human participant protocol was followed according to research procedures in Montenegro, informed by protocol in the United States. The Montenegro Olympic Committee approved the protocol for the research, which upheld ethical treatment of human participants, including the confidentiality of the responses and of the participants and the secure storage of data. All participants are identified by pseudonyms to ensure confidentiality.

The focus groups were conducted in Montenegrin and audio-recorded. Transcripts of the focus groups were transcribed verbatim in Montenegrin and subsequently translated to English by members of the Montenegro research team. Focus group transcripts were analyzed by members of the United States research team in consultation with a member of the Montenegro research team, the second author. Two researchers independently read the transcripts and analyzed the transcripts and coded the transcript using open coding procedures (Corbin & Strauss, 2007). Open coding allows researchers to examine in detail to uncover ideas and meanings of the participants. In the open coding, transcripts are read in detail. The open codes were reviewed for consistency and no discrepancy was found. The open codes were then further analyzed using axial coding procedures (Corbin & Strauss, 2007). In axial coding, thematic patterns between the codes that emerged in open coding are identified, and connections and linkages among the open codes are examined. These patterns were developed into major themes, which are reported in the results. To ensure the interpretive validity of the data, the research team performed member checking of themes. This involved the first and fourth author reviewing themes. Any discrepancies in the analysis and interpretation of data were discussed until agreement among the research team was reached.

In September 2011, the Wave I study was shared by the first and second authors with key stakeholders (Montenegrin Olympic Committee), governmental (Office of Gender Equity) and nongovernmental agencies (United Nations Montenegrin Office), as well as with the public through a press conference, which was picked up by major national newspapers and television news in Montenegro. The initial findings of the Wave II study were later distributed to the key stakeholders in Montenegro.

Results

Within six of the seven selected sports included in the report, a total of 6,576 individuals participate in football, volleyball, basketball, handball, judo, and track and field (see Table 9.1). Of this number, 4,376 were athletes. Among athletes, there were 2,995 men (68.4%) and 1,381 women (31.6%). There were a total of 340 coaches, of which 308 were men (90.6%) and 32 were women (9.4%). There were a total of 1,093 managers and decision-makers on both the level of clubs and associations, of which 989 were men (90.5%) and 104 were women (9.5%). There were a total of 212 medical staff, of which 153 were men (72.2%) and 59 were women (27.8%). There were a total of 490 referees, of which 425 were men (86.7%) and 65 were women (13.3%). There were a total of 65 delegates, of which 64 were men (98.5%) and only one was a woman.

The overall findings in relation to gender and sport participation were consistent across the different geographical regions (see Table 9.2), which suggests that geographic region may not play a meaningful role in influencing whether or not men and women participate in sport. There were, however, some differences in the types of sports men and women played in the different regions. This may indicate that some sports were more popular, accepted, or easier to access for women in the central regions, while other sports were more popular, accepted, or easier to access for women in the northern and southern regions. The greatest gender imbalance was noted at the level of National Sports Federations, where the ratio is nine to one, in favor of men.

The data showed that gender parity differed across sports (see Table 9.3). There was relative equality in participation rates for men and women in volleyball (51.3% women, 48.7% men) and handball (45% women, 55% men). However, each of the other four sports were male-dominated with approximately 75% or more of male participants: track and field (25.7% women vs. 74.3% men), judo (20% women vs. 80% men), basketball (13.4% women vs. 86.6% men), and football (12.7% women vs. 87.3% men). It should be noted that football and basketball had the lowest percentages of women. The greatest gender disparities occurred in football and basketball.

Table 9.1. Men and Women in Sports by Position

Gender				Position				Total
		Athlete	Coach	Managerial position	Medical staff	Referees	Delegates	
Male	Number	2995	308	989	153	425	64	4,934
	%	68.4	90.6	90.5	72.2	86.7	98.5	75.0
Female	Number	1381	32	104	59	65	1	1,642
	%	31.6	9.4	9.5	27.8	13.3	1.5	25.0
Total	Number	4376	340	1,093	212	490	65	6,576
	%	100.0	100.0	100.0	100.0	100.0	100.0	100.0

Table 9.2. Men and Women in Sports by Region

Gender				Region		Total
		Northern	Central	Southern	National level	
Male	Number	1,028	2,281	883	742	4,934
	%	72.9	71.7	76.0	90.0	75.0
Female	Number	382	899	279	82	1,642
	%	27.1	28.3	24.0	10.0	25.0
Total	Number	1,410	3,180	1,162	824	6,576
	%	100.0	100.0	100.0	100.0	100.0

Table 9.3. Men and Women in Sports by Sport

Gender				Sport				Total
		Football	Volleyball	Basketball	Handball	Judo	Track and Field	
Male	Number	1,309	250	570	530	1,234	1,041	4,934
	%	87.3	48.7	86.6	55.0	80.0	74.3	75.0
Female	Number	190	263	88	433	308	360	1,642
	%	12.7	51.3	13.4	45.0	20.0	25.7	25.0
Total	Number	1,499	513	658	963	1,542	1,401	6,576
	%	100.0	100.0	100.0	100.0	100.0	100.0	100.0

While women participated in many sport clubs, they were also underrepresented within sport clubs. Women were almost absent from decision-making positions in sport clubs and federations. Women typically occupied low entry-level positions such as secretaries, and there were very few, if any, female directors or managers. A similar pattern of findings emerged among coaches. There were some women coaches in a few sports, but male coaches tended to dominate even in the women's clubs.

Facilitators to Sport Participation

In the following sections we present the results from the focus groups. Female athletes and professionals (those working in sports as a coach, referee, delegate, etc.) were asked to discuss what factors led them to participate in sport. The major themes across all focus groups were family, friends, and "love for the sport."

Family and friends. Nearly half of female athletes said a male relative was a source of encouragement, such as a brother, father, or uncle who either played sport or was a coach who encouraged them to get involved. Female relatives also played a role. When asked what things made it easier for them to play sports, female athletes mentioned family and specifically their mothers. As Sanja explained, "Understanding and tolerance from the family is the most important, whether we talk about sports or anything else." Ljiljana agreed with the importance of parents in facilitating her sport participation, "the influence of parents in the early years is the most important since parents wish the best for their children, to take them off the street, to motivate them to do something else."

Other female athletes also mentioned that parents encouraged their children to participate in sport to "get them off the streets," which gave them something positive to do.

Many female athletes mentioned a sister or an aunt who played or a mother who encouraged them to sign up for sports. When asked about what helped get her involved in sport, Milica said, "Family and my mom! My family is a huge support and they push me to train." And in some cases, athletes said both their parents were important in supporting their participation. Abida said, "My parents are my biggest support, along with my friends, especially during competition." Maja, a footballer, explained, "Both my parents are athletes, our entire family is sports oriented so we were brought up with immense love for sports."

While family played a critical role in encouraging girls to sign up for sport and in providing role models for girls, friends were also mentioned as a factor in getting girls involved in sport. Many athletes discussed how they played sport because their friends, who also played, encouraged them.

"Love for the sport." The other major theme that emerged in the majority of the focus groups that female athletes attributed to enabling their sport participation was the "love for the sport." There were references to character, persistence, fighting spirit, winning spirit, and the challenge of sport, specifically the desire to disprove the notion that "boys are better." Female athletes discussed how they developed a passion for the game that became a part of who they are. Milena explained, "I started playing football when I was very young, and my love for the sport is the main reason keeping me in it."

It is this "love" for the game that kept women in sport, even when confronted with considerable barriers to their participation. Female athletes discussed how their love for sport helped them to overcome barriers and to make the necessary sacrifices to become a female athlete. The love for the sport served to get girls into the game and kept them in the game. In that way, love for the sport played a key role in facilitating girls' sport participation.

Most female professionals established a career in sport because they played sport when they were younger. Similar to their female athlete counterparts, female professionals also mentioned "love for the sport" as a key factor in their entry into sport and in facilitating their sport participation and professional sport careers. They discussed their desire to continue on in the sport and their love for the sport: "I love what I do and when I come to the practice and see those girls, I have a responsibility toward them and that is why I fight" (Vanja, football).

Moreover, female professionals discussed how "love for the sport" was critical in overcoming barriers.

> When I came here (from former USSR) in '91, we didn't have enough food to eat but we still practiced twice a day on a field that had no heating. Our club survived due to enthusiasm of its players and people who led the club. We had a deal—if we don't win the matches, we don't get what we signed our contract for. Some people stayed and some left. The results are incredible—a little country like Montenegro has the results that many larger countries don't. (Tina, handball)

Tina's discussion illustrates the importance of individual resilience in the face of significant barriers to participation. The lack of access to the basic necessities of life (food, proper shelter, etc.), let alone of sport, poses tremendous constraints on female athletes, yet Tina and others persisted in spite of these constraints. Yet individual agency is enacted in a complex web of interconnected social forces and, thus, experiences are not similar across all individuals. Put simply, although some female athletes were able to transcend these barriers to participation because of their "love for the sport," this does not indicate that these barriers did not constrain the participation experiences of other women. Indeed, some of the most robust and engaged discussions centered on the structural, cultural, and interpersonal barriers female athletes confront, which were more readily identified and more deeply engaged in the focus group discussions.

Barriers to Sport Participation

Both the female athletes and professionals in women's sports discussed the barriers women faced in sport. In most focus groups, discussions about barriers were often directly attributed to experiences with gender inequality (discussed in more detail below and including division of labor in the family, negotiation of school/sport balance, lack of resources, gender stereotypes, and so on). Forms of gender inequality were the principle barriers to girls and women's sport participation and to a professional career. Female athletes spent a great deal of time discussing the barriers and obstacles they had encountered. In comparison, the discussion of the facilitators to sport participation was relatively brief and rarely evoked detailed stories, examples, lived experiences, and emotions. This disparity in the findings suggests that barriers to sport participation were a more salient facet of women's sport experiences than facilitators. The key barriers that emerged are discussed below.

Family. While family dynamics often served as a facilitator to girls' participation, they also functioned as a barrier. Several participants discussed how their mothers explicitly discouraged them from participating in sport. After Sanja graduated from high school, she wanted to attend college so she could continue to participate in sports while in college. Instead, her mother advised her to stop playing sport and to focus on her education because, "after all, you're a girl." Sanja's mother's perspective illustrates both the reality that professional opportunities are limited for women in sports, as well as gendered cultural expectations of young women. Sanja explained that it was her father who encouraged her in sport, despite her mother's concerns. When Mira was young, she wanted to play football. Her mother, however, did not support this decision. Instead, her father got her involved in handball, a more culturally appropriate sport for girls and women. As Tanja, explained:

> Well, even some parents believe that their girls shouldn't play football. One of my friends was interested to join my club and I gave her the contacts. After a few days I asked her how it was going. She said that her parents don't agree with her playing football and they told her it would be better if she stuck with dolls. And that was the reason she cited for not starting the practice. Her parents thought football was too rough of a sport and that it is [*sic*] meant for boys only and she gave up.

Parents were also pressured by other family members to prohibit their daughters from playing sport. Ana's aunt begged her mother for a year to stop her from playing handball. Iva said that her grandmother asked her during visits, "How long will you keep this up [playing sport]? When will you get married and have kids?" Even when parents are supportive, they often are aware that others may feel differently. Maja explained that while her mom was very proud of her accomplishments in school and in sport, she does not tell people she plays football.

Several female professionals also discussed the family as a barrier to girls' participation. Gordana, a former coach and referee explained:

> Twelve years ago you couldn't see a female participating in sport or doing some running exercise. My uncle said to me: Stop playing sport and go and get married. Sadly, here it's all about entrenched stereotypes—if you are a woman, you need to stay home and give birth to babies and cook.

Gendered division of labor. In Montenegro, as in other countries, women who marry are expected to balance children and family obligations with their athletic career. Hochschild (2003) referred to the labor that employed women do inside the home, such as taking care of children, cooking and cleaning, as the "second shift." Men in general, and male athletes specifically, were not expected to participate in this "second shift." As Jelena said, "Men continue with sports after their 20s, while women, if they have kids or get a job, immediately stop with their (sport) career." As such, men do not face the same constraints on their time given that the gendered division of labor in households places the burden of domestic labor primarily upon women.

While female athletes were aware that the gendered division of labor was a barrier to a future career in sport, the female professionals had experienced it directly. The gendered division of labor produced a context wherein women were confronted by the choice between a family or a career in sport. For women who want both, in order to balance the conflicting responsibilities and obligations of having a family and being an athlete or a professional in sports, they explained that they must make difficult "sacrifices." One male professional in women's track and field said:

> I think it's more difficult for a woman to be away from the house for a long time with the family and kids, they often choose to stay at home and this in my view is the biggest barrier as I don't think it'd be logical for a mother to be away from her kids for long periods of time.

Many female athletes and female professionals discussed the sacrifices women have to make in order to play sport or to continue in a career in sports. As Iva observed, "If you are seriously involved in the sport and train professionally, there is very little time for anything else." Female athletes and professionals had to sacrifice school/education or family in order to be successful in sport. It is their "love" for sport or support from their parents, however, that helped them to overcome this specific barrier. Jelena said, "I don't think we could do what we do unless we really loved sports . . . but we have to think of our future. If we get injured then we have to have something to fall back on, and that's education."

Female professionals also discussed how they had to negotiate the expectations of being a wife/mother with their sport involvement. "When we get back from a game, he [her husband] goes in the shower and I go in the kitchen . . ." (Svetlana). Svetlana explained that if she made more money, they would be able to go to a restaurant to eat. Katarina stated she did not fly to sport events because she is a "responsible mother," but at the same time, she does not feel this is a form of gender inequality. Instead, she explained, "You have to sacrifice certain things and I did it on my own terms." Tina, now a single mother, said her husband left her because of her decision to continue with handball (at the professional level), a decision he did not approve of.

Female professionals were concerned with the lack of facilities and support for working women who are mothers, such as places to breastfeed. Zorka had to balance motherhood with sport. She explained, "I would run, breastfeed, then back to practice, diaper duty, for two years." Gordana, a referee, recounted an experience when she attended a conference in Rome. While at the conference, another female referee spoke about the difficulties in making it in the profession, given the challenges of family obligations. Gordana recalled, "She [the referee] cited the family support as the key variable that makes a difference. I don't have a child so I can dedicate more time to sports, but if I had, I don't know."

Female athletes were also aware that the gender division of labor would be a barrier that they too would eventually confront. Female athletes mentioned that as women get older, they have children and thus more responsibilities, while men have fewer as they get older. When asked why she thought there were not more women professionals in sport, Stasa explained, "Woman is the pillar of the family and she needs to take care of everything, and a man has less responsibilities." Jelena added, "They [female professionals and athletes] think they can't give 100% effort or they will neglect their child." Mirjana offered, "I agree that women have more responsibilities and in Montenegro men spend all their free time, of which they have more, for sport activities."

Female athletes also discussed the low pay with a career in sport: "When you commit to something, you expect to make a living out of it . . . if you are a woman working in sports, you have a very uncertain prospect in terms of financial compensation" (Mirna). Female athletes, particularly those from the North, were reluctant in their desire to have a career in sports (e.g., coach, referee, manager) after their athletic career ended. Milena said, "I don't know what the opportunities for women will be then, but under these circumstances, I wouldn't want to stick with sports." Mila also expressed a lack of hope in the future of sport. When asked why there was a lack of women in sports professions, Mila offered, "I think most of them give up when they see that there is no future."

Sport/school balance. While most female athletes in our study did not have children or family obligations, there were other sacrifices required to be a successful female athlete. Similar to the sacrifices women in sports careers must make to balance family and career, a key barrier discussed by the majority of female athletes was the challenge of balancing time commitments between sport and school. This was seen as a unique challenge for female athletes, as male athletes either have more opportunities to participate and earn money in sport, or they are "revered" at their school. Many female athletes realized there were either few opportunities to advance in their sport (either as an athlete or as a professional) or that being an athlete was a risky profession that could at any time end with an injury. This led female athletes to de-emphasize their sport training. Education was viewed as a necessary backup plan if or when their sport career ended. As Zana explained, "If you do sports and you are good, that can open a lot of doors in your life. But without the education, you don't have anything." Ljiljana noted, "School is something that provides us with a base. We know that we cannot do sports all our lives, so we simply need to plan on doing something else other than sports, so this is school." Iva wanted to go to college for physical education but planned to leave Montenegro after graduation. She said, "I don't think I could have a bright future in sports in Montenegro."

Sonja used to play handball professionally but now only plays occasionally because, "I tried studying and playing at the same time but it just didn't work." Tijana also said it was more difficult for female athletes: "Imagine how much money does one football player have? He is taken care of for his whole life. We have to dedicate our time to school because a female athlete has to have something on the side, because if she leans only on sports, she is doomed." Ana said, "There are girls who go to the most difficult high school, starts on a team, has all A's and gets all her obligations done—with guys this is different, they don't think, if I break my leg in ten years, what will I do?"

While emphasizing school was not inherently a "negative" outcome, the fact that female athletes did not receive the same types of support from the educational system as male athletes was perceived as a barrier. Radmila noted the lack of support she received from her school:

> Professors have very little understanding for women athletes and they often say, "Why the heck do you do sports? You won't be able to do anything with it in your life." So no matter how much I study and how many good grades I get, it doesn't make any difference.

Ana recounted a similar experience. Her teacher laughed when she said she played football. Ana's teacher did not support her absences for competition, whereas male students who are athletes were excused from classes. Ana explained:

> This past Saturday, we had to be in school to make up some lost classes but I had a game. So, I told my teacher, "I'll be away because of my game, but I'll bring a note from the club." When I came to school on Monday she asked me, "Where were you on Saturday?" I gave her a note and reminded her of our chat, but she said, "I don't care about sports." On the other hand, there is this guy who plays football and when he is away for a game he doesn't even have to bring in the note . . . he is excused.

Societal beliefs/gender stereotypes. In societies that uphold patriarchal beliefs, there often exists the "frailty myth," whereby women are thought to be physically and athletically weaker than men. According to the frailty myth, this gender difference is due to the natural, biologically inherent differences between men and women. However, researchers argue that once women were given the opportunity and access to sport participation, the so-called performance gap between men's and women's sport performances narrowed (Dowling, 2000). Yet despite women's improved performances, in the United States and in nations elsewhere, the ideology of male superiority in sport continues to persist. Female athletes discussed how these myths and stereotypes of women's natural inferiority served as a barrier to female athletic participation. As Tina explained, there is a belief in judo club that women do not "do anything while men sweat and practice hard." Moreover, she said the belief was that "Women can achieve results with much less effort than men." Indeed, a male professional illustrated this stereotypical perspective when asked in the focus group if there was gender inequality in sport.

> Girls are not serious in training, they chat around and can't wait for the training to end, while a guy kills himself. At the competition, with the little effort she put in, she wins a medal, while a guy who invests so much more than she did, can't make it through the first round.

As Ljiljana noted, even if natural differences exist between men and women, it should not matter. It does not prevent women from being as good of an athlete as a man. She explained:

> [Many people] think that women cannot do sports, maybe for physical, mental or some other reason. I don't know. This is really basic, but most people think that women cannot be as good an athlete as can be a man [*sic*]. Women and men cannot be compared on the basis of their natural physical predisposition, but a woman can be a great athlete, so women should be compared against other women, men with other men.

Similarly, there are myths regarding the influence of sport participation on the development of the female athletic body. Athletes discussed the societal stereotypes on how football causes "crooked legs" and basketball or volleyball makes one "tall." Slavica said, "One stereotype is that if you play volleyball or basketball that you'll be taller. You won't, especially if your parents are smaller." Sanja, added, "I play judo and often times people ask me if all girls who do judo are big." These stereotypes served as a barrier preventing girls and women from getting involved in sport. Some athletes thought that girls do not participate in sports because they believed sport would make them "look like men" (Tina, judo). Nikola, a male football coach, said he had to personally contact a principal to make sure his athletes were not made fun of in school. Nikola explained, "They [both teachers and students] verbally abuse my girls, telling them to stop playing sports as they'll look like men." At the same time, the pressure on women to conform to particular standards of beauty was a reason girls may participate in certain sports. For example, some female athletes said they thought girls participated in sport to lose weight. Yet none of the athletes interviewed said that weight loss was a reason they got involved or was a factor that facilitated their sport participation.

However, according to female athletes in this study, low body image leads to insecurities in physical education classes, and this may serve as a barrier to participation. "Boys make it worse. When they see that the girl is insecure, they start exploiting that weakness" (Mirna). Radmila added, "And girls take it not so well. We're girls after all and any comments that regard our physical looks are tough to take." Sanja explained, "Boys use words as compensation mechanism [if girls are better than them] to try and erect barriers."

Female professionals also confronted stereotypes regarding their abilities. The assumption many people held is that as women they were inherently not as competent or as capable as men in the same positions. Illustrating this belief, when asked if there was gender inequality in sport in Montenegro, a male professional said, "I don't think it's a sign of discrimination if we haven't had a woman be a president of a judo association. It's just the way things are. Someone with enough ambition needs to show up."

Female professionals in sport said they have to go beyond expectations to prove that they are capable at their jobs. "Men are in the key decision making positions, and if there is an attempt for a woman to break through it just fails. The stereotype says that men are reliable and women are not mentally stable" (Mila). Vesna, who is a basketball professional, explained, "Being a coach or other position requires a certain set of skills and competencies and that you [a woman] have to prove that you have them before you can do this job." Other women said they confronted the stereotype among men in the profession regarding their lack of abilities: "When I report back from a seminar they [men] laugh at me. As soon as you show that you may know a bit more than they do, that's it: a wall" (Vanja, football). "I think as girls, we have had to push and work much harder than guys to get certain things that they get as guys, in all different segments in sports" (Zorka, physical trainer). These stereotypes regarding the lack of women's competence served as a barrier to female professionals in sport.

Similar to most countries, sports in Montenegro are gendered. In other words, certain sports are viewed as culturally appropriate for men (e.g., football, basketball and judo), while others are viewed as culturally appropriate for women (e.g., volleyball). This gendered aspect of sport varies historically as well as cross-culturally. For example, while in most European and Latin American countries football is a male-identified sport, in the United States, given the historical development of American football, "soccer" is viewed as culturally appropriate for young boys and girls, particularly in suburban, White communities (Messner, 2009). However, regardless of the country, women who participate in stereotypically masculine sports encounter resistance. Female athletes in Montenegro that participated in stereotypically masculine sports said they too encountered resistance and lack of support. Iva, a volleyball athlete, explained, "In Montenegro, if a woman does football, people say 'what is she doing in football, that's a men's sport.' The society and family's stereotypes can act like a powerful hindrance for women to do sports."

Verdrana, a football player, also said that football (which she feels is not adequately represented in the media) was not accepted in Montenegro, "and when you say which sports you do, people usually say, 'What do you mean football, that is not for women.'" Ana, also in football, added:

> Usually men are associated with sports, while a girl will play with her dolls, play a piano and won't be taught (to throw) a ball or run out on a court. I stood out in my neighborhood when I played football while other girls played typical girls' games.

Female athletes resisted and challenged these sport-related stereotypes. Sanja did not agree that football is a men's sport. "Football is as much a male as it is a female sport, and in my case, I like football now as much as I liked handball before." When asked about the obstacles women in sports face, Stasa explained:

> Women tend to have more responsibilities and face more barriers. Guys do sports from a very early age and there are more guy athletes. Women in Montenegro don't do football because of a stigma that is a guy's sport. I think that our society is mainly responsible for that stigma.

Sanja added, "When I tell people I do judo they get into this defensive stance, and I feel like a monster. And they say, 'Uh watch out, there is that judo player, don't mess with her.'" Later in the focus group, she discussed how the boys in her school spread rumors about her, saying that she beats people up and she breaks their arms and legs.

Lack of opportunities, support, and resources. Female athletes, female professionals, and a few male professionals discussed the lack of opportunities, support, and resources available to female athletes as a key barrier to female sport participation. In the United States and elsewhere, women's sports advocates have been somewhat successful in their efforts to increase girls and women's access to sport and to improve the equitable distribution of funding and resources, as well as to ensure equal access to sport facilities. Without equitable access to sport opportunities, facilities, and resources, girls and women will have a difficult time overcoming cultural barriers.

One key barrier female athletes face is lack of support. They perceive a lack of support from their family, their sport association, and the society in general. Tijana said, "Imagine how difficult it is to cheer yourself on, to be your only support?" This lack of support from the sport association was especially salient for football players and for female professionals in football. Maja, a football player, said:

> The football association does not care if we compete or not compete. We don't have a league and sometime while we are en route to play a match against someone we find out that the game has been cancelled. (. . .) When girls start talking about sports, men all shut up and move elsewhere and start talking amongst themselves. They don't support what we do and I don't know why.

Nikola, a male professional in football, also stated there was a lack of support in the association for women's football. He said the association must be willing to change: "Women are marginalized in sports in Montenegro regardless of what we are talking about, that marginalization is higher in one (sport), lower in another, but present everywhere."

Another male professional agreed that the football association will continue to have problems because "they [the association] don't invest in women's football even though UEFA [Union of European Football Associations] is very strict and wishes to support development of women's sport." A female athlete in football said, "Our basic problem is, the Football Association of Montenegro does not want to develop (women's) football." A female professional in women's football alluded to the possible misappropriation of funds:

> I am sure the UEFA allocates funds for female football but who knows where that money is. They [UEFA] give us funds, specifically allocated for female football but the people from the association take it as "Well, they allocated funds to the association. We will spend as we see fit."

This lack of support from the sport association was not specific to football, although it seemed more salient to the experiences of athletes and professionals in that sport. Female athletes in other sports also noted the lack of support from their associations. Elvira said, "This year the women's junior national team [in track and field] was abolished, while men get to go all different types of competitions across Europe." Sanja lamented that the women's basketball team could not go to the European Championships.

Many female athletes identified a lack of facilities as a barrier to sport participation. Rajka explained, "When it comes to track and field, it is difficult to be a part of this sport when we don't have basic conditions to play, such as a field." There is only one track and field facility in the country, and it is located in the southern part of the country. This makes it difficult for athletes in the sport as they must travel or move in order to access the facility. Sanja posed an important question: "How will we accomplish success if we don't have anywhere to practice?"

In some cases where facilities existed, they were subpar. Several female football players said they practiced on fields that were smaller than regulation size because regulation size fields were not available. Some sport facilities had no heat, and in some communities, there was no indoor gym. As a result, female athletes, especially those from the northern region, lacked access to facilities to practice during the winter months. Pavle, a male professional in volleyball, said, "At one point we had about 100 girls playing in a very small hall. The last two years, we have a 10:00pm slot for practice and can you imagine a child that lives five kilometers out of town coming to practice at 10:00pm and going back home almost near midnight when temperatures are −20 Celsius."

In addition to an overall lack of facilities to practice and compete, a lack of equal access to facilities was discussed as a barrier. As Pavle mentioned in the above quote, women are relegated to the less desirable time spots for practice. Women's sport advocates in the United States have noted this is a key form of discrimination of female athletes. Slavica, a volleyball player, also concurred:

> Men get the best time slots for practice while girls have to do away with what we have or even try and practice in the bleachers. In our city, us and the gymnastics team never get any court time, whereas karate, where mainly men play, are OK.

The regular times we can use the court is either when we are already in school, or after 10pm.

Another key barrier is the lack of financing, funding, and sponsorships available to female athletes. This presents a barrier as the athletes or their families must pay for sport participation. The following quotes from female athletes illustrate the burden lack of funding poses:

I've been on a national team for five years. I am a professional athlete, yet the last stipend I paid was in 2009 and no one is asking me, how are you paying for the physical therapy, how are you handling the lack of equipment? (Tijana).

You have to get full equipment, transport to and from practice, everything else you need for practice; it isn't cheap. Plus, the municipality hardly ever pitches in. (Sonja).

Adding an additional burden, since most female athletes do not earn salaries in sport, they often must work to support themselves and to pay for the costs related to their training and participation.

A lot of girls try working and playing sports in order to maintain one source of funding going as you can't really make a living in most cases doing sports as a woman in Montenegro. It is difficult to do both. (Mila, professional, volleyball referee)

Female athletes also noted the unequal distribution of resources within the same club as a barrier. One female athlete said, "The men's team gets all the equipment for free. They even have salaries on the monthly level, while we have to pay for our own shoes and jerseys, not to mention salaries!"
Ljiljana said:

The amount of resources that they have relative to us was striking and evident, and when we travel they usually get a charter flight just for their team while we have to bum it with buses and red eye flights.

Female professionals and female athletes stated that funds were distributed when women's teams/athletes produced results. Nadu, a female professional in track and field, said, "I understand this logic but it is difficult when it is applied for female sports as there isn't many female athletes so it's a difficult thing to bank on one of them succeeding and then having an investment."
Several female athletes also talked about the perception that results bring in funding, but thought this logic itself was a barrier. Radmila explained, "In some cases it can be an excuse, as in 'we're expecting results and then we'll invest.' All the while they know that results will never come." Ana said, "Yes, it's all connected. We have to succeed to attract support, but we need support to succeed!"

Discussion

The International Working Group for Women and Sport (IWG) is a global coalition of organizations, foundations, and individuals committed to the use of the Brighton Declaration and other United Nations-based diplomatic instruments (e.g., Convention to Eliminate Discrimination Against Women, UN Beijing Platform for Action) to enhance opportunities and resources for girls and women in sport. The IWG has hosted major international conferences every four years since its inception in 1994. Each conference features a research report to document the status of efforts over the past quadrennial. Two examples of these documents offer hundreds of case studies that identify similar barriers as those we discovered in our examination of gender and sport participation in Montenegro (Fasting et al., 2014; White & Scoretz, 2002). These documents have examined women's participation and the barriers girls and women encounter in small island states (Trinidad and Tobago), Asian and Middle Eastern states (Malaysia, Saudi Arabia), and Central and South American states (Colombia, Nicaragua), as well as for Aboriginal and Native American peoples.

Similar to the girls and women in Montenegro, girls and women in these countries encounter similar barriers. These barriers include a need for sport policy and resources, education efforts to address the impact of negative stereotypes and myths about women, access to opportunities for physical activity and sport, fewer quality physical educators and coaches, fewer athletic role models for females, and lack of basic safety and sanitation provisions. A monograph produced by the United Nations (Division, 2007), two World Health Organization studies (2002, 2004), and a "sharing good practice" report issued by the International Council of Sport Science and Physical Education (ICSSPE; Kluka, Melling, & Scoretz, 2000) all reaffirm our findings regarding the barriers to female sport participation. Given the prevalence of research from a number of countries about the barriers for girls and women in sport, there can be little debate that action is necessary. What remains to be determined is the will of sport organizations and governments to act.

This study represents the efforts of individuals and institutions in Montenegro to address the current state of girls and women's sport in Montenegro, and as the first evidence-based study on gender and sport participation, represents the Montenegrin government's and sport organization's desire to address gender inequality. There have been tremendous gains made in women's sport in Montenegro, but efforts need to continue to achieve gender equality. Many of these gains are the direct result of individual efforts to develop female sports, and positive change has occurred because of individual people and their dedication and passion for women's sports. Individuals cannot be expected to carry this important task alone, although grassroots efforts are necessary to the successful development of girls and women's sport. This was a point reinforced in the focus group interviews with male professionals. Nikola, a football coach, explained, "The association is key. Women athletes are getting older without an opportunity to really showcase their talent. I am helping out, other individuals are helping out but without a system, without the institution, nothing will change." Pavle, a women's volleyball club founder, agreed: "Before you can think about having a change, you need support from the highest levels and support from your own environment." Dragan, also in football, noted the limits of individual efforts without institutional support: "What we have in Montenegro is a lot of enthusiasts and individuals who are fighting for different sports, but that's not sustainable."

Igor Vušurović, who at the time of the study was the director of the volleyball association in Montenegro, helped make volleyball illustrative of the successes possible in women's sport when individual efforts are supported and facilitated by institutions. Although volleyball does not have a long history in Montenegro, volleyball and handball are two sports that have gender equality in terms of sport participation. At the time of this study, there were more than 400 young girls participating in volleyball sport academies in Montenegro. These successes can be attributed in part to the success of the men's volleyball team in the 2000 Olympics (Igor Vušurović was a member of that team) and the efforts of individuals to develop the women's sport alongside the men's. Having a former professional male athlete employed full-time in a key decision-making position with a full support staff has enabled the development of the sport for women.

What this case illustrates is that while grassroots efforts are necessary, resources and support from the associations and key institutions in Montenegro must accompany those efforts. While efforts to improve female sport participation will take time, governmental offices must play a key role. Moreover, it is necessary that institutions such as the Ministry of Education and Sport and the Montenegro Olympic Committee continue their efforts to strengthen their partnerships with key stakeholders in order to successfully develop female sport in Montenegro.

In this regard, we encourage grassroots efforts to establish an NGO devoted to women's sport in Montenegro. This NGO would have the primary role of working with government, sport associations and communities to develop female sport/physical activity. The NGO could then partner with the International Working Group on Women and Sport by signing the Brighton Declaration. The IWG is a body of NGOs from around the world whose main goal is to promote and develop opportunities for girls and women in sport throughout the world (Meier, 2005). Several female athletes and female and male professionals agreed with the importance of establishing a committee or working group on women's sport. These individuals could be recruited to become members of this NGO.

In the United States and elsewhere, researchers and women's sports advocates have emphasized the importance of equal opportunity and equitable distribution of resources in sports offered in educational settings. In 1972 the United States legislature passed Title IX of the Educational Amendments. Title IX is federal legislation that prohibits educational institutions that receive federal funds from discriminating on the basis of sex. As most sport opportunities in the United States are offered in educational institutions, Title IX has made significant improvements in the distribution of opportunities for girls and women's sport. For example, before its passage in 1971, only 294,105 girls in the United States participated in high school sports. By 2009–2010 (the time of this study), that number had grown to 3,172,637

(National Federation of State High School Associations, 2009–2010). Moreover, Title IX has ushered in changes that have led to improvements in access to facilities, equipment, and resources necessary to participate in sport.

Although the sport system in Montenegro is much different than in the United States, as most athletes in Montenegro participate in club-based or professional sports, the reality that legislative action can produce significant gains in gender equality is one that may be considered in Montenegro. Legislation that ensures equal opportunities and equal distribution of resources and that has government oversight and is enforceable may facilitate the positive changes female athletes and professionals in women's sport wish to achieve.

These efforts are important not only to the individual athletes who will directly benefit but to Montenegrin society as a whole. The United Nations views sport as an integral way to empower girls and women by leading to improvements in women's physical, psychological health and by improving educational outcomes (Division, 2007). These improvements would positively contribute to the development of the Montenegrin society. More equitable gender relations in society can lead to overall improvements in family, education, politics, and the economy, as well as in other institutions. Indeed, international bodies and nongovernmental organizations—such as United Nations Educational, Scientific and Cultural Organization; United Nations Development Programme; United Nations International Children's Emergency Fund; Beyond Sport; Game Set Peace—all recognize that developing sport is a key way to achieve gender equality in society. Sport is also an important component in achieving the United Nations Millennium Development Goals (Meier, 2005; Division, 2007). The Montenegro Olympic Committee also recognizes a need to promote gender equality within the Olympic movement in Montenegro, and has established a Women and Sport working group to develop a strategy and four-year action plan for addressing women's sports.

We conclude with a quote from Vesna, a member of the basketball federation: "The success in Montenegro really ought to be measured by the number of girls participating. If we have a mass following, something good will happen for those girls and for the society."

Questions for Reflection and Discussion

Why do nations, particularly those that are transitioning or developing nations, view investing in women's sports as an important component to their overall development? In what ways were the experiences of female athletes similar to those in the United States? In what ways were they different? What factors contribute to those similarities and differences? What do you think is the role of sports for gender equality in the United States?

References

Brady, M. (2011). *Leveling the playing field: Building girls' sport programs and creating new opportunities*. New York, NY: Population Council.

Carpenter, L. J., & Acosta, R. V. (2004). *Title IX*. Champaign, IL: Human Kinetics Publishers.

Cooky, C. (2009). "Girls just aren't interested": The social construction of interest in girls' sport. *Sociological Perspectives, 52*, 259–284.

Corbin, J., & Strauss, A. (2007). *Basics of qualitative research: Techniques and procedures for developing grounded theory*. Thousand Oaks, CA: Sage.

Division for the Advancement of Women, Department of Economic and Social Affairs. (2007). *Women 2000 and beyond: Women, gender equality and sport*. New York, NY: United Nations. Retrieved November 6, 2014 from http://www.un.org/womenwatch/daw/public/Women%20and%20Sport.pdf

Dowling, C. (2000). *The frailty myth: Women approaching physical equality*. New York, NY: Random House.

European Union. (2008). *Montenegro 2008 progress report*. Commission of European Countries. Retrieved July 11, 2014 from http://ec.europa.eu/enlargement/pdf/press_corner/key-documents/reports_nov_2008/montenegro_progress_report_en.pdf

Fasting, K., Sand, T., Pike, E., et al. (2014). *From Brighton to Helsinki: Women and Sport Progress Report 1994–2014*. Valo: Finnish Sports Confederation.

Hochschild, A. (2003). *The second shift*. New York, NY: Penguin Books.

Kluka, D., Melling, C., & Scoretz, D. (2000). *Women, sport and physical activity: Sharing good practice*. Berlin, Germany: International Council of Sport Science and Physical Education.

Meier, M. (2005). *Gender equity, sport and development: A working paper*. Bienne, Switzerland: Swiss Academy for Development.

Messner, M. A. (2009). *It's all for the kids: Gender, families, and youth sports*. Berkeley, CA: University of California Press.

Montenegro Department of Gender Equality. (2007). Government database survey. Podgorica, Montenegro.

National Federation of State High School Associations. (2009–2010). Participation Data. Retrieved July 11, 2014 from http://www.nfhs.org/ParticipationStatics/PDF/2009-10%20Participation%20Survey.pdf

Sabo, D., & Veliz, P. (2008). *Go out and play: Youth sport in America*. East Meadow, NY: Women's Sports Foundation.

Sabo, D., & Veliz, P. (2013). More than a sport: Tennis, education and health. *United States Tennis Association (USTA) Serves*. Retrieved July 11, 2014 from http://www.ustaserves.com/resources/research/?intloc=headernavsub

Statistical Office of Montenegro. (2010). *Women and men in Montenegro*. Izdavač: Podgorica.

Staurowsky, E. J., DeSousa, M. J., Ducher, G., Gentner, N., Miller, K. E., Shakib, S., Theberge, N., & Williams, N. (2009). *Her life depends on it II: Sport, physical activity and the health and well-being of girls and women*. East Meadow, NY: Women's Sports Foundation.

Tucker Center for Research on Girls & Women in Sport. (2007). *Tucker Center Research Report: Developing Physically Active Girls: An Evidence-Based Multidisciplinary Approach*. Minneapolis, MN: University of Minnesota.

UK Sport. (2006). *Women in sport: The state of play*. London, England.

Walseth, K., & Fasting, K. (2003). Islam's view on physical activity and sport: Egyptian women interpreting Islam. *International Review for the Sociology of Sport, 38*, 45–60.

White, A., & Scoretz, D. (2002). *From Windhoek to Montreal: Women's sport progress report 1998–2002*. Montreal, Canada: International Working Group on Women in Sport. Retrieved October 1, 2014 from http://www.iwg-gti.org

World Health Organization. (2002). *Reducing risks: Promoting healthy lifestyle.* Geneva, Switzerland: World Health Organization.

World Health Organization. (2004, May 17–22). Global strategy on diet, physical activity and health. Presented at the *57th World Health Assembly (WHA)*, Geneva, Switzerland: World Health Organization.

Part III

The Gender of
Sports Media

• •

10

"It's Dude Time!"

• •

A Quarter Century of Excluding
Women's Sports in Televised
News and Highlight Shows

CHERYL COOKY, MICHAEL A. MESSNER,
AND MICHELA MUSTO

In the late 1980s, Margaret Carlisle Duncan and Michael Messner attended a conference put on by the Amateur Athletic Foundation of Los Angeles (AAFLA, now called the LA84 Foundation), attended mostly by representatives of the sports media. The AAFLA showed the audience clips from recent televised sports coverage that illustrated some extremely racist and sexist language and values projected by sports commentators. When the media people at the conference responded defensively and dismissed the clips they were shown as "anecdotal," Duncan and Messner volunteered to conduct a systematic social scientific study of gender in televised sports. The first study was released in 1989, and follow-up studies ensued in 1993, 1999, and 2004. In 2009, Cheryl Cooky joined Messner for that iteration of the study. The

Source: "'It's dude time!': A quarter century of excluding women's sports in televised news and highlight shows," by C. Cooky, M. A. Messner, & M. Musto, 2015, *Communication & Sport, 3*(3), pp. 261–287, doi:10.1177/2167479515588761. Copyright 2015 by the authors. Reprinted with permission of Sage Publications.

*following chapter is Cooky, Messner, and Michela Musto's 25-year follow-up, released
in 2015. A longitudinal study that measures quantity and quality of television sports
news and highlights programs' coverage of men's and women's sports across a quarter
century, this study allows unique insights into the unevenness of social change. Over
time, we have found that the quantity of such coverage has changed little if at all,
with women still receiving a tiny fraction of airtime in television news and highlights
shows. However, we did find a shift in the quality of gendered coverage, particularly
a decline in much of the overtly sexist coverage of women that we routinely observed
from the late 1980s through the early 2000s. Moreso than much of our other scholarly work, this study has reverberated outside of academia, garnering a good deal
of public exposure in mass media and the blogosphere and serving as useful data for
women's sports advocacy groups. In short, this study has provided a good opening for
us to become "public sociologists" who use research to advocate for greater equity and
fairness in media coverage of women's sports.*

—Cheryl Cooky and Michael A. Messner

Viewers of television sports news broadcasts watching Los Angeles local news
affiliates KNBC, KABC, and KCBS on the evening of July 14, 1989, saw no coverage of women's sports. Instead, several shots of female spectators were shown,
including one of a large-breasted woman wearing a tank top at a Minnesota
Twins baseball game. The commentator queried, "Isn't baseball a great sport? Just
brings out the best in everyone! Okay, I know we'll get complaints, but it's not
like we snuck into her backyard and took her picture. We're talking public place
here!" That same month, during the July 25, 1989, broadcast, the only mention of
a female athlete was essentially a gag feature. Footage showed golfer Patty Shee-
han driving her ball straight into the water. The commentator said, "Whoa! That
shot needs just a little work, Patty. She was out of the hunt in the Boston Big Five
Classic." The following story showed a man making a hole in one at a miniature
golf tournament, and the rest of the broadcast covered only men's sports.

On July 21, 2014, a day on which none of the Los Angeles network affiliate
news shows devoted a second of time to women's sports, KNBC spent 44 s covering Lakers's star Kobe Bryant playing in a celebrity softball game. "He showed
his home run swing!" the commentator gushed as viewers saw footage of Bryant's
"towering shot!" The same sports news segment devoted footage and coverage
of National Basketball Association (NBA) player LeBron James's 9-year-old son
who, the commentator predicted, in seven years "will likely be recruited by every
college basketball program in the country." Later that week, on July 26, during
their extended weekend broadcast, KNBC embedded in its coverage of mostly
men's baseball, football, and basketball a bland-but-respectful story on women's
NBA (WNBA) games, and KABC concluded its 11 p.m. show with a segment on
the world series of pro beach volleyball that included this commentary:

Your weekend wouldn't be complete without a little volleyball. Kerri Walsh Jennings and April Ross taking on team Slovakia in the semi-finals, looking for their 4th win of the tour. Easily dispatching the Slovakians in the first set, they lost the 2nd set, so it was decided in three. And team USA advances to that gold medal game, so if you've got nothing else to do, cool off tomorrow down at the beach in Long Beach.

At first glance, the presentation of gender in the televised sports news and the ESPN *SportsCenter* broadcasts we have now studied for the past 25 and 15 years, respectively, does not appear to have changed much. The shows cover men's sports nearly all the time, even to the point of featuring stories on out-of-season men's sports. However, the two segments we highlight above hint at some qualitative changes over time. Over the past 10 years, portrayal of women athletes has become increasingly "respectful," and news and highlights commentators have become far less likely to joke about women or portray women as sexual objects. Advocates of equity and fairness for women's sports will likely applaud the near disappearance of overtly sexualized and insulting coverage of women. The "good news" of the increasingly respectful coverage of women's sports is, we will show, more than eclipsed by two factors: The deepening quantitative dearth of coverage of women's sports and the ways in which the continuous cacophony of exciting coverage of men's sports is counterpoised with the tendency to present most of the few women's sports stories in a matter-of-fact, uninspiring, and lackluster manner.

In this study, we present the findings of the most recent iteration of our now 25-year longitudinal study of gender in televised sports news and highlights shows. In highlighting continuities and differences in the quantity and quality of coverage of women's and men's sports over time, we suggest that these patterns are best understood as indicators not of some "stalled revolution" but rather of the unevenness of social change. We end with several policy implications of our findings and analysis.

The Gender in Televised Sports Study

The longitudinal research for this study was first gathered in 1989, with follow-up studies conducted in 1993, 1999, 2004, 2009, and 2014, with each report from these studies published in the year following the data gathering. The Amateur Athletic Foundation of Los Angeles (1990, 1994, 2000, 2005), now called the LA84 Foundation, published the first four reports. The University of Southern California's Center for Feminist Research (2010) published the most recent study. The research reports, intended as public advocacy social science research, were widely distributed, reported in the mass media, featured in documentary films, used by organizations like the Women's Sports Foundation, and taught in schools of journalism.

The research from past iterations of this study was also disseminated in various scholarly publications (Cooky, Messner, & Hextrum, 2013; Messner, Duncan, & Cooky, 2003; Messner, Duncan, & Jensen, 1993; Messner, Duncan, & Wachs, 1996; Messner, Duncan, & Willms, 2006). The study has also been replicated by scholars both inside and outside the United States (Koivula, 1999;

Turner, 2014). The ongoing study contributed to a growing body of scholarly literature that explores the implications of gender inequitable and gender-biased coverage in sports media (e.g., Adams & Tuggle, 2004; Bernstein, 2002; Billings & Young, 2015; Caple, Greenwood, & Lumby, 2011; Cooky, Wachs, Messner, & Dworkin, 2010; Daniels, 2009; Eastman & Billings, 2001; Etling & Young, 2007; Farred, 2000; Kane, LaVoi, & Fink, 2013; Kian, Vincent, & Modello, 2008; Koivula, 1999; LaVoi, Buysse, Maxwell, & Kane, 2007; Rightler-McDaniels, 2014; Sheffer & Shultz, 2007; Tuggle, 1997; Turner, 2014; Webber & Carni, 2013; Whiteside & Hardin, 2012). This body of research, which includes studies of the coverage of live televised sports events and print, online, social, and televised news media coverage of sports, as well as the implications of media coverage for women's sports, consistently finds that—with a minor exception for quality of media coverage, particularly during the Olympics and for some collegiate-based media outlets (Billings & Young, 2015; Hardin, Chance, Dodd, & Hardin, 2002; Kane & Buyssee, 2005; McKay & Dalliere, 2009)—the vast majority of media coverage centers on men's sports and male athletes. For example, in their recent study comparing coverage of ESPN's *SportsCenter* and Fox Sports 1's *Fox Sports Live*, Billings and Young (2015) found that each program featured women's sports coverage less than 1% of the time, with some "modest gains" during the month of February during the Olympics. Moreover, women's sports continues to be covered in ways that convey the message to audiences that women's sport is less important, less exciting, and, therefore, less valued than men's sports (Cooky et al., 2013; Greer, Hardin, & Homan, 2009).

Our central aim of this study is to examine change and continuity over time. As such, in 2014, we replicated previous iterations of the study. The design and methods of data collection and analysis (both quantitative and qualitative) were identical to those of the 1989, 1993, 1999, 2004, and 2009 studies (see Cooky et al., 2013). As with prior studies (see Cooky et al., 2013), several research questions inform the 2014 study: In what ways do televised sports news media cover men's and women's sports events? What is the amount of coverage given to men's sports and to women's sports? Do the production values of men's sports differ from that of women's sports? If so, how? What is the quality of commentary of men's sports? What is the quality of commentary of women's sports? Are women's sports covered in ways that highlight athletic competence or in ways that trivialize women's sport? Does the coverage focus on the competitive aspects of women's sport, including games/matches, game highlights, scores and statistics, outcomes, and significance? Does the coverage sexualize, trivialize, or portray women as objects of sexualized humor? Does the coverage focus on women as wives, girlfriends, and mothers? Has the coverage of women's sports in this data sample changed or remained the same since prior data collection years? In other words, what are the continuities or discontinuities in the coverage over the past 25 years?

In Stage 1 of the data collection and analysis, we recorded each broadcast of the 6 p.m. and 11 p.m. sports news and highlights segments on the local Los Angeles network affiliates (KCBS, KNBC, and KABC) and the 11 p.m. broadcast of ESPN's *SportsCenter*. Also following the methodology of previous iterations, the sample was stratified by sport season and included three 2-week blocks (the second and third calendar week of each month) of televised news: March 16–29, July 13–26, and November 9–22. In addition to the local affiliates, we recorded three weeks of the one hour 11 p.m. ESPN *SportsCenter* broadcast. These three weeks corresponded with the first week of each of the three local network news segments: March 16–22, July 13–19, and November 9–15. As with previous iterations of this study, during our March sampling period, there were fewer 6 p.m. news broadcasts from KCBS because their parent network (CBS) broadcasts the National Collegiate Athletic Association (NCAA) men's basketball tournament games, which frequently preempted the news broadcasts.

In Stage 2, the research assistant (third author) received training on coding data, so as to ensure continuity in the analysis with past iterations of the study. The third author viewed all recordings and independently coded the quantitative and qualitative data for the month of March. Two undergraduate research assistants also received training on the quantitative coding and independently coded quantitative data for March. The percentage agreement (calculated using Holsti's formula) for interrater reliability on the quantitative codes (including visual and verbal commentary) was determined to be approximately 95%, well above what is considered an acceptable level of concordance (Fleiss, Levin, & Paik, 2005). We included all categories in this measure rather than calculating individual reliability scores for each code, as most codes were easily determined (for example, type of sport and competitive level). While few, any discrepancy in coding was resolved through a discussion with the authors until consensus was achieved. Once interrater reliability was established, the third author and the undergraduate research assistants completed the quantitative coding for the July and November broadcasts.

The study's codebook drew upon previous iterations of the study and included more than 20 distinct codes including gender of sport (male, female, and neutral), type of sport (basketball, football, golf, tennis, etc.), competitive level of the sport (professional, college, high school, youth, recreation, etc.), type of coverage (main, ticker, and score box), and time of the segment (measured from the start of an individual segment reported in total minutes/seconds; segments were defined based on the type of sport covered; timing of segment ended when either the competitive level of the sport changed or the gender of the sport changed). Codes were also included to quantify production values (coded as yes/no), including the presence or absence of music, graphics, interviews, and game highlights. We also coded the name, race (we acknowledge the limitations of determining race based on visual cues), and gender of each broadcast's sports anchor, ancillary anchor, and/or analyst. As in 2004 and 2009, most of the 2014 sports news and highlights programs (with the continued exception of KABC) in our sample included a continual running "ticker" at the bottom of the television screen. The ticker's written text displays game scores, headlines, and breaking sports news that may or may not be reported through the main conventional verbal commentary and visual images. We analyzed the ticker coverage for gender, time of the segment, type of sport, and competitive level of the sport.

In Stage 3, the third author independently viewed all recordings and, sensitized to themes from the quantitative findings, qualitatively analyzed the commentary, including visuals and verbal commentary. In Stage 4, the first author viewed all recordings and further developed the qualitative analysis from Stage 3 to confirm and expand upon the themes. In Stage 5, the first author ran descriptive statistics on the coded data. The first and second author then compiled an interpretation of the quantitative and qualitative results.

A Deepening Silence

As with previous iterations of our study, viewers of the news and highlights shows in our sample rarely see any mention of women athletes or women's sports. Among the three local network affiliates, only 3.2% of coverage was dedicated to women's sports. As Figure 10.1 shows, however, there is considerable difference in this regard among the three network affiliates we studied, with KABC devoting 5.2% of its main broadcast coverage to women's sports and KNBC 3.9%. Over the same 6-week sampling period, KCBS included only one story on women's sports—a scant 0.2% of its total sports news time. ESPN's *SportsCenter* did no better, devoting a paltry 2% of its hour-long highlight show to women's sports.

How do these 2014 findings compare with past studies? As Figures 10.1A and 10.2 illustrate, the three local affiliate news shows together devoted about 5% of their main broadcast coverage to women's sports in 1989 and 1993. In 1999, their

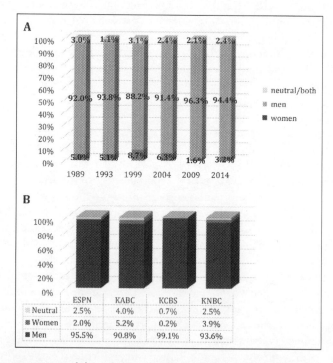

FIGURE 10.1. (A) Local Network Affiliates (KCBS, KNBC, and KABC) Main Coverage, by Gender. (B) Local Network Affiliates and ESPN *SportsCenter*'s 2014 Main Coverage, by Gender.

coverage of women's sports jumped to 8.7%. The coverage of women dipped slightly in 2004 to 6.3% and then plummeted to its nadir of 1.6% in 2009. The slight increase to 3.2% in our 2014 findings indicates that the news shows' coverage of women's sports remains substantially lower than its coverage 10, 15, 20, and 25 years ago. *SportsCenter*'s coverage, over the four time periods it was included in our sample, which spans 15 years (1999–2014), has remained remarkably flat, never rising above 2.5%, and in 2014, women's sports on the main broadcast coverage hovers at a paltry 2% of the total broadcast coverage.

Moreover, the dearth of coverage of women's sports is evidenced by the low number of segments (i.e., stories) in our sample. Of the 934 local network affiliate news segments (more than 12 hr of broadcasts), 880 were on men's sports (or approximately 11.5 hr), 22 segments (or nearly 18 min) were on gender-neutral sports (e.g., a horse race, coverage of the Los Angeles [LA] marathon, and a recreational sports event), and only 32 segments (about 23 min) featured women's sports. *SportsCenter*'s numbers were similar. Of the 405 total *SportsCenter* segments in our sample (nearly 14 hr), 376 covered men's sports (slightly over 13 hr), 16 segments were on gender-neutral sports (just over 20 min), and only 13 segments featured women's sports (approximately 17 min).

As in past studies, there was little or no difference between the 6 p.m. and the 11 p.m. editions of the three local network affiliate news shows in terms of coverage of women's sports. Also consistent with past studies, the November period of the 2014 sample included the least amount of coverage of women's sports. There was no coverage of women's sports in the month of November on the local network affiliates and only 44 s of women's sports coverage (two short segments on University of Connecticut's women's basketball team) on ESPN's *SportsCenter*. The scant coverage of women's sports was clustered in the March (3.0%) and July periods (4.6%).

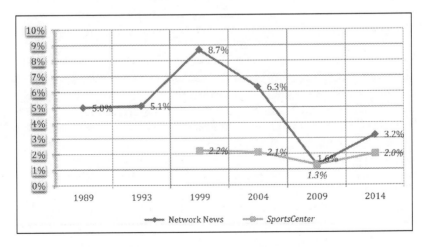

FIGURE 10.2. Main Coverage of Women's Sports (%), 1989–2014.

Lead Stories, Teasers, and Tickers

In addition to counting the total number of stories and amount of time devoted to women's and men's sports, we analyzed three other quantitative indicators of equity/inequity in coverage. First, every broadcast of sports news or highlights begins with a lead story, chosen by broadcasters because it is viewed as the most important story of the day and/or because it is deemed to be the most interesting "hook" with which to engage and hold the audience. As with previous iterations, none of the news and highlights shows in our 2014 sample led with a women's sports story. Second, transitions before commercial breaks in news and highlights shows are often marked by "teasers" that are intended to build interest and hold the audience for an exciting upcoming story. Of the 145 teasers we analyzed in the local network affiliate broadcasts, only one teaser alerted the audience to an upcoming women's sports story. Similarly, only three of *SportsCenter*'s 199 teasers were about women's sports.

SportsCenter and two of the local network affiliate sports news shows we analyzed (KCBS and KNBC) deployed running tickers at the bottom of the screen throughout the broadcast. Tickers display scores and breaking sports news, much of which is not covered in the sports anchor's main coverage. In 2014, *SportsCenter* devoted 2% of its ticker time to women's sports, similar to the show's proportion of main coverage devoted to women. The two network affiliates, on the other hand, devoted substantially more ticker time to women's sports, 6.1%. This proportion of ticker coverage represents an increase from the 3.2% ticker time devoted to women's sports by the two local affiliate news broadcasts in our 2009 study. But it is also notable that in 2014, KCBS and KNBC devoted far less of their main coverage to women's sports—0.2% and 3.9%, respectively—compared to KABC's 5.2% coverage of women's sports. It is reasonable to conclude, therefore, that this increased ticker coverage on KCBS and KNBC in 2014 is a dubious sign of "progress." Instead, it could be surmised that the scrolling ticker on these shows functions as a kind of visual and textual ghetto for women's sports, allowing the sports anchors to focus their main coverage almost entirely on men's sports while relegating women's sports literally to the margins of the screen.

Men's Big Three: "It's Never Too Early," "Too Soon," or "Too Late"

The coverage of sports on the local network affiliate news broadcasts typically comprises only a few minutes of the total news broadcast (extended sports shows on weekends, like KCBS's "Sports Central" are an exception). As a result, producers can only choose to cover a fragment of all of the sports taking place in a typical day. The findings of this study demonstrate that in nearly every broadcast, network producers decide to focus on men's sports rather than the many women's sports events that are taking place daily (see appendix for a sample of the women's sports events that occurred during the 6 weeks of this study). Moreover, as with previous iterations of the report, we found that even with broadcast time constraints, networks do find time to include frequent "human interest" stories on men's sports. Here are four examples that appeared during broadcasts wherein there was no coverage of women's sports:

- KNBC's March 18, 6 p.m. sports news included a 30-s segment about a swarm of bees invading a Red Sox versus Yankees game and a 20-s segment about an 18-in. corn dog available for purchase for US$25 at the Arizona Diamondbacks's stadium.
- KCBS's March 26, 11 p.m. sports news devoted 45 s to the ribbon-cutting ceremony for a new restaurant that opened at Chavez Ravine owned by former Dodgers manager Tommy Lasorda.
- KNBC's July 22, 11 p.m. broadcast devoted 40 s to discussing whether recently traded Lakers player Kendall Marshall would be able to find a good burrito in Milwaukee. This segment included a full-screen graphic showing a map from the Milwaukee basketball arena to a Chipotle restaurant while the commentator gave Marshall directions.
- KNBC's March 18, 11 p.m. broadcast included a 55-s segment about a stray dog that fans and players subsequently named Hank who had wandered into the Milwaukee Brewers's stadium. The story was about his adoption and the dog's new role as the "spring training mascot" for the Brewers.

These examples illustrate three dynamics that shape how news broadcasts build audiences for men's sports while positioning women's sports as unimportant and less interesting than men's sports. First, while being event driven, sports news is also presented as entertainment, often including stories that humorously portray the lighter and human side of men's sports. Second, if sufficient time exists to cover US$25 corn dogs, swarms of bees, the proximity of Chipotle to basketball stadiums, and stray dogs wandering into a professional sports stadium, it is simply untrue that there is not enough time to cover women's sports. Instead, producers and commentators actively choose to construct an exciting and pleasurable experience for consuming the coverage of men's sports, while ignoring women's sports. Third, as the case with the rest of the sports news coverage, most of these stories focus only on certain men's sports. Put another way, it is not just women's sports that are ignored on these shows. There is inequitable coverage across different men's sports as well. Billings and Young (2015) observe that men's sports other than the "big three"—like golf, National Association for Stock Car Auto Racing, and tennis—are often relegated to sports news secondary platforms (ESPN3, ESPNU, and other regional networks). Similarly, as with previous iterations of this study, the vast majority of reporting in 2014 was devoted to the big three—men's basketball (professional and college), men's football (professional and college), and men's baseball (mostly professional). As Figure 10.3 shows, the combined (main and ticker) coverage of all of the news and highlights broadcasts in our study devoted 74.5% of their time to the big three. This is slightly higher than the 68% proportion of coverage received by men's big three in our 2009 study.

As we noted in our 2013 publication (Cooky et al., 2013), although some argue that there are fewer women's sports events to cover, news and highlights shows keep the focus on the big three even during their off-seasons. Four examples illustrate this pattern:

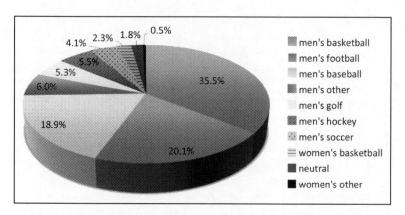

FIGURE 10.3. Total Sports Coverage (Main plus Ticker) on Local Network Affiliates and *SportsCenter*, 2014.

- On KABC's July 23, 6 p.m. broadcast, the news anchor introduced the sports anchor saying that he was "Gonna talk about college football, it's never too soon!" The sports anchor agreed and began discussing a 77-s story that previewed University of California, Los Angeles's (UCLA), and University of Southern California's (USC) season openers set to take place in late August.
- On KCBS's July 17, 6 p.m. broadcast, the sports anchor introduced the broadcast explaining to viewers, "When I say never, I mean it's never too early to start talking about the National Football League!" which began a 78-s story about the National Football League (NFL) media tour for Thursday Night Football.
- On KABC's July 15, 6 p.m. broadcast, the main news anchor introduced the sports anchor by saying, "And yep, it is a bit early in the year, but it's never too soon to think about the NBA." The sports anchor replied, "That's right, it's just around the corner." Although it was still midsummer, he acknowledged, "it's never too early to talk about opening night," which is "161 more shopping days" from now.
- On the July 17, broadcast of ESPN's *SportsCenter*, embedded in a longer segment on the NBA Cleveland Cavaliers's deal with LeBron James and an offer extended to Kevin Love, 25 s was spent on a story about a wedding in Akron, Ohio. ESPN featured a picture of a groom in his tux standing in front of his groomsmen, who all wore various LeBron James's jerseys.

Such gender asymmetries of out-of-season and in-season coverage of sports were especially evident in coverage of the NBA versus the coverage of the WNBA. During the playing season (and especially during the playoffs), the NBA receives bounteous daily coverage on news and *SportsCenter*, but it also receives frequent off-season coverage.

Table 10.1. NBA and WNBA Stories, In-Season and Out-of-Season, 2014

	March	July	November
WNBA on KABC, KNBC & KCBS	(out of season) 0 stories; 0:00	(in season) 10 stories; 7:11	(out of season) 0 stories; 0:00
WNBA on ESPN *SportsCenter*	(out of season) 0 stories; 0:00	(in season) 4 stories; 5:59	(out of season) 0 stories; 0:00
NBA on KABC, KNBC, & KCBS	(in season) 76 stories; 47:59	(out of season) 68 stories; 48:53	(in season) 71 stories; 01:10:23
NBA on ESPN *SportsCenter*	(in season) 56 stories; 1:12:23	(out of season) 16 stories; 40:05	(in season) 20 stories; 50:05

As Table 10.1 shows, the WNBA received neither this lavish in-season coverage nor a single instance of off-season coverage. Even the local angle for the Los Angeles WNBA team tended to deliver little positive news coverage. For example, on July 24, KABC included a rare story about the Los Angeles Sparks losing that day's WNBA game. The commentator joked with the news anchors, "Mark and Michelle, the Sparks: 3 and 9, their worst start in quite some time. They keep that up, we might not show 'em again! This is a town of winners!" The sports anchor's threat, however jokingly intended, stood in stark contrast with KABC's and the other news shows' continued fidelity to one of that year's biggest losers, the Los Angeles Lakers. Despite performing poorly for the season, the Lakers still received consistently high levels of airtime by all three local news stations, regardless of whether they were in or out of season. On the KABC's 6 p.m. broadcast on November 18, for example, the sports anchor lamented, "Watching the Lakers this year, you know, it's been really, really tough. It's kind of like ripping a Band-Aid off slowly." But anticipating the Lakers game to be played that evening, he added hopefully, "Well let's throw that band-aid away tonight, right?" Similar to the lived experience of racial minorities wherein they confront the expectation to be twice as good to receive half the credit, women's sports are held to a higher standard than men's: Women's sports are deemed deserving of coverage only if and when they are winners. Ironically, the sports media used this same logic to justify their own lack of coverage of women's sports; for example, women's college basketball was presented by some sports anchors as less interesting because "everyone knows UConn (or in previous seasons, Tennessee) is going to win."

On the rare occasion that women's sports were covered in 2014, basketball was by far the most commonly featured sport, with 81.6% of the combined main and ticker coverage, as shown in Figure 10.4.

This continues a shift toward attention to women's basketball that we noted in our 2009 study. In our past studies, women's tennis was most likely to receive coverage: 43% of all women's sports coverage in our 2004 study was devoted to tennis. By 2014, tennis had shrunk to 6.4% of women's sports coverage, a distant second to basketball (golf, at 5.9%, was third). This increased coverage of women's basketball may be attributed to the growth of live NCAA women's

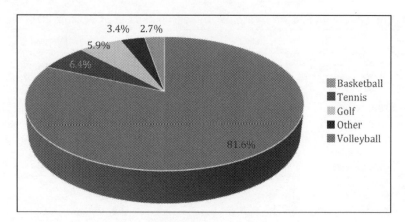

FIGURE 10.4. Women's Sports Coverage (Main Plus Ticker) on Local Network Affiliates and *SportsCenter*, 2015.

basketball television coverage during the past decade and some increase in live coverage of WNBA games. Yet as we will see in the following section, while women's basketball comprises the majority of women's sports coverage, when compared to the coverage of men's basketball, the gender disparity in the quantity and quality of coverage of basketball is evident.

March Madness, Still Mostly for Men

As in past iterations of our study, we found it useful to compare news and highlights coverage of the women's and men's NCAA basketball tournament. Unlike many sports where there are major structural asymmetries that at least partly explain differences in reportage—for example, the nonexistence of a women's equivalent to men's college football, the NFL, Major League Baseball (MLB), and the National Hockey League (NHL) or the fact that the WNBA has a far shorter season than the NBA and is scheduled during a different time of the year (summer)—the women's and men's NCAA tournaments are equivalent events, played during the same several week span. As such, they provide a source ripe for quantitative and qualitative comparison.

As Table 10.2 shows, the coverage of the women's and men's NCAA tournament during our March 2014 sample was highly uneven. Neither the local network affiliate news broadcasts nor *SportsCenter* devoted many stories in their main coverage to the women's tournament. There were 9 stories or 3 min 37 s of coverage of the women's NCAA tournament on the local affiliates, compared with 120 stories or 1 hr 26 min 6 s of coverage of the men's. ESPN had more coverage of the women's tournament than the local affiliates, 8 stories or 9 min 24 s, but it spent 2 hr 21 min 32 s covering 83 stories on the men's tournament. For the most part, these shows relegated coverage of the women to the ticker, though even that coverage was scant compared with ticker coverage of the men's tournament. For example, ESPN had just over 3 hr of coverage of the men's tournament

Table 10.2. Men's and Women's NCAA Basketball Stories, March 2014

	Men's NCAA Basketball	Women's NCAA Basketball
KABC, KNBC, & KCBS, main coverage	120 Stories; 1:26:06	9 Stories; 03:37
KABC, KNBC, & KCBS, ticker coverage	108 Stories; 1:14:10	24 Stories; 08:43
ESPN *SportsCenter*, main coverage	83 Stories; 2:21:32	8 Stories; 09:24
ESPN *SportsCenter*, ticker coverage	180 Stories; 3:00:55	18 Stories; 15:05

on their ticker and only 15 min of the women's tournament. This gender asymmetry echoed our findings in previous studies but was a bit surprising for two reasons. First, as we noted above, in recent years basketball has become by far the most reported-on women's sport (in the United States). Second, given that live coverage of the women's NCAA basketball tournament games (and regular season NCAA basketball games) has become far more prevalent over the past decade (ESPN has broadcast the tournament in its entirety beginning in 2003), and the quality of the women's live broadcasts has so vastly improved, we expected to see even more coverage of the women's tournament in our 2014 sample. Nevertheless, the coverage of the women's NCAA tournament remained dismally low, as it had been in 2004 and 2009.

Of the few times they did mention the women's tournament, commentators symbolically yawned at the predictable outcome of another University of Connecticut championship. Even the local angle for the Los Angeles news shows—appearances by USC's and California State University Northridge's women's team in the tournament—barely nudged the women's tournament into some local news broadcasts. On Monday, March 17, for example, the KNBC 6 p.m. broadcast sandwiched a story about a USC women's tournament game between two men's sports stories: on the front end, a 28-s segment about the grandson of St. Joseph's men's basketball head coach, Phil Martelli. The story included footage and commentary that described the 4-year-old "mini-Martelli" as "adorable" while mimicking his grandpa's sport coat, tie, and gestures during the game. The story concluded with the news that "St. Joseph's won the ball game earning a birth in the big dance!" In comparison, the 7-s segment on the women's tournament included only this verbal commentary, "Sticking with USC, congratulations to the Women of Troy who learned tonight they are a ninth seed in the women's basketball tournament. They'll play St. John's in the first round." The broadcast then transitioned to a 78-s segment on college football spring training practice and the relationship between the new head coach of the USC football team, Steve Sarkisian, and one of his assistant coaches. This broadcast illustrated two thematic patterns: First, news shows lavished a significant portion of their "March Madness" coverage time to a soft news story about the men's basketball—specifically about a coach of a team located in Philadelphia, Pennsylvania—than to a local Division 1 women's team that had made the NCAA tournament. Second, even when out of season, USC football received more coverage and higher quality coverage than a currently successful in-season USC women's basketball team.

Meanwhile on the men's side, the local angle apparently could not have been more exciting. A March 26 KABC story about the UCLA's men's team illustrates how news programs generate interest for men's basketball. The 73-s segment began in the newsroom, with one of the news anchors introducing the sports commentator, saying, "And tomorrow, oh boy, that game, UCLA, Florida, that could be a good one." The sports commentator nods and says, "I think it is. I think it's gonna go down to the wire." The sports anchor then proceeds with a story that includes an interview with UCLA coach Steve Alford, on-screen graphics that show the team's recent history in the tournament, and game footage and commentary about UCLA's opponent, the number one seed, "sensational" Florida Gators. The commentator then gushes longingly about UCLA's main hope for an upset, "6-foot 9 Kyle Anderson, a point guard, is a game-changer."

Building Excitement for Men's Sports

Although news and highlights on women's sports are still few and far between, the technical production and framing of these stories have improved over time. Unlike our early studies, when most women's sports stories were short verbal-only reports, many women's sports stories in 2014 supplemented verbal commentary with on-screen graphics and game footage in ways similar to reports on men's sports. However, we found that men's sports were presented with far more enthusiasm and excitement, the commentators consistently deploying vocal inflections, high-volume excitement, and evocative descriptors. Listening to commentators describe a women's sports event was usually like hearing someone deliver a boring afterthought, with an obvious lack of enthusiasm. Watching stories of men's sports was frequently akin to watching the classic 1960s "Batman" television show—(*Bam! Pow!*)—with viewers treated to plenty of visual action accompanied by a barrage of exciting spoken action descriptors. We collected many of the common action descriptors deployed by news and highlights commentators when presenting men's sports and present in the following paragraph. The reader should imagine male sports anchors delivering these descriptors in an excited, modulated, rapid-clipped, amplified voice—often literally yelling:

> Bingo, a thriller, rabid fans, smoked a laser, a battle, big shot, huge, threw down the dunk, hit an absolute bomb, awesome, exciting, smoked one to right field, ripped a double, drilling a ball to center field, unloaded a hit, clawed their way back into the game, a commanding lead, draining a great shot, he nails it, going full throttle, dialed in and in complete control, sending a rocket over the wall, punished the opponent, mowed down the batter, toe-to-toe battle, flying through the air, a great grab, sensational, really unbelievable, a great one, attacking, drilled one from long-range, a heavy-weight clash, a thunderous dunk, amazing, simply

mind-blowing, on fire, picture perfect, explosion, revved up and ready to go, gorgeous dunk—bam, spectacular, unbelievable, another beauty, electric, dominant, brilliant, outstanding, a master of the position, incredible, forceful, a weapon, a rock star, like a man possessed, that is just stupid good, instant awesome!

Such colorful commentary, so common in nearly every story about men's sports, plays an important role in generating excitement and ongoing interest in men's sports (Messner, Dunbar, & Hunt, 2000). *SportsCenter* is particularly adept at maintaining this level of enthusiasm for men's sports, a typical example of which came from their July 14, 2014, description of highlights from the MLB All Star Home Run Derby, during which one of the anchors says that a player brought José Bautista some Gatorade, "just to cool him down a little bit because he was on fire!" Later in the same segment, the sports anchor discusses Giancarlo Stanton's hit: "Wow! Take another look at this one. He just absolutely destroys them! You can see the speed on that swing in real time. And you just stand and admire a shot like that." One of Stanton's home runs is described as "an absolute bomb." As viewers are treated to more footage, Yoenis Céspedes is described as hitting "bomb after bomb after bomb," and a sports analyst gushes, "Céspedes kept getting better and better, and the home runs kept getting longer and longer and the numbers got bigger and bigger."

By contrast, when women's sports were covered at all, they were typically couched in what can only be described as a matter-of-fact style of commentary, akin to the July 26 KABC story we opened this chapter with of women's beach volleyball, a segment that was presented as a brief and bland afterthought with the accompanying commentary: "if you have nothing else to do." Frequently absent from such women's sports stories were the commentators' voluminous vocal inflections, exclamatory descriptions of athletic successes, and heartfelt laments of failures that saturate the commentary in men's coverage. The general lack of an excited tone and agentic language in most of the reporting on women's sports helps to mark women's sports as less interesting and, in many instances, even boring.

In our sample, there were a small number of exceptions that showed that commentators are capable of generating some enthusiasm for women's sports stories. For instance on KABC's July 24, 11 p.m. report of a WNBA game, the commentator declared, "the Mercury hotter than the weather! Diana Taurasi setting the pace with 18 points, and DeWanna Bonner? Was *boomin'* from here, there, and everywhere!" And on March 25, KNBC delivered a high-quality, local angle story on the Cal Poly Pomona women's basketball team's ascent to the Division II Final Four. With accompanying action footage, the commentator declared, "Just give that ball to Janet Blackwell and get out of the way! She scored a game high 35, lifting the Broncos into the Division II Final Four, with an 81–61 win over Edinboro." Footage of the team celebrating afterward was shown. Combining good technical production with enthusiastic reporting, this was one of highest quality segments about women's sports in our local network affiliate news sample.

Ambivalent Delivery

On several of the rare occasions when commentators mustered high technical production along with enthusiastic delivery for a women's sports story, they also infused a level of ambivalence into the story's frame. One of the longest (2 min 37 s) high-quality segments on women's sports in our sample was a July 22, KNBC story covering former USC (college) and LA Sparks (professional) basketball star Lisa Leslie's induction into the women's basketball Hall of Fame. The story featured some visual player footage and included respectful commentary that noted Leslie's many championships and awards. At the end of the segment, however, Leslie is shown holding her baby, as the commentator reports that Leslie "retired from the league in 2009, and now she enters the Hall of Fame!" Footage of her dancing on the court with her child is shown as she says, "Being a wife and a mom is just my favorite title. People always ask me if I miss playing basketball and I'm like, absolutely not, because I love being a wife, cooking and being home. I'm kind of a stay at home mom even though I have about ten jobs." She laughs as the segment ends. Similar versions of this story ran on the July 19, 11 p.m. broadcast (37 s) and again on the July 22, 11 p.m. broadcast (63 s), which represented nearly half (4 min 17 s of 10 min 30 s) of the total main coverage of women's sports on KNBC in our study. Thus an ambivalent story about a prominent, successful female athlete that framed her accomplishments alongside motherhood was the dominant representation of women's sports, both qualitatively and quantitatively, on KNBC.

SportsCenter's July 18th broadcast ran an in-studio interview with WNBA star Candace Parker, similar to the Lisa Leslie story in its length (1 min 38 s), its high quality, and also in its gender ambivalence. The segment opens with game footage clips of Parker scoring a basket along with commentary from the game, "Wow! Candace Parker! What a move!" Another clip of Parker holding a trophy above her head is shown. A graphic with her picture and "Candace Parker" in text along with the Sparks logo appears across the screen. The camera then transitions to interviewer Stan Verrett with Parker (in a dress and full makeup) in studio sitting in two chairs. As she is interviewed about the recent season and about her WNBA team's financial vulnerabilities, an on-screen graphic appears at the bottom of the screen showing Parker's statistics, including two-time WNBA most valuable player and three-time All Star. The interviewer then asked, "We always see you with your daughter, Lailaa [Parker, off camera, replies, 'Yeah'], How do you balance being the centerpiece of a franchise with being a centerpiece of a little girl's life as well?" Parker replies, "It's a lot of work. It's the hardest job I've had to do, but you know, seeing her smile and realizing, you know, when you walk through the door, basketball doesn't matter. She just wants me to be mom."

These two stories on Lisa Leslie on KNBC and on Candace Parker on ESPN were long segments with very high production values and respectful commentary. Both Leslie and Parker were featured because of their dominance and stature in the sport of women's basketball. But we found it notable that each piece eventually meanders to the theme of motherhood. Scholars have noted how professional women's sports are frequently framed by commercial interests and media in ways that highlight women athletes' heterosexual attractiveness and/or roles as mothers (Kane et al., 2013). "Other" women—those who are single, or who are lesbians, or who might not be viewed as conventionally attractive—are rarely given the same attention by media, sports promoters, or advertisers (Cooky et al., 2010). It is difficult to imagine a sports anchor or journalist questioning a prominent male athlete—say, LeBron James or Derek Jeter—"How do you balance being the centerpiece of a franchise with being a centerpiece of a little girl's [or boy's] life as well?" Yet as with previous iterations of the report, the framing of women as mothers is quite frequent, and yet it is a far cry from the overtly sexist and insulting stories that were found in our studies of 15 and 25 years ago. However, such framings of high-profile, successful women athletes, when juxtaposed with the fact that such issues are rarely, if ever, brought into stories about men athletes, reveal a gender asymmetry that subtly communicates ambivalence about women athletes (Duncan & Hasbrook, 1988). Indeed, we began to see this shift from overt sexism to ambivalence in our 2009 study, where we observed women athletes increasingly depicted not as sex objects or as jokes but as mothers, girlfriends, or girls next door (Cooky et al., 2013). When contrasted with the excited commentary and agentic tone utilized in the coverage of men's sports, this ambivalent delivery further marginalizes what little coverage of women's sports exists within the broadcasts, and as we noted in our 2009 study, it does little to build audiences for women's sports and reaffirms men's sports as the institutional center of sports (Messner, 2002).

"It's Dude Time"

During a November 14, 2014, broadcast of *SportsCenter*, the sports anchor introduced the show's NHL analyst, exclaiming, "It's dude time!" While it is common for sports anchors to present ice hockey as one of the more extremely aggressive masculine sports, the sports anchor's comment made us wonder: When are these shows *not* "dude time?" After all, nearly all of the segments we analyzed on *SportsCenter* and on the local network affiliate newscasts covered the major men's sports. Moreover, sports news and highlight anchors remain, as in the past, racially diverse but mostly male. Table 10.3 indicates that of all the news and highlights shows we analyzed, more than 95% had male anchors and coanchors at the helm (all of the women anchors in our sample appeared on KCBS, which included 11 of its 74 sports broadcasts anchored by a White woman and two by a Latina woman).

As Table 10.4 shows, at 14.4%, women are only slightly better represented as ancillary reporters on sports shows. During our sample period, sports shows (most often *SportsCenter*) also included "sports analysts" in the broadcasts, 96% of who were men.

"Dude time," therefore, is created in news and highlights shows by a nearly constant configuration of three intertwined patterns: (1) almost entirely men's sports content, (2) delivered almost entirely by men commentators, and (3) deploying an amplified, excited style of delivery. Together, these patterns give

**Table 10.3. Race and Sex of Anchors and Coanchors on
Local Affiliate Networks and ESPN, 2014**

	WM	BM	LM	AM	WF	BF	LF	AF	Other	Total
KNBC	55	0	25	0	0	0	0	0	0	80
KABC	36	1	0	41	0	0	0	0	0	78
KCBS	13	48	0	0	11	0	2	0	0	74
ESPN	24	12	1	0	0	0	0	0	0	37
Total	128	61	26	41	11	0	2	0	0	269
Total count (%)	47.6	22.7	9.7	15.2	4.1	0.0	0.7	0.0	0.0	100.0

NOTE: WM =White male; BM =Black male; LM =Latino male; AM =Asian/Asian Pacific Islander; WF = White female; BF = Black female; LF: Latina; AF: Asian/Asian Pacific Islander; Other: for example, Indian male, Armenian male.

**Table 10.4. Race and Sex of Ancillary Announcers on
Local Affiliate Networks and ESPN, 2014**

	WM	BM	LM	AM	WF	BF	LF	AF	Other	Total
KNBC	2	0	9	0	0	0	0	0	0	11
KABC	4	0	0	0	0	0	0	0	0	4
KCBS	3	1	0	0	0	0	0	0	0	4
ESPN	39	4	2	0	9	2	0	0	1	57
Total	48	5	11	0	9	2	0	0	1	76
Total count (%)	63.2	6.6	14.5	0.0	11.8	2.6	0.0	0.0	1.3	100.0

NOTE: WM =White male; BM =Black male; LM =Latino male; AM =Asian/Asian Pacific Islander; WF = White female; BF = Black female; LF = Latina; AF = Asian/Asian Pacific Islander; Other = for example, Indian male, Armenian male.

SportsCenter and the local network affiliates' sports news shows the consistent feel of what we refer to as a "mediated man cave"—a place set up by men for men to celebrate men's sensational athletic accomplishments. Based on the dearth of coverage of women's sports across a quarter century of analysis, it seems apparent that, similar to the sports talk radio studied by Nylund (2004), women are not welcome in the mediated man cave of televised sports coverage. Indeed, KNBC's March 22 broadcast included zero coverage of women's sports but did include a message to women fans: Don't get too close to the action. In a segment about the men's hockey match, Columbus Blue Jackets versus Montreal Canadiens, viewers see a woman fan banging on the glass and cheering. She suddenly gets sent flying back into her seat from the force of two hockey players colliding into the glass. The shot is replayed several times—in slow motion and from multiple angles—as the commentator says, "The force of that sends the fan flying back into her seat. Hockey is a tough sport for players and fans, and you gotta bet she'll think twice about getting that close again!"

The Unevenness of Social Change

More than four decades after the passage of Title IX, girls have dramatically increased their participation in youth and high school sports (Miller, Melnick, Barnes, Farrell, & Sabo, 2005; Sabo & Veliz, 2008). Yet stubbornly persistent conservative gender ideologies, structured inequities, and sex segregation continue to limit girls' challenge to boys' hegemony in sports (Cooky, 2009; Messner, 2011; Musto, 2014). As a tidal wave of girls' and women's participation from youth sports to college sports continues to swell, the waters of women's sport leadership as coaches and athletics directors have receded (Acosta & Carpenter, 2015; Messner, 2009). The larger picture of girls' and women's progress in sport, in short, looks less like a stalled revolution than a picture of the *unevenness of social change*, with truly dramatic, perhaps even revolutionary changes continuing in some sectors, while little or no change happens in others.

The mass sports media are certainly a site of such uneven social change in gender relations. Over the past 25 years, we have witnessed impressive growth in the quantity and quality of live televised coverage of some women's sports. Notably, when we began the gender in sports media study in 1989, there was almost no live coverage of women's NCAA basketball—even the NCAA Final Four games were, at best, televised on late-night tape-delay shot with extremely low production values. Today, ESPN, several national networks, and regional cable channels (like the Big Ten Network) broadcast many regular-season women's NCAA games and a large number of the women's NCAA tournaments. What's more, the production values of these broadcasts are improving dramatically, though still falling short in quality when compared with the broadcasts of the men's games. Viewers can also regularly watch live televised women's college volleyball, softball, and gymnastics, women's professional tennis, WNBA games, and other sports.

However, such growing media attention to women's sports, our study has shown, has not migrated to the nightly television news or to highlights shows like ESPN's *SportsCenter*. This has two broad implications. First, sports news and highlights shows are part of a larger media apparatus that actively builds audiences for men's sports (Cooky et al., 2013). As long as these daily shows remain mostly silent about women's sports, the building of enthusiastic and knowledgeable fan bases for women's sports will remain stunted. Second, news and highlights shows' continued silence about women's sports has implications for broader gender relations (Daniels, 2009; Messner, 2002). Modern men's sport has played a key historical role in bolstering ideologies of "natural" male superiority during a historical moment when girls and women have been moving affirmatively toward equality in many social institutions (Burstyn, 1999). The daily news and highlights shows' failure to equitably cover women's sports shrouds in silence women's historic movement into sport and the impressive accomplishments of women athletes, thus retaining sport as a potent site for the reproduction of ideologies of male superiority.

In another example of uneven change, despite the deepening dearth of coverage of women's sports in our study, we have found some notable changes in the quality of television news and highlights coverage over the past quarter century.

In 1989, television news shows devoted only 5% of their time to women athletes. And when they did cover women, it often was commonly either in the role of a comical object of the sports anchor's joke or as a sexual object. In fact, these two roles were often overlapping and were given significantly more airtime than were serious and respectful stories about female athletes. For instance, in 1989 by far the longest single story (3 min 50 s) on a woman in the 6-week period focused not on a female athlete but rather on "Morganna, the Kissing Bandit," a woman with enormous breasts who had made a name for herself by running out onto baseball fields and kissing players. What was most striking about these local network affiliate news broadcasts was the confluence of, on the one hand, the conspicuous absence of coverage of women athletes with, on the other hand, the ways that women were consistently placed in the role of sexualized comic relief.

Twenty-five years later, some things have changed while others have not. Similar to our observations in 2009, we saw little if any insulting and humorously sexualized stories about women athletes in 2014. Yet we found this "improvement" comes at a cost: the decline in the overall amount of coverage of women's sports over the past 25 years. It would appear that the sports media covers women's sports when it can do so in ways that conform to conventional gender norms that position women as either objects of men's (hetero)sexual desire or mothers, wives, or girlfriends. We suspect that the toning down of overtly sexist treatment of women on sports news and highlight shows is a result of public calls (including, we hope, our past research reports) for respectful coverage of women's sports. But a decline in overt sexism, while certainly welcomed by many, is not synonymous with respectful coverage.

What would respectful coverage of women's sports on news and highlights shows actually look like? Not simply, we emphasize, a lack of sexist verbal abuse directed at women but instead an active agenda of positive change that includes three policy benchmarks that producers, commentators, and sports anchors could achieve over the next 5 years:

1. Present a roughly equitable quantity of coverage of women's sports. Defining "equity" in this context would account for the fact that there are still more men's sports—especially big-time college and professional spectator sports—than equivalent women's sports. We suggest that a reasonable benchmark for equity would be to have proportional news broadcast coverage to the live broadcast coverage of women's sports. One reviewer suggested that approximately 6–9% of live broadcast coverage of sports events features women's sports. Under this rubric, the recommendation would be for the sports news media to triple their current coverage of women's sports from 2% to 6% on ESPN *SportsCenter* and from 3.2% to 9% on the local news. However, considering our longitudinal analysis, coverage of women's sports has been at 6–9% in 2004 and in 1999 and yet has declined in 2009 and 2014. Arguing to go back to what we argued in previous reports was dismal coverage seems unsatisfactory. As such, we recommend doubling the peak numbers and recommend women's sports coverage encompass

12–18% of broadcast coverage. A broadening conception of equitable coverage could also nudge producers of these shows away from their timid drift toward ever-increasing coverage of men's big three sports, instead including not only more women's sports but also a wider range of men's sports.

2. Present women's sports stories in ways roughly equivalent in quality with the typical presentation of men's sports. This refers, of course, both to the technical quality—deploying ample game footage, graphics, music, and interviews to accompany a story—and to the quality of the sports anchor's verbal presentation, including amplifying the enthusiasm in reporting women's sports to a level on the excitement meter that is equivalent with the usual presentation of men's sports.

3. Hire and retain on-camera sports anchors that are capable and willing to do steps 1 and 2. We find it notable that two of the three of the sports anchors on the network affiliates we studied are the same men who anchored the sports shows in 1989. While career longevity is not in and of itself a bad thing (Full disclosure: The second author of this study has held his same university position for nearly three decades, more than spanning the life of this televised sports study.), these men have shown little change over the years besides becoming less overtly insulting to women and devoting ever-larger proportions of their broadcast time to covering men's big three sports. Sports news and highlights shows need to open the occupation to more women (Tuggle, 1997; Sheffer & Schultz, 2007; Whiteside & Hardin, 2012). Perhaps just as important, hiring and retention decisions should prioritize anchors and analysts—women and men—who are knowledgeable about and love women's sports. It is unlikely that one can easily or effectively fake the sort of enthusiasm today's male commentators routinely show for men's sports and men athletes' accomplishments.

Twenty-five years is a long time for so little change to have taken place in sports news and highlights shows, especially against the backdrop of massive gender transformations and reforms in other areas of sport and society. To begin finally to move themselves into the 21st century, ESPN's *SportsCenter* and television sports news shows should take the three above benchmarks into account in their future decisions about hiring, retention, and programming.

Appendix

Selected Women's Sports Events during the Study Period

1. Intercollegiate Sports
   March 20–22, Division 1 NCAA Swimming Championship, University of Minnesota, MN.
   March 20–22, Division 1 NCAA Ice Hockey Championships—Frozen Four, Minneapolis, MN.
   March 20–23, NCAA Fencing Championship, Columbus, OH.

March 22–23, First Round NCAA Division I Women's Basketball Championship.

March 24–25, Second Round Division I Women's Basketball NCAA Championship.

March 29–30, Third Round (Sweet Sixteen) Division I Women's Basketball NCAA Championship.

November 22, NCAA Women's Cross Country Championship, Terre Haute, IN.

November 21–23, NCAA Women's Field Hockey Championship, College Park, MD.

2. Professional Basketball

July 13, WNBA, Indiana @ New York; Minnesota @ Tulsa.

July 14, WNBA, San Antonio @ Connecticut; Los Angeles @ Phoenix; Atlanta @ Seattle.

July 16, WNBA, San Antonio @ Washington.

July 17, WNBA, Tulsa @ Seattle; Atlanta @ Los Angeles.

July 18, WNBA, Chicago @ New York; Phoenix @ Los Angeles.

July 19, WNBA, Washington @ Indiana; Minnesota @ San Antonio; Connecticut @ Tulsa.

July 20, WNBA, New York @ Chicago, Connecticut @ San Antonio; Los Angeles @ Seattle.

July 21, WNBA, Indiana @ Washington; Atlanta @ Tulsa; Minnesota @ Phoenix.

July 23, WNBA, New York @ Indiana.

July 25, WNBA, New York @ San Antonio, Indiana @ Tulsa; Seattle @ Los Angeles.

3. Golf

March 20–23, Ladies Professional Golf Association (LPGA), JTBC Founders Cup, Tempe, AZ.

March 27–30, LPGA, Kia Classic, Rancho Mirage, CA.

July 11–14, RICOH Women's British Open, LPGA, London, England.

July 17–20, Marathon Classic presented by Ownes Corning & O-1, LPGA, Toledo, OH.

July 24–27, International Crown, LPGA, Owings Mills, MD.

November 7–9, LPGA, Mizuno Classic, Tokyo, Japan.

November 13–16, Lorena Ochoa Invitational Presented by Banamex, LPGA, Guadalajara, Mexico.

November 13–16, LPGA, Lorena Ochoa Invitational, Jalisco, Mexico.

November 20–23, CME Group Tour Championships, LPGA, Naples, FL.

4. Tennis

March 24–April 9, Sony Open Tennis, WTA, Miami, FL.

March 16–23, Innisbrook Women's Open, USTA Pro Circuit Event, Innisbrook, FL.

March 24–30, The Oaks Club, USTA Pro Circuit Event, Osprey, FL.

July 14, Swedish Open, WTA Tour, Båstad, Sweden.

July 21, Baku Cup, WTA Tour, Baku, Azerbaijan.

5. Other

March 15–16, Gymnastics Junior Olympic National Championships, Des Moines, IA.

March 10–16, World Junior Figure Skating Championships.

March 21–22, Professional Rodeo Cowboy Association (PRCA) Rodeo, Nashville, GA.

March 21–22, PRCA Rodeo, Ocala, FL.

March 21–22, PRCA Rodeo, Springfield, MO.

March 21–22, PRCA Rodeo, Kalispell, MT.

March 22–23, PRCA Rodeo, North Fort Myers, FL.

March 27–29, PRCA Rodeo, Lubbock, TX.

March 27–29, PRCA Rodeo, Nacogdoches, TX.

March 27–29, PRCA Rodeo, Graham, TX.

March 24–30, World Figure Skating Championships.

July 7–13, General Tire World Cup 9, USA Softball, Irvine, CA.

July 15–21, Canadian Open Fast Pitch International, Softball, Surrey, British Columbia, Canada.

July 15–19, USA Gymnastics Championships, Louisville, KY.

July 16, PRCA Rodeo, Hampton, IA.

July 16, PRCA Rodeo, Monroe, WI.

July 16, PRCA Rodeo, Cumberland, MD.

July 17, PRCA Rodeo, Benton, PA.

July 15–17, PRCA Rodeo, Nampa, ID.

July 16–19, PRCA Rodeo, Woodward, OK.

July 16–19, PRCA Rodeo, Pretty Prairie, KS.

July 17–20, PRCA Rodeo, Mitchell, SD.

July 17–20, PRCA Rodeo, Salinas, CA.

July 25–27, North American Roller Hockey Championships, Estero, FL.

November 19–23, Eastern Sectional Figure Skating Championships, Raleigh, NC.

November 19–23, Midwestern Sectional Figure Skating Championships, Geneva, IL.

November 19–23, Pacific Coast Sectional Figure Skating Championships, Spokane, WA.

November 19–20, AQHA Horsemanship Challenge Preliminary/Finals, Equestrian, Oklahoma City, OK.

November 21, PRCA Rodeo, Women's Professional Rodeo Association, Inverness, FL.

6. Professional Football

July 12, Postseason Week 2, Independent Women's Football League.

July 19, 2014, Playoffs—Final 4, Women's Football Alliance.

July 26, Postseason Week 3, Independent Women's Football League.

Questions for Reflection and Discussion

How can this sort of longitudinal study help us to understand the unevenness of social change in mass media? This study focuses narrowly on television news and ESPN's *SportsCenter*; what might we expect to find if we look at gender in live sports televised programming or online? What might explain the tighter focus, over the past 25 years, on the "big three" men's sports? What social changes might contribute to more and better quality coverage of women's sports or of men's sports other than football, basketball, and baseball?

Acknowledgments

The authors wish to thank Margaret Carlisle Duncan, Wayne Wilson, Emily Fogle, Randi Kass, and Orasio Becerra for their assistance on this and previous iterations of the study. Marj Snyder, Don Sabo, and the Women's Sports Foundation have been instrumental in providing support, and we appreciate their advocacy efforts for improving the media coverage of women's sports. Thank you to anonymous reviewers for their insightful reviews. A special thanks to Larry Wenner for his continued support of this project.

References

Acosta, V. R., & Carpenter, L. J. (2015). *Women in intercollegiate sport: A longitudinal national study, thirty-seven year update, 1977–2014*. Retrieved from http://www.acostacarpenter.org/

Adams, T., & Tuggle, C. A. (2004). ESPN's *SportsCenter* and coverage of women's athletics: "It's a boys' club." *Mass Communication and Society, 7*, 237–248.

Amateur Athletic Foundation of Los Angeles. (1990, 1994, 2000, 2005). *Gender in televised sports report*. Retrieved from http://www.la84.org/reports/

Bernstein, A. (2002). Is it time for a victory lap? Changes in the media coverage of women in sport. *International Review for the Sociology of Sport, 37*, 415–428.

Billings, A. C., & Young, B. D. (2015). Comparing flagship news programs: Women's sports coverage in ESPN's *SportsCenter* and FOX Sports 1's *Sports Live*. *Electronic News, 9*, 3–16.

Burstyn, V. (1999). *The rights of men: Manhood, politics and the culture of sport*. Toronto, Canada: University of Toronto Press.

Caple, H., Greenwood, K., & Lumby, C. (2011). What league?: The representation of female athletes in Australian sports coverage. *Media International Australia, 140*, 137–146.

Center for Feminist Research. (2010). *Gender in televised sports, 1989–2009. University of Southern California*. Retrieved from http://dornsife.usc.edu/cfr/gender-in-televisedsports/

Cooky, C. (2009). "Girls just aren't interested": The social construction of interest in girls' sport. *Sociological Perspectives, 52*, 259–283.

Cooky, C., Messner, M. A., & Hextrum, R. (2013). Women play sports, but not on TV: A longitudinal study of televised news media. *Communication & Sport, 1*, 203–230.

Cooky, C., Wachs, F. L., Messner, M. A., & Dworkin, S. L. (2010). It's not about the game: Don Imus, race, class, gender, and sexuality in contemporary media. *Sociology of Sport Journal, 27*, 139–159.

Daniels, E. A. (2009). Sex objects, athletes and sexy athletes: How media representations of women athletes can impact adolescent girls and college women. *Journal of Adolescent Research, 24*, 399–423.

Duncan, M. C., & Hasbrook, C. A. (1988). Denial of power in televised women's sports. *Sociology of Sport Journal, 5*, 1–21.

Eastman, S. T., & Billings, A. C. (2001). Sportscasting and sports reporting: The power of gender bias. *Journal of Sport and Social Issues, 24*, 192–213.

Etling, L., & Young, R. (2007). Sexism and authoritativeness of female sportscasters. *Communication Research Reports, 24*, 121–130.

Farred, G. (2000). Cool as the other side of the pillow: How ESPN's *SportsCenter* has changed television sports talk. *Journal of Sport and Social Issues, 24*, 96–117.

Fleiss, J. L., Levin, B., & Paik, M. C. (2005). *Statistical methods for rates and proportions*. Malden, MA: Wiley InterScience.

Greer, J. D., Hardin, M., & Homan, C. (2009). "Naturally" less exciting?: Visual production of men's and women's track and field coverage during the 2004 Olympics. *Journal of Broadcasting & Electronic Media, 53*, 173–189.

Hardin, M., Chance, J., Dodd, J., & Hardin, B. (2002). Olympic photo coverage fair to female athletes. *Newspaper Research Journal, 2*, 64–78.

Kane, M. J., & Buysse, J. (2005). Intercollegiate guides as contested terrain: A longitudinal analysis. *Sociology of Sport Journal, 22*, 214–238.

Kane, M. J., LaVoi, N. M., & Fink, J. S. (2013). Exploring elite female athletes' interpretations of sport media images: A window into the construction of social identity and "selling sex" in women's sports. *Communication & Sport, 1*, 1–31.

Kian, E. T. M., Vincent, J., & Modello, M. (2008). Masculine hegemonic hoops: An analysis of media coverage of March Madness. *Sociology of Sport Journal, 25*, 235–242.

Koivula, N. (1999). Gender stereotyping in televised media sports coverage. *Sex Roles, 41*, 589–604.

LaVoi, N. M., Buysse, J., Maxwell, H. D., & Kane, M. J. (2007). The influence of occupational status and sex of decision maker on media representations in intercollegiate athletics. *Women in Sport & Physical Activity Journal, 15*, 32–43.

McKay, S., & Dalliere, C. (2009). Campus newspaper coverage of varsity sports: Getting closer to equitable and sports-related representations of female athletes? *International Review of the Sociology of Sport, 44*, 25–40.

Messner, M. A. (2002). *Taking the field: Women, men and sports*. Minneapolis, MN: University of Minnesota Press.

Messner, M. A. (2009). *It's all for the kids: Gender, families and youth sports*. Berkeley, CA: University of California Press.

Messner, M. A. (2011). Gender ideologies, youth sports, and the production of soft essentialism. *Sociology of Sport Journal, 28*, 151–170.

Messner, M. A., Dunbar, M., & Hunt, D. (2000). The televised sports manhood formula. *Journal of Sport & Social Issues, 24*, 380–394.

Messner, M. A., Duncan, M. C., & Cooky, C. (2003). Silence, sports bras, and wrestling porn: The treatment of women in televised sports news and highlights. *Journal of Sport and Social Issues, 27*, 38–51.

Messner, M. A., Duncan, M. C., & Jensen, K. (1993). Separating the men from the girls: The gendered language of televised sports. *Gender & Society, 7*, 121–137.

Messner, M. A., Duncan, M. C., & Wachs, F. L. (1996). The gender of audience-building: Televised coverage of men's and women's NCAA basketball. *Sociological Inquiry, 66*, 422–439.

Messner, M. A., Duncan, M. C., & Willms, N. (2006). This revolution is not being televised. *Contexts: Understanding People in Their Social Worlds, 5*, 34–38.

Miller, K. E., Melnick, M. J., Barnes, G. M., Farrell, M., & Sabo, D. (2005). Untangling the links among athletic involvement: Gender, race, and adolescent academic outcomes. *Sociology of Sport Journal, 22*, 178–193.

Musto, M. (2014). Athletes in the pool, girls and boys on deck: The contextual construction of gender in coed youth swimming. *Gender & Society, 28*, 359–380.

Nylund, D. (2004). When in Rome: Heterosexism, homophobia and sports talk radio. *Journal of Sport and Social Issues, 28*, 136–168.

Rightler-McDaniels, J. (2014). Changes through the lens?: U.S. photographic newspaper coverage of female athletes. *Sport in Society, 17*, 1076–1094.

Sabo, D., & Veliz, P. (2008). *Go out and play: Youth sports in America*. East Meadow, NY: Women's Sports Foundation.

Sheffer, M. L., & Schultz, B. (2007). Double standard: Why women have trouble getting jobs in local television sports. *Journal of Sports Media, 2*, 77–101.

Tuggle, C. A. (1997). Differences in television sports reporting of men's and women's athletics: ESPN *SportsCenter* and CNN Sports Tonight. *Journal of Broadcasting & Electronic Media, 41*, 14–24.

Turner, J. S. (2014). A longitudinal content analysis of gender and ethnicity portrayals on ESPN's *SportsCenter* from 1999–2009. *Communication & Sport, 4*, 303–327.

Webber, J. D., & Carni, R. M. (2013). Where are the female athletes in *Sports Illustrated*?: A content analysis of covers (2000–2011). *International Review for the Sociology of Sports, 48*, 196–203.

Whiteside, E., & Hardin, M. (2012). On being a "good sport" in the workplace: Women, the glass ceiling, and negotiated resignation in sports information. *International Journal of Sport Communication, 5*, 51–68.

11

Reflections on
Communication and Sport
• • • • • • • • • • • • • • • • • • • •

On Men and Masculinities

MICHAEL A. MESSNER

Gender studies scholars have long pointed to the fact that when people mention "gender," they tend to think of women. This makes some sense, as it was the women's movement that first made gender "visible" to us. But feminism also raised critical questions about men and masculinity. Similarly, when someone says "gender and sports," many people think automatically about women's sports, including, as we point out in the previous chapter, how women's sports have been routinely ignored by the mass media. By contrast, however, the mass media presents us with a daily wall-to-wall cacophony of words and images about men's sports. In this chapter, I examine the ways that men's sports are covered in mass media and what this tells us about changes and continuities in our conceptions of men and gender relations. Though sports media offers up continuous stories of male glories, it also has to manage or make sense of frequent "problem stories," such as male athletes who are accused of sexual assault, domestic violence, or other crimes. I also discuss how the mass media handles problems that

Source: "Reflections on communication and sport: On men and masculinities," by M. A. Messner, 2012, *Communication & Sport, 1*(1/2), pp. 113–124, doi:10.1177/2167479512467977. Copyright 2012 by the author. Reprinted with permission of Sage Publications.

ensue from long-standing commercial links between men's sports and alcohol sale and consumption, as well as U.S. sport's joined-at-the-hip relationship to militaristic nationalism. Finally, I discuss how the rise in recent decades of strong and competent women athletes challenges the narrow forms of masculinity that have been so widely celebrated in sport since the mid-20th century.

—Michael A. Messner

Why Communication and Sport Matters

This morning, as with most mornings, I trudged toward wakefulness with a cup of strong coffee and with the *Los Angeles Times* spread on the table before me. Vegetables first: I scan the front section for the day's news. Then dessert, the sports section: Skimming by three full pages of stories on Dodgers and Angels baseball, University of California, Los Angeles, University of Southern California, and pro football, I land in the place that, since my boyhood years, has been my sweet spot, the baseball box scores. A Giants win, coupled with another Dodgers loss has stretched my team's September lead to six games. I had already known this good news last night; it even crossed my mind while I was still barely conscious in bed this morning, but still, I wanted to read it in the paper.

Yeah, there it is: a six-game lead over the Dodgers. I don't know, there may be a bit of a smirk on my face as my eyes scan to the facing page five—and then I see it. In the lower right corner of the page, below a boxing story with a photo of a victorious Sergio Martinez actually wearing a king's crown, my eyes settle on a one-eighth page ad, taken up mostly with a photo of a model—beautiful young woman showing plenty of skin, sitting on the edge of the bed and looking simultaneously sexy and sadly disappointed. Behind her, in soft focus, her male partner is crashed out; I can almost hear his snoring. The caption "PREMATURE ISSUE?" frames the photo, followed by the "guarantee" that "National Male Medical Clinics" can "solve ANY PE problem TODAY"—and starting with a mere $95 one-time office visit.

This juxtaposition begins to illustrate one reason it is important to think critically about men, masculinities, and sports media. On one hand, the sports page—or *Sports Illustrated*, or ESPN's *SportsCenter*, or sports talk radio—are seemingly harmless go-to places where every day, millions of boys and men enter an all-male world to "BIRG" (Bask In Reflected Glory) of the heroic exploits of male athletes (Beneke, 1997). Indeed, with the exception of the ad about premature ejaculation, the eight pages of this morning's sports section offer no clue that women even exist except for a tiny page two box that directs the reader to go to *latimes.com* if he or she would like to read a story about the U.S. women's soccer team. Not much room in the actual paper for that sort of thing, I guess—not when there is so much football happening. But the PE ad brings up another side of what is going on here and a hint about why it matters to think a bit more deeply about this topic. Such ads do not appear every day in the sports pages. They are rare on weekends, when the excitement of the day's games is still mostly ahead of us. But I have noticed over the years that such ads pop up with great regularity in the Monday paper—ads for treating erectile dysfunction (this past Monday had a full-page ad for Cialis), reversing hair loss, and losing that extra 20 pounds of flab. Advertisers seem to know that for men, Monday mornings can be a time of disappointment—not so much with our favorite team's performance, but with our own. Friday night's fantasy of excitement, triumph, and roaring sex has fizzled and withered into Monday morning's receding hairline. We are not the muscular boxer wearing the crown, we know; we are the guy in the PE ad, asleep and unable to satisfy the beautiful woman who, it appears, may be realizing that she had best move on to some other guy who is not such a loser.

This juxtaposition interests me, and I have always found it important: There is so clearly a disjunction between men's connection with mediated male heroes and our own less-than-heroic experiences with masculinity. We read the box scores, watch televised games and highlight shows, and check the Internet for scores and updates on our favorite teams. We experience this connection to sports as a go-to place of pleasure, a place that feels separate as an escape from the rest of life. But as a sociologist, I know that it is not separate at all. Sport has such power as a consumable item of culture that many of us experience it as a separate space; yet, our sports fantasies are tied to our own fears, inadequacies, even failures as men, as the Monday morning paper illustrates. More, the "sports–media complex"—that multibillion dollar partnership of commercial spectator sports with the mass media—linked with billions of dollars in advertising and consumer products—makes these connections for us every day, mostly without seeming to (Jhally, 1984). The sports–media–commercial complex consistently sells boys and men a glorified package of what masculinity is and should be, regularly nudges us with reminders that we do not measure up to this standard, and then offers compensatory products—beer, underwear, cars, shaving products, and, yes, erectile dysfunction medications—that promise transcendence from the shameful knowledge that, even if our team is in first place, we individual men are in fact losers (Messner & Montez de Oca, 2005; Wenner, 1991).

My Journey with Communication and Sport

Of course, there is far more to this topic than the commercial exploitation of tensions between masculine sports heroism and masculine failure. My interest in sports and masculinity as an academic topic started when, in graduate school in the early 1980s, I put my own lifelong attachment to sports into play with emergent feminist theories of masculinities. My first empirical project was an examination of men's lives as athletes (Messner, 1992). But my interests, inspired by feminism, went beyond concerns with the male life course—I wanted to explore sport as place where gender relations were being actively constructed. The 1980s were an opportune time to do this, as sport was transforming from an almost entirely homosocial institution to one with dramatically increasing participation by girls and women. How, I wondered, can we understand sport historically—not as some fixed patriarchal institution, but as a dynamic gender construction site? I postulated that while midcentury sport had been a nearly unambiguous site for the construction of binary conceptions of gender and for the ideological legitimization of hegemonic masculinity, late 20th-century sport had become a "contested terrain" of gender relations and meanings (Messner, 1988). The mass media was a key site for studying how these contested gender meanings would play out.

At the end of the 1980s, I met media studies scholar Margaret Carlisle Duncan at a miniconference that was held by the Amateur Athletic Foundation of Los Angeles (later renamed the LA84 Foundation). When the Foundation's jarringly critical clips of racist and sexist sports reporting were largely denied as anecdotal or "cherry picked examples" by the media people in the audience, Margaret and I offered to do some systematic research on televised sports for the Foundation. This began a productive collaboration on what became a longitudinal study. Duncan and I issued research reports on televised sports news every 5 years hence (adding ESPN's *SportsCenter* in for the 2000 report); Cheryl Cooky joined me in conducting the most recent update of the study in 2010 (Messner & Cooky, 2010).

In our first Gender in Televised Sports report, issued in 1990, Duncan and I showed that televised sports news was mostly ignoring women's sports, which got only 5% of all sports news airtime. Worse, when women (as athletes or not) did show up in the news, they were frequently trivialized, sexualized, and deployed as locker-room jokes. This combination of silence and trivialization spoke volumes, not only about deeply sexist attitudes toward women but also about the sports media's continued focus on sport as a terrain by and for the elevation of men as a superior sex class. This idea—that gender is always constructed *relationally*—became a foundational concern for thinking about men and masculinities. We could not understand the meanings of the (mostly) glorified cacophony of talk and images about men and sports without juxtaposing that noise with the silence and the "denial of power" within which the mass media couched women's sports (Duncan & Hasbrook, 1988; Eastman & Billings, 2001; Messner, Duncan, & Cooky, 2003).

And what did that cacophony of talk and images of men and sport say to us? In a study of televised sports that boys frequently watch, my colleagues Darnell Hunt and Michele Dunbar and I revealed what we called "the televised sports manhood formula," an overarching narrative about men and gender that cuts across live broadcasts and accompanying commercials (Messner, Dunbar & Hunt, 2000). The elements of the formula, we argued, constitute a pedagogy of manhood for young male viewers:

> What is a Real Man? A Real Man is strong, tough, aggressive, and above all, a winner in what is still a Man's World. To be a winner he has to do what needs to be done. He must be willing to compromise his own long-term health by showing guts in the face of danger, by fighting other men when necessary, and by "playing hurt" when he's injured. He must avoid being soft; he must be the aggressor, both on the "battle fields" of sports and in his consumption choices. Whether he is playing sports or making choices about which snack food or auto products to purchase, his aggressiveness will net him the ultimate prize: the adoring attention of conventionally beautiful women. He will know if and when

he has arrived as a Real Man when the Voices of Authority—White Males—say he is a Real Man. But even when he has finally managed to win the big one, has the good car, the right beer, and is surrounded by beautiful women, he will be reminded by these very same Voices of Authority just how fragile this Real Manhood really is: After all, he has to come out and prove himself all over again tomorrow. You're only as good as your last game (or your last purchase).

These research reports on gender in televised sports have been meaningful for me in a number of ways. First, the public nature of the reports has helped to stretch my work beyond academia; the reports have been used by women's sports advocacy organizations and in journalism schools. Second, the study's longitudinal nature has helped my thinking about looking at sport as a gender regime with a shifting and contested "state of play" in which certain sorts of men—particularly football, basketball, and baseball (and sometimes ice hockey) players—are given the vast majority of attention. Meanwhile, other men's sports are ignored and even sometimes trivialized in ways similar to how women's sports are treated. Put in the language of social theory, sports media does not simply construct hegemonic masculinity in relation to femininities but also in relation to marginalized or subordinated masculinities (Connell, 1989).

Focus: On Men and Masculinities

Over the past 20 years, a substantial body of literature has emerged that focuses on various aspects of men, gender, media, and sports. Here, I discuss four general areas of this scholarly work: case studies of male sports figures as "fallen heroes"; studies of the consumption of mediated sports as a male preserve; scholarship that explores the connections between mediated sport and larger historical, structural, and political processes; and discussions of how shifts in the coverage of women's sports affect the meanings of men's sports. In my brief overview of each theme, I will emphasize especially how shifting and contested images of women and men, mediated through sports media, have played mostly a conservative, reproductive role in gender relations.

Scandals and Fallen Heroes

Recent years have seen a decline of the past tendency in sports journalism to give famous men (be they politicians or athletes) a pass on off-field transgressions. The sports pages are peppered with stories of the latest athlete's DUI, drug test failure, arrest for possession of illegal firearms, assault, rape, or domestic partner violence. These stories hold the potential to disrupt the ideological association of male athletes as glorified icons of hegemonic masculinity. A number of years ago, media scholar William Solomon and I followed a story about boxer Sugar Ray Leonard's drug use and battery of his wife, looking at the ways that the story deployed "news frames" to render invisible the family violence part of the story and introduced a language of redemption for Leonard's "mistakes" with drugs and alcohol (Messner & Solomon, 1993). This frame, we argued, helped to defuse the potential of such stories to delegitimize the sport of boxing in particular and more generally to raise questions about the ways that sexism and violence are joined in men's sports.

Since that time, other scholars have deployed similar methods to analyze case studies of media coverage of scandals and fallen heroes, and these scholars have increasingly deployed sophisticated intersectional analyses—looking at the interplay of race, class, sexualities, and gender in the coverage of men's sports. Mary McDonald (1999) explored the gender and race dynamics in media coverage of well-known male figures in sport who were accused of domestic violence. Studies of media treatment of big-name male athletes who have contracted HIV have been especially useful in illuminating the intersections of gender with race and sexual orientation. For instance, McKay (1993) reflected critically on the ways that the media responded to basketball star Earvin "Magic" Johnson's revelation that he was HIV-positive by projecting Johnson's sexual promiscuity on to "wanton women." Dworkin and Wachs's (1998, 2000) comparison of mass media treatment of three stories of HIV-positive male athletes showed the ways that social class, race, and sexual orientation came in to play in the media's very different framings of these three stories. More recently, an intersectional analysis was deployed in examining the media's coverage of shock radio host Don Imus's scandalous statements about the Rutgers University women's basketball team (Cooky, Wachs, Messner, & Dworkin, 2010; Wachs, Cooky, Messner, & Dworkin, 2012). Together, these studies show how the sports media continues to play a largely reproductive—rather than critical or disruptive—role in the politics of sport and problems grounded in social inequalities.

Consumption of Sports Media as a Male Preserve

Another strand of research focuses more on men as consumers of sports media. As noted above, sports are often experienced by men as a separate gendered place, what Eric Dunning (1986) called "a male preserve" in an otherwise changing world. Researchers have explored how this male preserve is in fact connected to men's actual lives. In a classic study of in the *Sports Illustrated* "swimsuit issue," Laurel Davis pointed to how the popular annual magazine reflected and reproduced sport as a site of male, White, heterosexual, and even colonial privilege (Davis, 1997). Extending the analysis of the swimsuit issue and adding the televised coverage of the Super Bowl, Messner and Montez de Oca (2005) showed how beer and liquor ads position male consumers of "mega-sports media events" as losers who might hope to consume their way out of their insecurities.

David Nylund's (2007) fascinating analysis of men's relationships with sports talk radio shows how important the articulation of heterosexuality is in this cultural recuperation of a threatened masculinity. And in an innovative study, Sabo, Gray, and Moore (2000) interviewed women who had been physically abused by their male partners during or shortly after the men watched televised sports. This kind of study begins to give researchers and activists a handle on what the links might be between a man's act of violence against a woman partner and his acts of viewing violent sports, drinking alcohol, and gambling on sports. Similarly,

Wenner's (1998) and Curry's (2000) studies of sports bars begin to show the construction of (sometimes violent) masculinities within the context of an institution that thrives on men's collective consumption of televised sports and alcohol.

Sport, Masculinities, Politics, and War

While many studies of sports media and masculinities focus on the local or the case-study level, some scholars have also begun to examine this field in terms of large structural and transnational processes. This makes good sense, given the increasingly global nature of sports and sports media (Miller, McKay, Lawrence, & Rowe, 2001). Montez de Oca's (2005, in press) groundbreaking work on the historical rise of American football illustrates the central role of the mass sports media, especially television, in the post–World War II construction of the White male citizen. In a similar vein, scholars have pointed to the ways in which mass spectator sports, amplified by mass media, build narrow notions of patriotism that link masculinity, nationalism, and the glorification of warfare (Bairner, 2000; Jansen & Sabo, 1994; Malszecki & Tomislava, 2001; Trujillo, 1995).

Female Athletes as Visible Cultural Icons

Although my research with Duncan and Cooky reveals that televised news and highlight shows continue to treat women's sports as almost nonexistent, there has been a notable expansion of coverage of women's sports in other media outlets, and this has implications for how we view men and sport. Heywood and Dworkin (2003) have argued that women athletes have increasingly emerged, especially with younger girls, as cultural icons that signify a growing empowerment of women. This has occurred due to increased coverage of celebrity women athletes in advertising and in "new media" and also to some increases (albeit uneven and spotty) in live coverage of women's sporting events on television. For instance, although ESPN does not cover much of women's sports on its popular highlights show *SportsCenter*, over the past decade, the cable sports outlet has dramatically increased the quantity and quality of play-by-play coverage of certain women's sports like college basketball and softball. On one hand, these developments challenge "hard essentialism"—the hegemonic postwar ideology that naturalized men's and women's binary and hierarchical oppositions. When girls and women play sports—and especially if we pay attention to their abilities and accomplishments—then "what sports illustrates," according to sociologist Judith Lorber, is not a binary opposition between male and female bodies, but instead what Mary Jo Kane calls a "continuum of difference" between and among bodies of all sexes and genders (Kane, 1995; Lorber, 1996).

But the increased coverage of women's sports does not quite mean that it is "time for a victory lap" (Bernstein, 2002). The growth of coverage of women's sports within new media, in particular, might be seen as a containment or ghettoization of women's sports. For instance, ESPN has recently introduced ESPNW, a fledgling online site for the coverage of women's sports. While this may be a welcome development for fans who are hungry for more coverage of women's sports, it may also help to take mainstream media carriers off the hook in making any pretense of increased (much less fair or equal) coverage of women's sports. Put simply, creating the women's sports information ghetto ESPNW allows the much better funded and far more visible father station to remain, implicitly, ESPNM.

Further, though our most recent studies of gender in televised sports news and highlight shows revealed a decline in disrespectful trivialization and sexualization of women athletes, other research points to a continuation of these sorts of containments of women's power (Daniels & LaVoi, 2012). In addition to the familiar sexualization theme, a new frame seems to be arising in coverage of women's sports, and this seemed especially evident in the televised coverage of the 2012 Olympics, which focused on women athletes as family members and mothers who have made difficult individual choices to pursue their Olympics dreams. Conversely, men athletes' families are less often discussed; men are more likely to be looked at as "natural athletes." Elsewhere, I have referred to this emergent frame of women (flexible work–family choosers) and men (linear creatures, naturally disposed to sports and public life) as being at the heart of an emergent ideology of "soft essentialism" (Messner, 2011). The rise in popularity of men's combat sports (e.g., the continued popularity of football and the explosion of Ultimate Fighting) serves to bolster this emergent ideology. In the face of women's emergence as athletes, glorified images of massively built and violent male bodies may help erase or at least mitigate the extent to which women's increasing athleticism reveals a continuum of difference.

Most of the research I have discussed above—whether it looks at male sports heroes' scandals, sport as a site of gendered consumption, sports media's role in nationalism or global processes, or the reporting of women's sports—illustrates the largely reproductive nature of mass mediated sport, both in terms of content and consumption. However, neither sport nor sport media are seamless fields. Rather, there are increasingly evident fissures, contradictions, and disjunctures in the edifice of cultural formations of sport, men, and masculinities. In the final section, I will suggest ways that future research might explore these fissures as sites of possible social change.

Looking Ahead for Communication and Sport Research

Scholars of gender and sports media have engaged in a good deal of chicken-or-egg discussions in recent years: Will media interest in women's sports expand when actual audiences expand, or do audiences expand in the wake of increases in coverage? While the answer is, of course, "both-and," the question itself tends to oversimplify the complex dynamics at work. Clearly, the expanding athleticism and love of sports among girls and younger generations of women have begun to explode the mid-20th-century myths of categorical male bodily superiority. But the mass media's continued focus primarily on central men's sports mitigates the potentially progressive impact of female athleticism in the larger gender order. While there are market concerns (often very narrowly defined) in deciding which sports to cover and how to cover them, it is also likely that gender divisions of labor on the production end also figure into these decisions. While a few women have broken into sports reporting and commentating, this workplace is still dominated by men (Etling & Young, 2007; Sheffer & Shultz, 2007). For instance, in our 2010 televised sports report, we found that men commentators took up 99.5% of the sports news and 89% of *SportsCenter*'s airtime (Messner & Cooky, 2010). Scholars would do well to investigate sports journalism and commentary—print and electronic—as gendered work sites and to explore how these gendered worksites help shape assumptions and practices as to what to report and how to report it (Hardin & Whiteside, 2008; Kane & Disch, 1993).

Future studies should also focus on the consumption end of sports media. As an example of such research, Whiteside and Hardin (2011) show that women's lower levels of sports viewing are linked not to a lack of interest on their parts, but to the ways in which sports viewing for women too often does not mesh with family work. In short, in examining gender at the consumption end of sports media, it is necessary to explore not simply "tastes" but also how the consumption of sports media fits (or does not) with gendered divisions of labor at the juncture of leisure, work, and family life (Messner, 2009). Gender relations are strained and shifting at the nexus of these gender regimes. Under what conditions will this result in a degendering and equalization of sports, both as a product and as a field of consumption and leisure? And under what conditions do men respond to these strains by retreating to contemporary "man caves" to consume men's sports (and related products) pitched to them by male commentators? In other words, we need to more fully examine sports media not simply as "texts" but also at points of production and points of consumption in terms of larger gender divisions of labor and power.

Another potential site for change—and thus for critical research—concerns the emergence of "others" in sport who do not neatly fit within a gender binary. Scholars have focused for years on the ways that race/ethnicity complicates research on "men and sport" or "women and sport." But the analysis of race and sport in the United States too often has fallen into a Black–White binary. Does the recent explosion of interest in NBA player Jeremy Lin create an opportunity to deploy a multiracial analysis of men in sports media? Is such a prominent Asian American star framed as a "model minority" in ways that stabilize basketball as a "Black sport?" Similarly, recent stories of progay marriage statements by high-profile male athletes and professional teams create an opportunity to explore how or under what conditions hegemonic masculinity is still policed by homophobia and under what conditions hegemonic masculinity might be under reconstruction—no longer anchored by overtly cruel homophobia, but perhaps instead grounded in a seemingly benign "family friendly" heteronormativity. Offering an even more fundamental challenge to sex/gender binaries in sports media are stories of transgender athletes, though such high-profile stories have thus far been more about inclusion or exclusion of transgender athletes within women's sports (Cooky, Dycus, & Dworkin, 2012; Dworkin, Swarr, & Cooky, in press).

And finally, the recent burst of concern about head injuries and brain damage suffered by athletes—especially football players—creates an important opportunity for scholars of sports media. The mounting medical evidence, the continuing parade of sad stories of middle-aged men with advancing dementia, and the collective legal suits now being waged by former players against football leagues are all huge stories (Anderson & Kian, 2012). Do these stories simply operate in some parallel journalistic universe to the continued business-as-usual stories of football glory? Or does this story of the extreme "costs of masculinity" paid by our Sunday heroes sometimes bleed into the play-by-play broadcasts and the Monday headlines? If so, how and when does this happen? And when it does, might audiences—guys like me who like to read the sports pages—start to make the connection between the very real vulnerabilities of these sports heroes and our own vulnerabilities that are being tweaked by advertisers in these same newspaper pages? Today, people often bemoan the good old days when we could look up to our athletes as invulnerable heroes, as symbols of masculine perfection. I say the more the media can focus on athletes as real people—and especially as real bodies with all their human vulnerabilities—the better for the athletes and the better for all of us.

Questions for Reflection and Discussion

Many boys and men find sports media to be a go-to place for daily pleasures that enmesh them in images and stories of glorified masculinity: What do they learn when they go there? How might male sports media consumers be impacted if women's sports were covered more equitably on television, in print, and online? How are current social debates—for instance, about racism against African American men or about head injuries in football and other combat sports—impacting sports media, and how might these debates affect both the pleasures and the gendered meanings that sports fans derive from consuming sports media?

References

Anderson, E., & Kian, E. (2012). Examining media contestation of masculinity and head trauma in the National football league. *Men & Masculinities, 15*, 152–173.

Bairner, A. (2000). After the war? Soccer, masculinity, and violence in Northern Ireland. In J. McKay, D. Sabo, & M. Messner (Eds.), *Masculinities, gender relations, and sport* (pp. 176–194). Thousand Oaks, CA: Sage.

Beneke, T. (1997). *Proving manhood: Reflections on men and sexism.* Berkeley, CA: University of California Press.

Bernstein, A. (2002). Is it time for a victory lap? Changes in the media coverage of women in sport. *International Review for the Sociology of Sport, 37*, 415–428.

Connell, R. (1989). *Gender & power.* Palo Alto, CA: Stanford University Press.

Cooky, C., Dycus, R., & Dworkin, S. (2012). "What makes a woman a woman?" vs. "our first lady of sport": A comparative analysis of United States and South African media coverage of Caster Semenya and South African news media. *Journal of Sport and Social Issues, 37*(1), 31–56. doi:10.1177/0193723512447940

Cooky, C., Wachs, F., Messner, M., & Dworkin, S. (2010). It's not about the game: Don Imus, racism and sexism in contemporary media. *Sociology of Sport Journal, 27*, 139–159.

Curry, T. (2000). Booze and bar fights: A journey to the dark side of college athletics. In J. McKay, D. Sabo, & M. Messner (Eds.), *Masculinities, gender relations, and sport* (pp. 162–175). Thousand Oaks, CA: Sage.

Daniels, E., & LaVoi, N. (2012). Athletics as solution and problem: Sports participation for girls and the sexualization of female athletes. In E. Zubriggen & T. Roberts (Eds.), *The sexualization of girls and girlhood.* New York, NY: Oxford University Press.

Davis, L. (1997). *The swimsuit issue and sport: Hegemonic masculinity in sports illustrated.* Albany, NY: State University of New York Press.

Duncan, M., & Hasbrook, C. (1988). Denial of power in televised women's sports. *Sociology of Sport Journal, 5,* 1–21.

Dunning, E. (1986). Sport as a male preserve: Notes on the social sources of masculine identity and its transformation. *Theory, Culture & Society, 3,* 79–90.

Dworkin, S. L., Swarr, A. L., & Cooky, C. (in press). Sport and sex and gender injustice: The case of South African track star Caster Semenya. *Feminist Studies.*

Dworkin, S., & Wachs, F. (1998). Disciplining the body: HIV positive athletes, media surveillance, and the policing of sexuality. *Sociology of Sport Journal, 15,* 1–20.

Dworkin, S., & Wachs, F. (2000). The morality/manhood paradox: Masculinity, sport, and the media. In J. McKay, M. Messner, & D. Sabo (Eds.), *Masculinities, gender relations, and sport* (pp. 47–66). Thousand Oaks, CA: Sage.

Eastman, S., & Billings, A. (2001). Sportscasting and sports reporting: The power of gender bias. *Journal of Sport and Social Issues, 24,* 192–213.

Etling, L., & Young, R. (2007). Sexism and authoritativeness of female sportscasters. *Communication Research Reports,* 121–130.

Hardin, M., & Whiteside, E. (2008). Maybe it's not a "generational thing": Values and beliefs of aspiring sport journalists about race and gender. *Media Report to Women, 36,* 8–16.

Heywood, L., & Dworkin, S. (2003). *Built to win: The female athlete as cultural icon.* Minneapolis, MN: University of Minnesota Press.

Jansen, S., & Sabo, D. (1994). The sport/war metaphor: Hegemonic masculinity, the Persian Gulf War, and the New World Order. *Sociology of Sport Journal, 11,* 1–17.

Jhally, S. (1984). The spectacle of accumulation: Material and cultural factors in the evolution of the sports/media complex. *Insurgent Sociologist, 123,* 41–52.

Kane, M. J. (1995). Resistance/transformation of the oppositional binary: Exposing sport as a continuum. *Journal of Sport and Social Issues, 19,* 191–218.

Kane, M. J., & Disch, L. (1993). Sexual violence and the reproduction of male power in the locker room: The "Lisa Olsen Incident." *Sociology of Sport Journal, 10,* 331–352.

Lorber, J. (1996). Beyond the binaries: Depolarizing the categories of sex, sexuality, and gender. *Sociological Inquiry, 66,* 143–159.

Malszecki, G., & Cavar, T. (2001). Men, masculinities, war, and sport. In N. Mandell (Ed.), *Feminist issues: Race, class, and sexuality* (3rd ed., pp. 166–192.) Toronto, Canada: Pearson Education Canada.

McDonald, M. (1999). Unnecessary roughness: Gender and racial politics in domestic violence media events. *Sociology of Sport Journal, 16,* 111–133.

McKay, J. (1993). "Marked men" and "wanton women": The politics of naming sexual "deviance" in sport. *Journal of Men's Studies, 2,* 69–87.

Messner, M. (1992). *Power at play: Sports and the problem of masculinity.* Boston, MA: Beacon Press.

Messner, M. (2009). *It's all for the kids: Gender, families and youth sports.* Berkeley, CA: University of California Press.

Messner, M. (2011). Gender ideologies, youth sports, and the production of soft essentialism. *Sociology of Sport Journal, 28,* 151–170.

Messner, M., & Cooky, C. (2010). Gender in televised sports: News and highlights shows, 1989–2009. *University of Southern California Center for Feminist Research.* Retrieved from http://dornsife.usc.edu/cfr/gender-in-televised-sports/

Messner, M., Duncan, M. C., & Cooky, C. (2003). Silence, sports bras, and wrestling porn: The treatment of women in televised sports news and highlights. *Journal of Sport and Social Issues, 27*, 38–51.

Messner, M., Dunbar, M., & Hunt, D. (2000). The televised sports manhood formula. *Journal of Sport and Social Issues, 24*, 380–394.

Messner, M., & Montez de Oca, J. (2005). The male consumer as loser: Beer and liquor ads in mega sports media events. *Signs: Journal of Women in Culture and Society, 30*, 1879–1909.

Messner, M., & Solomon, W. (1993). Outside the frame: Newspaper coverage of the Sugar Ray Leonard wife abuse story. *Sociology of Sport Journal, 10*, 119–134.

Miller, T., McKay, J., Lawrence, G., & Rowe, D. (2001). *Globalization and sport: Playing the world*. Thousand Oaks, CA: Sage.

Montez de Oca, J. (2005). As our muscles get softer, our missile race becomes harder: Cultural citizenship and the "muscle gap." *Journal of Historical Sociology, 18*, 145–171.

Montez de Oca, J. (in press). *Discipline & indulgence: College football, media, and the American way of life during the Cold War*. New Brunswick, NJ: Rutgers University Press.

Nylund, D. (2007). *Beer, babes and balls: Masculinity and sports talk radio*. New York, NY: State University of New York Press.

Sabo, D., Gray, P., & Moore, L. (2000). Domestic violence and televised athletic events: "It's a man thing." In J. McKay, D. Sabo, & M. Messner (Eds.), *Masculinities, gender relations, and sport* (pp. 127–146). Thousand Oaks, CA: Sage.

Sabo, D., & Jansen, S. C. (1994). Seen but not heard: Images of black men in sports media. In M. Messner & D. Sabo (Eds.), *Sex, violence and power in sports: Rethinking masculinity* (pp. 150–160). Freedom, CA: Crossing Press.

Sheffer, M. L., & Schultz, B. (2007). Double standard: Why women have trouble getting jobs in local television sports. *Journal of Sports Media, 2*, 77–101.

Trujillo, N. (1995). Machines, missiles, and men: Images of the male body on ABC's *Monday Night Football*. *Sociology of Sport Journal, 12*, 403–423.

Wachs, F. L., Cooky, C., Messner, M., & Dworkin, S. L. (2012). Media frames and displacement of blame in the Don Imus/Rutgers University basketball team incident: Sincere fictions and frenetic inactivity. *Critical Studies in Media Communication*.

Wenner, L. (1991). One part alcohol, one part sport, one part dirt, stir gently: Beer commercials and television sports. In L. Vande Berg & L. Wenner (Eds.), *Television criticism: Approaches and applications* (pp. 388–407). New York, NY: Longman.

Wenner, L. (1998). In search of the sports bar: Masculinity, alcohol, sports, and the mediation of public space. In G. Rail (Ed.), *Sport and postmodern times* (pp. 303–332). Albany, NY: SUNY Press.

Whiteside, E., & Hardin, M. (2011). Women (not) watching women: Leisure time, television, and implications for televised coverage of women's sports. *Communication, Culture & Critique, 4*, 122–143.

12

It's Not about the Game

•••••••••••••••••••

Don Imus, Race, Class,
Gender, and Sexuality in
Contemporary Media

CHERYL COOKY, FAYE L. WACHS,

MICHAEL A. MESSNER,

AND SHARI L. DWORKIN

As we write the introduction to this chapter, it is nearly 10 years since radio show "shock jock," Don Imus referred to the Rutgers University women's basketball team as "some nappy-headed ho's." Even now, writing those words cause so much rage and disgust. As feminist scholars who are interested in the ways in which the news media cover women's sports and female athletes, we were particularly interested in this incident, in part because the comment itself trafficked in sexist, racist, and classist language, yet the media seemed to focus centrally on this as a "racist comment/joke" incident, ignoring the intersections of race, gender, sexuality, and class. We thought that this framing limited the possible meanings and thus the conversations regarding how to fully

Source: "It's not about the game: Don Imus, race, class, gender, and sexuality in contemporary media," by C. Cooky, F. L. Wachs, M. A. Messner, & S. L. Dworkin, 2010, *Sociology of Sport Journal,* 27(2), pp. 139–159, http://dx.doi.org/10.1123/ssj.27.2.139. Copyright by Human Kinetics, Inc. Reprinted with permission.

address the problems of such commentary. Of course, at the time we were conducting this research, we could not fathom that the normalization of sexist and racist language would not simply be an easy but horrific strategy of a radio host to garner attention and listeners but that this language would infuse the campaign strategy of the Republican candidate in the United States 2016 Presidential Election.

—Cheryl Cooky and Michael A. Messner

On Tuesday, April 3, 2007, the Rutgers University Scarlet Knights women's basketball team squared off in the National Collegiate Athletic Association's (NCAA) championship game against a perennial powerhouse, the University of Tennessee Volunteers. The following day, in a dialogue on *Imus in the Morning*, Don Imus, longtime radio talk show host and "shock jock," referred to the Rutgers University women's basketball team as "nappy-headed hos." Later that day, Media Matters for America, an independent media watchdog group, posted the transcript on their website, flagging the commentary due to the blatant racism and sexism in the dialogue (Ifill, 2007). The following is the full transcript of the segment:

> IMUS: So, I watched the basketball game last night between—a little bit of Rutgers and Tennessee, the women's final.
> ROSENBERG: Yeah, Tennessee won last night—seventh championship for [Tennessee coach] Pat Summitt, I-Man. They beat Rutgers by 13 points.
> IMUS: That's some rough girls from Rutgers. Man, they got tattoos and—
> McGUIRK: Some hard-core hos.
> IMUS: That's some nappy-headed hos there. I'm gonna tell you that now, man, that's some—woo. And the girls from Tennessee, they all look cute, you know, so, like—kinda like—I don't know.
> McGUIRK: A Spike Lee thing.
> IMUS: Yeah.
> McGUIRK: The Jigaboos vs. the Wannabes—that movie that he had.
> IMUS: Yeah, it was a tough—
> McCORD: Do The Right Thing.
> McGUIRK: Yeah, yeah, yeah.
> IMUS: I don't know if I'd have wanted to beat Rutgers or not, but they did, right?
> ROSENBERG: It was a tough watch. The more I look at Rutgers, they look exactly like the Toronto Raptors.
> IMUS: Well, I guess, yeah.
> RUFFINO: Only tougher.
> McGUIRK: The [Memphis] Grizzlies would be more appropriate.

This exchange exploded into a controversial, widely discussed and debated "media event," the contours of which reveal important insights about sport and the role of mass media in constructing hegemonic notions of race, class, gender, and sexuality. Following McDonald and Birrell (1999), we "read" Imus's remark as a sport "event" wherein mediated ideologies of race, gender, sexuality and class are articulated. First, we review the research on gender and race in sport media. A discussion of our theoretical framework and methodology follows. The chapter then explores the dominant media frames through a content and textual analysis. We examine these frames to critique hegemonic ideologies embedded in culturally relevant texts. We suggest possible "counter-narratives" of the Imus media event that offer "resistant political possibilities" (McDonald & Birrell, 1999, p. 295). The chapter concludes with a discussion of the implications of the media framings of the Imus/Rutgers controversy and asks what role the "sport–media complex" plays in the overall construction of these ideologies (Jhally, 1984).

Gender, Race, Sport, and the Media

The Imus dialogue on Rutgers University highlighted the ways in which female athletes continue to struggle to receive respectful quality coverage of their sport in mainstream news media. Research on the mainstream news media coverage of women's sport continually shows that representations of the female athlete are "contested ideological terrain" (Messner, 1988). Sociologists of sport have long noted the lack of coverage of women's sport in mainstream news media and, more importantly, the lack of respectful, serious coverage of women's sport, especially for female athletes of color (Douglas, 2005; Douglas & Jamieson, 2006; Lansbury, 2001; McKay & Johnson, 2008; Schultz, 2005), in mainstream print media (Bishop, 2003; Christopherson, Janning, & McConnell, 2002; Eastman & Billings, 2000; Eastman & Billings, 1999; Pratt, Grappendorf, Grundvig, & LeBlanc, 2008; Vincent, 2004; Vincent & Crossman, 2008; Urquhart & Crossman, 1999) and in mainstream televised media (Daddario & Wigley, 2007; Duncan & Hasbrook, 1988; Messner, Duncan, & Willms, 2006).

Despite attempts to educate the U.S. mainstream news media regarding stereotypical coverage of women's sport, there are consistent patterns that persist over time. As longitudinal research on the televised news media coverage demonstrates, women's sport is consistently ignored (Messner, Duncan & Willms, 2006; Messner, Duncan & Cooky, 2003). Research has found that the amount of coverage in local news and national sports highlight programs only gives approximately 3–8% of the coverage to women's sport (Messner, Duncan & Willms, 2006). Even when the media do cover women's sport, the coverage often trivializes women's athleticism and heterosexualizes female athletes (Heywood & Dworkin, 2003; Christopherson et al., 2002; Messner, 2002). Research on newspaper coverage of the Wimbledon championships in 2000 found that while the amount of coverage of the men's and women's events was relatively equal, the quality of coverage differed: The mostly male journalists who covered the tournaments devalued the athletic accomplishments of female tennis players by using cultural and racial stereotypes, trivialization, and sexual innuendo (Vincent, 2004). These trends in the coverage of women's sport, and specifically of African American female athletes, are not new to the post–Title IX generation. In her analysis of the print news media coverage of Alice Coachman and Althea Gibson, Lansbury (2001) found that White newspapers trivialized African American women's participation in sport, either by failing to cover the accomplishments of the athletes or by framing the athletes as masculine.

Research on contemporary media representations of African American female athletes has focused on African American women's participation in individual sports, like tennis, especially mediated representations of Venus and Serena Williams (Douglas, 2005; Schultz, 2005; Spencer, 2004). Indeed, this is logical given the American public's fascination with female athletes in individual sports and their feminine beauty, not athletic skill (Banet-Weiser, 1999a). This fascination is constructed, in part, by the media coverage of women's sport. However, when athletes are non-White, race in media representations also becomes salient. Douglas's (2005) analysis of the media coverage of the 2001 Indian Wells tennis tournament and the 2003 French Open, found that the media's "raceless" explanations for the hostile reception of the Williamses' sisters rendered race and White privilege invisible and upheld the marking of tennis as a "white" sport. Schultz (2005) argues that the popular media's representations of Serena Williams during the 2002 U.S. Open were "located within racialized discourses," albeit through the oppositional rhetoric that positioned Serena Williams against other White athletes on the tour (p. 338). For Schultz (2005), blackness in the media coverage of the 2002 U.S. Open was "constructed in contrast with discussions of normalized, white female tennis athletes" (p. 339). More recently, McKay and Johnson (2008) examined mainstream media coverage of Venus and Serena Williams and showed how, in the past, sport media has "othered" women as "objects of ridicule, inferiority and weakness . . . but currently is searching for new ways to disparage the powerful and therefore 'uppity' African-American sportswomen" (p. 492). They argued that despite the Williams sisters' unprecedented success in professional tennis, the mainstream sports media discursively positioned their bodies as simultaneously sexually grotesque and pornographically erotic.

Female athletes in basketball—and presumably other team sports—have to negotiate a "contradictory set of cultural images" (Banet-Weiser, 1999a). As scholars have long noted, women's participation in sport, and in particular team sport, is frequently accompanied by a questioning of the (hetero)sexuality of athletes (Cahn, 1994; Griffin, 1998). This is in part due to the fact that, unlike individual sports such as tennis and gymnastics, participation in a team contact sport like basketball is viewed in U.S. culture as a "masculine" endeavor (Banet-Weiser, 1999a). Thus female athletes are often confronted with cultural assumptions regarding their lack of femininity and therefore their lack of heterosexuality (Banet-Weiser, 1999a). These cultural assumptions regarding women's sport participation contribute to particular mediated representations of female athletes. For example, the WNBA's marketing strategy revolved around highlighting the heterosexual, emphasized femininity of WNBA players as models, mothers, or the girl next door (Banet-Weiser, 1999a; McPherson, 2000). In her analysis of the WNBA website, McPherson (2000) found that the players' familial relationships, ties, and responsibilities were highlighted. She argues this is not simply about rearticulating female athleticism within the domestic context; rather, it produces racialized narratives of Black femininity. Thus the negotiation of the contradictions in women's sport participation differs qualitatively for African American female athletes, given the ways in which African American women have long been portrayed in the media, and specifically sports media, as both hypersexualized and less feminine. As a result, African American female athletes are subject to particular "controlling images" in the media (Cahn, 1994; Collins, 1990).

As critical media scholars argue, basketball is a cultural site wherein blackness is both invisible and hypervisible (Banet-Weiser, 1999a; McPherson, 2000). Given the popularity of women's basketball and the fact that African American female athletes are overrepresented in basketball at the collegiate level (Smith, 1992), this study provides an analysis of media representations of female athletes in team sport contexts. As noted above, previous research reveals the agency of the media in shaping discourses of sport and female athletes in ways that are implicitly about race, gender, and sexuality. Building upon this research (Banet-Weiser, 1999a; Douglas & Jamieson, 2006; McDonald & Birrell, 1999; Schultz, 2005), we argue that media representations of female athletes of color cannot be analyzed outside of a consideration of the simultaneous, interlocking forms of oppression (gender, race, sexuality, class). This study differs from prior research in that we examine not only the framing or representation of a predominantly African American female team (here the Rutgers University women's basketball team) but also the media's framing of other key figures and the ways in which the media contextualized the "nappy-headed hos" dialogue, a comment that is simultaneously raced, gendered, and sexualized. Therefore, we explore the media's representation (framing) of African American female athletes (as the Rutgers team became racialized as "Black" through the dialogue despite the racial identities of individual players, of whom several were White) and whose voices were heard in the mainstream news media's framing of the event. Thus Collins's (1990) concept of representations of Black women, "controlling images," and her theory of intersectionality shed light on how multiple identities (race, gender, class, sexuality), privilege, and oppression converged in the media event (McDonald & Thomas, in press; Wingfield, 2008).

Theoretical Framework

According to Gramsci (1971), social order is maintained through a dynamic process of coercion and consent whereby dominant groups produce dominant cultural beliefs, called hegemonic ideologies, and subordinated groups consent to structural conditions that may be oppressive given the power of hegemonic ideologies. For Gramsci, consent is secured through the "cultural leadership of the dominant grouping" (Curran, 2006, p. 132). In the United States, the media operate as a part of this cultural leadership, particularly when the lines between the corporate elite and the media elite are increasingly blurred (Curran, 2006). Ideologies thus become "naturalized," or a part of commonsense, taken-for-granted understandings. However, Gramsci also recognized that subordinated groups can choose to oppose hegemonic dominance by creating alternative understandings of society that connect to people's social experiences and identities (Curran, 2006).

Patricia Hill Collins's theoretical framework was informed by Gramscian theories on the dynamics of domination and power in societies. Building upon Gramsci's hegemony theory, Collins (1990) argued that dominant groups control social institutions in society, such as schools, the media, and popular culture, which produce controlling images that are rife with stereotypes about subordinated groups. These controlling images are not passively accepted by marginalized groups, as there are cultures of resistance within subordinated communities. Collins (1990) explained, "Subjugated knowledges . . . develop in cultural contexts controlled by oppressed groups. Dominant groups aim to replace subjugated knowledges with their own specialized thought because they realize that gaining control over this dimension of subordinate groups' lives amplifies control" (p. 228). At the same time, Collins recognized there are segments of subordinated communities that internalize and perpetuate dominant ideologies. Thus the processes of domination and oppression are complex. The result is that "African-American women find themselves in a web of cross-cutting relationships, each presenting varying combinations of controlling images and women's self-definitions" (Collins, 1990, p. 96).

The concept of intersectionality refers to this "web of cross-cutting relationships" taking into account how various forms of oppression (e.g., race, class, gender, sexuality) interlock with one another (Collins, 1990). As such, "both/and perspectives" rather than "either/or perspectives" of social locations are used to understand the ways in which individuals (and social institutions) are situated within interlocking forms of privilege/dominance and oppression/subordination.

Therefore, we analyzed the Imus/Rutgers University controversy and the subsequent media framings to explore the tensions between the "controlling images" of African American women as "nappy-headed hos" and "women's self-definitions" of "young ladies of class." The Rutgers coach, players, and women's groups provided counterhegemonic discourses of African American women. Collins's theoretical framework allows consideration of how subordinate groups assert agency, despite a lack of institutional access or power, to also shape the media frames of the event. Thus this study critically analyzes the construction of media events by mainstream news print media to understand the "complex interrelated and fluid character of power relations" as they are constructed along axes of difference (McDonald & Birrell, 1999, p. 284).

Methods

Following Hall (2000), we acknowledge that media frames are both constructed within raced, classed, and gendered hierarchical relations of power and are read within those very same systems of domination. Also, building upon Gramscian theories of hegemony, Hall (2000) developed theoretical and methodological frameworks for understanding how meanings are produced and consumed. As

Hall notes, meanings are constructed through and within hierarchical structures of power wherein the preferred meanings, or the meanings intended by the producer, "have institutional, political and ideological power imprinted in them, and themselves become institutionalized" (Hall, 2000, p. 57). As such, preferred readings often limit the possible meanings encoded in texts by producers and thus limit the possible readings decoded by audiences (Hall, 2000; Hunt, 1999). Through a textual analysis, researchers can uncover both the denotative and connotative meanings of texts (Hall, 2000). From this methodological perspective, the media are viewed as creating and recreating narratives that can be linked to dominant ideas or ideologies that circulate in wider society.

Content analysis involves a systematic, quantitative analysis of content, usually texts, images, or other symbolic matter (Krippendorff, 2004). According to Payne and Payne (2004), "content analysis seeks to demonstrate the meaning of written or visual sources by systematically allocating their content to pre-determined, detailed categories and then both quantifying and interpreting the outcomes" (p. 51). It generally involves the researcher determining the presence, meanings, and relationships of certain words or concepts within the text. We used content analysis to systematically locate the preferred meanings of the text. Stokes's (2003) discussion of media methodologies recognizes that scholars can successfully combine content analysis with other interpretivist methods such as textual analysis.

We analyzed the major and regional newspaper coverage of the Don Imus/Rutgers University Women's Basketball controversy. Four of the top five national papers, based on circulation rates (Audit Bureau Circulation, 2006), were selected: *USA Today*, the *New York Times*, the *Los Angeles Times*, and the *Washington Post*. Eight regional papers were selected from different regions of the United States (Northeast, Midwest, South, and West) from the top 25 list, also chosen based on circulation rates (Audit Bureau Circulation, 2006). Regional newspapers included: *Chicago Tribune, Atlanta Journal Constitution, Houston Chronicle, Denver Post*, the *Philadelphia Inquirer, Boston Globe, San Francisco Chronicle*, and the *Seattle Times*. The *Star Ledger*, New Jersey's major newspaper, was also selected based on the location of Rutgers University to provide an understanding of "local" coverage of the story.

Articles were retrieved using the Lexis-Nexis database from April 4, 2007 (the day the comment aired) to April 19, 2007, using the search terms, "Imus" and "Rutgers University." This search yielded a total of 188 feature articles. We selected April 19, 2007, as the end date due to the shift in media coverage after the Virginia Tech shootings (a student went on a shooting spree, killing 33 people, including himself, and wounding 15 others), which became the new "media event" that dominated the newspapers and televised news programs.

The first and second author conducted a qualitative analysis of all articles to uncover the various media frames of the event. Thus the frames we subsequently analyzed in the content analysis were derived from this inductive approach. The initial qualitative analysis revealed eight emergent themes regarding media framing of the controversy, three of which we discuss in this chapter (due to space limitations). Emergent themes were discovered using open coding of data (Strauss & Corbin, 1990). First, we read the articles to determine who and what was left outside or marginalized in dominant news frames. Here, we focused on who and what was rendered invisible and silenced. Second, the frames for the Rutgers team were analyzed. Finally, we examined how the statement, "nappy-headed hos," was framed by the media. From these emergent themes, we created subthemes that we then quantitatively analyzed. For example, an emergent theme was what we labeled, "voices in the article." Upon our initial textual analysis, we noted which voices (as determined by direct quotes in the article) were included in the coverage (e.g., coach, Black leaders, women's leaders, players, politicians, and others). In the content analysis, we were then able to code whether an article mentioned and/or included quotes from specific individuals or groups. We then compiled descriptive statistics on the content of the subthemes. In the final step, we conducted a textual analysis, analyzing in depth the quantitative results from the content analysis (Hall, 2000).

Explanation of Events[1]

In 2007, Rutgers University had their first ever NCAA national championship appearance for women's basketball. The 2007 Rutgers squad, ranked number 19 and 21 by the Associated Press and the ESPN/USA Today polls, respectively, had struggled at the beginning of the season but won the Big East conference title against another powerhouse, the University of Connecticut. This was their first conference title in the history of the program (Rutgers Women's Basketball History, 2009). Rutgers continued its winning streak, defeating both Duke and Louisiana State University during the NCAA tournament. Rutgers's performance was surprising to many because Duke, a number one ranked team and top seed, had beaten Rutgers earlier in the season by 40 points. Rutgers's "Cinderella" season would end at the NCAA championship game, where they would face off against the University of Tennessee women's basketball team, a number one seed. Coached by Pat Summitt in her 33rd season, Tennessee won their seventh NCAA National Championship. The matchup should have provided a compelling story for journalists, given that Tennessee has been compared with other long-standing sport dynasties including Duke University's men's basketball program and Major League Baseball's New York Yankees ("Tennessee 5–0 against Rutgers in NCAA tournament play," 2007).

At the time, Imus's radio show, *Imus in the Morning*, was broadcast on WFAN, a CBS-owned radio station serving the New York City market with an average of 358,000 listeners daily (Carr, 2007, p. 7). In addition, millions watched a simulcast of the show on MSNBC. As noted in the introduction, the exchange on Imus's show on April 4, 2007, and its subsequent posting on Media Matters for America captured the attention of the mainstream news media, given the controversial nature of the dialogue.

Historically, the adjective "nappy" has served as a derogatory, racist stereotype to describe the hair texture of women of color. The term "ho" is a shortened slang version of the word "whore," which is a word to describe a sexually promiscuous or immoral woman (whore, 2009). In the United States, the word "ho" is part of pop culture vernacular, commonly heard in certain forms of rap and hip-hop music and on daytime talk shows such as *Jerry Springer*. It is often is used to refer to women who sexually manipulate men for economic compensation. In addition, the epithet "ho" typically evokes a woman of lower socioeconomic standing, whereas "escort" has higher socioeconomic connotations. According to pop culture usage, a "ho" can also refer to a woman who "steals" another woman's boyfriend or husband. The dialogue precipitated a series of events, which we outline below.

On Thursday, April 5, 2007, MSNBC issued a statement distancing itself from Imus and calling his comments "deplorable," while Imus claimed on his radio show that people should not be offended by "some idiot comment meant to be amusing." (Carr, 2007, p. 7). The National Association for the Advancement of Colored People called the remark "racist" and "unacceptable." On Friday, April 6, 2007, the National Association for Black Journalists issued a news release condemning Imus's remarks and called for his firing. NCAA President Myles Brand and Rutgers University President Richard L. McCormick also issued a joint statement strongly condemning Imus's remark:

> The NCAA and Rutgers University are offended by the insults on MSNBC's Don Imus program towards the ten young women on the Rutgers basketball team. It is unconscionable that anyone would use the airways to utter such disregard for the dignity of human beings who have accomplished much and deserve credit. It is appropriate that Mr. Imus and MSNBC have apologized. (Carr, 2007, p. 7)

Imus apologized on his radio show saying,

> We want to take a moment to apologize for an insensitive and ill-conceived remark we made the other morning regarding the Rutgers women's basketball team. It was completely inappropriate and we can understand why people were offended. Our characterization was thoughtless and stupid, and we are sorry. (de Moraes, 2007, p. C01)

WFAN and CBS also issued apologies. CBS issued the following statement: "We are disappointed by Imus' actions earlier this week which we find completely inappropriate. We fully agree that a sincere apology was called for and will continue to monitor the program's content going forward" (Carr, 2007, p. 7).

On Monday, April 9, 2007, Don Imus appeared on Reverend Al Sharpton's radio talk show. Reverend Sharpton, considered by the mainstream news media as a voice for "the African-American community," had spoken out frequently on racial issues in the past. On the show, Imus apologized once again for his remark. Sharpton accepted Imus's apology but called for his resignation. Moreover, the National Organization for Women mobilized its constituents to pressure the media networks to fire Imus. The Women's Sports Foundation posted a copy of the transcript on their website, asking their members to write or e-mail CBS and NBC to "do the right thing and not support bigotry on the airwaves." ("Protest Don Imus' Inappropriate Remarks," 2009)

In Chicago, Reverend Jesse Jackson, also considered a voice for "the African-American community" and a key leader in contemporary racial concerns, protested outside NBC's offices in Chicago. Claiming pressure from the mainstream news media and the organizational efforts of key figures like Sharpton and Jackson, as well as letters in protest from their own employees including Al Roker, a weather anchor for the *Today* show on NBC (who wrote on his *Today* show blog that Imus's comment was "vile and disgusting"), CBS Radio and MSNBC announced they were suspending Imus for two weeks.

Further adding to Imus's predicament, on Tuesday, April 10, 2007, the Rutgers team held a nationally televised news conference. Coach C. Vivian Stringer and the Rutgers athletes publicly accepted Imus's apology. However, Coach Stringer referred to Imus's comments as "racist and sexist remarks that are deplorable, despicable and unconscionable" (Horn & Gold, 2007, p. 11). Team captain Essence Carson put the controversy in perspective, noting, "It's more than about the Rutgers women's basketball team. As a society, we're trying to grow and get to the point where we don't classify women as hos and we don't classify women as nappy-headed hos" (Roberts, 2007, p. 1).

That same day, Alpha Kappa Alpha, a national sorority and a significant African American cultural institution with over 200,000 active members, issued a press release condemning Imus's comment and called for the firing of both Imus and his producer, Bernard McGuirk (Imus Press Release, 2007). Moreover, the president of Alpha Kappa Alpha sorority, Barbara A. McKinzie, urged members and their families to divest of any stock holdings in CBS, NBC, and their parent companies, including Microsoft and Westinghouse, and called on the members to boycott rap and hip-hop artists. McKinzie noted that the call for the boycott was a way for Alpha Kappa Alpha members to honor the legacy of another Alpha Kappa Alpha member, C. Delores Tucker, a politician and social activist who was one of the first women of color to call for a boycott of misogynist music and artists (Coach Stringer is also a member of the sorority). Also on Tuesday, April 10, 2007, key corporate sponsors of Imus's program pulled their support, including Proctor & Gamble, Staples, and Bigelow Tea. General Motors, GlaxoSmithKline, American Express, and Sprint followed the next day (Wednesday, April 11, 2007), leading MSNBC to cancel the simulcast of Imus's show.

On Thursday, April 12, 2007, CBS fired Imus. Several days later, the Women's Sports Foundation issued another press release supporting CBS and MSNBC for their decision to fire Imus (Women's Sports Foundation, 2007b).

Silence and Invisibility

The explanation of events outlines the myriad voices that could have been included in the media frames. A key aspect of media frames is the legitimation of some voices in a controversy and the exclusion of others that are silenced or rendered illegitimate or "outside the frame" (Dworkin & Wachs, 1998, 2009; Messner & Solomon, 1993). Thus we analyzed media coverage in terms of which individuals and groups were rendered visible or invisible. While "key players," whether they are inside or outside the media frame, exercised agency in speaking out on the issue, who is named and who is unnamed yields important insights regarding the hegemony of the media to shape ideologies and cultural understandings of the event.

As shown in Table 12.1, although the Rutgers team was named in the majority of articles (87.2%) the majority of articles did not name the coach, C. Vivian Stringer (78.2%) or specific players of the team such as Essence Carson or Matee Ajavon (87.8%). Although the story was about an insult directed at the Rutgers team and its players, the coach and the athletes were infrequently named or quoted. In other words, the mainstream media silenced their voices and perspectives. While it may appear that Rutgers was inside the frame, given that nearly 90% of the articles mentioned the Rutgers team, in most cases, the team was only mentioned once to provide context for the story. In a typical example, an article began, "Radio's Don Imus continued his public mea culpa Monday for calling female Rutgers basketball players 'nappy-headed hos'" (Johnson, 2007, p. 1D). The opening line was typically the first and only time the team was mentioned, discussed or quoted. Very few articles discussed the team's accomplishments, statistics, or the history and background of the team, including Rutgers's "Cinderella" season. The "Cinderella" narrative typically dominates the sport media frames, especially during the NCAA men's Final Four tournament. The absence of this narrative in the framing of the Rutgers team highlights the mainstream news media's continuing silence of women's sport (Messner, Duncan, & Willms, 2006).

Also nearly invisible in the media frame are the leaders of "women's groups" (e.g., president of the National Organization for Women, Kim Gandy; president of the Feminist Majority, Eleanor Smeal; the president of the Women's Sports Foundation, Aimee Mullins; and Alpha Kappa Alpha president, Barbara McKinzie); 92.6% of articles did not name one women leader or group (see Table 12.1). When a women's group was named, in most cases, it was the National Organization for Women, an organization that has been criticized in the past for its lack of inclusion of the voices and concerns of women of color.

While only 7.4% of articles mentioned a women's leader or group by name, 46.3% of articles included the name(s) of Black leaders or groups (defined as such by the media; see Table 12.1). In other words, the mention of Black leaders or groups was more than six times that of women's leaders or groups. Moreover, in the overwhelming majority that named or quoted "Black leaders," the leaders were Black men, while the "women's leaders" mentioned were White women. A few articles did mention C. Dolores Tucker, the first female African American woman to serve as Secretary of State and a Civil Rights leader who led a movement against misogyny in rap lyrics. She passed away in 2005 and thus could not be quoted in the articles, but other individuals who were quoted referenced Tucker's movement to end misogyny in rap and hip-hop.

Table 12.1. Invisibility

Key Figures or Groups Not Named	% (# of articles)
Imus (search term)	0 (0)
Stringer	78.2 (147)
Players	87.8 (165)
Rutgers team	12.8 (24)
Black Leaders	53.7 (101)
Women's Leaders	92.6 (174)
Politicians	67.6 (127)

N = 188. The percentages/number of articles may not add to 100% or 188 because not all articles included the frames analyzed.

Further adding to this missed opportunity to frame the story on the intersections of race, gender, and sexuality, the mainstream news media largely ignored the organized protests that occurred at the Rutgers University Women's Center. There were a few articles—particularly in the *Star Ledger*, a newspaper whose market includes Rutgers University—that mentioned the protests. Several included quotes from a letter written by Carolyn A. Brown, a Black female history professor at Rutgers University (Wentworth & Patterson, 2007). Alpha Kappa Alpha, as discussed earlier, also called for a boycott of Imus. Yet despite the diversity of voices, the articles framed Reverends Sharpton and Jackson almost exclusively as representatives or legitimate spokespeople. This positioning of Sharpton and Jackson, a routine part of mainstream media's packaging of "race stories," constructs a unitary Black community that shares a specific frame. Although these two leaders have been embroiled in past controversies, the media's uncritical positioning of Sharpton and Jackson as the primary spokespeople racialized the controversy. Moreover, this frame silenced intersectional ways of knowing, given that the quotations from Black leaders featured in the articles focused only the racial or racist aspects of the controversy while neglecting themes on race, gender, and sexuality in sport.

In addition to who was mentioned in the news articles, we analyzed whether these same individuals or groups were quoted (see Table 12.2). Black leaders were most frequently quoted (19.1%). There was little difference in the percentages of articles that included quotes from Coach Stringer (14.4%) or from Imus (15.4%). However, the voices of women's organizations (4.3%) and the Rutgers women basketball players (8.5%) were left almost entirely outside of the media frame. None of the articles quoted the Women's Sports Foundation (WSF) or the Alpha Kappa Alpha sorority despite both organizations issuing press releases. President Aimee Mullins of the WSF stated in the press release: "Race and gender bigotry are inexcusable." Alpha Kappa Alpha President Barbara McKinzie referred to Imus's comment as "racist and sexist." In short, the voices silenced in the media frames are the same voices that provide a context of intersectionality to Imus's comments. Given that Jackson and Sharpton are quoted in five times the number of articles as women's leaders and organizations, this further supports our analysis that race is the dominant frame in the mainstream print news media coverage.

Table 12.2. Silence

Key Figures/Groups quoted/paraphrased	% (# of articles)
Imus	15.4 (29)
Stringer	14.4 (27)
Players	8.5 (16)
NCAA/Rutgers University Administration	13.2 (25)
Black Leaders	19.1 (36)
Women's Leaders	4.3 (8)
Politicians	11.7 (22)

N = 188. The percentages/number of articles may not add to 100% or 188 because not all articles included the voices analyzed.

Media Framing of Female Athletes: Controlling Images versus Women's Self-Definitions

Imus's insult of the Rutgers University women's basketball team as "nappy-headed hos" suggests they "lack class," given their unwillingness, resistance, or inability to accept or adopt White middle-class standards of emphasized femininity. Most of the mainstream news media articles' quotations of the transcript failed to include the exchange that contrasted the "cute" Tennessee players with the Rutgers players who, in the eyes of Imus and his executive producer, were "like the Toronto Raptors," a men's NBA team known for their tough style of play. One exception was an article in the *San Francisco Chronicle* that included quotations from a University of California, Berkeley basketball player, Alexis Gray-Lawson, who thought the Tennessee team should have also been offended by the remarks because "casting them as the pretty team demeans their national title" (Knapp, 2007, p. B1). In sports such as gymnastics where subjective standards of beauty and "cuteness" become a factor in the evaluation of athletic performances, Chisolm (2001) argues that "cuteness" becomes a "female apologetic" to "minimize the transgressions of (gendered) social norms in sport" (p. 428). Imus's dialogue with his executive producer reproduced the gendered ideologies that female athletes historically have had to negotiate in their identities as athletes and as women (Cahn, 1994; Felshin, 1974; Festle, 1996).

The masculinization of female athletes historically has operated to "Other" women of color due to the ways that Whiteness and White privilege shape standards of beauty and femininity (Cahn, 1994; Schultz, 2005; Banet-Weiser, 1999b). In the sport of basketball, where athletic performances are based on performance standards separate from physical appearance, Imus's commentary regarding the "cuteness" of the Tennessee team serves to mark the athletes by both gender and race. The Imus incident also illustrates how the standards upon which female athletes are judged are not simply about the dichotomous category of Black/White; they also reveal the social value attributed to lighter skin. A journalist from the *San Francisco Chronicle*, Gwen Knapp, states that the Imus incident was not simply about race because there were as many African Americans on the Tennessee team as on the Rutgers team. Rather, it was about "who could 'pass' as part of mainstream culture" (Knapp, 2007, p. B1).

Table 12.3. Framing of the Rutgers University Women's Basketball Team

Frame Used	% (# of articles)
Innocent Victims	5.3 (10)
Young Ladies of Class	18.1 (34)
Both	10.6 (20)
Other	1.1 (2)
Article does not mention team	64.9 (122)

N = 188. The percentages/number of articles may not add to 100% or 188 because not all articles included the frames analyzed.

Given this, we were interested in how the Rutgers University women's basketball players were framed by the media (see Table 12.3). In most of the articles (64.9%), specific Rutgers players were not mentioned or quoted—that is, they were outside the frame. This finding supports our previous analysis of the invisibility and silence of the Rutgers University players and coach, which represented "subjugated knowledges" on the controversy (Collins, 1990). However, Rutgers's players and coach appeared inside the media frame after their nationally televised press conference on Tuesday, April 10, 2007. Of the 66 articles that discussed the players, more than half the articles (51.1%) framed the players as "young ladies of class." Of the articles that mentioned the players, 15% framed the players as "innocent victims" undeserving of Imus's verbal abuse. In this frame, the athletes were positioned as "vulnerable" or "meek" and "defenseless," lacking power in relation to Imus. Consider the following quote: "The Rutgers team had done nothing wrong but excel as history students and music majors, as big sisters and determined players" (Roberts, 2007, p. D1). In this quote, the Rutgers team is viewed as undeserving of Imus's verbal abuse. Several articles mentioned how Imus had "robbed them of their moment," likening the players to victims of a crime (Stanley, 2007, p. E1).

The mainstream news media coconstructed the frame of "young ladies of class" in their descriptions of the team, quoting or paraphrasing Coach Stringer, who defended her players by citing the educational accomplishments or leadership activities of the team. The following is an example of this frame: "These young ladies are valedictorians of their classes, future doctors, musical prodigies and yes, even Girl Scouts. They are all young ladies of class. They are distinctive, articulate" (Strauss, 2007, p. D3). The coconstruction of the frame illustrates the tensions between controlling images of African American women ("nappy-headed hos") and women's self-definitions. Coach Stringer represented the ways in which subordinated groups do not passively accept the controlling images put forth by the mainstream media. Challenging the image of African American women as "nappy-headed hos," Coach Stringer mentioned in the press conference that Essence Carson played musical instruments. In addition, she was quoted in several articles: "These young ladies are the best the nation has to offer and we are so very fortunate to have them here at Rutgers. They are ladies of class and distinction; they are articulate, they are brilliant" (Brennan, 2007, p. 12C). The Governor of New Jersey, Jon S. Corzine's comments on the team also coconstructed this frame: "The Rutgers Scarlet Knights women's basketball team embodies all that is great about New Jersey: intelligence, toughness, tenacity, leaders and, most of all, class" (Strauss, 2007, p. D3). Robert Mulcahy, the athletic director at Rutgers University, echoed the "class" frame. Articles noted how, during the press conference, Mulcahy introduced team captain, Essence Carson, as a "straight-A student, who could walk out of here and play 'Moonlight Sonata' on the piano without looking at the notes" (Strauss, 2007, p. D3). In short, the agency of Coach Stringer created counterhegemonic ideologies regarding female athletes that were then reproduced in the mainstream media's framing of the team.

A few articles (10.6%) fused the "innocent victims" and "young ladies of class" frames (see Table 12.3). These articles implied that because the players were outstanding citizens in the community and accomplished students and athletes, they were undeserving "innocent victims." For example, a *New York Times* article written by Gwen Ifill, a past target of Imus's "jokes," states, "For all their grit, hard work and courage, the Rutgers girls got branded nappy-headed hos." In the article, Ifill continues, "That game had to be the biggest moment of their lives . . . they are not old enough, or established enough to have built up the sort of carapace many women I know—black women in particular—develop to guard themselves against casual insult" (Ifill, 2007, p. A21). An article in the *Washington Post* describes the team as "a collection of bright, articulate young women, undeserving of Imus' attack" (Hicks, 2007, p. B01), and another *Washington Post* article used the descriptor "innocent women" to refer to the Rutgers players while later mentioning that "After all, at the heart of this discussion is a group of college-educated African-American women. A valedictorian. A musical prodigy. A budding young lawyer" (Hanretty, 2007).

In their analysis of the media coverage of golfer Nancy Lopez's farewell tour, Douglas and Jamieson (2006) argued that the "construction of whiteness relied upon discourses of sexuality and gender by maintaining cultural norms and values that were constitutive of dominant discourses of social power" (p. 128). In much the same way, White privilege is maintained and Whiteness is constructed through the ideologies of gender and sexuality that position the Rutgers University team as either "innocent victims" or "young ladies of class." Both frames reflect dominant ideologies, which maintain the cultural norms and values of White, middle-class, emphasized femininity.

Coach Stringer's description of the Rutgers women as "young ladies of class" deployed valued professional-class markers as a way of deflecting the negative confluence of race, gender, and sexuality with the lower-class life encoded in the "nappy-headed hos" epithet. The "young ladies of class" frame resists the "nappy-headed ho" label by challenging the "lack of class," "out of control," and "hypersexualized" Black female body. However, the largely successful (as seen in Imus's eventual firing) use of class markers to distance the young women of Rutgers from Imus's derision and the media's uncritical taking-up of this frame ignores the ways that "nappy-headed hos" implicitly invokes the tropes of gender, race, and (lower) class simultaneously. Working together with the dominant framing of the Imus event as primarily a "race story" and the narrative distancing of

Table 12.4. Outside the Frame: Sexism and Racism in American Society

Discussion Topic	% (# of articles)
Racism	35.6 (67)
Sexism	16 (30)
Article does not mention racism/sexism	51.6 (97)

N = 188. The percentages/number of articles may not add to 100% or 188 because not all articles included the topics analyzed.

the Rutgers women from "hos" implicitly normalizes this degraded status for women within poor Black communities.

Although researchers estimate that many African American female athletes come from low-income families, given disproportionate representation of African Americans among the poor and working classes in the United States (Smith, 1992), the Rutgers team was framed as "young ladies of class," transcending lower socioeconomic class locations. According to Collins's theory of intersectionality, some aspects of one's identity are sometimes privileged over others. The frame of "young ladies of class" puts forward the privileged aspects of the team's identity (in this case, upward class mobility) to counter the way race, class, and gender were disparagingly conflated. In this frame, "lower" class can be transcended for those who lack economic resources, which often confer a higher class status, through assimilation and acceptance of (White) middle-class norms of behavior and values such as playing a classical instrument and appreciating "high art."

Moreover, we argue that the label "young ladies of class" also implicitly positions women's basketball as moral (or classy) relative to men's basketball, which has faced long histories of accusations of a "lack of class" due to the participation of Black males from the urban underclass (Banet-Weiser, 1999a; Boyd, 1997). In this way, the comment deflects rather than underscores the history of sexualization (e.g., female athletes as "hos") that is so common in women's sports media coverage. At the same time, "young ladies of class" counteracts a long history of similarly disparaging frames of African American women in U.S. media more generally. As has been noted by Collins (1990), rarely are African American women framed in media outside of "sexualized," "lascivious," "wild," "primitive," "animal-like," "unfeminine," "welfare queens," or "matriarchal" frames. The Imus dialogue on April 4, 2007, touched on many of these historically racist and sexist frames by referring to women not only as "nappy headed" and "hos," but also as "grizzlies" who supposedly looked like the muscular NBA men's team, the Toronto Raptors.

Although some women internalize the (White, middle-class, heterosexual) standards of beauty in the United States, which leads to a devaluation of the skin color and hair textures of many African Americans, there is a long-standing tradition of a Black women's culture of resistance (Collins, 1990). This resistance illustrates that "hegemonic dominance is never totalizing or complete" and that the cultural context is a "fundamental site of resistance" (Collins, 1990, p. 228). In the case of Rutgers University, the athletes' resistant voices were allowed space in mainstream media, but they were ultimately framed to suggest that the controversy was the result of one individual's racism against an "undeserving" group.

Outside the Frame: Social Issues in Sport and Society

Missing from the media frames was critical self-reflexivity on the media's long-standing tradition of silence, trivialization, and sexualization of female athletes. Only a few articles actually dealt with issues pertaining to women's sport, such as gender discrimination in sport, the sexualization of female athletes in the media, or African American female athletes in sport. Moreover, the national newspapers in the sample included between two and three times the coverage of the Imus/Rutgers University controversy than on the *entire* 2007 NCAA women's basketball tournament (which spans 2–3 weeks). That one White man's insult can spur more print news media coverage than one of sport's major competitions illustrates the power of the mainstream to continually silence women's sport.

The findings also reveal that very few articles explored how female athletes are held to different standards than male athletes or how the hair texture of women of color is devalued in U.S. culture. When female athletes transgress gender norms and boundaries, even in a post–Title IX moment, they are still held to antiquated societal standards of emphasized femininity and feminine appearance by the mainstream news media.

Also outside of the media frame was a discussion of racism and sexism in the United States. Although more than half (51.6%; see Table 12.4) of the articles do not mention racism or sexism in U.S. society, the other half does tie the incident to racism and/or sexism in the wider society. Thirty-five percent of articles mention the prevalence of continued racism in U.S. society, while only 16% link the incident to continued sexism. In other words, there were twice as many articles that focused on racism than on sexism. A few articles acknowledged that although sexism played a role, racism in society is usually seen as more significant. J. A. Adande, a sports journalist for the *Los Angeles Times* notes that the story is "as much about sexism as it is about racism. It is sexist that looks even came into play while talking about a sporting event . . . but historically, racism trumps sexism" (Adande, 2007, p. D2). Similarly, Christine Brennan, a journalist for *USA Today* who covers women's sport notes, "When an issue like this explodes in our culture, the first outrage is usually racial, the second gender-related" (2007, p. C12).

Articles may have mentioned that the comment itself was sexist or linked the comment to the misogyny in rap music and "Black culture," but few discussed sexism in U.S. society. The *Star Ledger*, serving the New Jersey market, was one of the few newspapers to acknowledge the intersections of race and gender or how the comment was both racist *and* sexist. One article in the *Star Ledger* quoted Rutgers University history professor, Carolyn A. Brown: "Rutgers released a letter from Black female faculty at Rutgers writing Imus' slurs 'must be understood within a long history of oppression' in which African American women have suffered from racism and sexism" (Wentworth & Patterson, 2007, p. 1).

Summary and Conclusion

The Imus controversy, and the subsequent mainstream news media framing of the event, reminds audiences that female athletes' looks matter and racist notions of beauty remain alive and well. Our analysis shows that what was left outside the frame, in conjunction with what was highlighted inside the frame, created a dominant understanding of this media event as predominantly a *racial* event. This racial frame deflected the opportunity that the Imus controversy provided for an intersectional understanding of how gender, race, class, and sexuality operate in contemporary sporting contexts in the United States. We found that racial meanings of African American women/athletes were reproduced through gender, sexuality, and class as seen in the "young ladies of class" and "innocent victims" frames. Given the overall silence of women of color in the mainstream media, the dominant media frame on racism in society demonstrates that the mainstream media has the power to construct frames and to determine who and what is inside and outside the frame. Following Collins (1990), we observe that power operates to silence these subjugated knowledges that were outside or marginalized in the media frame. Thus other ways of knowing are obscured.

We conclude that the Imus dialogue stirred controversy and provoked debate in part because sport has been ideologically positioned as a "level playing field," particularly for African Americans (Smith, 2007; Hartmann, 2000). Ironically, the timing of Imus's comments coincided with the 60th anniversary of Jackie Robinson's breaking the color barrier in Major League Baseball. This historical event is significant due to the way it has served as an important symbol for the civil rights movement and has come to represent racial equality not only in sport but also in broader society. The contradiction between the anniversary and the dialogue on Imus's show highlights how "controlling images" of African American women continue to circulate despite the efforts of race- and gender-based progressive movements in the United States (Collins, 1990). An intersectional analysis illustrates how moments of resistance against race and gender domination that are mobilized around hegemonic middle-class values can be framed by the media in ways that defuse a broader critical analysis of the ways that power works in the sports–media complex.

Questions for Reflection and Discussion

Even though this incident happened a decade ago, what similarities do we see in the news media coverage of female athletes or of women more generally? In this chapter, we learn that the news media coverage of the "incident" garnered nearly two to three times the coverage than the entire NCAA women's basketball tournament combined. Based on what you've learned in this collection, what may be some factors to explain this? Why do you think the news media focus more on controversies in women's sports than the actual coverage of women's sports events? What does that tell us about gender relations in sports?

Acknowledgments

The authors would like to thank the editor, Pirkko Markula, and the anonymous reviewers for their constructive comments, suggestions, and feedback. A special thanks to Jennifer Schumacher for her assistance with data collection and entry.

Note

1   Information on the timeline of events found in Horn, J. (2007, April 13). The Imus scandal: Chronology and aftermath. *Los Angeles Times*, p. A21.

References

Adande, J. A. (2007, April 12). Pulling the plug on Imus should be an easy decision. *Los Angeles Times*, p. D2.

Audit Bureau of Circulation. (n.d.). Retrieved June 13, 2007 from http://www.accessabc.com

Banet-Weiser, S. (1999a). Hoop dreams: Professional basketball and the politics of race and gender. *Journal of Sport and Social Issues, 23*, 403–422.

Banet-Weiser, S. (1999b). *The most beautiful girl in the world: Beauty pageants and national identity.* Berkeley, CA: University of California Press.

Bishop, R. (2003). Missing in action: Feature coverage of women's sports in *Sports Illustrated. Journal of Sport and Social Issues, 27*, 184–194.

Boyd, T. (1997). *Am I black enough for you? Popular culture from the 'hood and beyond.* Bloomington, IN: Indiana University Press.

Brennan, C. (2007, April 11). Rutgers women stand tall in class. *USA Today*, p. 12C.

Cahn, S. (1994). *Coming on strong: Gender and sexuality in twentieth century women's sport.* New York, NY: Free Press.

Carr, D. (2007, April 7). Networks condemn remarks by Imus. *The New York Times*, p. 7.

Chisolm, A. (2001). Acrobats, contortionists and cute children: The promise and perversity of U.S. women's gymnastics. *Signs: A Journal of Women in Culture and Society, 27*(2), 415–450.

Christopherson, N., Janning, M., & McConnell, E. D. (2002). Two kicks forward, one kick back: Content analysis of media discourses on the 1999 Women's World Cup soccer championship. *Sociology of Sport Journal, 19*, 170–188.

Collins, P. H. (1990). *Black feminist thought: Knowledge, consciousness, and the politics of empowerment.* New York, NY: Routledge.

Curran, J. (2006). Media and cultural theory in the age of market liberalism. In J. Curran & D. Morley (Eds.), *Media and cultural theory* (pp. 129–148). London, England: Routledge.

Daddario, G., & Wigley, B. J. (2007). Gender marking and racial stereotyping at the 2004 Athens games. *The Journal of Sports Medicine, 2*, 30–51.

de Moraes, L. (2007, April 7). Sorry Excuses: MSNBC's Form Apology. *Washington Post*, p. C01.

Douglas, D. D. (2005). Venus, Serena and the Women's Tennis Association: When and where race enters. *Sociology of Sport Journal, 22*, 256–282.

Douglas, D. D., & Jamieson, K. M. (2006). A farewell to remember: Interrogating the Nancy Lopez farewell tour. *Sociology of Sport Journal, 23*, 117–141.

Dworkin, S. L., & Wachs, F. L. (1998). Disciplining the body: HIV-positive male athletes, media surveillance and the policing of sexuality. *Sociology of Sport Journal, 15*, 1–20.

Dworkin, S. L., & Wachs, F. L. (2009). *Body panic: Gender, health and the selling of fitness.* New York, NY: New York University Press.

Duncan, M. C., & Hasbrook, C. (1988). Denial of power in women's televised sports. *Sociology of Sport Journal, 5*, 1–21.

Eastman, S. T., & Billings, A. C. (1999). Gender parity in the Olympics: Hyping women athletes, favoring men athletes. *Journal of Sport and Social Issues, 23*, 140–170.

Eastman, S. T., & Billings, A. C. (2000). Sportscasting and sports reporting: The power of gender bias. *Journal of Sport and Social Issues, 24*, 192–213.

Felshin, J. (1974). The triple option . . . for women in sport. *Quest, XXX*, 36–40.

Festle, M. J. (1996). *Playing nice: Politics and apologies in women's sports*. New York, NY: Columbia University Press.

Gramsci, A. (1971). *Selections from the Prison Notebooks*. New York, NY: International Publishers.

Griffin, P. (1998). *Strong women, deep closets: Lesbians and homophobia in women's sport*. Champaign, IL: Human Kinetics.

Hall, S. (2000). Encoding/Decoding. In P. Marris & S. Thornham (Eds.), *Media studies reader* (pp. 51–61). New York, NY: New York University Press.

Hanretty, K. (2007, April 15). Imus' sin? Bad joke, wrong target. *Washington Post*. (n.p.)

Hartmann, D. (2000). Rethinking the relationships between sport and race in American culture: Golden ghettos and contested terrain. *Sociology of Sport Journal, 17*, 229–253.

Heywood, L., & Dworkin, S. L. (2003). *Built to win: The female athletes as cultural icon*. Minneapolis, MN: University of Minnesota Press.

Hicks, J. R. (2007, April 15). Drop the race card. *Washington Post*, p. B01.

Horn, J. (2007, April 13). The Imus scandal: Chronology and aftermath. *Los Angeles Times*, p. A21.

Horn, J., & Gold, M. (2007, April 11). Radio host skated close to the edge, and plenty went along. *Los Angeles Times*. p. A11.

Hunt, D. (1999). *O. J. Simpson facts and fictions: News rituals in the construction of reality*. Cambridge, England: Cambridge University Press.

Ifill, G. (2007, April 10). Trash-talk radio. *The New York Times*, p. A21. Imus called women's basketball team "nappy-headed hos." Retrieved October 16, 2007 from http://mediamatters.org/research/200704040011

Imus press release. (2007, April 7). Alpha Kappa Alpha, Inc. Retrieved August 1, 2009 from http://www.aka1908.com/news/imus/

Jhally, S. (1984). The spectacle of accumulation: Material and cultural factors in the evolution of sports/media complex. *Insurgent Sociologist, 12*(3), 41–57.

Johnson, P. (2007, April 10). Radio's Imus is suspended two weeks; Execs expect him to 'live up' to apology. *USA Today*, p. 1D.

Knapp, G. (2007, April 10). Women need to raise voices on Imus insult. *The San Francisco Chronicle*, p. B1.

Krippendorff, K. (2004). *Content Analysis: An introduction to its methodology*. Thousand Oaks: Sage.

Lansbury, J. H. (2001). "The Tuskegee Flash" and "the Slender Harlem Stroker": Black women athletes on the margin. *Journal of Sport History, 22*, 235–252.

McDonald, M. G., & Birrell, S. (1999). Reading sport critically: A Methodology for Interrogating Power. *Sociology of Sport Journal, 16*, 283–300.

McDonald, M., & Thomas, C. The Rutgers women's basketball team talks back: Intersectionality, resistance and media power. In S. Spickard Prettyman & B. Lampman (Eds.), *Learning culture through sports: Exploring the role of sport in Society* (2nd ed.). Lanham, MD: Rowman & Littlefield Publishers.

McKay, J., & Johnson, H. (2008). Pornographic eroticism and sexual grotesquerie in representations of African-American sportswomen. *Social Identities, 14*, 491–504.

McPherson, T. (2000). Who's got next?: Gender, race and the mediation of the WNBA. In T. Boyd & K. Shropshire (Eds.), *Basketball Jones: America above the rim* (pp. 184–197). New York, NY: New York University Press.

Messner, M. A. (1988). Sports and male domination: The female athlete as contested ideological terrain. *Sociology of Sport Journal, 5*, 197–211.

Messner, M. A. (2002). *Taking the field: Women, Men and sports*. Minneapolis, MN: University of Minnesota Press.

Messner, M. A., Duncan, M. C., & Cooky, C. (2003). Silence, sports bras and wrestling porn: Women in televised sports news and highlight shows. *Journal of Sport and Social Issues, 27*, 38–51.

Messner, M. A., Duncan, M. C., & Willms, N. (2006). The revolution is not being televised. *Contexts, 5*, 34–38.

Messner, M. A., & Solomon, W. S. (1993). Outside the frame: Newspaper coverage of the Sugar Ray Leonard wife abuse story. *Sociology of Sport Journal, 10*, 119–134.

Payne, G., & Payne, J. (2004). *Key Concepts in Social Research*. London, England: Sage.

Pratt, J., Grappendorf, K., Grundvig, A., & LeBlanc, G. (2008). Gender differences in print media coverage of the 2004 summer Olympics in Athens, Greece. *Women in Sport and Physical Activity Journal, 17*, 34–41.

Protest Don Imus' Inappropriate Remarks Regarding Rutgers Basketball Team. Retrieved July 11, 2009 from http://www.womenssportsfoundation.org/Content/Articles/Issues/Equity-Issues/P/Protest-Don-Imus-Inappropriate-Remarks-Regarding-Rutgers-Womens-Basketball-Team.aspx

Roberts, S. (2007, April 11). A first-class response to a second-class put down. *The New York Times*, p. D1.

Rutgers Women's Basketball History 1995–Present. (2009). Retrieved July 8, 2009 from http://www.scarletknights.com/basketball-women/history/history2.asp

Schultz, J. (2005). Reading the catsuit: Serena Williams and the production of blackness at the 2002 U.S. Open. *Journal of Sport and Social Issues, 29*, 338–357.

Smith, E. (2007). *Race, sport and the American dream*. Durham, NC: Carolina Academic Press.

Smith, Y. (1992). Women of color in society and sport. *Quest, 44*, 228–250.

Spencer, N. (2004). Sister Act VI: Venus and Serena Williams at Indian Wells: "Sincere Fictions" and white racism. *Journal of Sport and Social Issues, 28*, 115–135.

Stanley, A. (2007, April 11). Don Imus, suspended, still talking. *The New York Times*, p. E1.

Stokes, J. (2003). *How to do media and cultural studies*. Thousand Oaks, CA: Sage.

Strauss, A., & Corbin, J. (1990). *Basics of qualitative research: Grounded theory procedures and techniques*. Newbury Park, CA: Sage.

Strauss, R. (2007, April 11). Rutgers women send Imus an angry message. *The New York Times*, p. D3.

Tennessee 5–0 against Rutgers in tournament play. (2007). Retrieved July 11, 2009 from http://www.utladyvols.com/sports/w-baskbl/spec-rel/040307aaa.html

Urquhart, J., & Crossman, J. (1999). The Globe and Mail coverage of the winter Olympic Games: A cold place for women athletes. *Journal of Sport and Social Issues, 23*, 193–202.

Vincent, J. (2004). Game, sex and match: The construction of gender in British newspaper coverage of the 2000 Wimbledon championship. *Sociology of Sport Journal, 21*, 435–456.

Vincent, J., & Crossman, J. (2008). Champions, a celebrity crossover, and a capitulator: The construction of gender in broadsheet newspapers' narratives about selected competitors at Wimbledon. *International Journal of Sport Communication, 1*, 78–102.

Wentworth, B., & Patterson, M. J. (2007, April 11). Rutgers squad speaks out. *The Star Ledger*, p. 1.

whore. (2009). In *Merriam-Webster.com*. Retrieved July, 11, 2009, from https://www.merriam-webster.com/dictionary/whore

Wingfield, A. H. (2008). Bringing minority men back in: Comment on Anderson. *Gender & Society, 22*, 88–92.

Women's Sports Foundation. (2007a). Women's Sports Foundation responds to inappropriate comments made by Don Imus regarding the Rutgers women's basketball team. Retrieved July 11, 2009 from http://www.womenssportsfoundation.org/Content/Press-Releases/2007/Womens-SportsFoundation-responds-to-inappropriate-comments-made-by-Don-Imus-regarding-theRutgers-w.aspx

Women's Sports Foundation. (2007b). Women's Sports Foundation responds to CBS & MSNBC firing Imus. Retrieved August 1, 2009 from http://www.womenssportsfoundation.org/Content/Press-Releases/2007/Womens-Sports-Foundation-responds-to-CBS-MSNBC-firing-of-Don-Imus.aspx

13

"What Makes a Woman a Woman?" versus "Our First Lady of Sport"

● ●

A Comparative Analysis of the United States and the South African Media Coverage of Caster Semenya

CHERYL COOKY, RANISSA DYCUS, AND SHARI L. DWORKIN

In August 2009, 18-year old South African track and field athlete Caster Semenya won the 800 m event at the World Championships in Berlin, Germany. In that moment, Semenya went from relative obscurity to the subject of international news media debate and scrutiny. Given her "deep voice," "fast improvement in times" and "muscular frame," some of Semenya's competitors suggested she was not a "real

Source: "'What makes a woman a woman?' versus 'our first lady of sport': A comparative analysis of the United States and the South African media coverage of Caster Semenya," by C. Cooky, R. Dycus, & S. L. Dworkin, 2013, *Journal of Sport and Social Issues, 37*(1), pp. 31–56, doi:10.1177/0193723512447940. Copyright 2013 by Sage Publications. Reprinted with permission.

woman" and questioned whether she was eligible for competition in women's events. Subject to the International Association of Athletic Federations' (IAAF) gender verification policy, Semenya underwent sex testing to determine her eligibility, a process that lasted more than a year and resulted not only in a determination by which Semenya was deemed eligible for competition in women's events, the controversy also spurred the establishment of working groups within the IAAF and International Olympic Committee (IOC) tasked to reassess these policies. This chapter is part of a larger project wherein we also assess and critique sex testing policies in sports (see chapter 2). As feminist scholars, we were enraged by the media conversations regarding sex/gender, particularly the assumptions of female athletes as "mannish" or "not real" women unless they conformed to Westernized standards of femininity and beauty, as well as by the discriminatory treatment of Semenya in much of the international media. There were media accounts of the "leaked" test results, which ostensibly demonstrated Semenya was a "hermaphrodite" (a term considered offensive by many, especially for those in intersex communities), and even worse, news articles, blogs, and comment sections accused Semenya of being a man masquerading as a woman. This chapter uses a similar methodology and approach we had implemented in previous research on media framings of female athletes and controversies in women's sports. For this study we added in a comparison between American and South African media and were surprised by the stark differences in the ways in which the controversy was framed as well as how notions of sex/gender differed between the American and South African context. Not only does this empirical study illustrate the ways in which sex/gender is socially constructed, rather than biologically determined, it also illustrates the important role race, nationalism, and sexuality play in how sex/gender is constructed in a particular society/context. As I write this author note in the lead-up to the 2016 Summer Olympic Games, the IOC has changed its policies, yet it continues to police the boundaries of sex. Moreover, Semenya continues to remain a controversial figure, despite being determined by the IAAF and IOC to be eligible for competition in women's events.

—Cheryl Cooky

Introduction

Feminist theorists are concerned with the processes by which culture shapes and creates the body[1] (Balsamo, 1995; Butler, 1993; Dreger, 1998; Fausto-Sterling, 2000). As these theorists note, bodies are the products of historically specific practices and thus are not only determined exclusively by genetics but are also shaped by and through relations of power (Bordo, 1994; Butler, 1993; Dworkin & Wachs, 2009; Fausto-Sterling, 2000). For example, given the ways that specific social roles imbue bodies with particular capacities and physicality, there may be less in common biologically between bodies of female domestic workers and bodies of female athletes despite the specific sex categorization of those bodies (Gatens, 1992). Moreover, Butler (1993) argues that feminists should conceptualize and theorize the body as simultaneously produced by and constitutive of social meanings.

Feminist sport scholars locate these processes within sport contexts and highlight the ways in which sport reaffirms the sex/gender binary as inherent, natural, and inevitable (Birrell & Cole, 1994; Cavanaugh & Sykes, 2006; Cole, 2000; Kane, 1995; Sykes, 2006; Travers, 2008). Feminist sport scholars have also critically examined the policy of sex testing within the institution of sport and how it reinforces ideologies of natural, categorical sex difference, therefore excluding some women from sport participation. It was not until 2004, when the International Olympic Committee (IOC) established the "Stockholm Consensus," that male-to-female athletes were deemed eligible to participate in women's events at the Olympics (Sykes, 2006). However, Sykes argues that the Stockholm Consensus does not represent full acceptance of gender variance. Instead, there continues to be anxiety and resistance to gender variance in sport. In these ways, sport as an institution reaffirms and reproduces sex- and gender-based forms of social injustice (Cavanaugh & Sykes, 2006; Cole, 2000; Travers, 2008). We extend this scholarship to demonstrate how contemporary mainstream print media framings of gender-verification[2] testing in sport reproduce as natural and inevitable the ideological foundation of the sex/gender binary.

This article examines the tensions associated with sex, gender, race, nation, equality, and oppression as framed by the mainstream news media coverage of Caster Semenya. Semenya is a female track and field athlete from rural Limpopo, South Africa. She underwent gender-verification testing after she won the International Association of Athletics Federations (IAAF) 2009 World Championships in the 800 m event. Several media accounts claimed the tests were ordered because of her "deep voice, muscular build, and rapid improvement in times" (Associated Press, 2009). We use the media response to her gender-verification testing to explore race, gender, and sexuality injustice in sport. We examine whether and how media frames reinforce or challenge dominant binary notions of sex/gender, as well as the ways race, class, and nation intersect to produce culturally specific frames of Semenya and of gender-verification testing. Specifically, we asked how the United States and South African mainstream online and print media (newspapers) framed "gender-verification." We also ask how the United States and South African mainstream online and print media (newspapers) framed the controversy following Semenya's performance at the World Championships. That is, who or what was attributed to the suspicions surrounding Semenya's performance? What, if any, differences are there in the framings between the United States and South African media, and what do these differences reflect (and constitute) about each respective context?

The IAAF/IOC's historical policies only require sex testing of female athletes and transsexuals and are built on an assumption of categorical female frailty, male superiority, and physical dominance (Birrell & Cole, 1994; Cavanaugh & Sykes, 2006; Cole, 2000; Dworkin & Cooky, 2012; Kane, 1995; Travers, 2008). Similar to other athletes who have undergone sex testing, Caster Semenya was nearly denied the opportunity to participate in sport by having her sex/gender questioned. By holding Semenya's body up for scrutiny and suspecting her for her very success in the 800 m event, the "sport nexus" legitimated and perpetuated gender injustice (Travers, 2008). Paradoxically, even as gender-verification testing of Caster Semenya reaffirmed the sex/gender binary, this newsworthy event opened the door to rethinking not only the sex/gender binary in sport but also the ways that race, colonial legacies, and nationalism intersect with and shape understandings of sex testing. As we will argue, the events surrounding the "controversy" also opened the door for envisioning the transformative potential of sport, allowing new avenues for how sport might be restructured and reorganized.

We expected differences in media framings between the United States and South Africa given the relationship each country has to relations of privilege and oppression. Each country's social, political, and cultural context produces unique understandings of gender and of the role of sport in perpetuating or challenging race and gender inequalities (Dworkin, Swarr, & Cooky, 2013). Ostensibly for athletes, spectators, and citizens from the Global North, common sense understandings of gender-verification testing posit testing as an objective, scientific process that ensures a level playing field and thus "fairness" in sport competition. For athletes, spectators, and citizens from the Global South, this common sense understanding of the Global North is problematized, given the history of Western scientific knowledge of racial differences to justify and legitimate colonialism, slavery, and the exploitation of colonized peoples (Hoad, 2010; Nyong'o, 2010; Swarr, 2012). Moreover, it is important to acknowledge South Africa's apartheid past and the role that sport played, both materially and symbolically, to reinforce apartheid and to help South Africa partly overcome that history in contemporary terms (Hargreaves, 1997; Pelak, 2005). In South Africa, there is a historically specific understanding of sex testing as linked to and identified with Western scientific classifications of gendered and raced bodies. In this manner, sex testing aligns with past colonialist exploitation and contemporary forms of racial oppression, even in the postapartheid context (see Dworkin, Swarr & Cooky, 2013; Nyong'o, 2010). Thus for the Global South, Western scientific classifications of raced and gendered bodies are viewed as products of colonialism, European expansionism, and racism, not simply "objective" or "value-free" accounts that ensure equality in sport or in South African society.

We acknowledge these differing historical and sociocultural contexts and situate media framings accordingly. Yet the extent to which media frames may reaffirm the sex/gender binary in sport is central to our investigation. To this end, we conducted a content and textual analysis of mainstream print and online news articles from the United States and South Africa to examine media frames of sex/gender in sport. Our analysis reveals conflicting accounts of how womanhood is defined and which bodies are construed as "true" female athletes eligible to compete in international sport competitions. The comparative analysis also illustrates how differing cultural contexts produce contradictory understandings of sex/gender,[3] of gender-verification testing, and of notions of fairness in sport. We conclude the article with a discussion of transformative visions for sport, informed by postcolonial feminism and critical feminist sport studies (McClintock, 1995; Mohanty, 2003; Cole, 1994; Hall, 1996; Kane, 1995; Messner, 2002), imagining sporting practices as unfettered by the limits of the sex/gender system and by claims of a level playing field.

Sport, Gender Verification, and the Sex/Gender Binary

Prior to the late 20th century, we could not point to genes in the way we can today to define one's sex. However, the fact that we have knowledge of genetic components of sex identity does not mean we have the "ultimate, necessary, for-all-time answer to what it means to be of a certain sex" (Dreger, 1998, p. 9). Fausto-Sterling's (2000) critique of the binary sex system moves beyond genetic or biological classifications to offer new conceptualizations of sex categories. She states that "a body's sex is too complex. There is no either/or. Rather there are shades of difference" (p. 3). If nature allows for a continuum of sex, as Fausto-Sterling and other feminist theorists suggest, and if sport organizations' policies only accommodate categorical notions of sex alongside a separate-spheres requirement for women and men, then the incorporation and acceptance of bodies into sport that are not easily identifiable as male or female challenges the "cherished aspects" of sex-based forms of social organization in the United States (Kane, 1995; Travers, 2008). Thus gender-verification tests "constitute one element in a matrix of surveillance and policing practices of the boundaries around gendered bodies" (Cole, 1994, p. 20).

The justification for sex testing / gender verification as a way to uphold and ensure a "level playing field" (e. g., by identifying and policing women's sport spaces to prevent male "invaders") is built on the assumption that categorically all men are faster, stronger, and better at sport than all women. In this way, sport maintains the myth of absolute categorical sex/gender differences between men and women (Kane, 1995). Rather than viewing the relationship between sport and gender in binary terms—that is, categorically men are faster, stronger, and better at sport than women, Kane (1995) persuasively argued for the acknowledgment of sport performance as a continuum wherein many women outperform men in a range of sports, including traditionally male-dominated sports. Considering Fausto-Sterling's (2000) conceptualization of sex as a continuum furthermore disrupts the material and discursive ways that sport maintains the myth of a sex/gender binary rooted in natural differences as illustrated in and through sex-segregated sport competition. Thus sex testing / gender verification simultaneously reinforces the myth of a sex/gender binary and the subsequent justification to uphold this binary through sex-segregated sport competition. Ensuring that only "true" women compete with other "true" women—and that this category is distinctly different from "true" men—sex testing clearly constitutes and is constituted by sex segregation in sport.

Preventing women and men from competing with one another—a central role for sex testing—ostensibly ensures that sex-segregated sports are free from "intruders" who are not "real" (i.e., biological) women. As Kane (1995) argues, "This by definition creates the notion that sport is a naturally occurring binary divided along gender lines" (p. 204). However, female athletes who do not fit into traditional Western expectations of femininity are more likely to have their "biological standing as female athletes called into question" (Kane, 1995, p. 210). Cole (1994) adds, "The female athletic body was and remains suspicious because of its apparent masculinization and its position as a border case that challenges the normalized feminine and masculine body" (p. 20). Those female athletes that society views as nonconventionally feminine—that is, those deemed "deviant mutant" (Kane, 1995)—have the most potential to disrupt the sex/gender binary. This is because when "suspicious" athletes are sex tested, the ambiguities of sex and the social processes involved in constituting and reconstituting sex become exposed. This process thus challenges the underlying assumptions that sex/gender difference is inherent, natural, and most of all, can be categorically "known"—all assumptions through which the binary is upheld.

Given that these tests are administered primarily in international or Olympic competitions and that international sport bodies/federations are responsible for ordering, conducting, and interpreting the tests and for setting the policies for eligibility, the power of these organizations to constitute a singular meaning of sex/gender on a global scale cannot be underestimated. At the same time, international sport organizations are empowered to change policies on sex testing. The pressure from scientific and feminist communities has resulted in some changes, including the abandonment of mandatory testing in international competitions and the IOC's policy regarding the eligibility of transsexuals to participate in international competitions (for a critical analysis of these policies, see Cavanaugh & Sykes, 2006; Karkazis, K., B. Jordan-Young, G. Davis, & S. Camporesi, forthcoming).

Sex/Gender Binary in Local and Global Contexts

Current international governing bodies' policies on sex testing of "suspicious" female athletes impose understandings of sex/gender that do not necessarily resonate with local understandings of sex/gender. Although some may argue that definitions of sex/gender must transcend geographical and cultural boundaries within international sporting contexts in the name of "fairness" and "equality" in sport, understandings of sex/gender are culturally specific, constituted through race, class, and nation. Thus differing histories of sex, gender, colonialism, and racism produce historically and contextually specific constructions of sex/gender that have different implications for women from the Global North or the Global South. The treatment of Caster Semenya, and of other athletes who have undergone sex testing, implicates the role of sport in reproducing "natural" dichotomous sex/gender difference. It is this reproduction of "natural" difference that then serves to privilege male bodies and a masculinity linked to particular sexed (i.e., male) bodies, which thereby reaffirms and upholds sport as a male-dominated institution.

We acknowledge the potentially problematic position of White United States feminists from the Global North who wish to employ the Semenya case to "deconstruct" the discursive categories of sex/gender, especially given the local South African context wherein rights-based claims are directly founded on complex political histories and identity politics (Hoad, 2010). In theorizing "feminism without borders," postcolonial feminist Chandra Mohanty (2003) argues for a shift away from a biological or cultural basis for political or feminist alliances and, borrowing from Benedict Anderson, envisions an "imagined community (. . .), which suggests potential alliances and collaborations across divisive boundaries and communities in spite of internal hierarchies in Third World Contexts"

(p. 46). Indeed, this type of work is critical for social justice, for "If we pay attention to and think from the space of some of the most disenfranchised communities of women in the world, we are more likely to envision a just and democratic society capable of treating all its citizens fairly. Marginalized women provide the most inclusive paradigm for thinking about social justice" (Mohanty, 2003, p. 231).

Following Mohanty and the work of other postcolonial feminists (McClintock, 1995; Narayan, 1997), we too wish to draw an important distinction between "women as a discursively constructed group and 'women' as material subjects of their own history" (Mohanty, 2003, p. 23). In other words, a deconstruction of the categories by which bodies are placed in a sex/gender system seeks neither to deny nor to erase the material effects on the everyday lives of women. It is in this deconstruction of the category "woman" or in this specific case, "female athlete," that we wish to make visible how, on a global scale, international sporting contexts maintain sex- and gender-based forms of inequality, which are, in turn, shaped by nationalism, race relations, and colonial histories.

Method

Mediated messages (e.g., news media coverage) are not "objective" accounts of events. In other words, news media do not present an unmediated view of what "really happened" during an event. Instead, the media provide cues that encourage readers/viewers to interpret events in particular ways. In writing on the news media coverage of Renee Richards, Birrell and Cole (1994) explain,

> While the media appear simply to report what happened, they actively construct news through frames, values, and conventions. Having made the initial decision that an incident is worthy of treatment as news, reporters and editors make choices that foreground some elements of the potential narrative and obscure others, and they define and delineate issues through a series of word choices including headlines, descriptive word choices, photographs, who to authorize with an interview, and what to report. (p. 379)

Thus the media construct certain interpretations of newsworthy events while discouraging others (Fiske, 1996). In other words, what is included in the story and, more importantly, how it is discussed help "frame" an event for the reader or viewer (Fiske, 1996). As such, we analyzed newspaper articles for what was included inside media frames and what was excluded from the media frames. Examining what is inside and outside media frames provides insights into what Hall (2000) referred to as "preferred meanings" of texts.

As Hall (2000) notes, meanings cannot be conceived of as simply hegemonic, dominant, or totalizing; rather, "preferred meanings" are embedded in media texts. That is, the meanings intended by those responsible for the production of messages "have institutional, political and ideological power imprinted in them, and themselves become institutionalized" (Hall, 2000, p. 57). Hence even if not viewed as hegemonic in their meaning, texts have a finite set of interpretations given the preferred meanings encoded in texts by producers. Thus the encoding process by which producers embed preferred meanings into texts limits the possible meanings read by audiences (Hall, 2000). This imposes constraints on the possibility for alternative ways of knowing. Following Hall (2000), it is critical to highlight that media frames—and what is inside the frame and what is left outside the frame—are not only constructed within raced, classed, and gendered hierarchical relations of power but are also read by audiences who are positioned within the same systems of inequality. A combination of content analysis (quantitative counts of media framings) and textual analysis (qualitative examination of media frames) reveals how media create and recreate narratives, which are linked to dominant ideas or ideologies that circulate in wider society (for a detailed explanation of this methodology, see Cooky, Wachs, Messner, & Dworkin, 2010).

Using content and textual analysis to locate preferred meanings of texts, we analyzed newspaper coverage of the Caster Semenya controversy in the United States and in South Africa. For the United States sample, we selected major national and regional newspapers. The total sample included 13 newspapers. Four of the top five national U.S. papers were selected based on circulation rates (Audit Bureau Circulation, 2006): *USA Today*, the *New York Times*, the *Los Angeles Times*, and the *Washington Post*. Ten regional papers were selected using purposive sampling techniques in different regions of the United States (Northeast, Midwest, South, and West) from the top 25 list (Patton, 2001), which was also based on circulation rates (Audit Bureau Circulation, 2006). Regional newspapers included the *Star Ledger, Atlanta Journal Constitution, Houston Chronicle, Philadelphia Inquirer, San Francisco Chronicle, Cleveland Plain Dealer, Chicago Tribune, Denver Post, Boston Globe*, and *Seattle Times* (no articles were published on Caster Semenya during the time frame of the study in the *Chicago Tribune, Denver Post, Boston Globe*, and *Seattle Times*). For the South African sample, we were limited in part by the availability and accessibility of South African newspapers in the United States, as well as the language of the newspaper. As such, three South African print newspapers—*Business Day, Sowetan*, and *Mail & Guardian*—were analyzed. According to the Audit Bureau of Circulations South Africa, *Business Day* has a circulation of 36,110 and a readership of 76,000. *Sowetan* has a circulation of 125,490 and a readership estimated at 1,522,000, and *Mail & Guardian* has 50,230 readers and an estimated circulation of 428,000 (http://www.mediaclubsouthafrica.com, accessed May 27, 2011).

Print news articles from the above newspapers were retrieved using the Lexis-Nexis database from August 19, 2009, to January 21, 2010, using the search term, "Caster Semenya." January 21, 2010, was selected as the end date because the IOC convened to discuss sport organizations' policies on athletes with ambiguous sex identities. It was also announced that Semenya was allowed to keep her gold medal from the 2009 IAAF World Championships. *Mail & Guardian* was not available in the Lexis-Nexis database. Therefore, print news articles were accessed on the *Mail & Guardian* website using the above search criteria. This search produced a total of 215 articles, 53 from the United States newspapers and 162 from South African newspapers.

We developed a codebook based on emergent themes determined through an analysis of all 215 articles to uncover the various media frames of the event. Emergent themes were discovered using open coding of data (Strauss & Corbin, 1990). First, we read articles to determine who or what was left inside and/or outside (and therefore marginalized or erased) of dominant news frames. In this part of the analysis, we focused on which individuals and what groups were given voice and which were excluded or silenced. Second, we examined the ways the media described or discussed key stakeholders and groups that were involved in speaking on the controversy. Third, the media frames of Caster Semenya and other key individuals and organizations were analyzed. In this part of the analysis, we examined the text used to describe Semenya in terms of her sex/gender and how she was implicated in the controversy. We noted the following: Did the media frame Caster Semenya as innocent or guilty? Was Semenya framed as a woman, a man, a hermaphrodite, or intersexed? What was attributed to the suspicions surrounding Semenya? Were suspicions attributed to her athletic performance, her body and appearance, or other factors? Finally, we examined how the media discussed gender-verification testing. Here, we examined what terminology was used to describe the testing process and how the testing process was framed (e.g., ensuring a level playing field in sport, scientific, and socially constructed). Given the inductive approach of the textual analysis, we were open to all possible frames.

From these emergent themes, we created subthemes or codes that we subsequently analyzed in the content analysis. This analysis produced 99 codes in total. Thus the frames analyzed in the content analysis were derived from the inductive approach of the textual analysis. In the content analysis, we coded whether or not an article mentioned and/or included quotes from specific individuals and groups or included a specific type of framing. Two authors independently coded all 99 codes on 41 U.S. articles and 41 South African articles, or 38% of the total sample. The percentage agreement for interrater reliability was calculated at approximately 95%, well above what is considered an acceptable level of concordance (Fleiss, Levin, & Paik, 2005). Any discrepancies in coding were discussed with the last author and/or an independent senior researcher in sport sociology until consensus was reached. We then compiled descriptive statistics to determine the preferred meanings of the texts.

Background of the Event

Caster Semenya,[4] aged 18, University of Pretoria student and track athlete competed in the 800 m event at the World Championships in Berlin on August 19, 2009, and won the event in 1 min 55 s 45 ms (2 s slower than the World record). The silver medal went to Kenyan Janeth Jepkosgei (1 min 57 s 90 ms), 2.45 s behind Semenya. Earlier that day,[5] IAAF officials confirmed that Semenya was undergoing "sex-determination testing" to confirm her eligibility to race as a woman (Clarey, 2009). According to a *Los Angeles Times* article that quoted Nick Davies, a spokesperson for the IAAF, the IAAF began to "ask questions about Semenya" on July 31, 2009, when "she ran the fastest time in the world season, 1 minute 56.72 seconds, at the Africa Junior Championships" (Hersh, 2009, p. C1). By many media accounts, especially in the United States, the IAAF originally suspected doping. However, subsequent media reports confirmed that Semenya had undergone gender-verification tests on the request of the IAAF (Clarey, 2009). Pierre Weiss, general secretary of the IAAF, stated in a press conference that Semenya was undergoing testing because of "ambiguity" and not because the IAAF suspected her of knowingly cheating. Several athletes spoke out immediately after the championships. Elisa Cusma, an Italian runner who finished sixth in the race said, "These kind of people should not run with us. For me, she is not a woman. She is a man" (Clarey, 2009, p. 13). Russian athlete, Mariya Savinova, who finished fifth, told Russian journalists that she did not think Semenya would pass the gender-verification test stating, "Just look at her" (Clarey, 2009, p. 13).

Framings of Suspicion: "Too Fast," "Too Muscular" to Be a Woman versus Westernized/Racist Definitions of Beauty/Gender

More than one third of our total sample included some discussion of the suspicions surrounding Semenya's performance and/or appearance (see Table 13.1). According to media frames, Semenya's performance raised "suspicions" for several reasons. Media articles framed the suspicions as emerging because of her fast times in the World Championship (i.e., she's too fast to be a "real" woman) or her fast improvement over the brief course of her running career (i.e., since her performances at the African Junior Championships at the end of July and the World Championships in August). In addition, suspicions were said to emerge because of her "masculine," "muscular," appearance or because of both her appearance and her performance. Illustrative of the latter frame, for example, journalists in the United States noted that suspicions emerged because of Semenya's, "muscular physique and drastic improvement" (Longman, 2009a, p. B10) or her "improved speed and muscular build" (Longman, 2009b, p. D9).

A higher percentage of South African articles framed suspicions regarding Semenya's sex/gender compared to the United States articles. Of the South African articles to discuss the suspicions surrounding Semenya, most framed suspicions in one of three ways: because of both her appearance and her performance (36%), because her times were too fast at the World Championship (25%), or because her "performance improved too quickly" (20%; see Table 13.1). Of the articles that discussed suspicions in the United States sample, most articles focused on her masculine appearance, deep voice, or muscular build (32%), although more than half of the articles (54%) attributed the suspicions to a combination of her time being "too fast" at the World Championship (18%), too fast times at the Africa Junior Championships (18%), or that her "performance improved too quickly" (18%). Only a few articles in the United States sample included both frames of appearance and performance to justify the suspicions. For example, a *New York Times* journalist explained it was because "she improved her times drastically in the 800 and 1500 meters and became the world leader in the 800"

Table 13.1. Media Frames: Suspicions of Semenya's Sex/Gender

	Too fast time (World)	To fast time (Africa Junior Championship)	Appearance (masculine, deep voice)	Both appearance/ performance	Too fast times (at World and Junior)	Too fast increase in performance
U.S. papers	18% (4)	18 % (4)	32% (7)	14% (3)	0% (0)	18% (4)
S.A. papers	25% (14)	7% (4)	11% (6)	36% (20)	2% (1)	20% (11)

NOTE: Results only include the articles that had an explicit frame of suspicions.

(Longman, 2009b). This, along with her "improved speed and muscular build," led to "sex verification testing" (Longman, 2009b).

The United States articles framed the suspicions as objective accounts and very few offered a critical assessment of the validity of the suspicions or the assumptions that undergirded them. In contrast, when mentioning her fast times as a cause for suspicion, South African newspapers were critical of this explanation and implied or stated outright that racism instead was to blame for the suspicions. For example, in an op-ed article published in *Sowetan*, the author wrote, "We all know that her crime is that an African girl outran everybody to clinch the women's 800m final" (Mofokeng, 2009). In a more explicit reference to racism, another *Sowetan* op-ed article condemned the IAAF, stating, "The conduct of the international body was racist and humiliating" ("The IAAF is a Disgrace," 2009).

Although nearly 46% of the United States articles and 47% of South African articles included some discussion of Semenya's body and appearance as responsible for raising suspicions regarding her sex/gender identity, there are important distinctions across the two regions. The textual analysis revealed that the "appearance" frame in the United States newspapers was often used as justification for the suspicions of other athletes or sport organizations, thus legitimating the need for the IAAF to enact their sex testing policy. For example, the *Los Angeles Times* wrote, "The concerns about whether she met standards to compete as a female athlete were prompted by still and television images of the teenager" that implied it was her appearance that led the IAAF and others to question her eligibility to participate as a female athlete in women's sport events. In a frame that seemed to attempt to explain Semenya's gender expression, a journalist for the *Los Angeles Times* explains, "Semenya . . . has grappled with the consequences of looking boyish all her life" (Dixon, 2009, p. A1).

In the South African sample, especially in *Mail & Guardian*, articles were critical of the implication that Semenya's masculine corporeality, strength, or muscularity meant that she was not a "true" woman eligible to compete as a female athlete. Highlighting the linkages among appearance, sex/gender, and race, a *Mail and Guardian* journalist underscored the role that racism plays when Westerners impose White standards of femininity in the global sporting arena. This particular journalist, in a somewhat sarcastic tone, implied that the whole controversy could have been avoided if Semenya had only made "herself appear more girly," and taken "beauty tips from her peers in Berlin," who "glam up for the start with lip gloss, enough gold jewelry to outshine the medals, and even false eye lashes" ("A Better Balance," 2009). Another op-ed article in the *Sowetan* notes that suspicions regarding Semenya's sex "seem to rely on patriarchal sexist stereotyping of women as weak and soft, which Caster does not fit into because she is considered to be too strong and muscular to be a woman" (Langa, 2009). This questioning of a female athlete's gender in the sex/gender binary is not unique to Semenya. Historically, female athletes—especially White, heterosexual, middle-class athletes—must negotiate mutually exclusive constructions of gender where muscularity and strength are linked to masculinity and beauty and glamour are linked to femininity (Cahn, 1994; Dworkin, 2001; Dworkin & Wachs, 2009; Hargreaves, 1994; Heywood & Dworkin, 2003). In mainstream media coverage, female athletes who do not conform to dominant notions of femininity continue to be the subject of ridicule and the targets of racist and sexist commentary (Cooky et al., 2010).

Also as part of this frame, politicians and political leaders spoke out on behalf of Semenya, critical of the ways in which Semenya's appearance was blamed for raising suspicions. The following was a quote from an African National Congress (the ruling political party in South Africa) press release, "We condemn the motives of those who have made it their business to question her gender due to her physique and running style. Such comments can only serve to portray woman as weak" ("South Africa Lashes Out," 2009). An op-ed article in the *Sowetan* was quite angry in tone at the "ignorance" of society speculating how to rid the world of "gender Nazis." The author wrote, "Now poor Caster has to be publically shamed simply because she does not look the way society dictates a woman should look" (Lategan, 2009).

Some articles, in both South Africa and in the United States, provided a discussion of how these standards are "racist" or based on White/Western notions of beauty. An op-ed writer in *Sowetan* noted, "It is very clear that the IAAF used Western stereotypes of what a woman should look like as probable cause, and that is racist and sexist since many of those making the determination are fat and ugly European men" (Anderson, 2009). In addition, the *Mail & Guardian* reported, "Although the debate is ostensibly about sex, many in South Africa believe it has a racial dimension. Political leaders have accused Western 'imperialists' of a public lynching" (Smith, 2009). In the United States, articles reported this perspective as the response from South Africa and not necessarily indicative of sentiments in the United States. For example, an article in the main section of the *Los Angeles Times* echoed the South African frame critical of Western standards of beauty and femininity: "Other black South Africans find something more sinister in the controversy erupting around Semenya: another example of demeaning Western attitudes toward black Africans, particularly women" (Dixon, 2009, p. A1).

Of interest, the "appearance" frame in the South African articles that specifically referenced Semenya's "masculine" appearance was used primarily as a physical descriptor of Semenya and was not invoked to justify the IAAF's gender-verification test, as it was in the United States frames. Nor did the mention of Semenya's masculine appearance necessarily signify that she was not a "girl." In this way, South African media frames simultaneously challenged the

Table 13.2. Media Frames: How is Semenya Described in Terms of Her Gender?

	Girl, woman, lady	Not a "real" girl/ woman	Both/intersex	"Hermaphrodite"	Ambiguous	Total
U.S. papers	50% (8)	2% (6)	6% (1)	6% (1)	16% (4)	16
S.A. papers	95% (57)	0% (0)	0% (0)	3% (2)	1% (1)	60

sex/gender binary, describing Semenya as masculine, although reaffirming the binary by asserting her identity as "our girl" and "golden girl" (Mdlesthe, 2009), a frame we discuss in the following section.

Frames of Semenya's Sex/Gender: "What Makes a Woman a Woman?" versus "Our First Lady of Sport"

South African media accounts frequently included quotes and images that identified Caster Semenya as "our golden girl," "our first lady of sport," and "golden heroine" (see Table 13.2). For example, many articles used these frames in the descriptions of Semenya: "Golden girl Caster Semenya yesterday thanked South Africa for supporting her" (Moeng, Mbamba, & Ratsatsi, 2009). "Caster Semenya is our golden girl," wrote an author in an op-ed in the *Sowetan* ("Semenya is Not a Cheat," 2009). Pictures of the crowd holding signs reading "100% woman" during a rally for Semenya's welcome back to South Africa featured in media articles, intentionally countering questions about Semenya's sex. Print media coverage offered confirmation of her sex through quotes from family members, sport fans, and even government officials. A fan awaiting Semenya's arrival home at the airport says, "At the end of the day, she is our hero. She is our African girl and there's no need to question that" (Brooks, 2009). An article appearing in *Sowetan* quoted Semenya's father: "She is my little girl. I raised her and I have never doubted her gender" (Sowetan Reporters, 2009).

Although not a dominant frame, there were several articles in the South African sample that challenged the sex/gender binary by recognizing that having "both male and female characteristics" did not provide evidence that Semenya was not a "girl." An op-ed published in *Business Day* noted, "It is, therefore, not true that we are either male or female, or masculine or feminine. In nature there is more. . . . Unfortunately even good scientific explanations are contaminated by subjective conclusions" (Matshiqi, 2009). The *Mail & Guardian* published an article that questioned the binary and noted how South African politicians' "constant reiteration that she is a woman . . . reinforces the same binary that is the cause of the problem: men have to be men and women have to be women" (Schuhmann, 2009).

It should be noted that the ostensibly celebratory embrace of Semenya's gendered nonconformity by politicians and the public was not representative of South Africa's treatment of transgendered individuals or gender nonconformists. In one of a few articles that raised this issue, Schuhmann (2009) situated the Semenya controversy in the specific historical and cultural context, informing readers that "feminine masculinities and masculine femininities are not normally celebrated so overtly." On the contrary, women who defy gender norms in

South Africa are often the targets of hate crimes, "curative" rape, and homophobia. Although in 2009 Semenya earned heroine status in South Africa, in April of 2008, South African Black lesbian football star Eudy Simelane was gang-raped and murdered. These "corrective rapes" (a term used by activists and scholars) are intended to punish lesbians for their sexuality and "convert" them to heterosexuality (Dworkin, Swarr, & Cooky, forthcoming; Gevisser, 2009; Swarr, 2012).

Moreover, at the same time that South Africa frames focused on the "subjective" aspects of sex (although erasing the transphobia and homophobia inherent in their celebration of Semenya as a "true woman"), the dominant frame in the United States centered on the "medicalized" aspects of sex/gender. These debates largely took place among scientists and academics on whether or not "sex tests" could identify and verify "real" female athletes (see Table 13.3). Twenty percent of the United States articles compared to only 7% of South African articles included this frame (see Table 13.4). We discuss the framing of Semenya's gender-verification test in the following section.

Frames of Semenya's Gender-Verification Test: "A Reasoned Choice among Imperfect Options" versus "Violation of Human Rights"

The "medicalized" frame acknowledged the scientific limitations of using sex testing / gender verification to determine sex/gender (see Table 13.2); 35% of articles in the United States sample framed gender-verification testing in this way. Illustrative of this frame, Alice Dreger wrote an article for the *New York Times* that discussed the limitations of gender-verification testing, which included quotes from a professor in human genetics and pediatrics, a pediatric endocrinologist, and a professor of epidemiology on whether or not a process of sex testing, even one that included an interdisciplinary panel (genetics, endocrinology, anatomy, psychology), could determine one's sex in a definitive way that would ensure someone with an "unfair advantage" was not allowed to compete. Although this article and others like it provided a critical assessment of the limits of sex testing, rightly acknowledging the complexity of determining an individual's sex, outside the frame was a critical discussion of the legitimacy or purpose for sex testing female athletes (see Table 13.5). This absence left unquestioned the assumptions on which gender-verification tests are based. Thus the sex/gender binary and the need for sport to be sex segregated went unchallenged in the United States media frames. One scientist said the "IAAF must acknowledge that all it can do is make a reasoned choice among many imperfect options" (as quoted in Dreger, 2009, p. SP8).

Surprisingly, inside this frame were quotes from the IAAF and other experts to assure audiences that Semenya's sex/gender would be determined once the testing was complete and the results made public, despite the fact that many of the same articles also acknowledged the limitations of gender-verification testing to determine one's sex. In other words, Semenya's sex and/or her eligibility to compete would be "known" once the IAAF had the results of the test, even though scientists in the articles said the test itself was problematic. As such, the United States articles "medicalized" debates about sex/gender and gender-verification testing, presenting the limitations of assessing male and female

Table 13.3. Media Frames: Process of Sex Testing / Gender Verification

	Socially constructed	Determines true identity	Scientific	Human rights violation	Racist	Equal playing field	Can't determine sex/ gender
U.S. papers	5% (1)	0% (0)	0% (0)	30% (6)	20% (4)	10% (2)	35% (7)
S.A. papers	18% (14)	17% (13)	7% (5)	37% (28)	13% (11)	0% (0)	8% (6)

NOTE: Results only include the articles that had an explicit frame of testing process.

Table 13.4. Does the Article Include a Scientific and/or Academic Discussion of Sex/Gender?

	Yes	No	Total
U.S. papers	20% (11)	80% (42)	53
S.A. papers	7% (12)	93% (150)	162
Total	11% (23)	89% (192)	215

bodies, and yet they were still concerned with how we can determine the "truth" surrounding Semenya's sex/gender. Thus the United States frames reinforced a binary between male and female sport performances that ultimately served to naturalize sex/gender difference.

Unlike articles in the United States that framed sex testing / gender verification as a scientific process, although one with limitations, the South African media framed gender verification as a lingering artifact of South Africa's apartheid past and the racist history of Global North/Western culture's scientific scrutiny of African women's bodies (see Table 13.3). More than half of the South African sample included a discussion of the process of sex testing as a human rights violation or as racist (although the U.S. newspapers also had human rights and racism as a dominant framing of the process of testing, these articles quoted or referenced the South African response). These articles offered a critique of the policies of sex testing as "sexist and racist" rather than a scientific attempt to determine true sex/ gender (Brooks, 2009). "It is the ghoulish, white-coated scientists of the IAAF who would do well to look into their hearts and ask whether the overwhelming evidence of Caster's life as a girl in South Africa does not count as science" (Brooks, 2009). Such responses are understandable given a long racist and colonial history wherein Black women's bodies were objectified (Dworkin et al., 2013; Ray, 2009).

Inside this frame were statements from politicians and South African sport stakeholders that the IAAF's policy on gender verification was in violation of Caster Semenya's human- or gender-based right to compete as a female athlete in women's sport competition. This is not surprising given burgeoning human rights discourses in postapartheid South Africa and the growing attention given to women's rights in sport and broader society (Banda, 2005; Hargreaves, 1997; Pelak, 2005: Robins, 2008). To that end, an article in *Sowetan* reported that the South African parliament planned to petition the United Nations to investigate the "'abuse' of running sensation Caster Semenya's human rights" and quoted Butana Komphela, the head of Parliament's sports portfolio committee, who

Table 13.5. Media Frames: Is There a Critical Discussion of Limitations of Sex/Gender Testing to Determine Sex/Gender?

	Yes	No	Total
U.S. papers	15% (8)	85% (45)	53 articles
S.A. papers	7% (12)	93% (150)	162 articles
Total	9% (20)	91% (195)	215 articles

said the IAAF "had committed a 'gross violation of Semenya's human rights'" (Majavu, 2009). "The Athletics South Africa (ASA) council took issue with the IAAF's 'failure' to observe the confidentiality required to handle the Semenya issue with sensitivity and infringed upon the human rights of the athlete" (Moreotsene, 2009). The president of South Africa, Jacob Zuma, was also quoted in this frame: "Miss Semenya had also reminded the world of the importance of the right to human dignity and privacy, which should be enjoyed by all human beings" ("Continue to Walk Tall," 2009). The South African frames thus seemingly empowered Semenya, acknowledging her human right to participate in women's sport competitions without being subjected to the humiliation of gender-verification testing, although mostly through the voices of political leaders and South African sport stakeholders.

At the same time that this frame delegitimized scientific claims of Semenya's sex/gender, it also positioned Semenya's family members, coach, teammates, representatives of Athletics South Africa, and South African political leaders and stakeholders as "experts" to verify Semenya's sex, in spite of any pending results of the IAAF's gender-verification tests. Absent from this frame were academic experts or scientists to discuss the validity of gender-verification testing. Instead, articles included quotes from Semenya's mother, father, uncle, grandmother, friends, fans, and other members of the community verifying that Semenya was indeed a girl, and as such, there was no need to conduct or to await the results of the gender-verification tests. Approximately 12% of the articles in the South African sample (only one article in the United States sample) included this frame. These quotes frequently verified Semenya's gender as a "girl." A *Mail & Guardian* article quoted Semenya's uncle: "Caster is a girl . . . I am not worried about that too much. I know where she comes from. For myself, I know Caster is a girl" (Brooks, 2009). Semenya's mother, Dorcas Semenya, reflecting on the controversy, said, "I cannot comment about the scientists and the professors, all I know is that I gave birth to a girl in 1991" (Moeng, Mbamba, & Ratsatsi, 2009). Thus in the South African media frames, culturally relevant "local" definitions of gender were inside the frame, whereas scientific determinations and the legitimacy of international sport organizations' policies were dismissed as either violating Semenya's human rights or an example of Western imperialism and racism.

Framings of Semenya: Inside and Simultaneously Outside the Frame

Although every article in our sample was about Caster Semenya, Caster Semenya the athlete and human being was almost always outside the frame. And although she was framed in the South African articles as a "golden girl" and "our first lady of sport," which positioned her as a representative of the South African nation-state, this frame constructed only a symbolic representation of South African nationalist identity and largely lacked any substantial discussion of Semenya's experiences from her own voice or perceptions. Semenya's agency was constrained in her silencing by South African political leaders and stakeholders who discouraged her from speaking during press conferences. As a result, in the majority of mainstream print news media coverage of the controversy, her voice, experience, and perspective were outside the frame. Indeed, Semenya was quoted in only five (approximately 9%) of the United States newspapers and in only eight (approximately 5%) of the South African newspapers.

When Semenya was asked to provide her own perspective on the events, quotes centered on her response immediately after the race and not on the subsequent controversy: "I took the lead in the 400 meters and I killed them, they couldn't follow. I celebrated the last 200 cause I knew, man" (Bearak, 2009). In a rare example of an article where Semenya's perspective is inside the frame, she was quoted in a *Mail & Guardian* article demonstrating resilience, perseverance, and acceptance, "God made me the way I am and I accept myself. I am who I am and I'm proud of myself" ("Caster is a Cover Girl," 2009). The absence of her voice in mainstream media articles and the way in which her experience was rendered invisible served to deny the subjective aspects of her becoming an international phenomenon at the age of 18. She became an international phenomenon not because of her sport performance but as a result of the gender controversy her performance elicited in local and global contexts. Thus the exclusion of Semenya's voice and her subsequent invisibility deflected any challenge that her perceptions of her own experience would pose to the "controlling images" of Black women that circulate in the mainstream news media (Collins, 1990; Cooky et al., 2010).

Summary

The controversy surrounding Semenya's performance at the 2009 World Championship provides an analytical framework for a critique of sexism, racism, and homophobia that is embedded in the logic of gender verification. As discussed earlier, Western scientific classifications of raced and gendered bodies are not simply "objective" or "value-free" accounts. Rather than framing the gender-verification tests as a scientific process necessary to "ensure" a level playing field, as did the United States news media, the South African news media framed the process as racist, a human rights violation, and a product of Westernized standards of femininity and beauty. In the United States' media frames, gender-verification testing and Western definitions of sex/gender were "global" processes by which capitalist, neoliberal notions of fairness, equality, and competition omitted the "local" knowledge of Semenya's sex and gender.

Looking beyond Western/Global North cultural constructions of sex/gender may appear to offer liberatory imaginings of sex/gender, given that self, family, and community-based understandings held more currency in South Africa (and in the South African media frames) than did Western scientific definitions. However, similar to media framings of tennis star Renee Richards (see Birrell & Cole, 1994), the United States and the South African media both discussed whether or not Semenya was a "real" woman. In United States and South African print news media, dominant frames illustrated print media's reinforcement of limiting, binary definitions of sex/gender, although in differing ways.

Moreover, the United States media frames engaged scientific debates regarding Semenya's "real" sex/gender and discussed the science of sex testing. Several newspapers in the United States quoted medical and academic experts who outlined the limitations of existing technology to determine or verify one's sex or gender. Ultimately this medicalized understanding of sex and gender reinforced the sex/gender binary, which allowed the legitimacy of sex testing and the need for sex-segregated sport to remain unquestioned.

Conversely, in South Africa media frames, the sex/gender binary was upheld through nationalist identity claims of Caster Semenya as South Africa's "first lady of sport" and a "golden girl." Although the South African media framed gender verification as illustrative of the lingering effects of racism, colonialism, and apartheid past, sex segregation in sport remained unquestioned in both countries' news media frames.

Although there were distinctions in the ways that the sex/gender binary was upheld in each context (scientific vs. local definitions), similarities were evident. Outside the news media frames in each country was a discussion of how the sex/gender binary in sport serves to maintain gendered hierarchies and inequalities both in sport and in wider society. Only a few articles in our sample offered any critique of the sex/gender binary or acknowledged that sex and gender are not as neatly aligned as dominant cultural and scientific understandings would suggest. Moreover, only three articles (approximately 1%) of the entire sample discussed the possibility or desirability of abandoning sex segregation in sport.

Most of the groups, organizations, and institutions whose representatives were quoted in the news media from both countries were male-dominated, and the individuals who were inside the frame were mostly men. In the U.S. context, it was predominantly male scientists and male members of international sport organizations that were framed as "experts" to determine Semenya's identity. In South Africa, it was male political leaders, male sports stakeholders, and family members (male and female) who were framed as "experts" with the right to speak for Semenya. These groups made essential claims to Semenya's identity to support her right to participate in sport as a woman. Indeed, South African politicians suggested that Semenya's human rights had been violated in the process of undergoing gender-verification testing; the President of South Africa, Jacob Zuma, spoke on her behalf, defending her identity and her right to participate in an institution for which women had fought to be included. Yet outside the frame were Semenya's voice and her own perspectives on her experiences. As the IAAF and Athletics South Africa strongly encouraged Semenya not to speak at press conferences, Semenya's voice remained outside the frame, even though she was discursively positioned as a representative of the South African nation-state.

Transformative Visions

Women athletes throughout history have played a unique role in constituting femininity and national identities through their sport participation (Ritchie, 2003). Caster Semenya is no exception. In South African media frames, Semenya was positioned as a national icon and a representative of the democratic, postapartheid, South African nation-state. Multiple constructions of her femininity and claims of her essential femaleness largely ignored, however, the reality of ambiguities surrounding the boundaries of race, sex, and gender in that nation (Swarr, 2012). The mobilization of nationalist rhetoric in the South African papers and the defense of Semenya's "true womanhood" suggest a reliance on the gender binary to defend what was perceived by many in South Africa as a racist assault.

One might interpret "transforming" sport as a call for recognizing how sports, in their current manifestations, provide a space for transformative visions and new ways to reimagine sporting practices. Reading the Semenya controversy through the lens of postcolonial feminism (Mohanty, 2003), transformative visions come to light that simultaneously allow for and reject the inclusion of the sex/gender binary in sport. Indeed, Caster Semenya, as an agent in the framing of her experience, receded into the background of the story, and she was outside the frame. Yet Semenya speaks to us, feminists from both the Global North and the Global South, in and through her sport performance. Semenya, both in her corporeality and in the media framing of her performance, presents a challenge to persisting forms of racism and sexism, both within and outside of sport, in global and local contexts.

In the coverage of Caster Semenya, mainstream media frames reaffirmed the legitimacy of gender-verification testing (in the United States) and the sex/gender binary (in both countries), and thus reproduced social injustice in sport and in society. Given that print news media, especially sports news media, have historically been male-dominated institutions (Messner, 2002; Serra & Burnett, 2007), it is not surprising that mainstream media frames concerning female athletes would reinforce gender ideologies and present female athleticism in sexist and racist ways (for a similar case study, see Cooky et al., 2010). Thus the framings of Semenya and the controversy itself lead us to reinforce calls for the inclusion of a diversity of voices, multiple standpoints, and contextually specific understandings in print news media. This inclusion of multiple voices and perspectives provides a critical challenge to the dominant meanings in media frames, which often uphold sex and gender injustice in sport.

The power of international sport organizations to constitute a singular meaning of sex/gender on a global scale cannot be underestimated. Some have argued that any transformation of sport requires abandoning sport policies that maintain the idea of dichotomously sexed and gendered bodies, including sex testing / gender verification (Cavanaugh & Sykes, 2006; Travers, 2008). To do so means abandoning the sex/gender binary in societies that define sexed/ gendered bodies in oppressive and limiting ways. Although these suggestions are compelling, we recognize they may be difficult to achieve.

At the same time, there is evidence that the controversy and the subsequent outcry in South Africa and elsewhere regarding the treatment of Semenya has led to changes in international sport-governing policies on gender-verification testing. As of May 1, 2011, the IAAF released its latest policy titled, "IAAF Regulations Governing Eligibility of Female Athletes with Hyperandrogenism to Compete in Women's Competition." This 14-page policy outlines the process, rules, and procedures of determining the eligibility of female athletes. As part of this new policy, the IAAF no longer uses the terms "gender verification" or "gender testing" and has strict procedures to ensure the confidentiality of the process. Also, female athletes with hyperandrogenism may be eligible to compete in women's competitions if they submit to a test and agree to be compliant with the IAAF's policies. Athletes who refuse a test, are found to have androgen levels higher than the "normal male range," or have androgen levels within the "normal male range" but are deemed to derive a competitive advantage from those androgens, could be ineligible for competition by either the expert medical panel's recommendation or the IAAF officials' decision. This latest policy suggests a movement toward addressing the complex ways that sex/gender is expressed, yet it remains problematic in that it upholds the rationale for sex segregation in sport.

We suggest that if sport-governing bodies continue to maintain the need for such tests, they should track the countries from which athletes undergo testing. This would ensure that certain countries are not inadvertently or overtly targeted and would also ensure that race and national profiling of certain femininities/ masculinities do not occur. Moreover, to level the playing field, the policy of sex testing should be applied equally and consistently to male and female athletes. Male athletes who have endogenic levels of testosterone or androgens that exceed the "normal male range" should also be prevented from participating as a male athlete in men's competitions, given that these athletes would have an "unfair advantage" over other male competitors who have lower levels of testosterone. Some may argue that doping controls already assess athletes for the illegal use of synthetic hormones, steroids, and blood doping. However, we are suggesting that in addition to testing for steroids or other forms of doping, male athletes should also submit to a test to determine their eligibility to participate as a "normal" male athlete. Moreover, the numbers of male and female athletes who are tested must be monitored and, if inequalities exist, athletes or national sport federations would be able to file a sex discrimination violation.

Although proposing to "sex test" male athletes along with female athletes challenges the assumptions of female frailty/male superiority embedded in sex testing, this proposal ultimately reproduces the sex/gender binary by reinforcing the assumption that "male" and "female" are mutually exclusive categories. Scientific experts acknowledge that the IAAF (and other sport-governing bodies that implement sex testing) is making a "reasoned choice among many imperfect options," which we argue offers a convincing rationale to eliminate sex testing in sport.

A way to accomplish this goal is for local and global sport communities and societies to reject the assumptions on which sex testing is based. According to the IOC and the IAAF, the rationale for sex testing is to ensure a "level playing field" for women in sport by preventing men, or women with too much testosterone/androgen levels, from competing in women's events. To address sex/gender injustice in sport, therefore, we need to deconstruct and dismantle the myth of sport as a "level playing field."

This transformative change has the potential to extend beyond the sex/gender binary in sport to address other inequalities. This is because the myth of sport as a level playing field reproduces other forms of inequalities, such as racism, classism, ableism, and others. In some ways, this type of transformative potential can easily be realized, given that sport is not—and arguably has never been—a level playing field. The media framings of Semenya shed light on the need for global sport communities and especially those individuals in positions of power to dictate sport policies and organizational structures and to acknowledge that sports competitions (and other institutionalized sporting practices) in their current manifestations are imbued with inequality and injustice.

Only certain bodies (i.e., male, White, Western/Global North, affluent, heterosexual, able-bodied, etc.) are privileged in most sporting contexts. Transformative visions see the ways contemporary sport institutions and organizations at the amateur or Olympic and professional levels are rife with various inequalities. They also recognize that these inequalities are often accepted as part of the sport (here consider that economic resources confer better access to training facilities, equipment, and coaches, all of which enhance sport performance). These transformative visions move us toward an understanding of injustice in sport, one that identifies and locates inequalities to challenge the myth of sport as a level playing field.

By exposing what myths in sport exist and how these operate to mask the production and reaffirmation of inequalities opens the door to transforming the ways sport is organized, structured, and understood. In Western countries, the notion of sport as a level playing field serves to normalize competition and hierarchies that are found in broader society. As such, sport is a key socialization agent that serves to maintain social inequalities. Thus, rather than attempt to maintain the myth of a level playing field by sex testing athletes to ensure no one has an "unfair" sex/gender "advantage," there should be a clear recognition and acceptance that sport is not a level playing field. This effectively eliminates the need to sex test athletes, male or female, in the first place. This may be an effective route through which to begin to transform sport and to assist with the eradication of sex, gender, race, and sexuality injustice.

Questions for Reflection and Discussion

In what ways did the news media coverage of sex testing / gender verification differ in the United States compared to South Africa? What may be some of the factors to explain why the coverage differed? In both this chapter and in chapter 2, we advocate for the elimination of sex testing/ gender verification policies in sports. On your own, look up the current IOC eligibility policies regarding women's participation. Based on your assessment of the policies, do you agree with the authors that we should abandon sex testing / verification in sports? Why or why not?

Notes

1   We acknowledge the potentially problematic use of the term "body," given that it reproduces the mind/body dualism in an article where our central argument is a critique of binary understandings of sex/gender. Here, we use the term "body" even though recognizing the limitations of language.

2   It should be noted that media reports referred to the testing in various ways such as gender verification, sex testing, gender testing, physical tests, and so on. This was included in our analysis; however, given the focus of this chapter, we report these findings elsewhere (Dworkin, Swarr, & Cooky, 2012).

3   Given the ways in which sex and gender are conflated, the understandings of Caster Semenya, and the media representations we analyzed, we use the term "sex/gender." The IAAF's own policy on "gender verification" speaks to the conflation of gender with sex. Moreover, following Fausto-Sterling (2000), we recognize that "our beliefs about gender—not science—can define our sex . . . and effect what kinds of knowledges scientists produce about sex in the first place" (p. 3).

4   We respect Semenya's self-identity, and thus throughout the article, we refer to Semenya using feminine pronouns. Based on the textual analysis, most articles in the United States and in South Africa also refer to Semenya using feminine pronouns.

5   Media accounts in the United States and in South Africa differed in the sequences of events, of who knew what and when, who ordered the tests, when they took place, and why. Thus, there was little agreement in media accounts of the "timeline" of events.

References

A Better Balance. (2009, August 21). Retrieved from http://mg.co.za/article/2009-08-21 -abetter-balance

Anderson, L. (2009, August 24). On what basis was Caster tested? *Sowetan*. Retrieved from http://www.sowetanlive.co.za/sowetan/archive/2009/08/24/on-what-basis-was-caster -tested

Associated Press. (2009, September 16). *IAAF: Semenya decision in November*. Retrieved from http://sports.espn.go.com/oly/trackandfield/news/story?id=4464405

Audit Bureau of Circulation. (n.d.) Retrieved from http://www.accessabc.com

Balsamo, A. (1995). *Technologies of the gendered body: Reading cyborg women*. Durham, NC: Duke University Press.

Banda, F. (2005). *Women, law, and human rights: An African perspective*. Oxford, England: Hart.

Berack, B. (2009, August 26). Inquiry about sprinter's sex angers South Africans. *The New York Times*, p. A6.

Birrell, S., & Cole, C. L. (1994). Double fault: Renee Richards and the construction and naturalization of difference. In S. Birrell & C. L. Cole (Eds.), *Women, sport and culture* (pp. 373–397). Champaign, IL: Human Kinetics.

Bordo, S. (1994). *Unbearable weight: Feminism, Western culture and the body*. Berkeley, CA: University of California Press.

Brooks, C. (2009, August 25). *Warm welcome home for champ Semenya*. Retrieved from http://mg.co.za/article/2009-08-25-warm-welcome-home-for-champ-semenya

Butler, J. (1993). *Bodies that matter: On the discursive limits of sex*. New York, NY: Routledge.

Cahn, S. (1994). *Coming on strong: Gender and sexuality in twentieth century women's sport*. New York, NY: Free Press.

Caster is a cover girl. (2009, September 8). Retrieved from http://www.mg.co.za

Cavanaugh, S. L., & Sykes, H. (2006). Transsexual bodies at the Olympics: The International Olympics Committee's policy on transsexual athletes at the 2004 Athens summer games. *Body & Society, 12*, 75–102.

Clarey, C. (2009, August 20). Gender test after a gold medal finish. *New York Times*, p. B13.

Cole, C. L. (1994). Resisting the cannon: Feminist cultural studies, sport and technologies of the body. In S. Birrell & C. L. Cole (Eds.), *Women, sport and culture* (pp. 5–30). Champaign, IL: Human Kinetics.

Cole, C. L. (2000). One chromosome too many? In K. Schaffer & S. Smith (Eds.), *The Olympics at the millennium: Power, politics and the games* (pp. 128–146). New Brunswick, NJ: Rutgers University Press.

Collins, P. H. (1990). *Black feminist thought: Knowledge, consciousness, and the politics of empowerment*. New York, NY: Routledge.

Continue to walk tall, Zuma tells Semenya. (2009, August 25). Retrieved from http://mg.co.za/article/2009-08-25-continue-to-walk-tall-zuma-tells-semenya

Cooky, C., Wachs, F. L., Messner, M. A., & Dworkin, S. L. (2010). It's not about the game: Don Imus, race, class, gender, and sexuality in contemporary media. *Sociology of Sport Journal, 27*, 139–159.

Dixon, R. (2009, August 21). Gender issue has always chased her: The African runner accused of being a man was often teased as a child. *Los Angeles Times*, p. A1.

Dreger, A. (2009, October 25). Seeking simple rules in complex gender realities. *The New York Times*, p. SP8.

Dreger, A. (1998). *Hermaphrodites and the medical invention of sex*. Cambridge, MA: Harvard University Press.

Dworkin, S. L. (2001). "Holding back": Negotiating a glass ceiling on women's strength. *Sociological Perspectives, 44*, 333–350.

Dworkin, S. L., & Wachs, F. L. (2009). *Body panic: Gender, health, and the selling of fitness*. New York, NY: New York University Press.

Dworkin, S. L., & Cooky, C. (2012). Sport, sex segregation, and sex testing: Critical reflections on this unjust marriage. *American Journal of Bioethics, 12*(7), 21–23. doi:10.1080/15265161.2012.680545.

Dworkin, S. L., Swarr, A. L., & Cooky, C. (2013). Sex and gender and racial (in)justice in sport: The treatment of South African track star Caster Semenya. *Feminist Studies* 39: 40-69.

Fausto-Sterling, A. (2000). *Sexing the body: Gender politics and the construction of sexuality*. New York, NY: Basic Books.

Fiske, J. (1996). *Media matters: Race and gender in U.S. politics*. Minneapolis, MN: University of Minnesota Press.

Fleiss, J. L., Levin, B., & Paik, M. C. (2005). *Statistical methods for rates and proportions*. Malden, MA: Wiley InterScience.

Gatnes, M. (1992). Power, bodies and difference. In M. Barrett & A. Phillips (Eds.),

Destabilizing theory: Contemporary feminist debates (pp. 120–137). Stanford, CA: Stanford University Press.

Gevisser, M. (2009, August 30). Castigated and celebrated. *Sunday Times*. Retrieved from http://www.timeslive.co.za/sundaytimes/article34966.ece

Hall, M. A. (1996). *Feminism and sporting bodies: Essays on theory and practice*. Champaign, IL: Human Kinetics.

Hall, S. (2000). Encoding/Decoding. In P. Marris & S. Thornham (Eds.), *Media studies reader* (pp. 51–61). New York, NY: New York University Press.

Hargreaves, J. (1994). *Sporting females: Critical issues in the history and sociology of women's sports*. London, England: Routledge.

Hargreaves, J. (1997). Women's sport, development and cultural diversity: The South African experience. *Women's Studies International Forum, 20*, 191–209.

Hersh, P. (2009, August 20). Gender issues: Others in 800 meters raise questions about surprise winner Caster Semenya of South Africa; international officials start inquiry. *Los Angeles Times*, p. C1.

Heywood, L., & Dworkin, S. L. (2003). *Built to win: The female athlete as cultural icon*. Minneapolis, MN: University of Minnesota Press.

Hoad, N. (2010). "Run, Caster Semenya, run!" Nativism and the translations of gender variance. *Safundi: The Journal of South African and American Studies, 11*, 398.

The IAAF is a disgrace. (2009, August 24). *Sowetan*. Retrieved from http://www.sowetanlive.co.za/sowetan/archive/2009/08/24/the-iaaf-is-a-disgrace

Kane, M. J. (1995). Resistance/transformation of the oppositional binary: Exposing sport as a continuum. *Journal of Sport and Social Issues, 19*, 191–218.

Karkazis, K., Jordan-Young, B., Davis, G., & Camporesi, S. (2012). Out of bounds? A critique of the new policies on hyperandro-genism in elite female athletes. *American Journal of Bioethics 12*(7): 3-16.

Langa, M. (2009, August 24). IAAF decision sexist and insulting to women. *Sowetan*. Retrieved from http://www.sowetanlive.co.za/sowetan/archive/2009/08/24/iaaf-decision-sexist-andinsulting-to-women

Lategan, H. (2009, August 25). Semenya tests a disgrace to human society. *Sowetan*. Retrieved from http://www.sowetanlive.co.za/sowetan/archive/2009/08/25/semenya-tests-a-disgraceto-human-society

Longman, J. (2009a, November 20). South-African runner's sex-verification result won't be public. *New York Times*, p. B10.

Longman, J. (2009b, December 27). A question of gender topples a track official. *The New York Times*. p. D9.

Majavu, A. (2009, August 25). Parliament to petition UN over "abuse." *Sowetan*. Retrieved from http://www.sowetanlive.co.za/sowetan/archive/2009/08/25/parliament-to-petition-unover-abuse

Matshiqi, A. (2009, Aug. 28). Finding the words for Caster Semenya. *Business Day*. Retrieved from http://www.businessday.co.za/articles/Content.aspx?id=799

McClintock, A. (1995). *Imperial leather: Race, gender, and sexuality in the colonial contest*. New York, NY: Columbia University Press.

Mdlesthe, C. (2009, August 24). She is "nice lovable." *Sowetan*. Retrieved from http://www.sowetanlive.co.za/sowetan/archive/2009/08/24/she-is-nice-lovable

Messner, M. A. (2002). *Taking the field: Women, men, and sports*. Minneapolis, MN: University of Minnesota Press.

Moeng, K., Mbamba, M., & Ratsatsi, P. (2009, August 26). Thanks for all your support. *Sowetan*. Retrieved from http://www.sowetanlive.co.za/sowetan/archive/2009/08/26/thanks-for-all-your-support

Mofokeng, J. (2009, August 26). Millions rejoice for golden girl. *Sowetan*. Retrieved from http://www.sowetanlive.co.za/sowetan/archive/2009/08/26/millions-rejoice-for -golden-girl

Mohanty, C. (2003). *Feminism without borders: Decolonizing theory, practicing solidarity.* Durham, NC: Duke University Press.

Moreotsene, L. (2009, September 14). Tests on golden girl are "invalid." *Sowetan*. Retrieved from http://www.sowetanlive.co.za/sowetan/archive/2009/09/14/tests-ongolden-girl -arEe-invalid

Narayan, U. (1997). *Dislocating cultures.* New York, NY: Routledge.

Nyong'o, T. (2010). The unforgivable transgression of being Caster Semenya. *Women & Performance: A Journal of Feminist Theory, 20*, 95–100.

Patton, M. Q. (2001). *Qualitative evaluation and research methods* (3rd ed.). Newbury Park, CA: Sage.

Pelak, C. F. (2005). Negotiating gender/race/class constraints in the New South Africa: A case study of women's soccer. *International Review for the Sociology of Sport, 40*, 53–70.

Ray, C. (2009, November 4). Caster Semenya 21st century "Hottentot Venus"? *New African*. Retrieved from http://newafricanmagazine.com/blogs/lest-we-forget/caster-semenya -21stcentury-hottentot-venus

Ritchie, I. (2003). Sex tested, gender verified: Controlling female sexuality in the age of containment. *Sport History Review, 34*, 80–98.

Robins, S. (2008). *From revolution to rights in South Africa: Social movements, NGOs and popular politics after apartheid.* Durban, South Africa: University of KwaZulu-Natal Press.

Schuhmann, A. (2009, August 31). Feminine masculinities, masculine femininities. *Mail & Guardian*. Retrieved from http://mg.co.za/article/2009-08-31-feminine -masculinitiesmasculine-femininities

Semenya is not a cheat. (2009, September 14). *Sowetan*. Retrieved from http://www .sowetanlive.co.za/sowetan/archive/2009/09/14/semenya-is-not-a-cheat

Serra, P., & Burnett, C. (2007). The construction and deconstruction of gender through sport reporting in selected South African newspapers. *South African Journal for Research in Sport, Physical Education and Recreation, 29*, 147–158.

Smith, D. (2009, August 23). Semenya sex row causes outrage in SA. *Mail & Guardian*. Retrieved from http://mg.co.za/article/2009-08-23-semenya-sex-row-causes-outrage-in-sa

South Africa lashes out at "racist" world athletics body. (2009, August 20). *Mail & Guardian*. Retrieved from https://mg.co.za/article/2009-08-20-sa-lashes-out-at-racist-world -athletics-body

Sowetan Reporters. (2009, August 20). Leave my girl alone, pleads Caster's dad. *Sowetan*. Retrieved from http://www.genderlinks.org.za/article/leave-my-girl-alone-pleads -castersdad-sowetan-2010-02-16

Strauss, A. C., & Corbin, J. M. (1990). *Basics of qualitative research: Grounded theory procedures and techniques.* Thousand Oaks, CA: Sage.

Swarr, A. (2012). *Sex in transition: Remaking gender and race in South Africa.* New York, NY: SUNY Press.

Sykes, H. (2006). Transsexual and transgender policies in sport. *Women and Physical Activity Journal, 15*, 3–13.

Travers, A. (2008). The sport nexus and gender injustice. *Studies in Social Justice, 2*, 79–101.

About the Authors

CHERYL COOKY is an associate professor of American Studies at Purdue University. She is an associate editor of the *Sociology of Sport Journal* and past president of the North American Society for the Sociology of Sport. She is the author of numerous book chapters and is published in a diverse array of journals including *Gender and Society, American Journal of Bioethics, Cultural Studies<=>Critical Methodologies,* and *Contexts: Understanding People in Their Social Worlds,* among others.

MICHAEL A. MESSNER is a professor of Sociology and Gender Studies at The University of Southern California. He is the author of many books, including *Some Men: Feminist Allies and the Movement to End Violence Against Women* (coauthor; Oxford University Press, 2015) and *Taking the Field: Women, Men, and Sports* (University of Minnesota Press, 2002), and he is the editor of *Child's Play: Sport in Kids' Worlds* (Rutgers University Press, 2016), among other titles.

About the Contributors

MARKO BEGOVIC is the head of Public Procurement at the Directorate for Youth and Sports in Montenegro.

SUZEL BOZADA-DEAS is a PhD student at the University of Southern California and an adjunct instructor of sociology at Sonoma State University.

SHARI L. DWORKIN is a professor in the Department of Social and Behavioral Sciences and associate dean for academic affairs in the School of Nursing at University of California, San Francisco. She is the author of *Body Panic: Gender, Health and the Selling of Fitness* (NYU Press) and coauthor of *Built to Win: The Female Athlete as Cultural Icon* (Minnesota Press). She has authored numerous articles and book chapters on sport, inequality, and bodies. Her articles have appeared in *Gender and Society, Sociology of Sport*, the *Journal of Sport and Social Issues*, the *Journal of Sex Research*, and other journals.

RANISSA DYCUS is an attorney in Indianapolis, Indiana.

MICHELA MUSTO is a sociology PhD candidate at the University of Southern California.

CAROLE OGLESBY has been in the professoriate for more than 40 years, 27 of them at Temple University. She was a department chair at Temple from 1992 to 1995 and at California State University, Northridge from 2003 to 2009. She was the principle author/contributor for a UN-Division for the Advancement of Women monograph entitled *Women, Gender Equality and Sport*.

LAUREN RAUSCHER is an associate professor of sociology and the director of the Women's Leadership and Mentorship Program at Robert Morris University.

DON SABO is a professor emeritus in health policy at D'Youville College, where he founded the Center for Research on Physical Activity, Sport, and Health. He is the former research director of the Women's Sports Foundation and now serves as its senior health policy advisor. He has directed and coauthored dozens of nationwide reports such as *Beyond X's and O's: Gender Bias and Coaches of Women's College Sports* (2016) and *Her Life Depends on It III: Physical Activity and the Health and Well-Being of American Girls* (2015).

MARJORIE A. SNYDER is the senior director of research and programs at the Women's Sports Foundation and a faculty member in the George Washington University Sports Philanthropy Certificate Program.

FAYE L. WACHS is a professor of sociology at California State Polytechnic University, Pomona. She is the coauthor of *Body Panic: Gender, Health and the Selling of Fitness* (NYU Press, 2009).

Index

Printed in the United States
By Bookmasters